Climate and Evolution

Climate and Evolution

RONALD PEARSON
*Department of Zoology
The University of Liverpool*

1978

ACADEMIC PRESS
LONDON   NEW YORK   SAN FRANCISCO
A Subsidiary of Harcourt Brace Jovanovich, Publishers

Academic Press Inc. (London) Ltd
24–28 Oval Road
London NW1

US edition published by
Academic Press Inc.
111 Fifth Avenue,
New York, New York 10003

Copyright © 1978 by Academic Press Inc. (London) Ltd

All Rights Reserved

No part of this book may be reproduced in any form,
by photostat, microfilm or any other means,
without written permission from the publishers.

Library of Congress Catalog Card Number: 77–93200
ISBN: 0–12–548250–7

Text set in 11/12 pt V.I.P. Bembo, printed by photolithography,
and bound in Great Britain at The Pitman Press, Bath

Preface

Climatic changes, whatever their causes, have far-reaching effects upon living organisms. It is such changes, and their probable effects during the last thousand million years, that are the subject of this book. Their involvement in biotic history can take three different forms. First of all they can affect the rate of evolution by varying the intensity of the selective pressures acting at given moments of world history. This, it is suggested, gave rise to the changing faunal and floral associations of geological time. Secondly, changing climatic conditions shaped the environments in which Man and all other species evolved, and in which present-day species achieved their distributions. Finally, and during the last few thousand years, continuing changes of a less extreme nature have exerted crucial influences on many important historical events.

February 1978   RONALD PEARSON

Acknowledgements

Many of my colleagues and friends have encouraged me but I would like to express my particular gratitude to the following. Emeritus Professor Sir Harry Godwin, FRS, formerly of the Botany School, Downing Street, Cambridge; the late Professor P. M. Sheppard, FRS; Professor A. J. Cain, Professor C. J. Duncan, Dr G. A. Parker, Dr M. Begon and Mr E. P. Chell, of the Zoology Department, Liverpool University; and Mr W. E. Wilkes, the Science Librarian. I would also like to extend my especial thanks to Miss D. S. Paterson, and particularly Miss A. Callaghan upon whom fell the burden of typing out two drafts of the manuscript. Needless to say they are in no way responsible for any inadequacies the book may have.

I must also express my appreciation for permission to use illustrations from the following sources: *Annals of the New York Academy of Sciences; Biological Reviews; Bulletin of the Geological Society of America; Journal of Geology; Nature; Oikos; Paleogeography, Paleoclimate and Paleoecology;* and *Science*. I owe further similar debts to Professor H. H. Lamb; Dr W. H. Zagwijn; Mrs H. Phillips; Almqvist and Wiksell Forlag, AB; BBC Publications; Benjamin-Cummings Publishing Co., Inc.; Elsevier Scientific Publishing Co.; Ferdinand Enke Verlag; Holt-Saunders Ltd; The Institute of Biology; Litton Educational Publishing International; Methuen and Co. Ltd; Peter Davies Ltd; Thames and Hudson Ltd; The Society of Economic Paleontologists and Mineralogists; Weidenfeld and Nicolson Ltd; and Yale University Press.

Lastly I would like to thank Academic Press and, in particular, Dorothy Sharp and Arthur Bourne.

Contents

Preface v

Acknowledgements vii

CHAPTER 1 INTRODUCTION 1

1. General considerations 1
2. The Phanerozoic time scale 4
3. Brief history of the concept of evolution 5
4. Physical factors limiting animal dispersal etc. 10
5. Environmental change and natural selection 15

CHAPTER 2 A BRIEF HISTORY OF HISTORICAL CLIMATOLOGY 17

1. General introduction 17
2. The Lagrange–Croll–Milankovič theories 19
3. Elsworth Huntington and the pulse of Asia 23
4. Abbot and volcanism 27
5. Brooks and British meteorologists 29

CHAPTER 3 MORE RECENT KNOWLEDGE OF CLIMATIC CHANGE 35

1. The climate of the 1960s and 1970s 35
2. Periodicities of climate 43
3. The Camp Century ice cores 53
4. Climatic data from historic time 57

CHAPTER 4 GEOMAGNETIC CONSIDERATION — 62

1. The earth's magnetic field — 62
2. Magnetic disturbances — 66
3. The atmospheric dynamo — 69
4. The upper atmosphere — 71
5. Magnetic effects and climate — 73
6. The magnetisation of rocks — 81
7. Variations in atmospheric ^{14}C content — 93

CHAPTER 5 LONG-TERM CONSIDERATIONS — 98

1. Ancient ice ages — 98
2. Possible galactic causes of periodic glaciations — 100
3. Continental drift — 105
4. Periodic vulcanism and tectonism — 108
5. Volcanic eruptions and climate — 112

CHAPTER 6 THE PALEOZOIC ERA — 115

1. Introduction — 115
2. Continental dispositions — 117
3. Paleoclimatic considerations — 119
4. Paleozoic extinctions — 124

CHAPTER 7 THE MESOZOIC ERA — 135

1. Introduction — 135
2. Continental drift — 138
3. Climatic periodicity — 140
4. Geomagnetic determinations — 142
5. Paleotemperature data — 144
6. Mesozoic climates — 149
7. Some faunal considerations — 154

CHAPTER 8 THE TERTIARY PERIOD — 159

1. Introduction — 159
2. Tertiary floras — 160
3. Theoretical considerations of climate — 165
4. Isotope data on Tertiary marine paleotemperatures — 168
5. Neogene planktonic biostratigraphy — 173

CHAPTER 9 THE QUATERNARY SUCCESSION — 177

1. Introduction — 177
2. The period involved — 177

CONTENTS

3	The United Kingdom succession	184
4	Sea-level variations	187
5	The last glaciation	189

CHAPTER 10   LATE WEICHSELIAN AND FLANDRIAN TIME — 196

1	Introduction	196
2	The late Weichselian period	198
3	The Flandrian period	200
4	^{14}C age determination	202
5	Climate during the Flandrian period	206
6	Radiocarbon variations in the atmosphere	208

CHAPTER 11   CLIMATE AND HISTORY — 211

1	Introduction	211
2	Nomadic incursions	213
3	Chinese history	220
4	North and Central America	224
5	British history	227

References — 230

Subject Index — 267

1

Introduction

1 GENERAL CONSIDERATIONS

The history of ideas includes many ironies. Concepts have frequently risen to prominence, or sunk into disrepute, along with the changing whims of fashion. Some ideas are speedily accepted and become widely influential from the moment of their formulation whilst others lack this initial phase of enthusiastic acceptance and remain decried, disputed, or simply unheard of, their existence known to relatively few people for long periods after their inception. Time and time again valid concepts have only been recognised as such long after their initial promulgation. Neither history guarantees the continued acceptance of such ideas despite evidence that they are correct. Indeed there seems to be a pronounced cycle. Ideas gain acceptance in one generation, become *passé*, and are then rediscovered, often independently of the early literature, by a later generation. It is difficult, indeed impossible, to point to any universal, common factor in such cases, apart from saying that the ideas are, at various times, unacceptable to certain arbiters of fashion. Retrospectively their history clearly says more about those arbiters, and the socio-political environment in which they lived, than about the ideas themselves.

One example that is particularly relevant to the subject matter of this book can be considered briefly here. Others, which relate to historical climatology, occur in subsequent chapters. At the time that "The Origin of Species by Natural Selection" was published many paleontologists still shared the view of Cuvier (1769–1832) and Alcide d'Orbigny (1802–1857) that the history of life on earth had been marked by a series of catastrophic extinctions. Actually the cataclysmic nature of natural processes was far from being peculiar to the theories of Cuvier and occurred elsewhere in the works of Lomonosov (1711–1765), Hutton (1726–1797), von Hoff

(1771–1837) and even Lyell (1797–1875). All such thinkers regarded floods, volcanic eruptions and earthquakes as natural phenomena that were just as relevant to the past as to the present; although Lyell emphasised the slow and uniform effects rather than episodic changes. Whilst he noted that the specific conclusions of such workers bear relatively little direct relationships to modern ideas, Newell (1967) pointed out that the "stratigraphic column" was certainly characterised by discontinuities of both lithology and fossil content. There is actually nothing in the fossil record to justify "catastrophism" as Cuvier himself understood it, nor, for that matter, a literal interpretation of Lyell's uniformity, but, nevertheless, in the early nineteenth century the known facts of paleontology seemed to justify the former. However, following the publication of Darwin and Wallace's ideas on evolution, considerations of episodic phenomena were largely abandoned by zoologists because it was considered that they conflicted with the tenets of natural selection. Indeed it was really only the publication of Umbgrove's book (1947) that led to long-term periodic phenomena, other than those relating to Quaternary climates, being considered by biologists again.

Many workers would, today, admit that there have certainly been some four or five critical environmental revolutions in the past (cf. Berkner and Marshall, 1964; Fairbridge, 1967; and Valentine, 1973). These may be listed as:

1. The appearance of the first living systems, $c.\ 3 \cdot 8 \pm 0 \cdot 3 \times 10^9$ years B.P.
2. The appearance of the first photosynthetic systems, O_2, $c.\ 2 \cdot 8 \pm 0 \cdot 2 \times 10^9$ years B.P.
3. The first carbonate shells, $c.\ 6 \pm 0 \cdot 3 \times 10^8$ years B.P.
4. The great coal age, $c.\ 3 \cdot 5 \pm 0 \cdot 3 \times 10^8$ year B.P.
5. The appearance of carbonate plankton, $c.\ 1 \cdot 0 \pm 0 \cdot 2 \times 10^8$ years B.P.

During the period that has elapsed since the publication of Umbgrove's book a number of authors have also drawn attention, often quite independently, to other somewhat periodic aspects of world faunal and floral history. Clearly any change in environmental conditions affects a variety of taxa to a greater or lesser extent, but the principal problem with which such ideas are concerned relates to possible, contemporaneous, world-wide changes of the environment that have affected the existing biota and given the varying faunal and floral associations of the past. It is upon these that the classical divisions of geological time are based. Complementary and related problems refer to periods of geological time within which there appear to have been widespread extinctions.

Simpson (1952), considering the vertebrate record, concluded that episodes of "explosive evolution" cannot be defined as limited to, or caused at, any particular point in time. In particular, it was not, in his opinion, possible to demonstrate a causal relationship between such supposed episodes of extinction and periodic, diastrophic periods affecting the earth's crust. However, in the same symposium, Newell (1952, see Fig. 1) drew contrasting conclusions when he considered

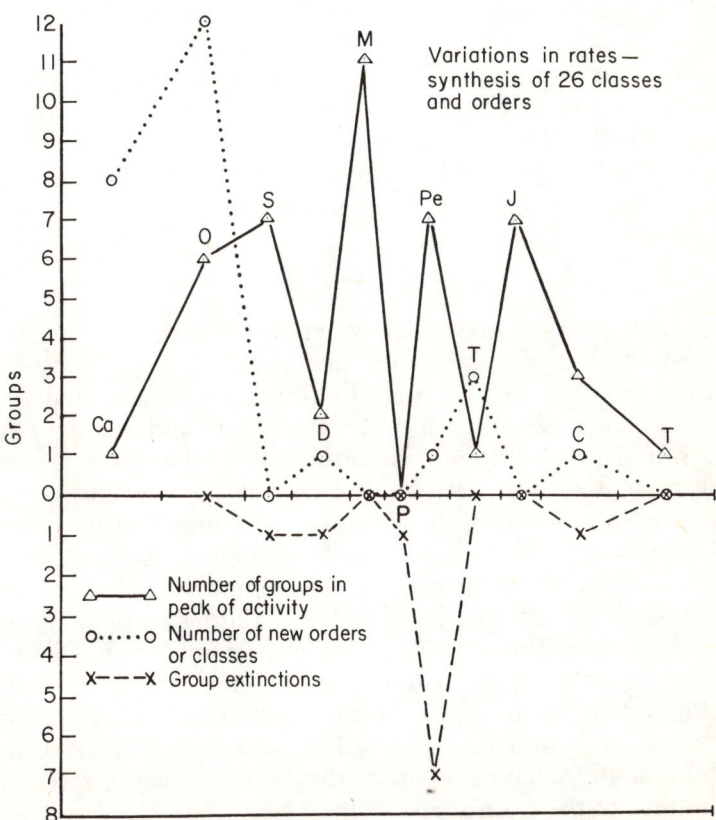

Fig. 1. A synthetic graph showing the times at which there appear to have been the highest rates of generic differentiation, together with the suggested times of the first appearance and the disappearance of the major taxa of invertebrates (Newell, 1952). Ca, Cambrian; O, Ordovician; S, Silurian; D, Devonian; M, Mississippian; P, Pennsylvanian; Pe, Permian; T, Triassic; J, Jurassic; C, Cretaceous; T, Tertiary. Compare Figs 46 and 49.

the invertebrate succession. He favoured climatic explanations for such periods of extinction and these were subsequently proffered, often independently and alongside periodic orogenic activity, by van der Hammen (1961), Pearson (1964), Ager (1973) and Budyko (1974). Such explanations envisage periodic or sporadic climatic changes as the "cosmic clutch" that has varied the pace of evolution by changing the intensity and precise nature of the selective processes acting at given moments of world history. Emergent data on geophysics and climatology now go a long way towards supporting such suggestions.

Although various suggestions which involve other parameters have been proposed, the discovery of geomagnetic reversals, and their association with climatic changes, has now focussed attention on this basic thesis. Complementarily, our knowledge of plate tectonics, which demands differing geographies in the past, as postulated by Köppen and Wegener (1924), necessarily implies changing environmental and climatic régimes.

2 THE PHANEROZOIC TIME SCALE

Relative time scales for geological events were established in the last century by the use of stratigraphy and paleontology. Those sequences which existed in particular localities were correlated on an international basis by comparing the type fossils, and components of faunal assemblages. Although the initial values that were given for the various ages on this basis now seem hilarious it is essential to view them in the context of the historical, and, more particularly, the biblical background of the times. Such age determinations undoubtedly had a great influence upon contemporary conclusions about evolution. In 1893 Walcott proposed that the Paleozoic had lasted some $17\frac{1}{2}$ m.y. (million years), the Mesozoic 7 m.y., and the Cenozoic 3 m.y. Around the same time Lord Kelvin suggested that a minimum of 20 m.y., and a maximum of 400 m.y., had elapsed since the earth was molten. These figures were subsequently corrected by Goodchild, in 1897, who concluded that 704 m.y. had elapsed since the beginning of the Cambrian.

It was only with the advent of modern, radiometric methods of age determination that it became possible to establish an independent absolute chronology with any degree of certainty and an interesting review of the early attempts at age determination is provided by Wager (1964). Reviews of more modern work are provided by Holmes (1959), Faul (1960), Kulp (1961), Evernden and Richards

(1962) and York and Farquhar (1972). The most comprehensive analysis is provided by the symposium volume (1964) of the Geological Society of London.

In principle the easiest method of assigning dates to given periods is to collect fossiliferous material from their initial and final phases and apply to it the radiometric techniques that are currently available. In practice this is not an easy process, because of the great difficulty experienced in obtaining reliable dates from sediments, and two other approaches have therefore been favoured. These comprise dating volcanic rocks that are interbedded between sediments of proven stratigraphic position, or dating igneous intrusives that have been obtained under comparable circumstances. Volcanic rocks can be dated in a number of ways which are broadly dependent upon their composition. Minerals such as sanidine, biotite, plagioclase, and whole rock basalts are exposed to the K-Ar or, occasionally, the Rb-Sr techniques. The dating of igneous intrusives is usually accomplished by Rb-Sr whole rock analysis coupled with the analysis of component minerals by the Rb-Sr and K-Ar techniques. However, a hazard of such approaches lies in the fact that plutonic bodies may have spent a considerable time at depth during which time they lost daughter isotopes and therefore give a wrong value. Complementarily, intrusives are frequently difficult to place in their correct stratigraphic position and are therefore less reliably ascribed than the lavas noted above.

For these and other reasons the various values included in the *QJGS time scale* are of varying validity. For example, McCartney *et al.* (1966) concluded that 560 ± 11 m.y. was reasonable for the base of the Cambrian but York and Farquhar (1972) favoured 590 m.y. It was, however, the Silurian which had the worst radiometric coverage of all and the QJGS values were modified by the last-named authors. Their conclusions on these and other periods are summarised in Table 1.

3 BRIEF HISTORY OF THE CONCEPT OF EVOLUTION

In general terms Linnaeus epitomised the view that all species are fixed and immutable, and declared in his "Fundamenta Botanica" (1736) that nature "has as many species as were created in the beginning". Nevertheless, prior to Linnaeus and Ray it was widely thought that any species could give rise to practically any other one, so that, far from being an obstacle to scientific progress, the views of Linnaeus introduced some order where confusion had previously

TABLE 1

The Phanerozoic time scale (after the QJGS, 1964, and York and Farquhar, 1972)

	m.y.		m.y.
CENOZOIC		PALAEOZOIC	
Quaternary		*Permian*	
Pleistocene	1·5–2??	Upper	240
Tertiary		Lower	280
Pliocene	c. 7	*Carboniferous*	
Miocene	26	Upper	325
Oligocene	37–38	Lower	345??
Eocene	53–54	*Devonian*	
Palaeocene	65	Upper	359
MESOZOIC		Middle	370
Cretaceous		Lower	395?
Upper	100	*Silurian*	430–440???
Lower	136?	*Ordovician*	
Jurassic		Upper	445?
Upper	162	Lower	c. 500?
Middle	172	*Cambrian*	
Lower	190–195	Upper	515?
Triassic		Middle	540?
Upper	205	Lower	570?
Middle	215		
Lower	225		

reigned, and the known occurrence of hybrids etc., forced even these concepts to remain open to some discussion. Adanson in his "Histoire des Familles des Plantes" (1763) argued against the absolute fixity of species, conceiving that transformations were related to the action of such external factors as domestication and climate. Buffon, who devoted much of his time to the problem of species, and tried to cross dogs with wolves, rabbits with hares, and goats with sheep, also came down in favour of limited variability, and expressed his "transformist" views most clearly in discussions of the "degeneration" of animals under the influence of climate and domestication.

Maupertuis was one of the first people to overtly accept and promulgate "transformist" ideas, and his "Essai sur la Formation des Corps Organisés" (1754) is a fairly definitive landmark in natural history. An analogous contribution of great importance was the

"Zoonomia, or the Laws of Organic Life" by Erasmus Darwin (1794), which contained a theory of the gradual "transformation" and "perfection" of the animal kingdom. "Improvements" were here considered to result from responses to a variety of external stimuli such as climate, habitat, food, diseases and domestication. Apart from rather "Lamarckian" ideas about how the trunks of elephants enable them to feed on high branches, the Zoonomia included the beginnings of such Darwinian notions as protective coloration, sexual selection etc. Indeed, by this point at the close of the eighteenth century the new doctrine of "Transformism" was clearly fairly firmly entrenched.

It was at this time that Lamarck's position at the Natural History Museum in Paris, in which he was given the job of reclassifying the collections, led him to reject the belief in the immutability of animals and in his "Philosophie Zoologique" (1809) he propounded a theory of evolution. In this he concluded that new needs "create" new organs, with the degree of development of these organs being proportionate to the use made of them, and, perhaps more important in view of subsequent controversy, that everything which an individual acquires during the course of its life is preserved and transmitted to its descendants. He was supported by Sainte-Hilaire (1772–1844) but Cuvier was one of his most overt critics.

A large part of Cuvier's own scientific activity was directed towards paleontology. His first paper on the subject, in which he compared extinct and extant species of proboscideans, was followed by a series of similar studies that culminated in the first edition (1812) of his "Récherches sur les Ossemens Fossiles ou l'on Établit les Caractères de Plusieurs Animaux dont les Révolutions du Globe ont Détruit les Especes". A second edition embodying many new facts was published in 1821–1824, whilst a third edition (1825) only differed from the foregoing in a number of alterations to the "Preliminary Discourse" which was also published under the title "Discours sur les Révolutions de la Surface du Globe". According to Cuvier, three distinct faunas had inhabited the globe during three distinct epochs. The first included giant fishes and reptiles but only a few small mammals; the second, during which land mammals came to the fore, was represented by *Paleotherium* and *Anoplotherium*; whilst the third comprised the mammoths, mastodons, hippopotami and rhinoceroses. The methods he used were, at least in essence, those which are still used today, and even his precipitate denial of the existence of any intermediate forms evinced an extensive search for them which guided paleontology into its later channels. However, the conflict between his simplistic "catastrophism" and the complexity of the fossil deposits which were even then being described, resulted in his seminal idea bearing little relationship to the data of this book.

It is undoubtedly a truism to say that the reception given to new ideas changed between 1789 and the first decade of the nineteenth century. Received with enthusiasm in the later decades of the eighteenth century, they were later to be inextricably confused, in the minds of European literati, with the horrors of the "Terror". This appears to have had an influential and unfortunate effect on the ideas put forward in biology. It was, perhaps, the publication of Lamarck's thesis that led three physicians, Wells, Prichard and Lawrence, to independently repudiate the concept of the inheritance of acquired characters. Their views, which were published in the second decade of the nineteenth century, all advanced, in varying degrees, the alternative theory of natural selection which had been foreshadowed by the writings of Erasmus Darwin. However, it was not a propitious moment for the publication of such ideas. Lawrence's book "The Natural History of Man" argued that the differences which exist between the various races of man are hereditary, have arisen by such changes as one can observe amongst litters of rabbits or kittens, and are maintained by barriers against their interbreeding. He also considered that such changes were unrelated to direct effects of food, climate etc.; concluded that men could be improved or ruined by selective breeding, just as domestic animals could be; and drew a political moral by using the European royal families and aristocracies as examples. It was almost certainly this thesis that led to the legal withdrawal of the book immediately after its publication. His suggestion that the European royal families, together with corrupt and mentally deficient aristocrats, could be improved by applying the processes of stockbreeding, would have fallen on many receptive ears and the influential figures, horrified by the recent history of France, might reasonably have been expected to attempt to suppress it. Furthermore, his discussion of the orang-utan theory of man's origins, relieved by vivid references to the buttocks of Hottentot women and what he called the "rites of Venus", was eminently readable. As Darlington (1959) remarked, the clergy read it, probably enjoyed it, and denounced it. The laity read it and enjoyed it. From Lawrence they could learn the principle of sexual selection and the analogy with animal breeding which was later to be inextricably associated with, and ascribed to, Charles Darwin. Alongside this were discussions of mutation; a comparative study of skulls which was later improved by T. H. Huxley; and ideas about "eugenics" which, as a science, was later invented by Galton. The government's reaction was inevitable. The Lord Chancellor proscribed it, whilst pamphlets denounced the folly and wickedness of the "Surgeon Lawrence" whose name was linked with that of Paine. Lawrence, faced with the options of becoming a martyr to science or renouncing his scientific opinions, chose the second path. However his work persisted and nine editions had appeared by 1848 (cf. Darlington, 1959). Its fame or infamy was extensive. Young naturalists probably studied it, including Mathew, whose priority was later to be acknowledged by Charles Darwin, and Blyth who, according to Darlington, developed the theory of natural selection. Darlington considered that the main problem for Darwin was that the idea of evolution, perhaps popular with uneducated people, was both far from respectable in academic circles and contrary to the prevailing concepts of naturalists who liked to think of their species as fixed for all time. Furthermore, it was widely identified with Lamarck's concepts. Darwin's contribution was immense, and his success was due to his great dedication to observation; to his industry; and to his patience; but it may have been assisted by half a century of "illicit" speculation amongst those people who were so disposed.

The concept of natural selection was, of course, subject to extensive controversy after Darwin and Wallace had put it forward but, once accepted, proved to be a germane and powerful influence. The immense number of publications that have ensued during the subsequent century or so are surveyed in a plethora of review articles, books and papers on evolution. However, as biologists have bent their energies to its extensive proof they have frequently closed their eyes to the one outstanding characteristic of the fossil record—the contemporaneous faunal changes which delineate the boundaries of successive periods. Nevertheless, over the last thirty years there has been a gradual, and progressively more intense, build-up of articles on this latter topic. A variety of explanations have been put forward to explain so-called catastrophic extinctions. Ager, Budyko, Newell, Pearson and van der Hammen have already been cited. Amongst other workers one can cite Schindewolf (1955) and Uffen (1963), who followed Wilser (1931) in attributing faunal discontinuities to occasional bursts of cosmic or ultraviolet radiation. Schatz (1957) proposed variations in the atmospheric oxygen content as an influential factor, whilst Cloud (1959) favoured varying levels of trace elements. Beurlem (1956) and Fischer (1965) wondered whether variations in oceanic salinity were the cause, whilst Bramlette (1965) and Tappan (1968) suggested that falls in oceanic productivity were influential. Finally, following the discovery of geomagnetic reversals a number of authors have implicated these, either directly or indirectly, as causative factors. Thus Uffen (1963) viewed decreased geomagnetic values as intimating transitory increases in cosmic radiation, whilst Hays (1971) and Mann (1972) considered that increased radiation had exerted a direct effect by increasing the mutation rates. In contrast Harrison (1968) saw geomagnetic reversals as being implicated via climatic changes that resulted from changed atmospheric conditions.

4 PHYSICAL FACTORS LIMITING ANIMAL DISPERSAL ETC.

Many textbooks and review articles exist which survey the basic tenets of biogeography and detail the environmental parameters which are currently limiting, either directly or indirectly, the distributions of animals and plants. It is not the intention of this book to provide an exhaustive, or indeed even an extensive, survey of such work, but certain general considerations need emphasising. In the northern hemisphere the northerly limits of numerous species distributions are defined by low temperatures, the most southerly limits by high temperatures. Specific examples of these considerations can be considered in a moment but first of all one may consider the more general, and well known, laws that describe anatomical characteristics in terms of climate.

The best established of these (Mayr, 1942) are Bergmann's rule, Allen's rule, Gloger's rule—and certain additional ones enunciated by Mayr for birds alone. The first, Bergmann's rule, states that amongst related species of animal those found in warmer regions are smaller than those in colder areas. This is widely true for altitudinal as well as latitudinal temperature differences and is, in general, well established. Nevertheless, exceptions do occur (cf. Carter, 1954) where some other environmental factor, such as short growing season, prevents the animal attaining large size. The rule has long been considered to reflect the value of maintaining body heat in homoiotherms, as the heat loss from the surface of a larger body will be relatively less than that from a smaller body.

Allen's rule reflects similar considerations and simply states that the extremities—tails, ears and beaks, tend to be shorter in a cool environment thereby reducing the surface area and reducing heat loss. Gloger's rule, that dark colour due to melanin pigmentation is more strongly developed in warm and humid environments, is clear in man but needs qualification elsewhere. Clearly the needs of crypsis in a dark coloured environment will lead to its selection. Mayr's additional rules involved the number of eggs in a clutch being larger, the digestive and absorptive parts of the gut being larger, wings being longer, and migratory behaviour being more developed, in birds of colder climates. Figures 2 and 3 show that analogous rules

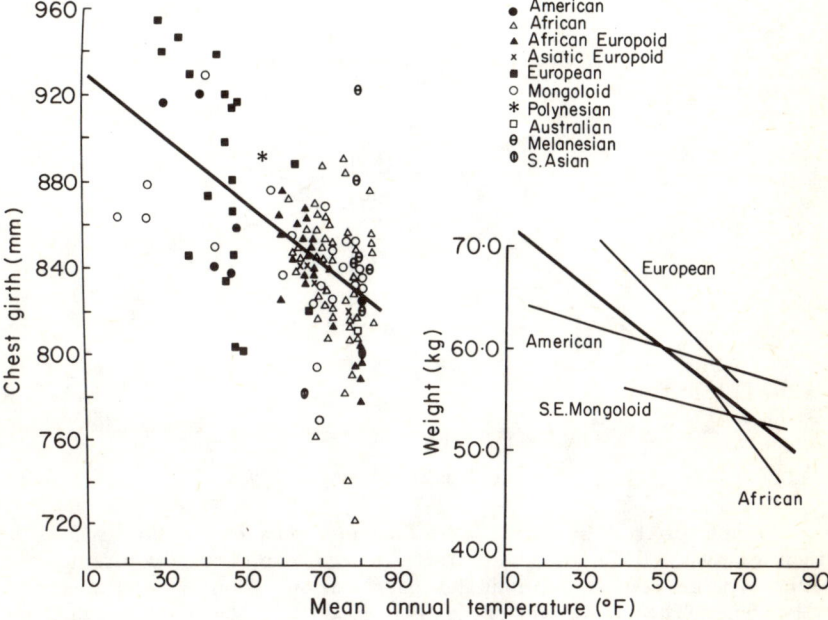

FIG. 2. Some correlates of Bergmann's rule in human populations. Chest girth and weight, which are both correlated with the ratio of body surface to volume, decrease with increasing average temperature. Only aboriginal males are included in the samples used for this Figure. (Roberts, 1973.)

are applicable to human morphology although Coon (1966), amongst others, emphasised that in the case of man, whose variation is perhaps best known, each subspecies has its own clinal system, with some being the exact opposite of others. In terms of stature he concluded that Europeans are tallest along the 25° January frost line whereas in Mongoloid Asia the optimum temperature is a few degrees colder. In Negro Africa the tallest peoples live in hot humid swamps of the upper Nile whilst the tallest pygmies inhabit the cool slopes of Mt. Ruwenzori. The tallest Australian aborigines inhabit the hottest, dampest part of their continent in the north and stature diminishes as one goes southward to Tasmania. Experimental work shows that Mongoloids achieve cold tolerance by an increase in basal metabolism, whereas Australian aborigines and Lapps achieve it by heat transfer between outgoing arterial blood and incoming venous blood. Europeans, in general, derive insulation from subcutaneous

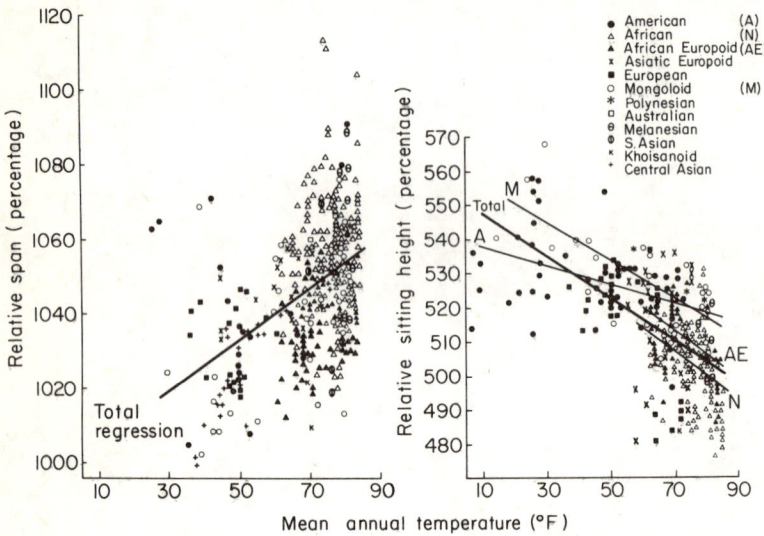

FIG. 3. Some correlates of Allen's rule in human populations. Relative span is the distance between finger tips, with arms extended, expressed as a percentage of stature. A larger relative span indicates that the arms are longer in relation to the overall height. The relative sitting height is a measure of the length of the trunk, plus head and neck, expressed as a percentage of stature. A smaller relative sitting height indicates that the legs are longer in relation to the overall height. Both measurements show a tendency towards a decreasing relative limb length in colder climates. (Roberts, 1973.)

fat, although such fat gives Negroes, who can be just as corpulent as Europeans, much less protection against the cold.

Lowry (1967) discussed many of the important environmental parameters in his book on biometeorology. These included, besides temperature itself, lapse rates at the surface and above; soil heat budget; relative humidity; vapour pressure; wind; advection and turbulent transfer. A plethora of other papers also deal with the physical factors that limit species distributions and again these involve many parameters. Temperature, in particular, was considered by Dahl (1952), Connolly and Dahl (1970), Pearson (1965), Haram and Pearson (1967) and Stuckenberg (1969). The latter author, following Bailey (1960), was principally concerned with "effective temperature", a criterion which is related to the mean annual temperature together with the mean annual temperature range. Dahl and Pearson suggested that the southern limits of the distribution of numerous arctic-alpine taxa, including species of angiosperms, coleopterans, crustaceans and fishes, are defined by

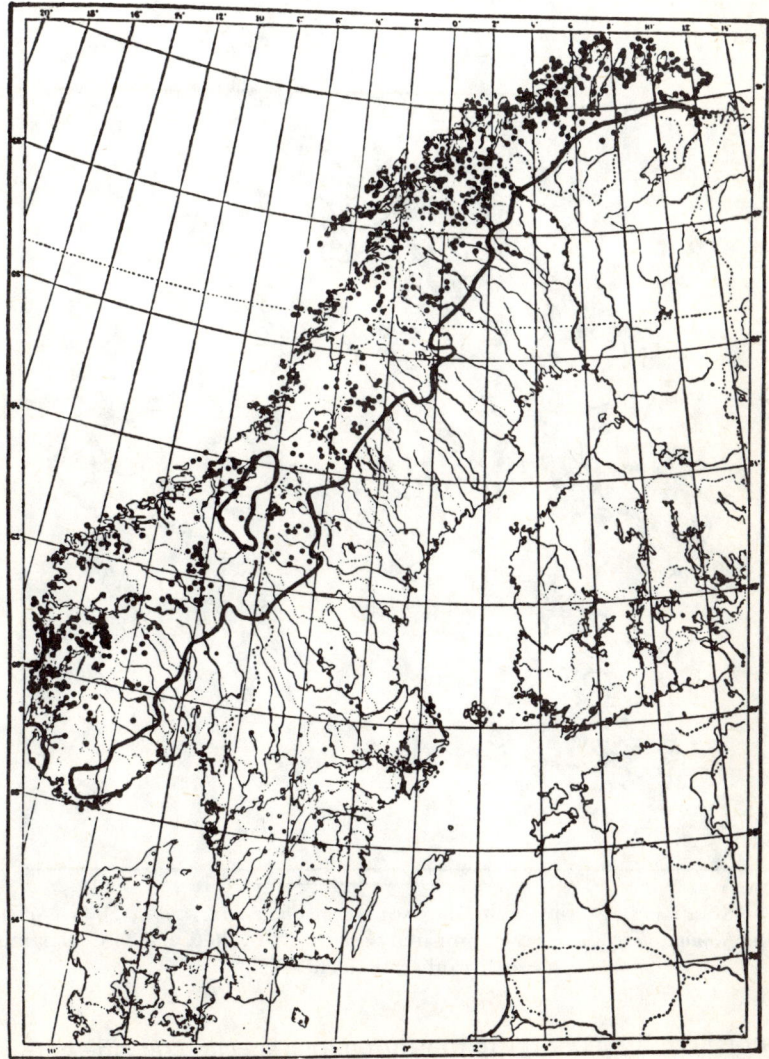

FIG. 4a. Distribution of *Sedum rosea* in Fennoscandia compared with the 25°C maximum summer isotherm.

maximum summer temperature. A number of examples are represented in Fig. 4. Complementarily, Pearson also pointed out that

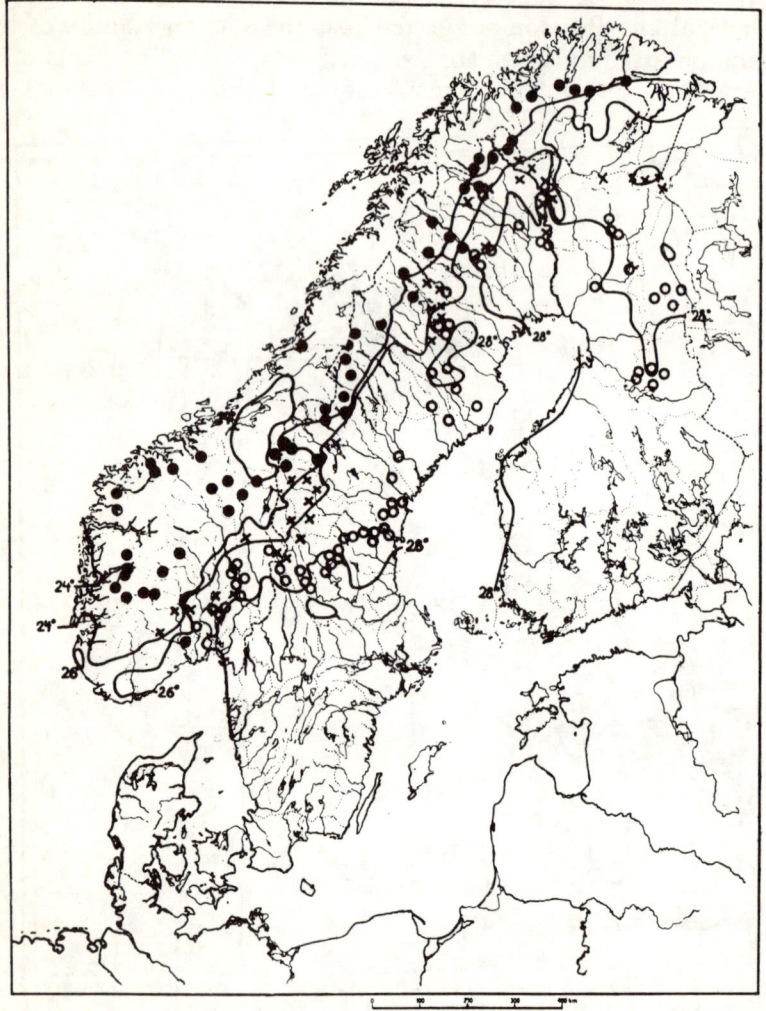

FIG. 4b. South and easternmost localities of *Gnaphalium norvegicum* (O), *G. supinum* (X) and *Ranunculus glacialis* (●), compared with the 28°C, 26°C and 24°C maximum summer isotherms (Dahl, 1952).

the northern limits of more thermophilous species coincide with the comparable winter minimum isotherms. Analogous data also exist for numerous marine and terrestrial biota whose distributions are now known to have varied in a coordinated fashion during the climatic deteriorations and ameliorations of the Quaternary era (see Chapters 9 and 10). Clearly the influence of such temperature limitation can be direct, acting directly on the enzyme systems of the species concerned, or indirect, and act via limitation of food supply etc.

Many older works also considered the part played by environmental factors in cycles of abundance. Such papers identified two principal types of cycle. The first, a 3–4 year one, was typified by the fluctuations of the numbers of lemmings, voles, hares and ptarmigan in temperate latitudes. The second type had a periodicity of $c.$ 10 years and concerned grouse, hares and their various predators in high latitudes. Explanations of such cycles invoked sunspots (Elton, 1924; Wing, 1935); weather conditions (Elton, 1929; Shelford, 1943); or fluctuations in the nutritional value of food (Nordhagen, 1928; Heape, 1931; Rowan, 1950). However, in his review of the occurrence of terrestrial vertebrates in arctic and alpine habitats, Hoffmann (1974) concluded that sunspots are no longer given any serious consideration—a slightly anachronistic conclusion in view of the greatly increased interest in such phenomena during the seventies.

5 ENVIRONMENTAL CHANGE AND NATURAL SELECTION

The coloration of animals has long interested naturalists and, in recent decades, it has formed the basis for numerous important works on natural selection. The most important of these are undoubtedly those of Kettlewell (1942; 1955a, b; 1956; 1957a, b; 1958a, b; 1961a–c; 1965; 1972), Cain and Sheppard (1950; 1952; 1954), Cain (1953), and Sheppard (1951a, b; 1952a, b; 1953; 1956; 1958). Whether dealing with the changing percentages of industrial melanic moths, or the banding and colour of the snail *Cepaea nemoralis* in the face of thrush predation, these papers all demonstrate the effects of the environment upon the balance and nature of predator–prey relationships. They, together with other similar works on ecological genetics, were summarised by Ford (1965). Cain and Currey (1968) then subsequently compared the situation which is represented by subfossil shells that were deposited during the interval between the Flandrian climatic optimum and the present day, with those prevailing today.

In the case of *Biston betularia* the increased proportions of melanic forms in areas of industrial pollution, and the decrease which occurs if pollution is reduced (Cook *et al.*, 1970), are clear examples of environmental changes inducing changes in the genetic composition of animal populations. Analogous changes are also well known amongst plants in the face of heavy metal concentrations in the soil (Bradshaw, 1965; Bradshaw *et al.*, 1965).

The proportions of the various banding and colour types of *Cepaea nemoralis* were shown at an early stage to differ from one "colony" to another, with the commonest phenotypes at any given location being those which are the least conspicuous against the prevailing background. Thus in green areas the most advantageous shell colour is yellow, which appears greenish if the animal is inside. Elsewhere pinks are advantageous on leaf litter, and reds or browns in beech woods with their reddish litter and patches of black soil. Furthermore, in a diversified habitat such as a hedgerow the least obvious patterns are the banded ones. In relatively uniform conditions selection favours unbanded ones and changes in the predominant background necessarily change the selective pressures and lead to changes in the predominant morph.

A rather different predator—the malaria parasite—is a further illustration of the diverse nature of such selective agents and effects. Malaria is well known and widespread. Practically all the people in malarial areas are subject to attack, and mortality, which is either directly or indirectly due to the disease, is very high. The parasite is therefore a very powerful selective agent. The interpretation of the selective advantages of the sickle cell anaemia and thalassemia heterozygotes in the presence of the parasite was originally advanced by J. B. S. Haldane on the basis of the similarity between the geographical distributions of the organism and the alleles concerned. Once again environmental changes which affect either the parasite or its vectors will necessarily change the selective pressures acting upon the sickle cell and thalassemia alleles. The significance of such effects to, say, the development of agriculture in Africa and Malaya was discussed by Wiesenfeld (1969), and many other suggestions about human adaptations in the face of physical or biotic factors have been confirmed. These are widely cited in the literature on physical anthropology, genetics etc. (cf. Bodmer and Cavalli-Sforza, 1976).

2
A Brief History of Historical Climatology

1 GENERAL INTRODUCTION

In the general considerations of Chapter 1 some reference was made to the fate of non-fashionable ideas. The periodicity of climatic phenomena is a case in point. During the early decades of the present century the data collected by Brückner, Huntington and, later, Brooks, were widely influential. Indeed they remained so until the 1940s. A brief glance at the dates of the various editions of Brooks's "Climate Through the Ages", or an inspection of Toynbee's consideration of nomadic incursions from the steppes, will easily establish this. However, even during this period their concepts were gradually falling into disrepute amongst workers with different interests. Two factors contributed to this. On the one hand some of their generalisations about climatic trends seemed to be contradicted by certain events in the thirties, and, on the other hand, Huntington's own interests changed somewhat—he became more interested in racial history. The relevant works gradually passed out of topical discussions, grew old on library shelves, and a younger generation of climatologists turned to what they saw as more immediate and tractable problems. It is interesting that one person whose preoccupation with the effects of climate on history increased during this period was Markham whose book on climate and the energy of nations was published in 1942. It seems highly significant that he had previously been the personal secretary of Ramsay MacDonald during the heartbreak of the 1920s and early 1930s, since the renewed interest in climatic change that has taken place during the last decade has also been accentuated by the recent economic recession.

In his essay "Of the Vicissitudes of Things" that appeared

sometime prior to 1625 Francis Bacon noted that in the low countries it had been observed that the same kind of weather recurs every 5 and 30 years. However it was not until 1890 that such cycles were rediscovered by Brückner who found evidence for them in a number of different and rather unrelated spheres. He studied the variations in the levels of European rivers; the level of the Caspian Sea; cold winters in Europe together with widespread rainfall and temperature measurements; and concluded that cycles were apparent which, in world-wide terms, comprised 10–12 cold years with excessive rainfall alternating with spells of dry years of equivalent length. In Britain it was found that the cycle could be detected in tree rings and that a 200-year-old yew tree in the Forest of Dean had grown more rapidly in the dry intervals than in the wet ones. The well-marked growth maxima occurred around 1790, 1830, 1860–1870 and 1900. Under the inspiration of Elsworth Huntington such dendrochronological studies were then carried to immense lengths in the USA.

Such data evinced an actual 33 years periodicity which was identified by the eponymous title of "The Bruckner Cycle", and substantiated by a study of the growth rings in giant sequoias from California. The Austrian's conclusions found immediate acceptance and the subsequent flurry of interest was later sustained by Brooks's studies. Nevertheless a 33 year cycle is only apparent if all the irregularities in the data are ruthlessly swept aside (see Chapter 4) and a further complicating factor is the occurrence of several other cycles with different periodicities. In the case of the British Isles the most obvious of these proved to be a rainfall cycle of 51 years 8 months, but again a number of individual years can occur "out of turn". For example, the wet year 1903 occurred in a dry period, and the exceptionally dry year 1921 occurred during a wet phase. Other weather cycles with periods of 11, 9·5, 4·7, 2·1 and 1·7 years were also apparent.

There then emerged the correlation between weather and sunspots. A relatively recent example of this that predates the present boom in interest comprises the correlation between high sunspot numbers in 1906, 1917, 1927, 1937, 1947, 1957, and high levels of Lake Victoria. However, during the period 1890–1920 there were times when the changes of the lake's level were out of phase with solar cycles. The German climatologist Baur then found that, in Central Europe, two waves of increased rain were associated with the maxima of the sunspot cycle. This led Lawrence of the Meterological Office to conclude, from available data relating to the period 1945–1962, that when the sunspot values exceed 100 the variations of global temperature are nearly in phase with them. If, however, the values fall below 100, then the global temperature and sunspot curves are in opposing phases.

2 THE LAGRANGE–CROLL–MILANKOVIČ THEORIES

Three factors have long been thought to influence the total incident solar radiation and its latitudinal distribution. The first of these is the obliquity of the ecliptic, or the angle which the plane of the equator makes with that of the earth's orbit around the sun. The second is the relative eccentricity of the earth's elliptical orbit itself; and the third is the precession of the equinoxes (Milankovič, 1930; 1938). These variables have, during the last decade, again achieved a wide notoriety and their values have recently been calculated with increased precision (see Van der Vlerk and Florschutz, 1956; Zeuner, 1952; Fairbridge, 1961a; Jardetzky, 1961; Bernard, 1962; Kutzbach *et al.*, 1968; Calder, 1974; Gribbin, 1976; Weertman, 1976). Nevertheless, the basic tenets of the climatic theories that are associated with them are now of considerable age, certainly predate Milankovič by some 140 years, and owe a considerable amount of their past fame to Milankovič's forerunner Croll. The imprecision of the available knowledge about planetary parameters, coupled with the scanty and erroneous data on geological time, made these various earlier conclusions either less precise or simply wrong.

Croll (1875) summarised the history of these ideas in what was, at the time, a widely influential book. The climatic significance of the earth's elliptical orbit was clearly appreciated by Mairan in 1765, and by 1782 Lagrange had undertaken calculations to determine its varying eccentricity. Further calculations were carried out by Laplace in 1801. Neither Herschel nor Lyell seem to have been aware of these calculations although both were well aware of the climatic implications of any orbital variations. The former (1830) concluded that the total amount of heat which is received by the earth at any particular moment in time is proportional to the length of the minor axis of the ellipse and, in the same year, Lyell made a brief reference to such ideas in the first edition of "The Principles of Geology". This consideration was somewhat expanded by the ninth edition in 1853 but his conclusions were greatly influenced by those of Arago, who denied that the orbital variations were of sufficient magnitude to affect the earth's "thermometry", by which he appeared to mean its heat balance. Other authors, who also reflect the early nineteenth century interest in such considerations, are Humboldt, Adhenar, de la Beche and Bakewell. More precise and informed calculations were then undertaken first of all by Leverrier and then by Stockwell (cf. Croll, 1890).

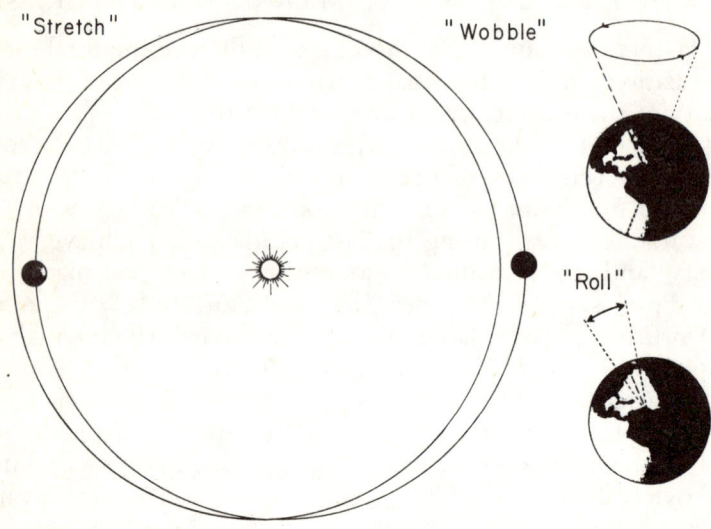

FIG. 5. Variations in the earth's orientation relative to the sun, and the "stretch" of its orbit around the sun, can change the amount of heat received by the northern hemisphere in summer (Calder, 1974; see also references in text).

The obliquity of the ecliptic causes the seasons and the greater the obliquity the greater is the contrast between the heat received in summer and winter (Fig. 5). Milankovič assumed a variation between 22° and 24·5° with a periodicity of 40,400 years. At present the earth is tilted at 23·4° relative to the plane of its orbit around the sun. During July the north pole nods towards the sun, in January the south pole does. However, the earth's orbit around the sun is not exactly circular and reaches out 3 million miles further in July than in January. As a result, summer in the northern hemisphere is not quite as warm as that in the southern hemisphere, with the difference amounting to about 7 per cent of the total solar heat incident on earth.

The Croll–Milankovič theory relates to the variations which occur in this pattern (see Figs 6 and 7). First of all the earth's orbit around

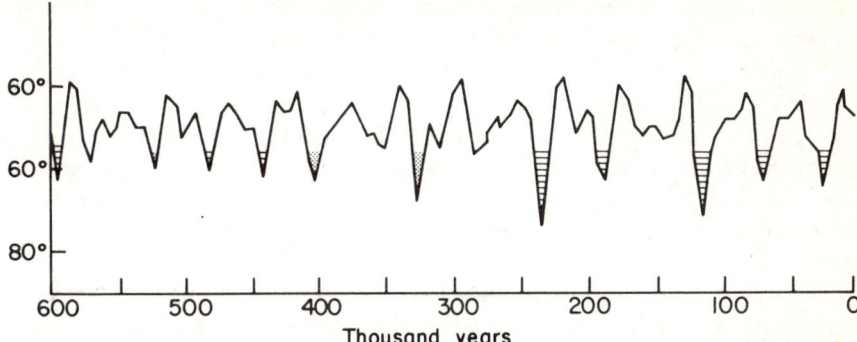

Fig. 6. Solar radiation curves calculated for the past 600,000 years at latitude 65°N. Ordinate equals latitude equivalent. During the great interglacial (between Mindel 2 and Riss 1) there are minima, the greatest of which compare with the "Mindel" and "Riss" glacial phases (Schwarzbach, 1963).

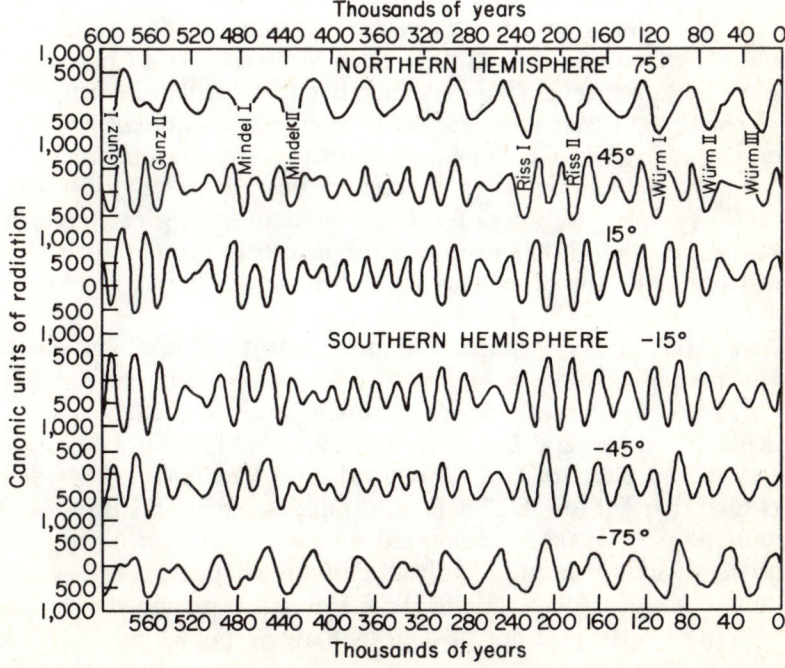

Fig. 7. Schwarzbach's (1963) comparison of solar radiation curves for the southern and northern hemispheres.

the sun varies from being almost circular to being rather more elliptical. This cycle occupies somewhere between 90,000 and 100,000 years and the most extreme effect probably reduces the intensity of incident solar energy by c. 30 per cent.

Another variable is whether the north or south pole is most closely directed towards the sun. Although current summers are warmest in the southern hemisphere, 10,000 years ago it was the northern hemisphere that had the hotter summers and this *wobble* has a 21,000 year periodicity.

The third and final contributor to the Croll-Milankovič effects, a "roll" of the earth which varies the tilt of the axis from c. 21·8–24·4°, has a rough periodicity of c. 40,000 years and the greater the tilt the more pronounced is the difference between summer and winter. During the last 10,000 years of the post-glacial or Flandrian climatic amelioration, the tilt has been diminished and this should, all other things being equal, produce cooler summers and warmer winters. The interactions of these three components of the so-called Milankovič effect produce a relatively complex pattern whose resemblance to the ice-age pattern was emphasised by Milankovič, Emiliani, Zeuner, van der Vlerk and Florschutz etc. Fairbridge (1961) also concluded that such astronomic cycles received a large measure of support from sea-level changes, and that the calculations implied a ±1·5° change in mean annual effective radiation in the sensitive 65°N latitudinal zone. He also concluded that the retardation factor for the warming of air temperatures in western Europe was c. 4,000–6,000 years. The world rise in sea level exhibited an even greater retardation of some 2,000–4,000 years with respect to air temperature which he attributed to the albedo of the albeit waning, but residual ice sheets.

Calder (1974) also carried out the relevant calculations and his curves are represented in Fig. 8. The upper curve is derived from oxygen isotope determinations, the lower one from calculations of the Milankovič effects. Lamb (1972), citing additional calculations carried out by Bernard (1962a, b; 1964) and Kutzbach *et al*. (1968), concluded that, although of *unproven reality*, such results do seem to tie into the pattern that is exhibited by the last glaciation, together with late Weichselian and Flandrian climatic changes.

Emiliani (1955a; 1955b; 1956; 1958; 1966) also provided a detailed discussion of early versions of the calculations, but Donn and Shaw (1967) concluded that his correlation of the deep-sea climatic record and the Croll–Milankovič curves was invalid. However, answering them point by point (1967), he, like Bé (1960), Ericson (1961),

Ericson *et al.* (1961), and Ericson and Wollin (1956; 1964), suggested that criticism would continue to be voiced in the future because a general evaluation of such a field is very difficult. At the present time

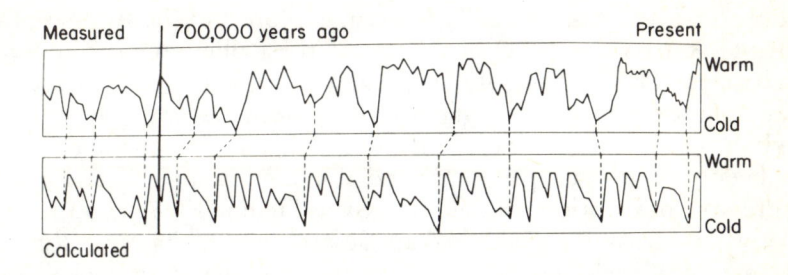

FIG. 8. The known record of past ice ages (top) compared with theoretical changes in northern hemisphere summer sunshine based on the Milankovič effect. The measured record depends on an interpretation of oxygen isotope ratios in marine fossils: the predicted values reflect Calder's recalculation of the Croll–Milankovič curves (Calder, 1974).

the increased precision of recent calculations has led to a wide acceptance of the general conclusions.

3 ELSWORTH HUNTINGTON AND THE PULSE OF ASIA

Huntington's theories provide a prime example of the way in which ideas can fall into disrepute, disappear from current knowledge, and then stage a re-emergence. They continued to be known to a relatively small band of people since readers of his own books, and of Toynbee's "Study of History", could hardly be unaware of them. Nevertheless, it is certainly true that, as Chappell (1971) said, Huntington's work fell under a pall of neglect during the middle decades of the century. Much of the neglect may be attributable to the conclusions of works such as Sauer (1936) and Murphy (1951), and Toynbee (1975) makes no reference to climate although, by then, some of the relevant works were being reissued in America.

There can be little doubt that Huntington's climatic theories were succinctly stated in his very first book, "The Pulse of Asia". His subsequent publications up to 1923 were then largely refinements of his initial thesis, and the whole was summarised in his last book (1945). In the Tarim Basin of Chinese Turkestan he had, during

1905–1906, observed numerous ruined dwellings which had apparently been abandoned during the first millennium A.D. He also observed dead vegetation within dry watercourses which penetrated into deserts for long distances beyond the limits of streams that were then water-filled. Like the early Russian explorers of the area (see, for example, Kropotkin, 1899) he attributed these phenomena to climatic changes. This was hardly surprising in view of the widespread acceptance of Brückner's conclusions. Indeed he was particularly emphatic—witness the title of his book—that such climatic changes had been of a pulsating nature, and not merely an uninterrupted, progressive desiccation. In contrast, Sven Hédin (1903), who led an expedition across the Taklamakan desert, became famous for his explanation of such observations in terms of a "wandering lake" and was so enthralled with concepts of such wandering watercourses, which do, of course, occur, that he ascribed all evidence of changed conditions to them alone, and tended to deny any overall climatic changes.

Huntington's thesis was, however, subsequently accepted and gained intellectual support from the emerging evidence for longer-term climatic variation which was epitomised by Penck and Brückner's (1909) paper on the glaciations of the Alpine and Tyrolean regions. In an endeavour to obtain evidence for the widespread nature of the climatic pulsations that he envisaged, Huntington later carried out field observations in south west Asia and North America (1911; 1914b). The resulting evidence from south-west Asia proved less convincing, and generated more controversy, than his earlier work. Many geographers and historians who were prepared to accept his earlier conclusions now baulked at these more recent ones. Nevertheless, he was himself quite clear about the world-wide nature of such climatic variations, and the immense influence which they had exerted upon the course of history. Indeed he proceeded to devote many years to its proof.

Bearing in mind the wide dissemination of Brückner's ideas and the equally wide influence of Croll's albeit incorrect conclusions, it is not surprising that Huntington soon sought solar factors to account for his data. Without any doubt one of the most impressive successes of such climatic work in the early decades of the century was the link that then emerged between Huntington's climatic conclusions and sunspots, which Chappell (1971) thought were still little known. Little known in 1970 perhaps, but widely influential in the twenties.

Huntington suggested that sunspots may exert their influence via charged particles rather than by "ordinary" radiation. Discovering

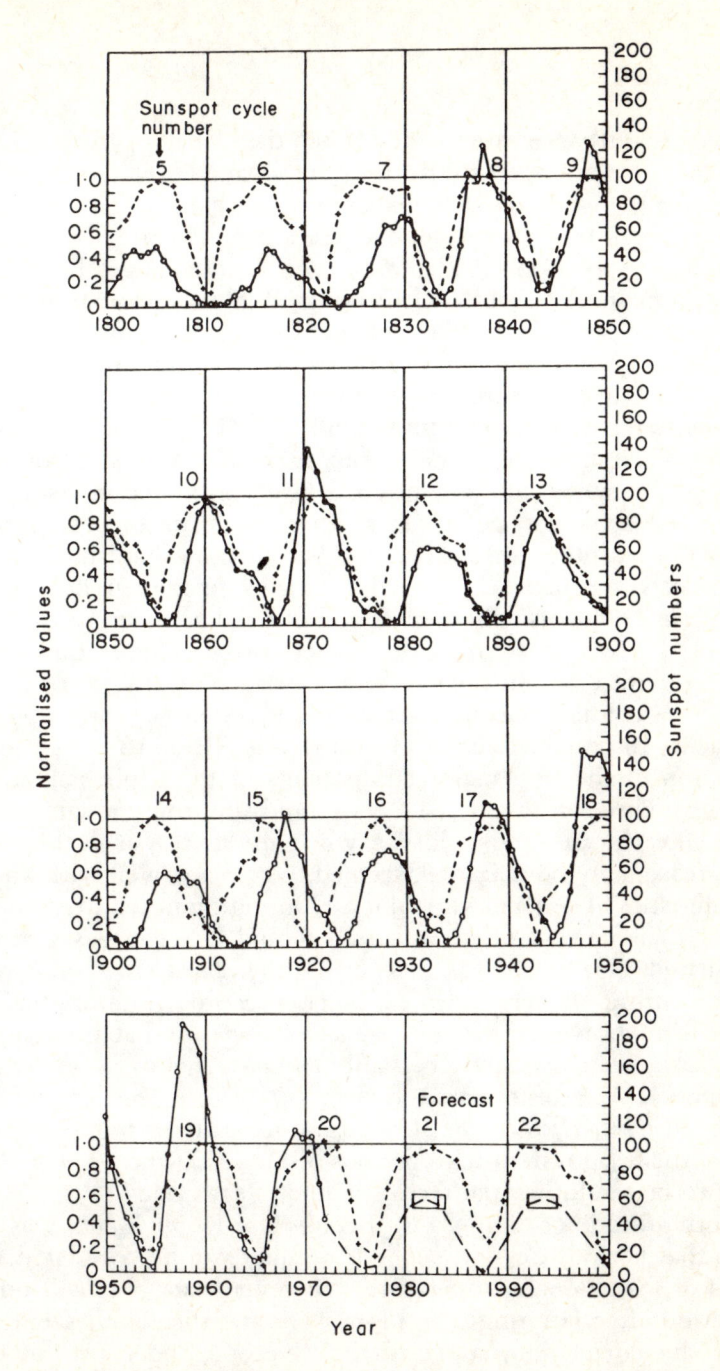

FIG. 9. The dashed line shows variation in sunspot number, and the solid line the normalised value of the tide raised on the sun by the tidal planets (Gribbin, 1976, after Wood).

that solar disturbances are greatest when the planets, particularly the larger ones, are arranged so that they are separated from one another by 90°, he then predicted ionospheric disturbances from tables of planetary positions. In recent decades analogous predictions have been made by Nelson (1952; 1962), who acknowledges his debt to Huntington, and by Gribbin (1976) (Fig. 9). Huntington himself was also clearly indebted to workers such as Brown, Birkelund and Wolf, and said so quite explicitly (1923). In particular, Brown had considered the orbital periodicity of Jupiter, which could reasonably be expected to have the maximum individual influence, and pointed out that this is just under 12 years—compare the 11·2 year sunspot cycle. Furthermore, when Jupiter's influence was considered in association with that of Saturn (9·93 years) there was an incontrovertible correlation with the sunspot cycles. The actual mechanism by which such effects are manifest actually remains unproven but, at the present time, it is usually seen as reflecting the changing centre of mass of the solar system as the planets orbit. This might have a "stirring" effect within the sun.

With less credibility Huntington also suggested that the 80–90 year periodicity of certain sunspot phenomena is related to the period of revolution of the two major components of the triple star Alpha-Centauri. This period is *c.* 81·2 years and the times at which they approach each other most closely, when any force which they exert might reasonably be maximal, seemed to coincide well with known characteristics of sunspot variability. Huntington noted that the next year of their close mutual approach would be 1956—as Chappell emphasised 1957–1958 was the period of highest sunspot number known during the centuries of precise records. Huntington and Visher were, however, at some pains to emphasise that any relationship between solar activity and Alpha-Centauri was wholly hypothetical. In recent years (cf. Gribbin, 1976) it has become clear that the *combined effects of the planets* produce patterns in the centre of mass of the solar system with periods of 11, 22, 30 and 80 years. This seems to be the influential factor in an 80 year cycle.

Huntington, in common with Brooks and Köppen etc., was well aware that periods of high sunspot number can be correlated with phases of low global temperature. However, data obtained during the period after Huntington's ideas were at their zenith seemed to negate this correlation, suggest a positive one, and contributed, in part, to the diminution of his fame. Huntington actually considered that the most direct global result of increased sunspot number was an increased *storminess* and, in saying this, he was following the conclusions of Kullmer, a German professor at Syracuse University. Kullmer had mapped the path of cyclonic storms in North America in relation to sunspot activity and demonstrated that such storms intensify within the central part of their track during phases of high sunspot number (cf. Kullmer, 1933). Complementarily, they are more diffuse during phases of low sunspot activity. One important feature that also emerged was that the northern hemisphere cyclonic belt was clearly centred on the magnetic rather than the geographical pole. Support for this solar-cyclonic hypothesis then came from the observations of a Dr Veeder (cf. Huntington, 1917). He had discovered that auroral displays are at once followed by an intensification of both high and low pressure cells, and then, after a further few days, by increased meridional exchange. Explanations of these observations envisaged a transfer of air from higher to lower altitudes, thereby reinforcing the high-pressure centres, and such conclusions are clearly coincident with many more recent ones that have apparently frequently been made in ignorance of Huntington's work (cf. Chapter 3) although Chappell certainly drew attention to the support which the meteorology of 1968–1969 gave to Huntington's theories. That winter brought record-breaking extremes of both cold and moisture to many parts of western North America, to the northern great plains, and to the area where cyclonic storms converge near the St Lawrence River. All such areas lie in the cyclonic belt and therefore, according to Huntington's theories, within the path of increased storminess. Corroborative evidence seemed to be provided by the flooding of South California and the high levels in Lake Galilee, the southern California floods being the worst since 1938 which was also a year of very high sunspots.

There remains the problem of *heterochronism* (Gumilyov, 1964; 1966a; 1966b). Huntington was well aware that different global areas show different responses at times of sunspot maxima and minima. He therefore suggested that *non-cyclonic* areas do not reflect *sunspot activity* but rather show an increase in temperature during phases of high sunspot number which may be the result of radiation from faculae. These, he thought, had a maximum effect when sited near the centre of the sun.

4 ABBOT AND VOLCANISM

Chapter 5 includes a discussion of periodic tectonic and volcanic activity. It is, however, appropriate to mention Abbot's work at this point. Dr C. G. Abbot was over a hundred years old when he died in

December 1973. In his classical work (Abbot and Fowle, 1913) he considered, not only sunspots, but the periodicity of volcanic eruptions and their effects on climate. This topic has since been discussed with varying credibility by a number of workers in recent years (cf. Lamb, 1967; Winkless and Browning, 1975). Abbot plotted the decrease in incident solar radiation following volcanic eruptions (Fig. 10) and then combined these transmission data with curves of sunspot periodicity. The combined curve $P + S$ he considered to exhibit a high degree of correlation with mean annual global

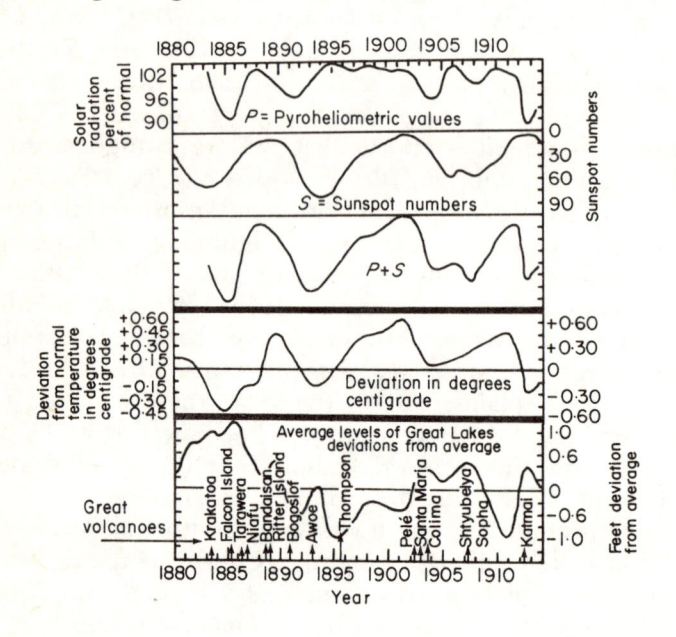

FIG. 10. A comparison of the great volcanic eruptions (arrows at bottom) with various climatic and solar parameters (after Abbot and Fowle, 1913, from Winkless and Browning, 1975).

temperatures. This idea that volcanic dust may have important climatic effects is actually, once again, very old. Benjamin Franklin had suggested that the hard winter of 1783–1784 was due to dust released by Icelandic eruptions or to disintegrating meteorites. Other references occur in the intervening period but it was the eruption of Katmai in 1912 that stimulated the interest of Abbot and Fowle and also Humphreys (1913). Defant (1924) made a study of the strength of the atmospheric circulation during the two years following each of the four great eruptions, Krakatoa, Tarawera, Bandai San and the

West Indies (1883, 1886, 1888, and 1902, respectively), and considered that the circulation was strengthened for the subsequent two years. In contrast, Brooks and Hunt (1929), taking the eruptions of 1875, 1912 and 1914 into consideration, decided that the strengthening of the circulation only persisted for some six months.

As recently as 1972 Dr Abbot is reported as complaining that few people took his cyclic work seriously. He personally worked on solar power for his last decade and Winkless and Browning (1975) consider that his cyclic studies on weather had been totally "discredited".

5 BROOKS AND BRITISH METEOROLOGISTS

In his individual papers Brooks made considerable contributions to the contemporary knowledge of world climate. Furthermore, in his synoptic works (1934; 1949) he reviewed a wide variety of other data elucidated by Huntington and many other workers in a variety of fields. In the revised edition of "Climate Through the Ages", he considered oceanic circulation, solar radiation, the astronomical components of world climate, cloudiness, continentality and orogenesis. He then followed these with a consideration of continental drift, Carboniferous and Quaternary glaciations and the climate of the historical period. One caveat needs to be mentioned at this point. Toynbee, in his study of nomadic incursions from the Eurasian steppes etc., leant heavily upon Huntington's conclusions about climate. In his later works Brooks then used Toynbee's conclusions to corroborate climatic data. Clearly such circular considerations have to be approached with care.

When considering the overall climatic characteristics of the geological past, Brooks concluded that one of the principal features of the "warm" periods, which he considered had predominated for much of world history, was a relatively small difference between the polar and equatorial climates. As a meteorologist he was acutely aware that no single factor could explain the diversity of such past climates. He was equally clear that any causal factor suggested as an explanation for such spatio-temporal diversity must affect both the atmospheric and oceanic circulations, but that the part played by these circulations was by no means fully understood.

An equal diffidence characterised his attitude to the contemporary knowledge of solar radiation and its variation during sunspot cycles. Well acquainted with Huntington's theses he laid particular stress on the known occurrence of apparent 11 year cycles in Australian

Carboniferous clay deposits. The interest in Chinese dynastic annals as a source of climatological information was also reflected in his quoting Chu's and Wittfogel's studies, whose conclusions seemed to suggest that marked sunspot maxima had occurred towards the close of the eleventh century and in 1372. Indeed the latter seemed to be the highest during the last two millennia. Although the relationship between such maxima and terrestrial climatic conditions certainly remained obscure Chu (1926) had found that, in China, the number of severe winters per century fell to a minimum between A.D. 600 and 800, and then rose to a maximum between A.D. 1100 and 1400, and the variations seemed to parallel very closely those known from independent European evidence.

Indeed it was, perhaps, for his studies on the available data about climatic changes during historic time in Europe that Brooks was best known. In this he has subsequently been followed by Lamb and Manley. He collated an immense number of data from European history and, like Easton (1928), drew careful generalised conclusions from them about annual temperatures, wind direction, the severity of winters and the warmth of summers. From the available Sinic data he also decided that the fourth, sixth and seventh centuries, together with the fifteenth and sixteenth centuries, stood out as particularly dry—the second, third, eighth, twelfth and fourteenth as wet.

Figure 11 gives generalised curves, illustrating those derived by

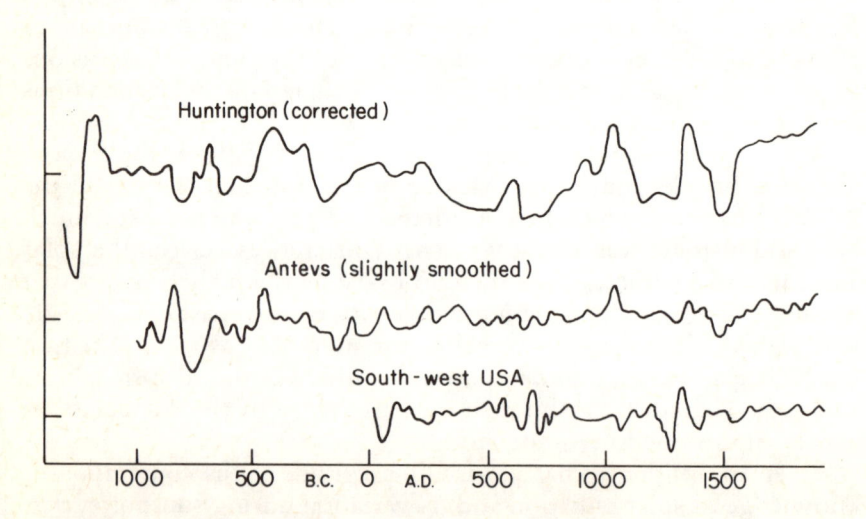

FIG. 11. A comparison of the long-established suggestions relating to rainfall variation in the USA (Brooks, 1949).

Brooks for the rainfall of Europe, Asia, North America and East Africa according to the data of Huntington *et al.* (1925). The first 3 regions seemed to him to exhibit a good deal of resemblance and certain specific discrepancies might, he suggested, merely reflect the inherent difficulties of dating in the absence of an absolute time scale. East Africa was certainly the most discordant but the dating was, in that case, entirely conjectural. The first 3 are, in fact, regions lying between 35°N and 65°N, regions in which Brooks considered rainfall to be the result of barometric depressions. In contrast his 4th set of curves was constructed with the intention of reflecting variations in the equatorial, low-pressure belt. This is separated from the foregoing by the subtropical high-pressure belt of monsoon rainfall. Even 30–50 years ago the available information suggested that this last-named area exhibits variations that are opposite in character to those observed farther north—the rainfall being greatest when the general atmospheric circulation is weakest.

Brooks favoured a variety of solutions to the problem of short-term cycles. The 9·5 year periodicity was considered to be related to the movements of the great subtropical anticyclones. These appeared to move from north to south and back again with a period of 19 years, giving two periods of maximum and minimum rainfall respectively in middle to high latitude countries such as Britain and Scandinavia. He thought that the cause of the 4·7 year cycle was correlated with the movement of ice by the East Greenland current. Very large amounts of ice were apparently brought to Iceland in every fourth to fifth year and were associated with a strong polar high-pressure system moving southwards—causing Atlantic depressions to assume a more southerly track. As a result Britain received more rain than usual. However, very short rainfall cycles of 2·1 and 1·7 years complicated the overall pattern. More widespread correlations also emerged, with a poor Nile flood in summer often being followed in the succeeding winter and early spring by low barometric pressure and consequent stormy weather within the triangle bounded by Britain, Iceland and Norway.

Synoptic explanations of such interrelationships relied heavily upon Walker's papers (cf. 1924). He had established that global changes (compensations) of barometric pressure were not haphazard but followed fairly clearly defined patterns which he embodied in rules. For example, he considered that when pressure is higher than is usual in a region which is normally characterised by high pressure, such as the subtropical anticyclone areas, then there is a tendency for the pressure to be higher than average in all such regions. Complementarily, in those areas that usually have rather low pressure it is simultaneously lower than usual. If pressure is above normal in the Azores region it will tend to be equally high in a more or less circumglobal belt running from Hawaii to North Mexico, across Bermuda and North Africa. On the other hand it will be below average over the stormy belt running from Kamchatka and the Aleutian Islands, across Canada, Newfoundland and Iceland, the British Isles, Norway and northern Asia. There is also a simultaneous tendency for pressure to be below average near the equator. He was convinced that these contrasting pressure conditions were controlled by, or related to, sunspot cycles. Increases in the number of sunspots were associated with pressure increases in zones of normally high

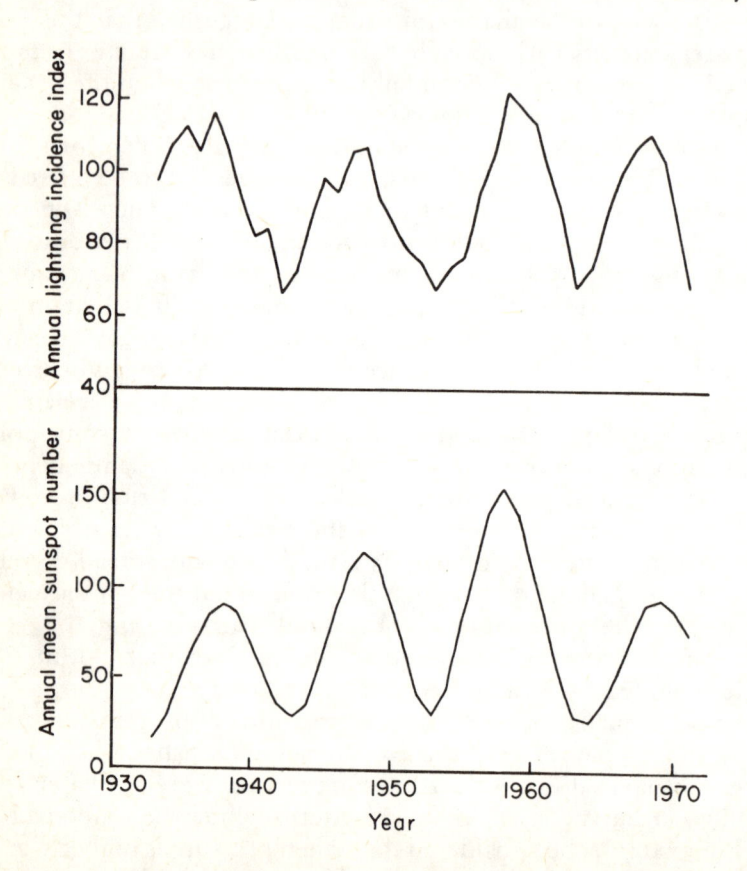

FIG. 12. Annual lightning index (above) calculated as the mean number of thunderstorm days raised to the power of 1·9, compared with the yearly mean sunspot number (Stringfellow, 1974).

pressure, and decreases in those zones normally characterised by low pressure (cf. Huntington and Visher, 1923).

After further studies Clough (1933) stated that 11, 37, 83 and 300 year cycles are apparent in auroral data, the frequency of severe winters, Chinese earthquakes, Nile floods, tree growth in Arizona and wheat prices in England. Brooks (1934) had also confirmed that the annual frequency of thunderstorms was closely correlated with sunspot number (compare Fig. 12). The incidence of such storms in northern latitudes—Siberia, Sweden, Norway and Scotland—and in southern latitudes—the West Indies, south eastern USA and southern Asia—appeared to be greatest when sunspots were most numerous. Between these two belts lay a region including England, Wales, Holland, and Germany, together with the northern and western parts of the USA, in which such a relationship seemed less clear but was still generally positive. As rainfall is associated with such thunderstorms in the interior of continents this evinced an association between sunspot number and rainfall maxima.

At about the same time Sir George Simpson (1929) discussed the probable effects of large oscillations in incident solar radiation, comparable with those predicted by Milankovič. He concluded that the first effect of an increase in radiation would be to raise the temperature everywhere on the earth's surface, but more particularly in low latitudes. This would then increase the rate of evaporation of water and the strength of the atmospheric circulation. More evaporation would then lead to an increase in global cloud cover and in precipitation. However, as clouds reflect a large part of the incident solar radiation, an increase in cloud cover then lowers global

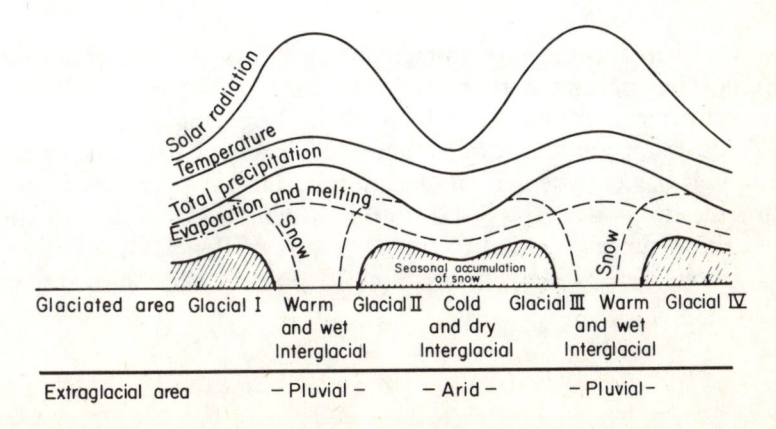

FIG. 13. A summary diagram of G. C. Simpson's glacial theory (Schwarzbach, 1963).

temperatures. In high latitudes and altitudes a large part of the total precipitation falls as snow and, as the radiation increases, the proportion of the precipitation which falls as snow decreases, but for a time this decrease was seen as being slower than the increase in total precipitation. Hence snow falls increase initially but, with a further increase in the incident radiation, the general rise of temperature would cause so much less of the precipitation to fall as snow that the total snowfall would diminish (Figs 13 and 14). Accumulation of

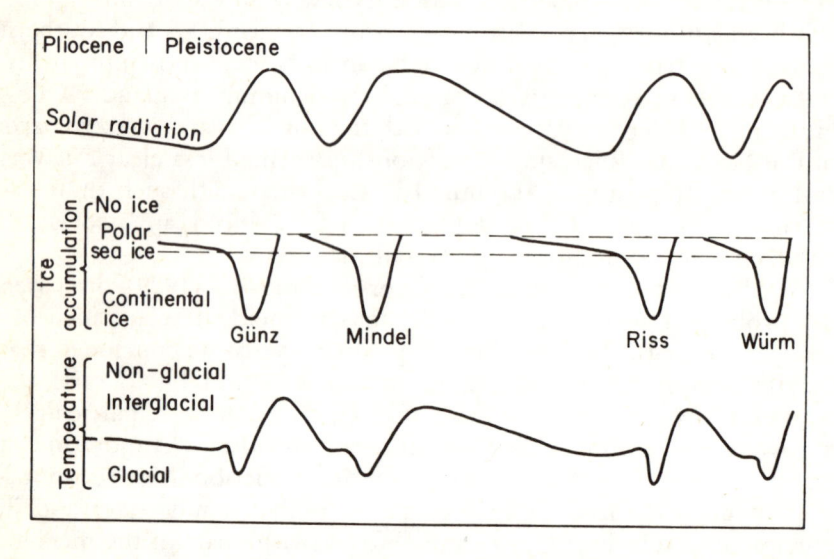

Fig. 14. G. C. Simpson's glacial theory as modified by Bell (after Schwarzbach, 1963).

snow to form ice-sheets results from an excess of snowfalls over melting. The melting is represented in curve IV of Fig. 13, and, as long as summer temperature remains below freezing point, it is very low. With rising temperature it increases slowly at first but, as soon as the melt has exposed the underlying surface, it proceeds rapidly. Figure 13 shows the effect of a double oscillation of solar radiation and as these curves seemed to fit the results of Penck and Brückner (1909) they were widely quoted (cf. Brooks, 1949; Schwarzbach, 1963).

3
More Recent Knowledge of Climatic Change

1 THE CLIMATE OF THE 1960s AND 1970s

Our modern conceptions of atmospheric organisation are portrayed in Figs 15 and 16 whilst Chapter 2 demonstrates the long-standing and often well-informed interest in climatic change. At the present time a phase of global cooling has reversed the previous upward trend of temperature and the misery caused by this changing situation, coupled with a widespread ignorance of earlier works on historical or synoptic climatology, has led to a spate of publications in recent years. One may cite, for example, the works of Lamb himself (loc. cit.) and works such as Calder (1975) or Gribbin (1976). These have attempted to both verify and publicise the widespread nature of the trends observed.

The disasters resulting from such climatic events have been most horrific within the latitudinal belt 10–20°N, and particularly in its African zone. In the Sahelian region, in Mauretania, Senegal, Mali, Upper Volta, Chad and the Cape Verde Islands, there has been a succession of drought years, accompanied by heart-rending famines. The FAO estimated that in the Sahel zone of West Africa many thousands of people, and some $3\frac{1}{2}$ million head of cattle, died in 1973. In Ethiopia too, the catastrophic deaths and famine finally hit world headlines despite earlier attempts of the local establishment to cloak the situation in unrelieved secrecy. Similar problems beset other areas in comparable latitudes. India, Bangladesh, Trinidad and Mexico all suffered to varying degrees. By the early 1970s such examples clearly hinted, except to very perverse eyes, that a latitudinal anomaly in the general atmospheric circulation must be the underlying cause. Workers such as Western and Praet (1973) were certainly quite clear that ecological changes in East African game reserves were predominantly climatic in origin and that both overgrazing and damage by elephants were secondary effects.

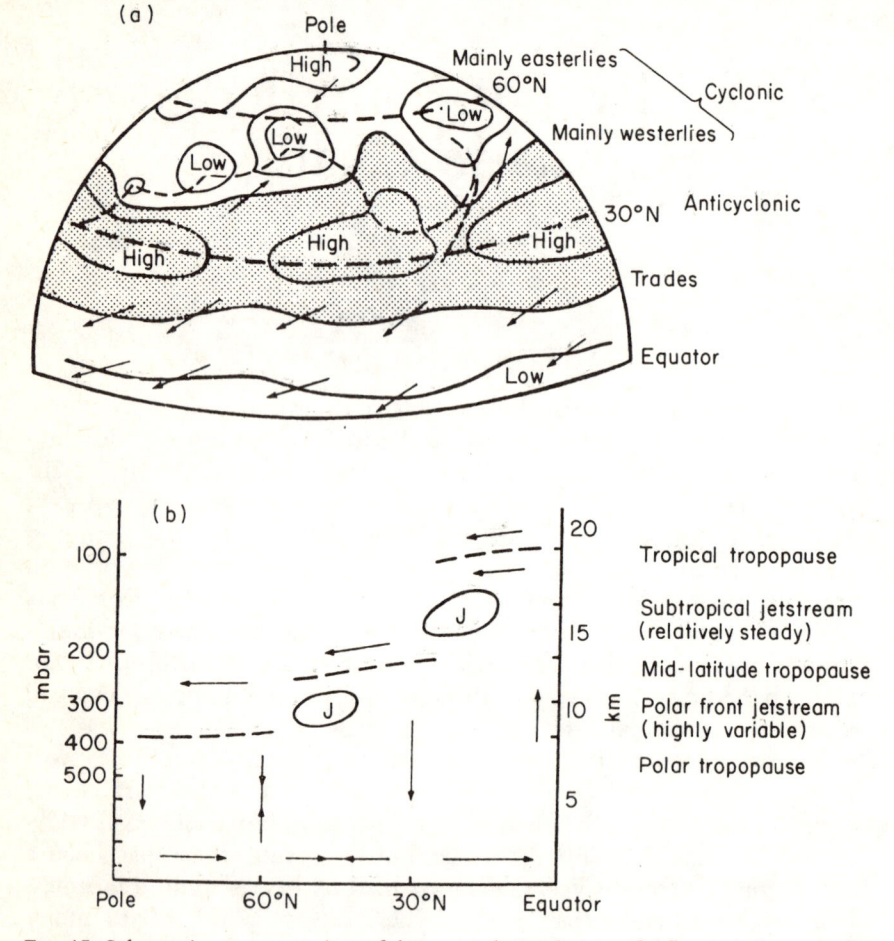

FIG. 15. Schematic representation of the general circulation of the atmosphere on an idealised earth, ignoring the effects of continents, oceans and the seasons. (a) The surface pressure pattern as it may be on one day. The long period average would show simple zones of low and high pressure. (b) A vertical cross-section from pole to equator. (After Sutcliffe, 1966.)

In the southern hemisphere the floods and desert blooms of Australia led to similar conclusions although Salinger and Gunn (1975) and Salinger (1976) pointed out that the climatic curves for New Zealand do not exactly parallel those for other global areas.

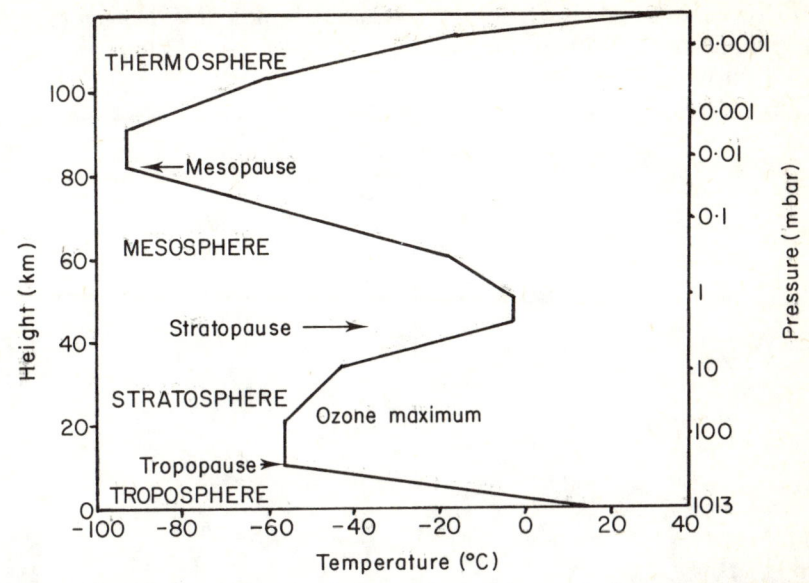

FIG. 16. Overall representation of pressure and temperature changes with height up to about 110 km. Note in particular the tropopause and the zone of maximum ozone concentration and the warm layer above it. (Courtesy of McGraw-Hill Book Co.)

They concluded that New Zealand was cooling from 1880 to 1900, and that it had its coldest period from 1900 to 1935, when the northern hemisphere was experiencing warm years. Conversely, their data suggested that during the last three decades New Zealand has warmed up whilst the northern continents have been cooling. Temperatures there rose by 1°C over those years and the recent retreat phases of west coast glaciers show a good relationship with mean annual temperatures.

During the quinquennium 1968–1972 the records of the average temperature recorded by nine North Atlantic weather ships stationed between 35°N and 66°N fell 0·5°C below the values of the 1940s. Between the mid-1940s and 1970 global mean temperatures seem to have fallen by 0·33°C (Gribbin, 1976) and the dates for the annual harvest were some 9 days later during 1960–1973 than during the foregoing 20 years—indicating the longer growing period that was required. However, Hawson (1974) was unable to find any evidence for a persistent trend of average atmospheric temperature, whilst Miles and Follard (1975), who detected a slight trend of the subpolar pressure minimum towards the equator, concluded that there was no trend for the maximum of the westerlies. They felt that concepts which envisaged a shift of the climatic zones towards the equator were untenable. Nevertheless, Kukla and Kukla (1974) reported a rapid increase in snow and ice-cover during 1971–1972 that persisted into following years (see Fig. 17), and Wahl and Bryson (1975),

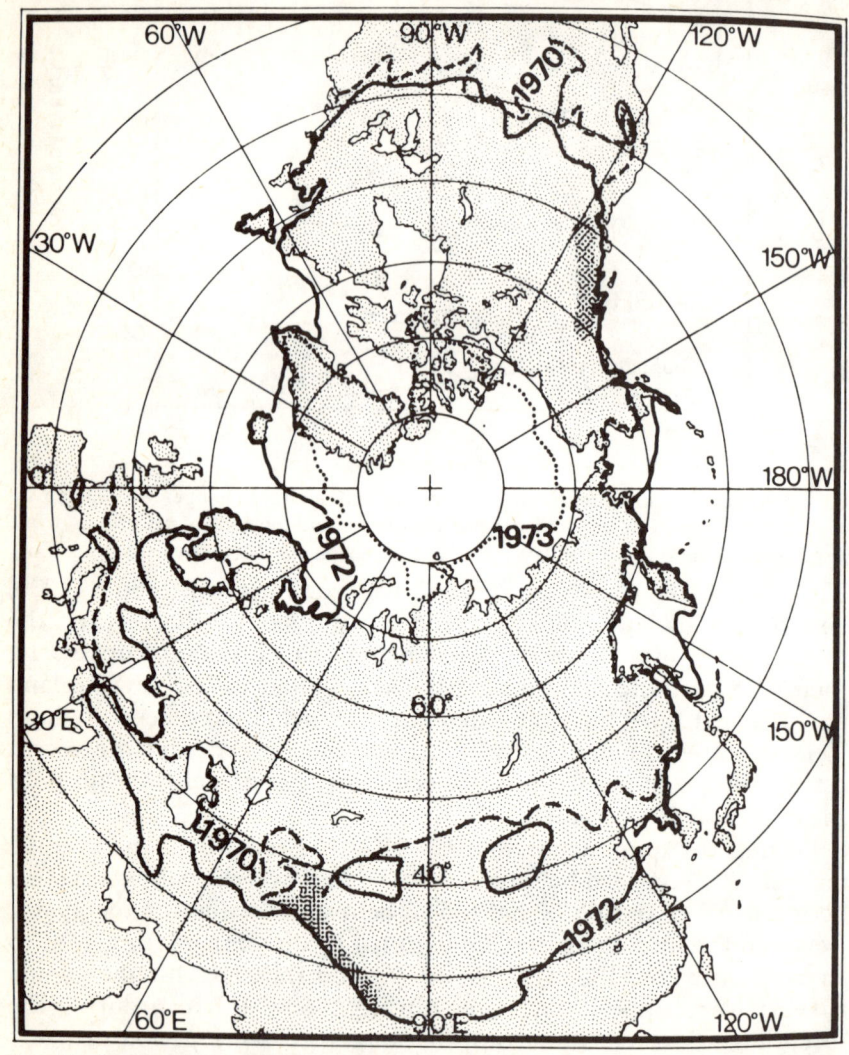

FIG. 17. Snow and ice-cover boundaries for the northern hemisphere. The dashed line shows the boundary at the beginning of 1970, and the solid line the boundary at the beginning of 1972. The dotted line around the North Pole marks the maximum extent of pack ice in September 1973, covering large areas of formerly open water. Heavily stippled areas correspond to mountainous regions where snow failed to melt in the summers of 1971, 1972 and 1973. (Kukla and Kukla, 1974.) (Copyright American Association for the Advancement of Science.)

considering North Atlantic surface temperatures, concluded that the change from the Little Ice Age conditions (q.v.) to those of the present century were more or less wiped out between 1951 and 1972. Furthermore, although Whillans (1976), using radio echo-sounding equipment, concluded that the West Antarctic ice sheet had undergone no "important" changes during the last 30,000 years, data from the south east quadrant of the Ross ice shelf (Thomas, 1976) indicate that, near the grounding line, the ice shelf is growing thicker by almost 1 m year^{-1}. This would imply an advance of 1 km year^{-1} for the grounding line between the west Antarctic ice shelf and the Ross ice shelf.

On Baffin Island seasonal running means for temperature and precipitation during the period 1960–1969 showed a marked decrease, by as much as 2·1°C, for the mean temperature of the ablation season (June–August). However, the complicated nature of the events is reflected by the fact that the accumulation season (September–May) exhibited an equally pronounced increase—by as much as 2·0°C (Bradley and Miller, 1972). Aerial photography showed that the established snowbanks generally decreased in area between 1949 and 1960, but then increased markedly in the sixties. In contrast the termini of glaciers continued to recede, although in 1970 two cirques, snowfree in 1960, contained glacierets. Namias had previously suggested that a new climatic régime began over the North Pacific and North America in 1961 as a direct result of warmer water replacing cold surface water in the North Pacific. This rise in oceanic temperature was conceived as amplifying the standing long wave pressure pattern in the northern hemisphere. Under these circumstances Baffin Island is situated in a critical position and slight changes in the upper air trough over eastern North America significantly affect its climate. In fact, immense numbers of papers deal with the changing conditions on glaciers etc. Krenke (1974), who summarised the climatic conditions for glacier formation and the occurrence of glacial climates, emphasised that all the climatic zones are considerably displaced during those epochs in which there is an anomalous recurrence of zonal processes. He pointed out that the shapes of glaciers are extremely sensitive to variations in the strength of cyclonic activity, and that all glacial districts of the Arctic are associated with low-pressure troughs on averaged charts. The deeper these troughs are, the greater the icing which occurs.

Lamb (1976), taking into account Winstanley's conclusions (see below), suggested that what has happened in the northern hemisphere in recent years can be largely attributed to a change in the prevailing wave positions of the circumpolar vortex. This, in spite of the fact that we remain ignorant of the causes of such shifts involving the centre of the polar cap itself. He intimated that during 1971 the Canadian Arctic became overwhelmingly involved in the cooling that had set in sharply elsewhere in the far north in 1961. Just as sharply the coldest centre was transferred to the Canadian sector. This resulted in an increase in the south to north thermal gradient between the western Atlantic and northern Canada, particularly during winter, and greatly increased the energy of the atmospheric circulation over the North Atlantic. Mild air was driven towards Europe, and more saline water to Iceland, although these conditions do not seem to have penetrated so far into the Arctic as did the general warming of the twenties and thirties. Doubts about whether this situation can lead to a restoration of the conditions prevailing prior to 1960 are strengthened by the observation that the centre of the polar cold régime, together with the waves in circumpolar vortex, returned to their 1960s positions for a few months in both 1973 and 1975. The ice then subsequently increased again in the sector east of Greenland and once more approached the coast of Iceland in July and August 1975—perhaps for the first time this century in those particular months. Reverting to suggestions that are similar to those made by Brooks in an earlier decade, Lamb commented that the great variations to which both the volume of water transported by the east Greenland current, and the southward penetration of this water in the East Iceland current, are prone, may be one of the more interesting and important aspects of climatic change. It may affect both the development of major ice ages and also the Little Ice Age of recent centuries.

In this context it is worth noting that Mason (1971) provided a review of the global atmospheric research programme and Belrose *et al.* (1975) showed the extent to which wind changes at different altitudes are mutually interrelated. General surveys of the relationships which exist between weather systems and both the polar and subtropical jet streams are provided by various works on synoptic and dynamic meteorology (e.g. Barry and Chorley, 1971). However Winstanley (1973) demonstrated that records from a selection of representative stations within the summer, monsoon, rainfall zone of the northern hemisphere display a striking parallel with the overt frequency of the westerly weather type over the British Isles (Lamb, 1972). Since reaching the peak values of the 1920s and 1930s there has been a downward trend in rainfall of the monsoon type, and this trend increased sharply around 1950–1955. He suggested that this was closely related to the contemporary, recent cooling of the Arctic.

The frequency of westerly weather over the British Isles since 1900 indicates that highly mobile weather systems which give mild wet winters over England are linked to strong, zonal circulation in the mid-tropospheric, circumpolar westerlies. The influence of such systems seems to have reached a peak in the 1920s and to have been decreasing since then. Many other data indicate that the strength of the zonal circulation also achieved a maximal value around 1930 in the northern hemisphere, and about 1900–1910 in the southern hemisphere (Lamb, 1968; 1972). Fluctuations in this zonal circulation are almost exactly paralleled by fluctuations of the monsoon rainfall, and exactly opposed by fluctuations in the winter–spring rainfall of the Mediterranean and Middle East. Rainfall levels in England are closely parallel to the strength of the zonal circulation, reach a peak around 1930, and then decrease. Over longer periods of time both the strength of the the zonal circulation and the amount of rainfall seem to have peaked in the 13th century and subsequently to have declined and achieved minimal levels around 1700. They then rose again to a peak around 1930.

From this close relationship between the strength of the zonal circulation and the rainfall over England Winstanley concluded that it was reasonable to assume that long-term trends of summer rainfall in the Sahel and north-west India closely parallel rainfall trends in England. Conversely, winter–spring rainfall over the Mediterranean and Middle East are probably opposite to this. Such close correlations of trends both within and between rainfall belts intimated the existence of mechanisms controlling rainfall on an intercontinental scale. Winstanley suggested that the causal relationships lay in the sympathetic responses exhibited by both large-scale horizontal eddies in the circumpolar vortex, and the meridional circulation in the tropics, to changes in the strength of the general circulation. With a strong zonal circulation relatively long, small amplitude waves in the circumpolar westerlies tend to be restricted to mid-latitudes: that is, the circumpolar vortex is contracted (see Fig. 18). Highly mobile depressions and ridges travel eastwards across the Atlantic to give changeable weather and high rainfall over the UK whilst troughs in the circumpolar westerlies do not extend very far south into the subtropical latitudes so that the rainfall over the Mediterranean and Middle East regions is low. In the tropics the meridional circulation is strong and extends well to the north, as do the monsoons. Such conditions are associated with a general warming of the northern hemisphere. Thus when the zonal circulation is increasing in strength

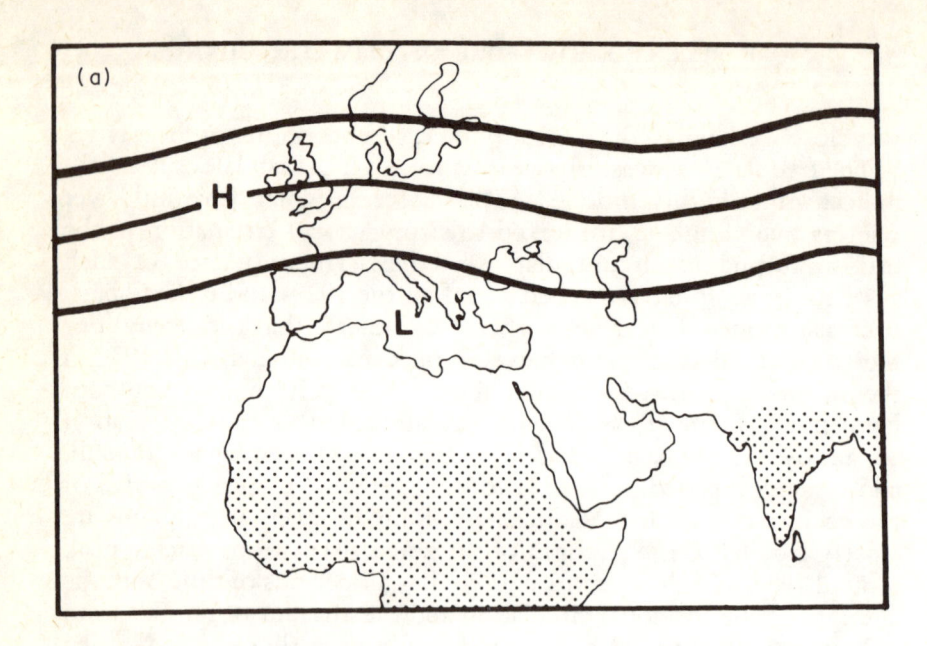

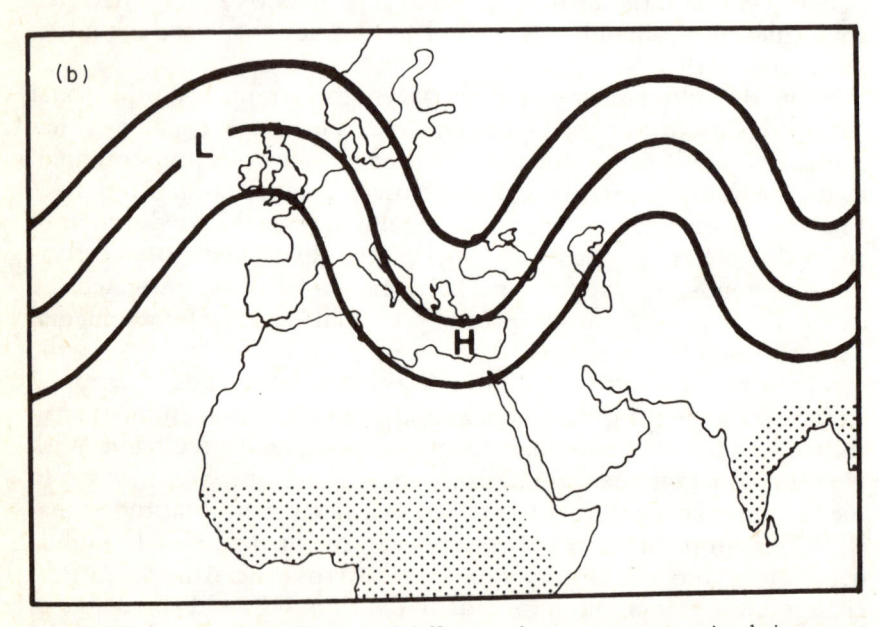

FIG. 18. Diagram indicating principal differences between extreme circulation types and associated rainfall patterns. (a) Strong zonal circulation produces high rainfall over Britain and allows monsoon rains to extend well to the north in India and Africa; (b) weak zonal circulation leads to low rainfall over Britain and suppresses the northward extent of the monsoon rains. H, high rainfall; L, low rainfall. The change in the boundary of the dotted area shows the change in the extent of the monsoon region. (Winstanley, 1973.)

the monsoon rainfall of the Sahel and Northwest India is increasing, as is the UK rainfall, and that over the Middle East and the Mediterranean is decreasing. There is a northward shift of the principal climatic zones. Such trends seem to have characterised the centuries immediately prior to 1200 and also the years before 1930.

In contrast, when there is a relatively weak zonal circulation, as at present, there are relatively short, large amplitude waves in the circumpolar westerlies, and the strongest westerly flow tends to be shifted southwards. The circumpolar vortex is expanded. In association with this the weather systems in the middle latitudes move more slowly and persistent anticyclones develop which block eastward moving depressions, deflecting them either to the north or to the south. In the UK both the rainfall and the frequency of westerly winds decrease; westerly troughs extend into the subtropical or even tropical latitudes; and rainfall over the Mediterranean and Middle East is increased. This explains the well-known synoptic relationship between blocking over western Europe and heavy rainfall over the Mediterranean. However, as the circumpolar vortex expands so the tropical, meridional circulation contracts. As a result monsoon rains do not extend so far north. This all reflects a general cooling of the northern hemisphere and a concomitant southward shift of the principal climatic belts. In recent years the rainfall over both the UK and the Sahelian region has been low, that over the Mediterranean and Middle East high.

2 PERIODICITIES OF CLIMATE

2.1 *Periodicities of less than a century*

The data referred to in the foregoing chapter demonstrate that the older workers had little doubt that the apparent vagaries of climate are definitely related to solar phenomena, and in particular to the solar wind and its sources in the sun. Apart from the works already referred to, and others which are referred to in subsequent chapters, some of the important works which have discussed the overt results of these relationships are Willett (1961), who summarised climatic data from prior to 1940 in terms of 80–90 year sunspot cycles, and Gleissberg (1944), Flohn (1951), Baur (1956), Julian *et al.* (1957), Berlage (1961), Brier (1961), Dzerdzeevskii (1961), Ward and Shapiro (1961) and Schell (1961), who all dealt with related topics. Schove (1954; 1955; 1961) and Lamb (1961) gave updated summaries of the well-attested solar and climatic characteristics of historic time, whilst

Manley (1961; 1971) summarised a variety of meteorological conclusions relating to the postglacial period. In broad terms they bridge the gap with the earlier generation of climatologists, epitomised by Brooks (1949), maintained a continuing thread of interest in the importance of sunspot cycles, and both heralded and stimulated the most recent chapter of research into climatic change. Some idea of this recent interest is provided by the works of Lamb and all such papers draw conclusions that are analogous to, if perhaps more precise than, those in the works outlined in Chapter 2.

A wide variety of correlations, apart from the obvious annual ones, undoubtedly exist between climatic and astronomical cycles. They vary from short ones that are associated with the lunar cycle and are measured in days, to others involving periods of months, and yet others that are related to the 11+ year sunspot cycle and its harmonics. For example Rosenberg and Colman (1974) observed a 27 day cycle in the rainfall records of Los Angeles which, although challenged (cf. Rosenberg, 1975), they tie in with the earlier observation that there is a significant correlation between the surface, semi-permanent, East Pacific, high-pressure cell, and the meridional lunar force over the 27·3 day lunar cycle in declination. Green (1975) also re-examined north-west European climatic trends and noted that some significant correlations exist between certain weekly or monthly periods in summer and winter. This is illustrated by the February–June relationship. A regression demonstrated quite clearly that the mean temperature in February is inversely related to that in June. In 30 out of 35 years this correctly predicted whether the June temperature was higher or lower than that in the foregoing year. In 25 out of 35 years this prediction was within 1·0°C, and in 14 years it was correct to within 0·5°C.

Wing (1961) had previously demonstrated that tests of a variety of terrestrial data—such as temperature, run-off, barometric pressure and geomagnetic variation—against cycles of 5·115 days, 3·635 quarter years, 4·465 quarter years, 4·222, 9·6 and 11·08 years, all showed correlations with solar phenomena. Indeed he concluded that latitudinal passage, from the pole to the equator, occurs on earth simultaneously with latitudinal passage of sunspots on the sun. Arai (1958) had also provided a harmonic analysis of 5 day and monthly mean 500 mbar charts of the northern hemisphere for 1946–1956 and concluded that the higher the sunspot number the less the eccentricity of the circumpolar vortex.

Sunspot characteristics do, of course, exhibit a number of periodicities of which the best known are $c.$ 5½, 10–12, 22–23, 80–90 and 170–200 years. Less conclusive data also intimate the existence of a 400 year cycle. The 5·7 year cycle is widely considered to be a harmonic of the 11+ year cycle and to reflect the fact that this last-named is not a true sinusoidal curve. Furthermore the 22–23 year cycle is known as the Hale cycle in recognition of his demonstration that the magnetic polarity of sunspots reverses from one 11+ year cycle to the next. Longer-term considerations are epitomised by Bray (1967) who defined a solar activity index and concluded that its mean values, during the period from the sixth century B.C. to the present, indicate that groups of 3 or more cycles with indices averaging 107–137 alternate with periods during which these indices fall below 100. The reliability of this index was intimated by the highly significant negative correlation coefficients which can be derived between mean annual sunspot number and the length of the *c.* 11+ year cycle from 1699 to 1964; the cycle length from 527 B.C. to A.D. 1964; and the low or high atmospheric ^{14}C levels in "active" or "weak" cycles, which give inverse changes in 22 out of 24 cases.

As far as climatic effects are concerned both Baur (1956) and Lamb (1972), reflecting the earlier conclusions of workers such as Huntington, Walker and Brooks (cf. Chapter 2), concluded that:

a. a high pressure exists over the polar regions around sunspot maxima;
b. a strong development of middle latitude westerlies, sub-polar lows and subtropical anticyclones occurs around the middle of the declining phase of solar activity;
c. there is a weakened circulation around sunspot minima;
d. there are strong meridional and cellular circulation systems at some stage during the most rapid rises of solar disturbance;
e. strong middle latitude westerlies, strong sub-polar lows and subtropical anticyclones typify the increasing phases;
f. severe winters in central Europe cluster at sunspot extremes;
g. summer rainfall in central Europe is significantly lower two years before both solar maxima and solar minima and in the second summer after maxima;
h. average summer temperatures at New Haven, Connecticut, have high values two years before sunspot minima, and low values one year before maxima;
i. the complex wave of thunderstorm activity in Europe appears, according to Lamb, to be inverse to the tendency for dry summers. Thundery years involve the subtropical anticyclone failing to move north in summer so that the continent is dominated by cyclonic activity.

Power spectrum analysis, which involves Fourier analysis and auto-correlation, is a widely accepted technique for separating "signals" from "noise" in temporal sequences of rapidly fluctuating elements (cf. Landsberg et al., 1959). Mitchell (1965) carried out such an analysis on the annual mean Zurich temperatures and was able to demonstrate 5·7, 11 and 90 year periodicities but not the Hale cycle. A comparable analysis of recent Adriatic varves (Seibold and Weigert, 1960) demonstrated rather different tendencies, with peaks occurring at 6, 8 and 14 years, but only a weak 11+ year periodicity. A complex of peaks falling between 2 and 6 years in such analyses was thought by Anderson (1961) to either represent noise (?), or some factor that is analogous to those highlighted by Brooks.

Periodicities of 2·0, 2·5 or 2·7 years have in fact been reported for Icelandic pressure; Swedish winter temperatures; snow-cover in the USSR; temperature, pressure and precipitation in Europe and the USA; precipitation in India; North Atlantic and Norwegian sea-surface temperatures; floods in the Nile Valley; tree rings in western USA; and varves in North and South America, Scandinavia and India (cf. Landsberg, 1962; Stachy, 1970). Certainly the opposing motions, around the hemisphere, of the stratospheric anticyclones formed by winter warming in roughly alternate years, have kept in phase, throughout the period of records, with the winds at the same height over the equator. Westerly and easterly movements alternate with an oscillation of 25–28 months' duration and this swamps seasonal and lesser variations.

The cause of such a 26 month cycle is still controversial but Lamb (1972) thought that there is a case for considering that the phenomenon represents a slow overturn of the stratosphere in rather shallow meridional cells. Although he felt that it would be inappropriate to ascribe this to a special atmospheric sensitivity to the fifth harmonic of the 11+ year cycle, he concluded that, for whatever reason, the atmosphere does not complete its heat budget within a single year but needs this longer period to do so. Luxemburg wine vintages certainly show that between 1626 and the mid-nineteenth century the phase in which either the odd or even years were the better ones recurred at 16 year intervals. This would suggest that, during the period concerned, the basic recurring unit was 2·3 years. In fact in the long term the periodicity seems to vary from 2·15 to 2·3 years although its length *is always one fifth of the current sunspot cycle*.

Periodograms of the barometric pressure difference between Madeira and Iceland, or between Siberia and Iceland, as well as those for the maximum area of Baltic Sea ice, all present period lengths of

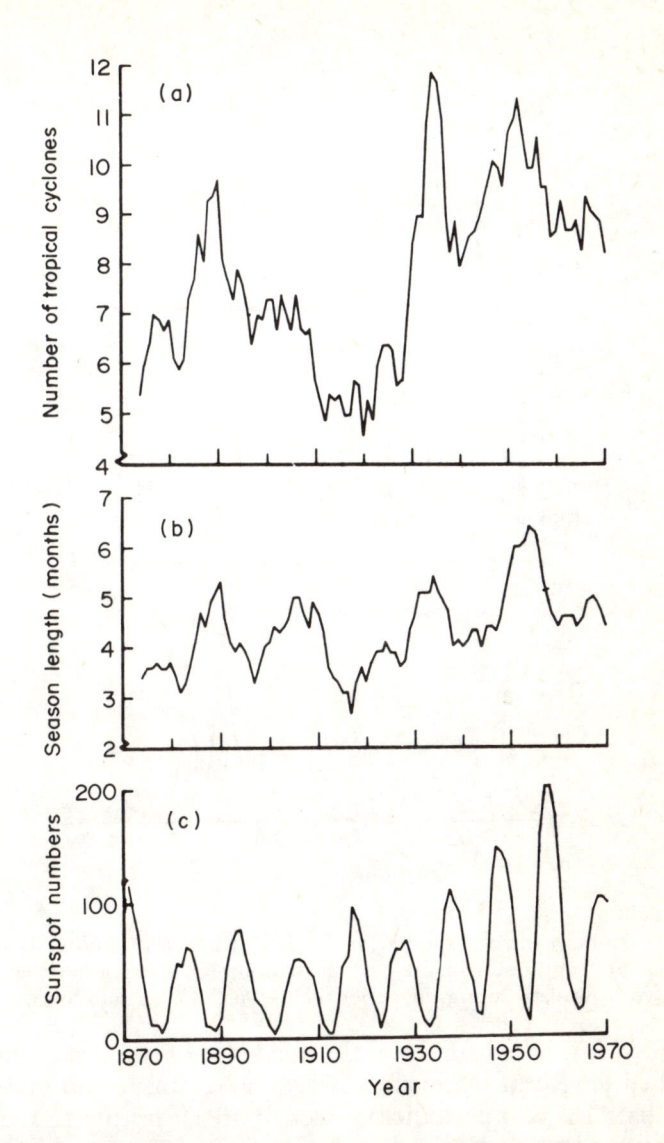

FIG. 19 (a) Seven-year running mean number of Atlantic tropical cyclones; (b) seven-year running mean length of Atlantic tropical cyclone season; (c) twelve-month running mean sunspot numbers. See further Fig. 20.

5–6 years, and, interestingly, of 21–23 years which is comparable with the Hale cycle (Voltzinger, 1966). Hints of other periodicities such as 2–3, 11–12, 14–15 and 18 years also occur. Cohen and Sweetser (1975) have recently applied maximum entropy spectral

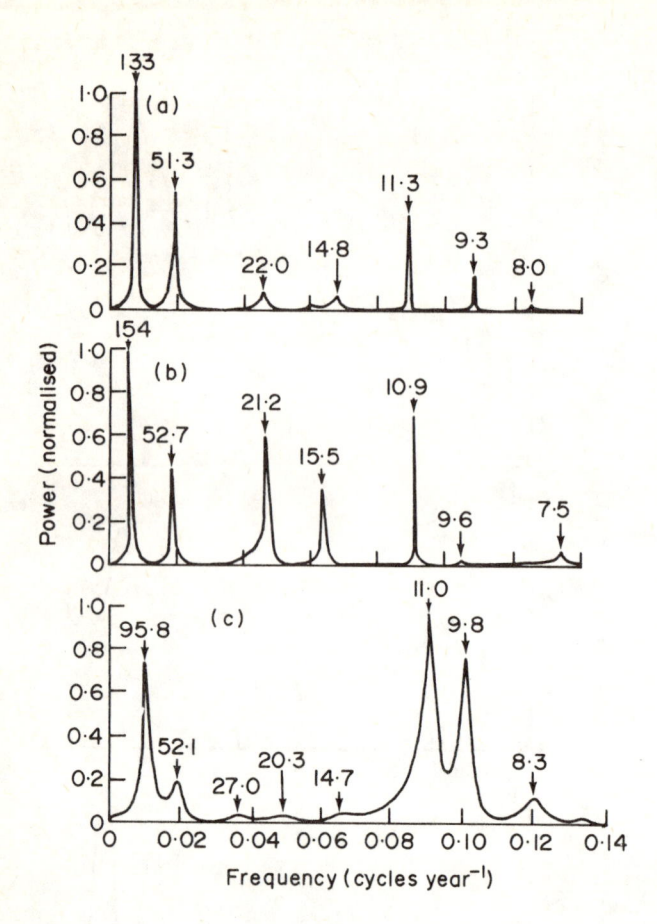

FIG. 20. Maximum entropy spectra for the data of Fig. 19. (a) Number of tropical cyclones; (b) length of tropical cyclone season; (c) sunspot numbers. Spectra computed from data during the period 1750–1963. (Cohen and Sweetser, 1975.)

analysis to smoothed curves of the incidence of tropical cyclones, the smoothed length of the cyclone season and sunspot numbers. They found that 11+ year periodicities were quite clear; that 15 and 22 year ones emerged from the cyclone data but were only weakly visible in sunspot numbers; and that there were also pronounced long period components of 133 and 154 years. These last were associated with cyclone data and might, they felt, represent ill-defined estimates of a 96 year component of sunspot data. It was not possible to establish whether the 22 year peak definitely had its origin in the reversal of magnetic fields associated with Hale's cycle (see Figs 19 and 20).

A wide variety of other comparable conclusions exist in the

literature. Rainfall in Europe during the period from 1800 to the 1960s again shows a 2–2·5 year cycle; Baltic ice-cover exhibits 3, 5–6, 8, 11–14 and 21–24 year cycles; and the zonal index, that is to say the strength of the zonal component of the mean circulation as measured by the average pressure difference between latitudes 35°N and 55°N, exhibits a 2·2 year periodicity (cf. Lamb, 1972). Mock and Hibler (1976) demonstrated a pervasive $c.$ 20 year oscillation in the January mean temperatures over a substantial part of North America using maximum entropy spectral analysis, and Currie (1974) detected a 10·5 year spectral peak by similar methods. Maksimov and Sleptsov (1963) had previously found an 11 year cycle of mean atmospheric pressure. This had an amplitude of 0·5 mbar between 0–35° latitude and 1·5 mbar in the polar regions. Gasjukov and Smirnov (1967) detected analogous variations, with a maximum of 2·0 mbar, over Alaska.

Complementarily numerous $c.$ 80–90 year cycles have been described. These do of course characterise sunspot numbers, and have been attributed by Huntington and Visher (1923) and Gribbin (1976) to the Jupiter effect. English rainfall from the twelfth century has a detectable 100 year periodicity; the severity of European winters from 1215 to 1905 has an 89·5 year recurrence cycle (Easton, 1928); the Greenland and Barents Sea ice a 71–77 year periodicity; and the pressure differences of southerlies over the North Sea both a 18–23 year and a 55–80 year periodicity (Lamb and Johnson, 1966). Similarly the latitudinal distribution of the Siberian anticyclone belt in January, and the North Atlantic anticyclone belt in June, appear to exhibit 80–85 and 85–110 year cycles respectively.

Abbot (1963) correlated the recurrence of severe droughts over the American great plains area with the Hale cycle and with multiples such as 46 and 91 years. The European winters of 1895, 1917, 1940 and 1963 certainly fit such a pattern although the sunspot cycle itself averaged 10·2 years from 1917 to 1963, and the winters do not recur in this way at dates prior to 1895 when the double cycle was closer to 23 years (Lamb, 1972).

Data of this type can, of course, arise from a wide variety of sources and a number of biological analyses which lead to similar conclusions also exist. Southward *et al.* (1975) submitted the surface temperatures of the English Channel to power spectrum analysis and demonstrated a 10–11 year cycle. They were able to show that thermophiles such as hake, John Dory, red mullet, megrim and *Chthamalus* are positively correlated with temperature, whilst a negative correlation was shown by cold water forms such as cod, haddock and *Balanus*. In some of their examples the 11 year periodicity was relatively inconspicuous by comparison with the secular trend but they concluded, for example, that the number of pilchard eggs in autumn is certainly correlated with an 11 year temperature cycle. They then went on to predict increasing quantities of cod etc. in the English Channel on the basis of a continuing trend up to 1990.

In contrast Bryson and Dutton (1961) concluded from their dendrochronological studies that there was little evidence for any important periodicity in tree ring thickness. There was a hint of 2+ and 3+ year effects but no evidence for sunspot periodicity. Nevertheless positive correlations were described at that time by Bray (1968) who found that the mean basal area growth of certain trees was 9·6 cm^2 year^{-1} for 1934–1964; 9·4 cm^2 during the active sunspot cycles between 1723 and 1799; and 9·7 cm^2 during the four active cycles 1834–1879. In contrast it averaged 8·8 cm^2, 8·7 cm^2 and 8·9 cm^2 for the weak sunspot cycles of 1699–1723, 1799–1823 and 1879–1923. Complementarily a correlation coefficient of +0·75 was established between the growth of Taiwan cypress trees and Zurich sunspot numbers for 1749–1950. Cycles of 6, 11, 20–22 and 100 years could all be detected (Outi, 1961).

The study of two long-term fertiliser experiments at Alltcailleach forest, on Upper Deeside, demonstrated that the growth of *Pinus sylvestris* exhibits several regular oscillations each of which can be related to a particular climatic cycle. Some of these are peculiar to low rainfall areas like the Grampian rain shadow. During the 40 years 1933–1972 average ring widths declined linearly and 3 climatic parameters were significantly and independently related to the width. Two of these, annual temperature and the previous May–June rainfall, were linearly related. Spectral analysis of the ring width deviations and the 3 climatic parameters, followed by repeated curve fitting about the indicated harmonics, elucidated 3 significant oscillations, and one that was just short of significant, each of which could be matched by a climatic oscillation (Table 2).

Relationships between sunspot cycles and factors such as glacial advance or isotope content are less easy to establish because there is a pronounced lag period prior to the terrestrial response. However, Bray (1968) thought that 75–80 per cent of all the known, major advances occurred during periods of weak solar activity and Schiegl (1975), using 5 year means, found a reasonable correlation between the deuterium content of *Picea* and summer temperatures. Moran and Blasing (1972) also showed that, in the case of glacial characteristics, retreat fluctuations exhibit an immediate response to climatic parameters and further lagged responses to various independent modes of co-variance of these primary factors.

TABLE 2

Correlations observed during fertilizer experiments in the Alltcailleach forest

	Period (years)	Significance of fit	Amplitude	Mean	Lag between climate and ring width
Annual temperature	42	P 0·01	0·34°C	6·48°C	None
May rain	23	P 0·01	17·9 mm	62·5 mm	0·6
May rain	11·9	P 0·01	21·0 mm	62·5 mm	None
June rain	4·44	P 0·05	15·1 mm	50·9 mm	1·2

Many recent data certainly support the suggestions of Herschel, Wolf, Brückner, Jevons, Garcia-Mata and Shaffner (see Williams, 1961) who all demonstrated that correlations exist between harvests or world commodity prices on the one hand, and solar cycles on the other. The world wheat production figures for 1949–1973 exhibit such a relationship (Anon, 1975). Solar maxima occurred in 1957 and 1968. Global wheat production was greater in 1958 than in each of the subsequent five years, and greater again in 1968 than in each of the next four years. It was correlations of this sort that stimulated the historic works of Brückner and also, probably, that of Markham. Nevertheless it is essential to emphasise that by no means all the workers who have studied long-term climatic phenomena accept such correlations. For example, Starr and Oort (1973) when discussing a five-year climatic trend for the years 1958–1963, during which the mean atmospheric temperature fell by 0·60°C, considered that the causes were wide open to speculation. Although they were at least aware of the possibility of astronomical causative factors they indicated that "internally" generated cycles reflecting "reverberation" within the atmosphere–ocean–cryosphere system may be the sole factors involved. Nevertheless these systems are themselves universally acknowledged to depend upon incident solar radiation for their energy budget.

2.2 Periodicities in excess of a century

Many of the works cited in both the foregoing and subsequent sections demonstrate the existence of cycles which exceed a century in length. The ^{14}C content of the atmosphere is mentioned in terms of a 100–200 year cycle in Chapter 4. European temperatures since 1760 were shown to suggest a 170–200 year repetition period by Brunt (1925) and Landsberg (1962), whilst English temperatures from A.D. 1100 to the present day show similar characteristics (Lamb, 1965; 1966; 1972). More or less identical conclusions emerged from a study of the pattern of south westerly winds over England from 1340 to 1965. These winds appeared to recur at 200 year intervals (Lamb, 1967) and English rainfall from 1100 to now shows both a *c.* 100 year, and a 170–200 year periodicity. In contrast night cloudiness in China since 2300 B.C. was thought by Link (1958; 1964) to follow a 400 year recurrence pattern. Krivsky (1953), Yamamoto (1967) and Rubashev (1964) suggest that both *c.* 90 and 170–200 year cycles are indicated by the annual rainfall in central Europe; the Bai U rains of Korea; and the sea level at the periphery of the Atlantic. The relationship of such factors to food production was discussed by Willett (1964).

Tetrode (1952) emphasised that, for those places in Europe and North America for which temperature measurements extend back far enough, the two warmest periods of 36 months coincide with the highest observed sunspot maxima together with the two subsequent years. These were 1778–1780 and 1947–1949. The slightly lower sunspot maxima of 1787 and 1957, which preceded a decline in solar activity, had slightly lower temperatures.

Biological data suggest even longer-term cycles. Tallantire (1972) concluded that the climatic conditions which permit the spread of *Picea* in Fennoscandia have recurred at *c.* 900 year intervals, with the prerequisite fall in winter temperature having enabled it to gradually extend its range further and further west during successive favourable epochs. At least 3 variables seem to be involved. One is the overall strength of the atmospheric circulation. A second comprises changed circulation indices and related shifts of the cyclone tracks, and the third involves long-term changes in the air and sea temperatures. These last seem to have maintained a progressive downward trend since the end of the postglacial climatic optimum. Tallantire considered that the principal causative feature may be the geomagnetic skewing effect on atmospheric circulation, with the centres involved being Canada east of the Rockies (A.D. 1800), the mid-Pacific (A.D. 1300), and Russia just east of the Urals (A.D. 800).

3 THE CAMP CENTURY ICE CORES

During the late sixties it became clear that the two large ice sheets in Antarctica and Greenland contain detailed climatic data (Hansen and Langway, 1966; Arnason, 1969; Dansgaard et al., 1969; 1971; 1975). The index of concentration, δ, of oxygen-18 and deuterium in high-latitude precipitation is mainly determined by its temperature of formation which causes seasonal fluctuations of δ in accumulated snow and ice, as well as long-term fluctuations due to climatic change. Herein lies an extremely accurate method of determining the temperature variation within an ice core. If the δs increase as one moves up the core it indicates climatic warming; decreasing values indicate cooling. However, as other factors also influence the isotopic concentrations a vertical profile of δ in a glacier should not be interpreted simply as a paleotemperature record and this is particularly true in the case of temperate glaciers where re-freezing of the melt-water, and isotopic exchange between snow and water, complicate the picture. Although high polar glaciers can be investigated with a high degree of precision, dating of the older levels is difficult—indeed impossible if the ^{14}C technique is used.

In a preliminary study Dansgaard et al. (1969) found that the δs of the ice-core increments, if plotted against time values, showed a good correlation with the main features of climatic change as determined by other studies (see Chapters 9 and 10 for example). The upper part of the core spans the last 780 years (Fig. 21). The δ values are plotted to the right, as a function of t, and the hatched areas represent relatively warm periods—that around 1930 and those in the middle of the eighteenth and sixteenth centuries. Low δs reflect relatively cold periods, e.g. the 1820s, the Little Ice Age from 1600 to 1740, and the generally cool conditions of the fifteenth century that finally severed the links between Iceland and the Norse colonies of Greenland. On the face of it one might estimate that 10 maxima (indicated by arrows) exist between 1240 and 1930. This would correspond to a climatic oscillation with a periodicity of c. 63 years, and would conform well with the 66 year periodicity suggested by faunal studies in Greenland (Vibe, 1967). However, the step curve might be expected to reflect systematic oscillations superimposed upon irregular deviations due to unusually large amounts of isotopically heavy summer snow. Fourier analysis of the step curves gives a power spectrum that exhibits 2 dominant peaks that correspond to periods of 78 and 181 years. This is in striking conformity with the data on sunspots and climate derived by the other workers already mentioned.

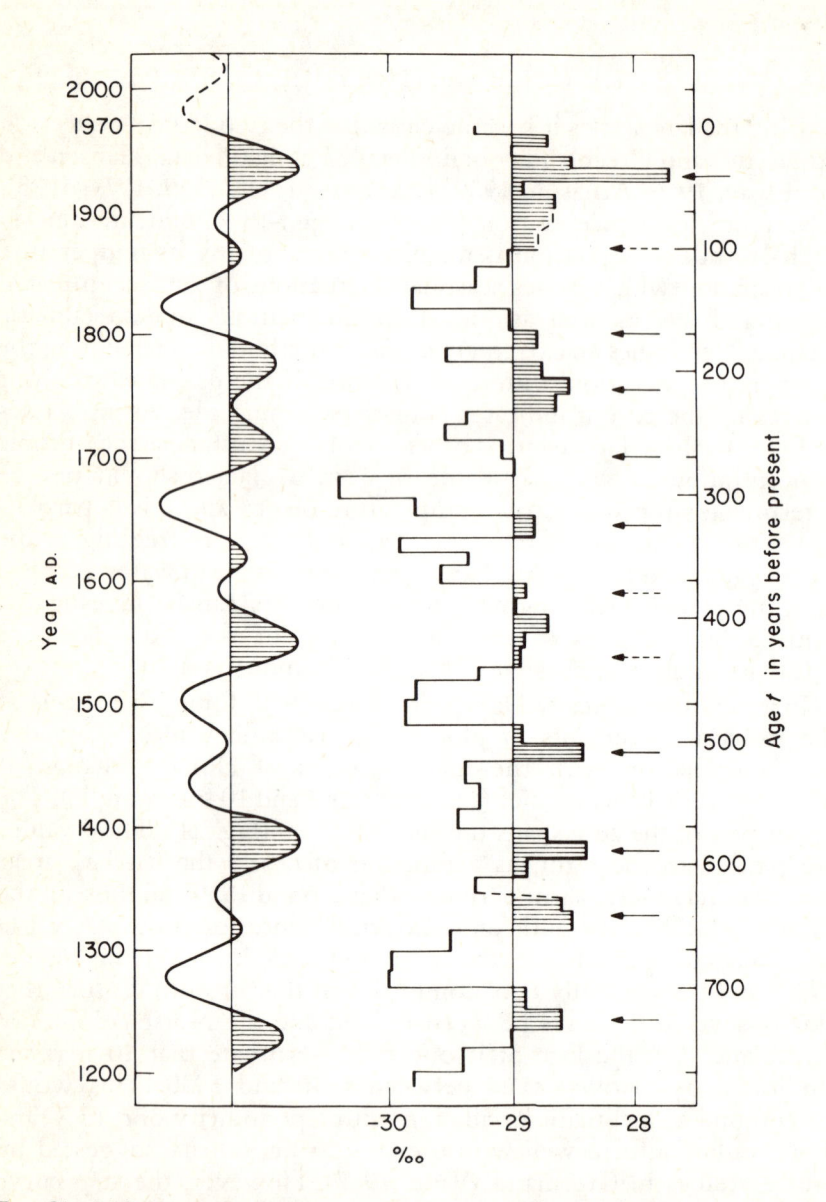

FIG. 21. *Right:* Oxygen-18 values of an ice core from Camp Century plotted against time t since the deposition of the ice. The hatched areas correspond to relatively warm periods. *Left:* A synthesis of the two harmonics that dominate the step curve, judged from the spectral analysis. The dashed extrapolation suggests the probable future climatic development as a continued cooling through the next one or two decades, followed by a warming trend toward a new climatic optimum around the year A.D. 2015. (Dansgaard et al., 1971.)

This conformity is supported by more precise analyses. Maximal lengths of the sunspot "cycle" (~12 years) occurred around 1662, a rather aberrant period, 1728, 1816 and 1895. These dates are all close to minima. Complementarily minimum lengths (~10 years) occurred around 1706, 1770, 1850 and 1930 which are all close to δ maxima. In addition, relatively long time intervals with short sunspot cycles occurred around 1560–1590; 1750–1790; and 1900–1950 (Schove, 1955). These periods broadly coincide with the last 3 maxima in the 180 year component of the δ curve. Thus, as would be expected from the foregoing chapter and sections, it was considered that the 180 and 78 year periodicities seem to originate in changing solar conditions.

The larger part of the core then spans the period back to 10,000 B.P. and is of relevance to Chapters 9 and 10. Fourier power spectra for this period suggest a dominating 350 year periodicity which Dansgaard *et al.* (1971) suggested may correspond to the *c.* 405 year periodicity detected in atmospheric ^{14}C fluctuations (cf. Suess 1970; and Chapter 4).

Proceeding back from the present the last millennium seems to have been colder than the foregoing one; and the first halves of both the 3rd and 4th millennia B.P. were also cool or cold. The postglacial or Flandrian climatic optimum is represented by an almost continuous series of high δs from 4100 to 8000 B.P., with two extremes close to 5000 and 6000 B.P. Furthermore, the classical Bølling and Allerød periods are clearly depicted (cf. Chapters 9 and 10). There appeared to be a pronounced 2,000 year periodicity back to 45,000 B.P., and a 4,000 year periodicity prior to 100,000 B.P. However, in view of the antiphase correlation of Holocene δs, and a 2,400 year period in the ^{14}C concentration of tree-rings, Dansgaard *et al.* were loathe to believe this change of periodicity, and instead assumed that it reflected the progressive deviation of the time scale from absolute chronology as the bottom of the ice sheet was approached. The principal features certainly substantiate the long-established division of the Wisconsin glaciation into three intervals (cf. Chapter 9). An early phase from 73,000 to 59,000 B.P. corresponds to the main cooling of the last interglacial; a Middle Wisconsin period from 59,000 to 32,000 B.P. has generally more stable conditions; and, a Late Wisconsin phase from 32,000 to 13,000 B.P. comprised the coldest part of the glaciation. In broad terms the abrupt transition to the Holocene also supported suggestions (cf. Broecker *et al.*, 1960) that the disappearance of the ice sheets was a much faster process than their creation. The δ data also confirmed that a slow, general

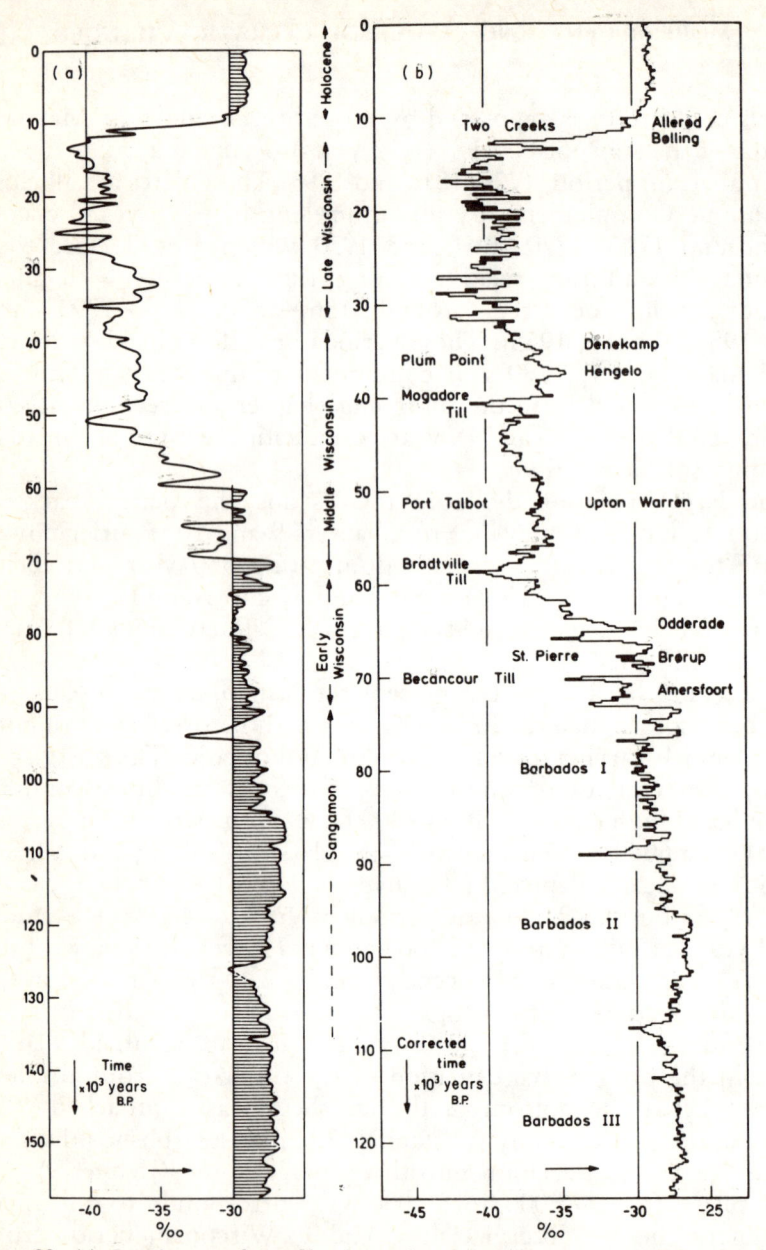

FIG. 22. (a) Continuous δ profile along the entire ice core except for the deepest 17 metres, plotted on the preliminary time scale (Dansgaard et al., 1971). (b) $\delta^{18}O$ in 200 year intervals plotted on the corrected time scale. Tentative interpretations in European and American terminology are shown to the right and left respectively. At the far left is a proposed division of the Wisconsin glaciation in accordance with the characteristic features of the δ curve. (Dansgaard et al., 1971.)

amelioration from 18,000 to 12,500 B.P. was interrupted by numerous minor climatic deteriorations that were coupled with glacial advances.

Bray (1972) then tested data taken at 25 year intervals from two cores, against cycles of from 100 to 2,800 years. The results of this analysis showed that the maximum χ^2 values occurred in a pronounced peak from 1,275 to 1,350 years, and that the maximum value actually coincided with 1,325 years and a division point at 300 B.P. The known dates of ice advance and retreat correspond closely with the data of this 1,325 year cycle and suggest that glacial resurgences have occurred at every colder interval of such a cycle. The Bølling, Older Dryas and Younger Dryas periods (q.v.) all fit well into this scheme and the implications are therefore quite clear. The same temporal pattern characterised the expansion and contraction of both the large-scale Late Pleistocene ice sheets and also the smaller-scale Holocene polar and alpine glaciers. Like so many before him, Bray emphasised that by placing more emphasis on the timing of major and minor glacial pulsations it may be possible to ascertain the causative mechanisms involved.

4 CLIMATIC DATA FROM HISTORIC TIME

Various authors cited in the foregoing sections have provided discussions on historic climates. Lamb (1972) is the most outstanding. In addition Bloch (1965) gave a slightly controversial account of sea-level changes. He suggested that the present sea level seems to have been reached in the sixteenth century, and that since that date *no* indications of a permanent change of an order greater than 30 cm can be detected. In contrast, there are definite signs that one or more distinct sea-level minima and maxima occurred between A.D. 700 and 1600. During the fifteenth and sixteenth centuries a general rise in the price of salt all over Europe was one reason for political unrest and he linked this with the fact that salt producing broads, meres, clairs and kogs, in East Anglia, Holland, France and Friesland respectively, were *flooded* so that peat salt production ceased. Complementarily both peat cutting and salt production started on the Broads between A.D. 700 and 800 whilst the Domesday book records at least 1,200 salt producing areas (Salinae) which Bloch interpreted as reflecting a lower sea level than that of today.

Various other data of varying provenance exist. In the eleventh century the island of Walcheren had a thriving community and the apparent absence of any protective dykes may indicate a lower sea level—even if one admits the possible existence of sandbars. Similarly Haithabu, near Schleswig, flourished around A.D. 900 and it has been suggested that the land was a metre higher above the sea than is the case today. At about the same time the Vikings occupied the low-lying island of Noirmoutier on the Atlantic coast of France, and, at A.D. 860, the similar low island in the Camargue. Simultaneously the Crimean salterns in the Black Sea were emerging and being occupied by a Viking task-force, whilst the popes had solar salt pans on the Ostian flats although such activity had previously ceased after Trajan because of flooding. The fortunes of all such salt producers in lowland areas certainly suffered disastrously from flooding in A.D. 1362 and A.D. 1634 (Bantelmann, 1960). The destructive power of these and other floods was thought by Bloch to have been enhanced by a general rise in sea level—as deduced by dyke-building activity, designed to counteract it, along all the threatened coasts during the last 600 years. A low sea level prior to the flooding of the Somerset levels was indicated by Godwin (1943) and confirmed by Willis (1961). Furthermore, in the Crimea, ports and towns founded and inhabited from 500 to 300 B.C., are now under water. A rise in sea level around 400 B.C. may, indeed, be indicated by the rise in salt prices in Athens and by the simultaneous selection of new salt-pan sites in the Ostian region. An earlier (c. 1200 B.C.) high level is, perhaps, also indicated by the Rameses II canal linking the Nile to the Red Sea which was re-used by Trajan and later by the Arabs in A.D. 650 (see also Toynbee, 1975).

Multidisciplinary studies, initially stimulated by Huntington, all point to a warm climate that lasted for some centuries around A.D. 1000–1200 and was followed by a decline of temperature until, between 1500 and 1700, the coldest phase since the last ice age occurred. Lamb (1965) concluded that around A.D. 1200 and A.D. 1600 changes of the prevailing temperature and rainfall, over periods of some 50–150 years, probably amounted to 1·2–1·4°C and 10 per cent respectively. He suggested that, although the differences between the climate of A.D. 1000 and 1200 and that of the present day were sufficiently small to explain earlier ignorance and scepticism (cf. Chapter 2), nevertheless the Arctic pack ice was so much less extensive than today that appearances of drift ice near Iceland, and Greenland south of 70°N were apparently rare in the 10th century and unknown between 1020 and 1194 when a rapid increase of frequency caused a permanent change of the shipping routes (cf. Koch, 1945). Brooks (1949) suggested that, as in the climatic optimum, the Arctic Ocean became ice-free in the summers of that epoch, but Lamb thought that it was more probable that some permanent ice persisted north of 80°N. Evidence of early Norse burials in south-west Greenland, together with plant roots deep in the now permanently frozen ground, certainly seem to suggest temperatures some 2–4°C above the present ones and neighbouring sea temperatures were probably up by some, perhaps comparable, amount. Vebaek (1962) suggested that by the fourteenth and fifteenth centuries the ground was once again permanently frozen close to the surface. Chard and Giddings (1962) also suggested that the archaeological evidence intimates that North American eskimoes of the Thule culture first occupied Ellesmere Land c. A.D. 900. They then expanded their range north-west, as far as the New Siberian Islands, and north-east around the north of Greenland. Whaling and fishing were important to them and they used considerable quantities of driftwood for building. By the sixteenth century all this activity had ceased. Ellesmere Land, and both northern and north-eastern Greenland, were deserted, houses were smaller, there is less evidence for driftwood, and there had also been battles, for the first time, between southward moving eskimoes and the settlers of the old Viking colony of Greenland. This last ultimately succumbed. Fritts (1962) certainly cited suggested, average, summer temperatures for the north Alaska region in the eleventh century that are 2·3°C warmer than the 1851–1950 average.

Elsewhere, in the temperate latitudes, the settlements and forest clearance that appear to have been more or less static since the early Iron Age spread rather rapidly further up the valleys and hillsides in the course of some two centuries from around A.D. 800. They then retreated decisively in the fourteenth century, partly because of the Black Death, and the higher farms were subsequently left unoccupied for hundreds of years (cf. Holmsen, 1961). In some areas additional farms were then subsequently vacated in the face of glacial advance as late as 1743 (Lamb, 1965). In central Europe, prior to some time variously placed at A.D. 1300 and 1450, vineyards were cultivated both farther north and up to 220 metres higher above sea level. Similar data apply to the British Isles (Fig. 23). At the same time the tree line in central Europe is thought to have been some 70–200 m above the present limits (Firbas and Losert, 1949). Dansgaard et al. (1975) were at some pains to point out that this period, during which vineyards occurred in England, could actually have begun prior to A.D. 1000, and that the initial onset of the medieval warm period has yet to be established. It is certainly much more uncertain than the time at which it ended. Archaeological evidence (see also Chapter 11) from the Western Great Plains, the upper Mississippi Valley, and the arid south-west of the USA, indicates a moister régime giving enough rainfall to support small agricultural settlements that were progressively abandoned from 1250 onwards (Griffin, 1961).

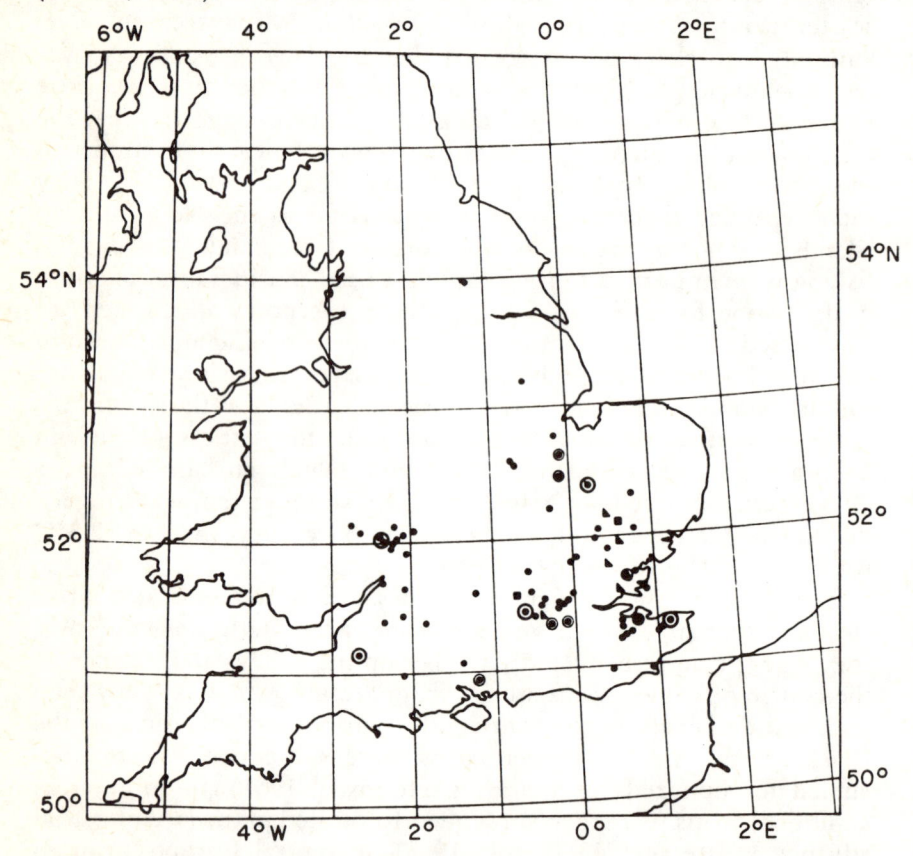

Fig. 23. The distribution of English vineyards during the period A.D. 1000 to 1300. (Lamb, 1965.) ●, Vineyard, usually 1–2 acres or size not known; ▲, vineyard, 5–10 acres; ■, vineyard, over 10 acres; ◉, denotes evidence of continuous operation for 30–100 years; ◉, denotes evidence of continuous operation for over 100 years.

In a consideration of other latitudes Brooks (loc. cit.) suggested that the Middle Ages were marked by a wet period in Yucatan, and probably Cambodia, and that there was a relatively moister period in the Sahara from A.D. 1200, or earlier, until c. A.D. 1550. Butzer (1958) also cites evidence of greater rainfall and larger rivers in the

Mediterranean and Middle Eastern regions. In fact, numerous investigations have led to our knowledge of the climatology of the tropical zone (cf. Brooks, 1954; Lamb, 1966; Mitchell, 1963; Maley, 1973), and these all provide data on the lowered pluviality and rapid increase in temperature during the last century or so. Butzer (1971) demonstrated that a low stand of Lake Rudolf was concomitant with a small but definite low in the regional temperature. Mitchell, who had previously established a temperature curve for latitudes 30°N–30°S, suggested that a close relationship existed between temperature and the level of Lake Chad, with the evaporation linked to local air temperatures. Maley also concluded that an *above average* rainfall is closely associated with decreased maximal temperatures. Such observations conflict, however, with suggestions that the monsoon passes towards the continental interior at times of high temperature.

Not unexpectedly the fluctuations in the level of Lake Chad itself during the last millennium are by no means isolated events. For example, the level of the Nile has been recorded since the seventh century, albeit with a few interruptions in the sixteenth and seventeenth centuries, and Brooks summarised the data:

a. low or average levels typify the seventh to sixteenth centuries, with a very low one around A.D. 1500;
b. a very high level occurred around A.D. 1600. This is followed by a period for which we lack data but the level seems to have been consistently low;
c. a very high level occurred in 1750;
d. a low characterises the beginning of the nineteenth century;
e. a highstand occurred around 1880;
f. lows characterise the period from the beginning of the present century to 1950.

Reviewing all the foregoing information one can reasonably conclude that the average temperatures were some 1–2°C above the present ones during the period from A.D. 1000 to 1200, and possibly over a longer period, although the differences may have been less in those latitudes south of 40°N where increased moisture and precipitation are the main indications. The temperature anomaly was also possibly bigger—? 4°C (Lamb, 1966)—near the coast of Greenland and possibly elsewhere along the rim of the Arctic Ocean. A present-day parallel suggested by Lamb would be the Svalbard (Spitsbergen) archipelago where the average annual mean temperature for 1930–1940 was almost 4°C above that in 1912–1920.

4
Geomagnetic Considerations

1 THE EARTH'S MAGNETIC FIELD

Our present knowledge of the characteristics of the earth's geomagnetic field, together with the variations which they undergo with time, has now got a very considerable history. A correlation with the sunspot cycle was certainly known to Chapman and Bartels (1940) and was implicit if not overt in the later writings of Huntington (see Chapter 2) (cf. Fig. 24). Numerous investigations, particularly those involved in both theoretical and practical studies of radio transmissions, had led, by the 1930s, to an extensive awareness of many related phenomena—such as the ionic concentration and temperature of the ionosphere on the one hand and solar wave radiation on the other (see, for example, Chapman and Bartels, 1940; Vestine, 1961; and synoptic historical accounts of which Ratcliffe, 1970, is perhaps the most readable).

The international geophysical year then inaugurated a dramatic increase in our knowledge of the earth's external magnetic field. Present concepts are emphasised by Fig. 25 which compares "classical" ideas of a dipole in space with more recent conclusions which envisage the earth surrounded by a magnetosphere and exposed to a persistent, if variable, solar wind. Numerous papers describe the dependence of magnetosphere characteristics on this solar wind, the ionosphere and associated currents.

The geomagnetic field has two main characteristics. One is its dipolar nature, with two positions where the inclination (dip) of the field is vertical, and the other is the systematic change of direction and intensity between the two poles. The intensity is about 0·6 Oe at each dip pole, and about 0·3 Oe at the equator. The present magnetic dip poles are at approximately 73°N, 100°W and 68°S, 143°E. They are not antipodal but correspond to an inclined, eccentric magnetic dipole that is situated some 400 km from the centre of the earth. Spherical harmonic analysis also suggests that more than 99·5 per cent of the earth's field is of internal origin and that 80 per cent can be

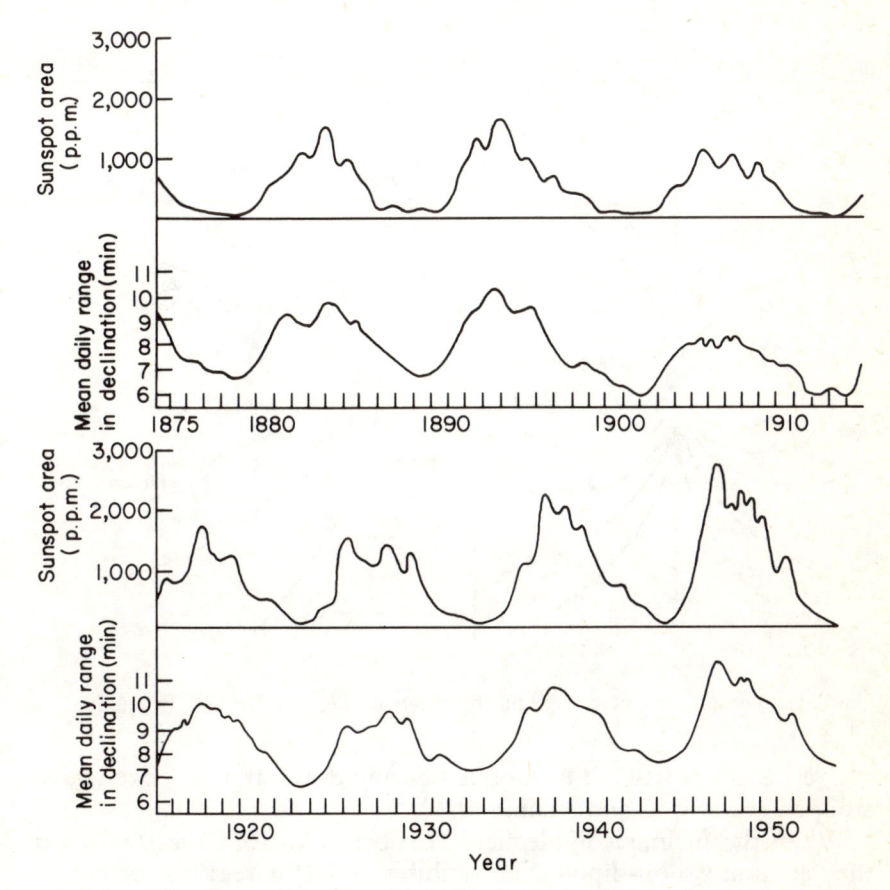

Fig. 24. Twelve-month running means of sunspot area (parts per million of the visible hemisphere) and the daily range of geomagnetic declination (minutes of arc). (Curves reproduced by permission of the Controller of Her Majesty's Stationery Office and the Astronomer Royal from "Sunspot and Geomagnetic Storm Data, 1874–1954", by the Royal Greenwich Observatory.)

attributed to a single geocentric dipole that is inclined at $11\frac{1}{2}°$ to the earth's axis of rotation, has a magnetic moment of $8 \times 10^{25}G$, and an axis that intersects the earth's surface at the geomagnetic poles (78·5°N, 69·1°W; 78·5°S, 110·9°E). Most of this dipole field is attributable to a single dipole along the axis of rotation, the remainder to one or more dipoles in the equatorial plane.

The available data also suggest that a westward drift of the main dipole axis has been going on since at least the time of Halley in 1693. Present values for such motion (0·00 years^{-1}N, and 0·06 years^{-1} E)

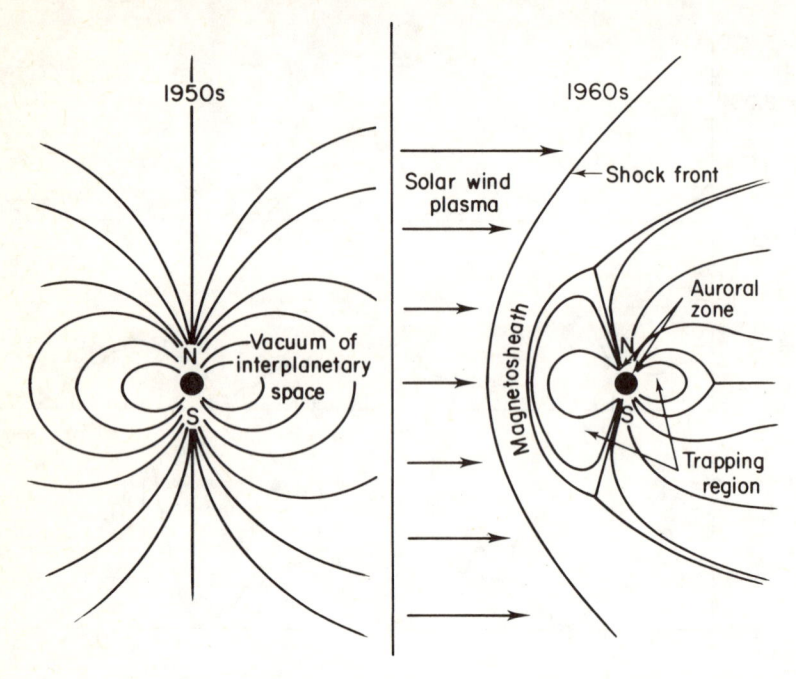

FIG. 25. Old (left) and new ideas on the external magnetic field (O'Brien, 1967).

suggest that a westward motion is slowing down and may even have stopped (Harwood and Malin, 1976).

When the inclined dipole field is subtracted from the total field the remaining non-dipole field exhibits some 8 regions, of continental dimensions, which have either positive or negative values and an amplitude of 0·15 Oe. These regions are asymmetrically distributed, are particularly strong in the southern hemisphere, and notably weak in the Pacific area.

Measurements of the various magnetic elements as a function of latitude long ago established that these exhibit a roughly diurnal variation. Such conclusions were actually the immediate consequence of nineteenth-century magnetic determinations but analogous investigations have been carried out in large numbers during the last decade. For example, Schutz *et al.* (1974) concluded that fluctuations in the field which are detectable at the earth's surface are caused by overhead ionospheric currents. Furthermore Fourier analysis (cf. Garland, 1971) demonstrates that besides an overt 24 hour variation there is also a 25 hour periodicity. This is related to lunar effects and changes in both amplitude and phase through the month in such a manner that on a few days in each month there is a virtually pure 24 hour period. The individual solar and lunar components of the variation are usually designated S_q and L_q respectively. An analysis which was based upon potential theory long ago suggested that, although the causes were, indeed, predominantly external, an internally produced component is by no means negligible. Just prior to this, and long before the structure of the atmosphere had been elucidated, Balfour Stewart (1882) had proposed a dynamo action in the upper levels of the atmosphere which reflected solar and lunar tidal motions. This "dynamo theory" has been the subject of much discussion and correction but it remains the most potent explanation of diurnal effects.

One early difficulty was the absence of any pronounced 12 hour periodicity in the observed magnetic effects which would be expected on the basis of tidal motions. The first major advance (Chapman, 1919) focussed upon the fact that, if the conductivity of the upper atmosphere arises from photo-ionisation of the constituent molecules, then it must be dependent upon the sun's hour angle. Hence the dynamo effect is greatest on the sunlit side of the earth. Pekeris et al. (1973) are among those authors who have reconsidered such problems in recent years and they concluded that their model also necessitated a dynamo mechanism in the outer part of the liquid core.

Variations in relation to solar effects feature in sections 5 and 7, but we can note in passing that Courtillot and Le Mouel (1976) found clear evidence for such relationships. Using Burg's maximum entropy spectral analysis these workers studied both the monthly, and the annual, mean values for the absolute elements of the geomagnetic field as determined at a number of world observatories. After they had removed the parabolic trend which accounts for much of the secular variation of *internal* origin, the residual variations clearly exhibited a world-wide character and most of the power found in the spectra for periods of between 2 and c. 20 years was clearly related to the solar cycle. Marked peaks occurred around 10–12 years and the first two harmonics.

2 MAGNETIC DISTURBANCES

The daily variations which were referred to above are rarely seen in a wholly unmodified form on any given day because they are subject to distortion by irregular disturbances. These are usually referred to the international index figure K, which reflects the range of magnetic components during three-hour periods. The average values for these indices, as determined at a number of observatories, are then used to provide a universal index, K_p. This ranges from 0 to 9 on a quasi-logarithmic scale and thereby covers the variability from extremely quiet conditions (0), to those typical of a severe magnetic disturbance—a magnetic storm.

Despite the fact that such irregularities vary considerably from one storm to another all storms share certain characteristics in common. The typical form of the disturbances during such a storm are represented in Fig. 26. There is an abrupt onset with an initial phase

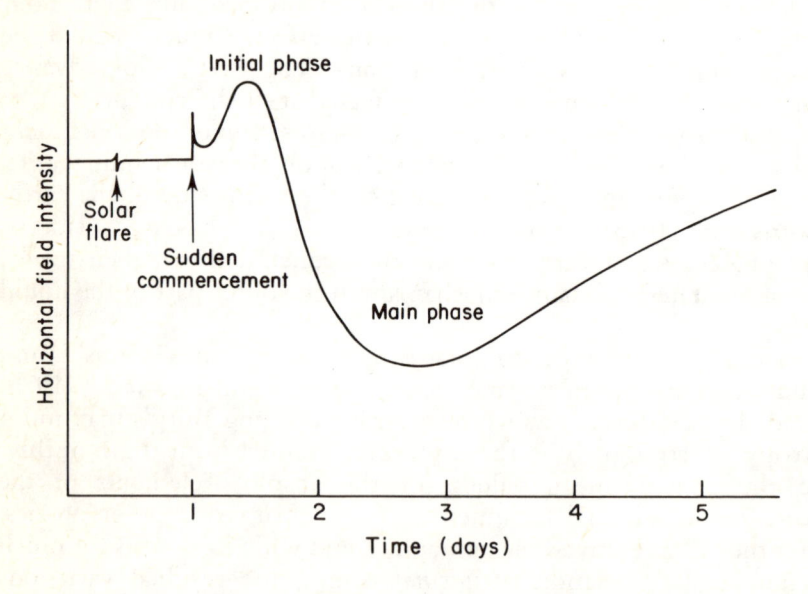

Fig. 26. The characteristic sequence of events during a magnetic storm, idealised from records of horizontal magnetic field intensity.

during which H (the horizontal component) is increased. The field then exhibits a striking decrease followed by a more gradual recovery, and data abound which demonstrate that such phenomena are essentially of solar origin (cf. Garland, 1971). There is a close correlation with the levels of sunspot activity and, what is more, between pronounced storms and particular sunspots. Storms also have a repetitive occurrence with a periodicity of 27 days which is the time taken for the sun to rotate on its axis. It has long been assumed that such observed effects on the earth's geomagnetic field are the result of streams of charged particles from the sun, and the changes of H which characterise the principal phase of a storm intimate that a current is circling the earth in an equatorial plane. Modern concepts (cf. Fig. 25) envisage material of solar origin arriving as the solar wind, perhaps in the form of a neutral plasma, and, following the trapping of particles in the earth's geomagnetic field, there is charge separation. Burton *et al.* (1975), who studied the geomagnetic disturbances during 1967 and 1968, for which solar wind observations are available, concluded that the magnetosphere acts as a half wave rectifier of the interplanetary electric field.

Ionized material of solar origin and varying intensity, principally emitted by sunspots, continually sweeps past the earth and may carry with it a "frozen" magnetic field from the sunspots. As the material approaches the earth the geomagnetic dipole increases and the solar plasma is prevented from approaching closer. Explorer 33 also provided data which showed that the interplanetary magnetic field irregularities are enhanced in the region of interaction where a fast solar wind-stream overtakes a slower one. Careful comparisons with geomagnetic indices then showed that these irregularities enhance the level of geomagnetic disturbances (Garrett *et al.*, 1974).

A strong burst of solar wind leads to a compression of the lines of force of the earth's field, because they cannot enter the plasma, and, at the earth's surface, this is reflected by the sudden initiation of a magnetic storm. Aggregations of particles from the solar wind then become trapped in the earth's field and spiral around the lines of force. It is these particles which constitute the well-known radiation belts and oscillate between mirror points. Simultaneously there is a small longitudinal drift, which is of opposing nature for negative and positive particles, and gives a net single ring current over the equator. The mirror points themselves are normally high above the earth and the trapped particles do not interact with the atmosphere to any appreciable extent. However, distortion of the dipole field by an intensified solar wind disrupts the mirrors so that charged particles can enter the atmosphere and are then slowed down by collisions which produce aurorae etc. A greatly enhanced electrical conductivity within the auroral zone is associated with these phenomena and a current—the auroral electrojet—is concentrated within it. This is thought to be the source of a number of the phenomena that have been noted during magnetic storms. Gurnett and Akasofu (1974) certainly concluded that it is enhanced ionospheric conductivity, rather than the electric field, that is responsible for large increases in the auroral electrojet during a substorm.

As charged particles escape from the radiation belts the concentration within these returns to "normal", the ring current decreases, and the geomagnetic field at the global surface returns to its "usual" value. Table 3 contains examples of the relative magnitudes of the times involved for trapped particles of different energies.

TABLE 3

Examples of the characteristic times for trapped particles of different energies (Akasofu and Chapman, 1961)

Particle	Radius of gyration (km)	Period of gyration (s)	Period of oscillation (s)	Period of drift
Electron, $1·07 \times 10^3$ KeV	3·38	$7·48 \times 10^{-7}$	0·67	14 min
Proton, 2 KeV	3·38	0·433	400	6·6 days
Proton, 479 KeV	67·6	0·433	20	21 min

Garland also summarised the various time variations involved. Energy fluctuations have a periodicity that is comparable with that of sunspots, because of the higher incidence of disturbances during periods of maximum sunspot activity; a periodicity of six months which reflects the greater ability of the geomagnetic field to trap particles when one pole is tilted towards the sun; and a periodicity of 27 days because of the cyclical recurrence of magnetic storms after one solar rotation. A band of periodicities ranging from one to several hundred seconds represent micropulsations (Troitskaya, 1967) that are thought to be the magnetic effects of hydromagnetic waves which are trapped in the magnetosphere. Higher frequencies arise from natural oscillations of the earth–ionosphere complex as a whole, and from the electromagnetic radiation associated with lightning discharges. Long period effects are due to overall reversals of the main field.

An abnormally high range of solar-induced, daily variation of the horizontal, geomagnetic field occurs at stations +3° from the magnetic equator. This is explained (Rastogi, 1974) as due to a belt of strong eastward current, known as the equatorial electrojet, which is flowing in the ionosphere at E region heights (see section 4 below) and reflects an enhanced conductivity that is created there by inhibition of the vertical, Hall, polarisation field.

Furthermore, Aldredge (1975) showed that sudden changes—impulses—in the rate of magnetic secular variations often occur simultaneously at many widely spaced observatories. As the horizontal component is correlated with sunspots he therefore concluded that these effects are most likely to be due to changes in sources such as the ring current and both the equatorial, and polar, electrojets. He also (1976) demonstrated by Fourier analysis that the annual means for the horizontal and vertical geomagnetic components are most easily explained by a westward flowing ring current that increases as sunspot numbers increase, but lags behind them by a year or two.

As the northward component of the interplanetary magnetic field increases a characteristic current system appears in the polar cap. This comprises (Maezawa, 1976) two current vortices on the dayside polar cap, one in the pre-noon sector, and the other in the afternoon sector. On the other hand when the interplanetary magnetic field is directed southward a transpolar current sheath appears and covers the whole polar cap. Svalgaard (1973) suggested that the very pronounced seasonal variation of the intensity of the polar cap currents may indicate a dependency upon either the ionospheric conductivity or the tilt of the magnetic axes of the earth. Nishida *et al.* (1966) had earlier suggested that the varying shape of the magnetosphere during the year, which is the result of variations of both the solar wind velocity and the geomagnetic dipole axis, should give a seasonal variation in the vertical component of the polar magnetic field.

3 THE ATMOSPHERIC DYNAMO

The dynamo theory suggests that atmospheric movements drag the conducting ionosphere across the earth's magnetic field so that voltages are induced and currents flow. Any calculation of the characteristics of these currents necessitates a knowledge of the air movements, and of the ways in which the motion of electrons and ions is affected by collisions with neutral air particles or by the earth's magnetic field. The motion of the air at ground level has now been investigated by measurements of barometric pressure which have been spread over a long enough time to enable persistent oscillations of half a solar day, and half a lunar day, to be defined. This shows that the solar oscillation is about 16 times as strong as the lunar one. It is now thought that the lunar oscillation is a tidal one, driven by gravity, whereas the solar oscillation is driven by the heat put into the atmosphere by the sun's radiation. Malin (1973) summarised more recent data relating to the diurnal lunar and solar actions on both the ionosphere and oceans. However, even in the thirties it was possible to use estimates of both the solar oscillation and ionospheric conductivity to calculate the currents that would flow in the atmospheric dynamo and to see whether they would be expected to produce the observed diurnal changes of terrestrial magnetism.

Detailed calculations demonstrated that the oscillation at a height of 100 km is c. 200 times greater than that at ordnance datum. However, even with this enhanced movement the calculated changes of the magnetic field were less than the observed values by a factor of c. 400. Some time elapsed before the source of error was discovered. Around 1950 it was realised that although currents can flow horizontally in the ionosphere they cannot flow vertically for they would have nowhere to flow to. This modified the possible motions of ions and electrons and made important differences to the magnitude of the calculated conductivity. Revised conductivity estimates, combined with an estimated air speed at 100 km, gave calculated geomagnetic variations that were then similar to the observed ones. One important result was that, near to the equator, where the earth's magnetic field is horizontal, the conductivity, and hence the currents, would be much enhanced. This conclusion provided a satisfactory explanation of the long-established observation that the geomagnetic variations which occur near the equator are particularly large.

The advent of rockets carrying equipment into the high atmosphere subsequently enabled the actual experimental location of the dynamo currents. It was found that as the height increased the strength of the field at first decreased, as would be expected if the earth behaved like a magnetised sphere. However above 100 km the field began to vary in a different manner. This was taken as indicating that dynamo currents were flowing and subsequent investigations confirm that these do, indeed, flow at heights of about 130 km.

The permanent geomagnetic field not only affects the direction and magnitude of the current but it also exerts a force upon it and causes it to move. This itself causes movements of the ionospheric region of current flow so that the atmospheric dynamo at 100–130 km can drive a current in the F layer above it (see Fig. 27 below). This would be much smaller than that in the E layer but would be large enough to experience an important force in the presence of the permanent magnetic field and therefore to explain some anomalies observed in the F layer. Various approaches demonstrate that movements of considerable magnitude must occur in the F layer but it is only in the case of the equatorial anomaly that these are easily related to the observed anomalies.

When the sun is overhead at the equator the maximum electron concentration in the peak of the F layer is not found at the equator but on lines that approximately parallel the geomagnetic dip equator and are removed from it by some 20°. Explanations of this phenomenon point to the fact that the distribution of electrons depends on the movements resulting from the motor action as well as their own rates of release, loss or diffusion. Since diffusion only occurs across a magnetic field with difficulty, it will follow the field lines rather than passing vertically. This led to the suggestion that the diurnal ionisation which can be detected in the F layer at the equator is first of all driven upwards by the action of the underlying dynamo, and then diffuses obliquely downwards along the lines of force. As a result, the maximal electron concentrations build up on two lines—one on each side of the equator—and such a movement is known as the fountain effect.

Kamei and Maeda (1976) have, more recently, demonstrated that "tides" resulting from lunar factors may have an effect on the dynamo region and produce significant changes in the ring current of the magnetosphere.

4 THE UPPER ATMOSPHERE

Our knowledge of the upper atmosphere has changed very considerably since the early 1920s. At that time the air at ground level was known to mainly comprise oxygen and nitrogen together with a very small proportion of helium. These gases were mixed in the lower 20 or 30 km but, above that height, they separated out and at sufficient heights the lightest, helium, predominated. The temperature was also known to decrease in the first 12 or 15 km above the ground and, at some indeterminate height, to increase again. On the day side of the earth solar radiation impinging upon the atmosphere produced a layer of ozone at $c.$ 25 km and caused the oxygen to exist in atomic rather than molecular form at heights above 150 km. It also ionised the air at some unknown height, thereby rendering it conducting so that it reflected radio-waves. This solar radiation could be photons of uv or X-radiation, or a stream of charged or uncharged particles. Whichever it was due to, it clearly waxed and waned with the c. 11 year solar cycle. From 1924 onwards radio-waves were used with the express purpose of investigating the electron content of the upper atmosphere and subsequently, in 1951, experimental equipment was sent in space vehicles to make direct measurements at great heights (cf. Ratcliffe, 1970).

To decide whether it was particles or photons that were involved advantage was taken of the differences between their speeds. Because photons travel with the speed of light any ionisation produced by them would diminish during a visible eclipse. In contrast, any similar effects involving more slowly moving particles would occur at other times. In fact, while particles are traversing the distance between the moon and the earth the moon moves through a similar distance. When detailed calculations are carried out it turns out—somewhat unexpectedly—that the eclipsed particle stream will impinge on the earth *before* the visible eclipse. Here was the basis for the crucial test and it was found that the penetration frequencies of the E and F_1 layers were markedly reduced during an eclipse but not before. The factors causing the effects were clearly travelling with the speed of light although data for the F_2 layer were confusing and some particulate penetrations may occur at this level.

Routine measurements of penetration frequencies were commenced during the early investigations in 1927 and it is now clear that the electron concentrations of the layers vary within solar cycles. Even during quiet times, when none of the extreme variations accompanying magnetic storms occur, the electron concentration in the ionosphere varies from day to day. Some of these variations reflect the 27 day rotation of the sun whilst others seem to be more randomly distributed.

Recent ideas about the factors influencing the production of ionisation at different heights are summarised in Fig. 27. Each atmospheric gas can only be ionised by radiation with wavelengths shorter than a certain ionisation limit. This last is represented along the horizontal scale. No gas of any importance can be ionised by radiation with a wavelength that is longer than 1,200 Å, but radiation which cannot ionise oxygen or nitrogen is nevertheless absorbed by these gases and the broken line indicates the levels to which it penetrates prior to the strength being reduced by a factor of $1/e$. The F region is produced by radiation with wavelengths of 200–800 Å, which ionises molecular nitrogen and atomic oxygen between 150–170 km. The E layer near 100 km is produced jointly by X-rays with wavelengths less than c. 100 Å, which ionise oxygen and nitrogen, and by uv with a wavelength in the region of 1,000 Å, which ionises oxygen.

The D region below 90 km is more complicated. Figure 27 shows

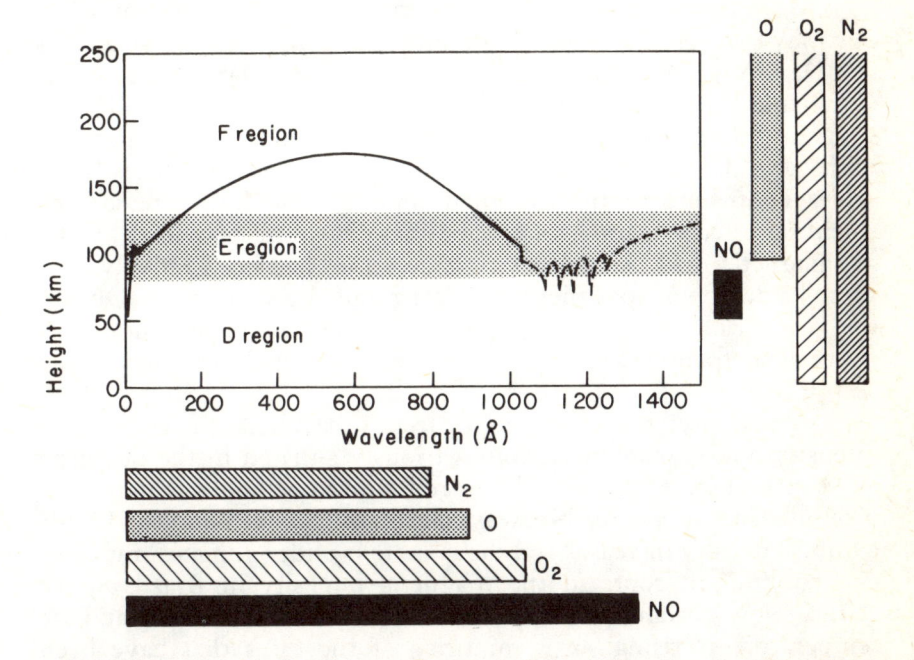

FIG. 27. The formation of the ionospheric layers. The gases available to be ionised are distributed in height as shown on the right, whilst the wavelengths of radiations that ionise them are shown below the horizontal scale. Radiations that cannot ionise the major gases are shown by the broken line. (Ratcliffe, 1970.)

that X-rays with a wavelength of less than 20 Å can ionise all gases present at that level, but the other radiations, with wavelengths in excess of 1,130 Å, cannot ionise any of the gases which are normally present. If, however, some other gas that is capable of being ionised by the longer wavelengths is present, e.g. NO, then the resulting electrons would be important. Rocket and satellite measurements of the Lyman-alpha and X radiations that are not absorbed by the atmosphere show that they are strong enough to contribute about equally to the ionisation of the D layer.

5 MAGNETIC EFFECTS AND CLIMATE

Although the suggestion that there may be a relationship between the earth's geomagnetic field and global climate had been made at various times during some 50 years it is only relatively recently that convincing correlations have emerged. A number of these are mentioned in the context of atmospheric ^{14}C content in section 7 but one may cite here the work of Willett (1953), DeVries (1958), Egyed (1961), Libby (1967), Damon (1968), Harrison (1968), Bucha et al. (1969) and Wollin et al. (1971; 1973). One may note that Wollin et al. suggested that a higher magnetic intensity produces, or is associated with, a colder climate. Magnetic phenomena may therefore themselves contribute to the modulation of climate by virtue of the shielding effects against solar radiation which are provided by the geomagnetic field. Analogous considerations had been actively canvassed a decade or so earlier by DeVries and also by Damon. During the last decade several symposia have helped to clarify the issues concerned, focus attention on the salient points, and educate the sceptical.

Particular interest focusses on the trends that characterise magnetic intensity and climate at stations variously situated in the northern and southern hemispheres. These are found to be opposite in nature. The intensity curves for Norway, Germany, Sweden and the USSR exhibit intensity increases and the climate is undergoing a simultaneous cooling. In contrast, the magnetic intensity in Brazil, South Africa, New Zealand and Samoa has recently been decreasing and the temperature is rising. In a minority of the cases that have been studied the trends of 10 year mean values for air temperature do not correlate with the magnetic intensity variations but at some of these the intensity trends do show a correlation with *winter* temperatures. Furthermore at some observatories there are abrupt changes of magnetic intensity from year to year and these are accompanied, or followed, by equally abrupt changes of climate. Wollin et al. (1973) therefore concluded that a close, if not causal, link exists between climate and the earth's geomagnetic field (Fig. 28). They may of course show independent parallel effects that are both caused by solar variations.

For longer periods of time the same authors demonstrated a correlation between the magnetic intensity curves of a deep-sea sediment, the *Globorotalia menardii* climatic curve and the variation of oxygen isotope ratios. However Amerigian (1974) suggested that the changes of magnetisation in sediments depend upon composition and grain size and that correlations between climate and the magnetisation may reflect variable inclination errors induced by bottom current velocity changes.

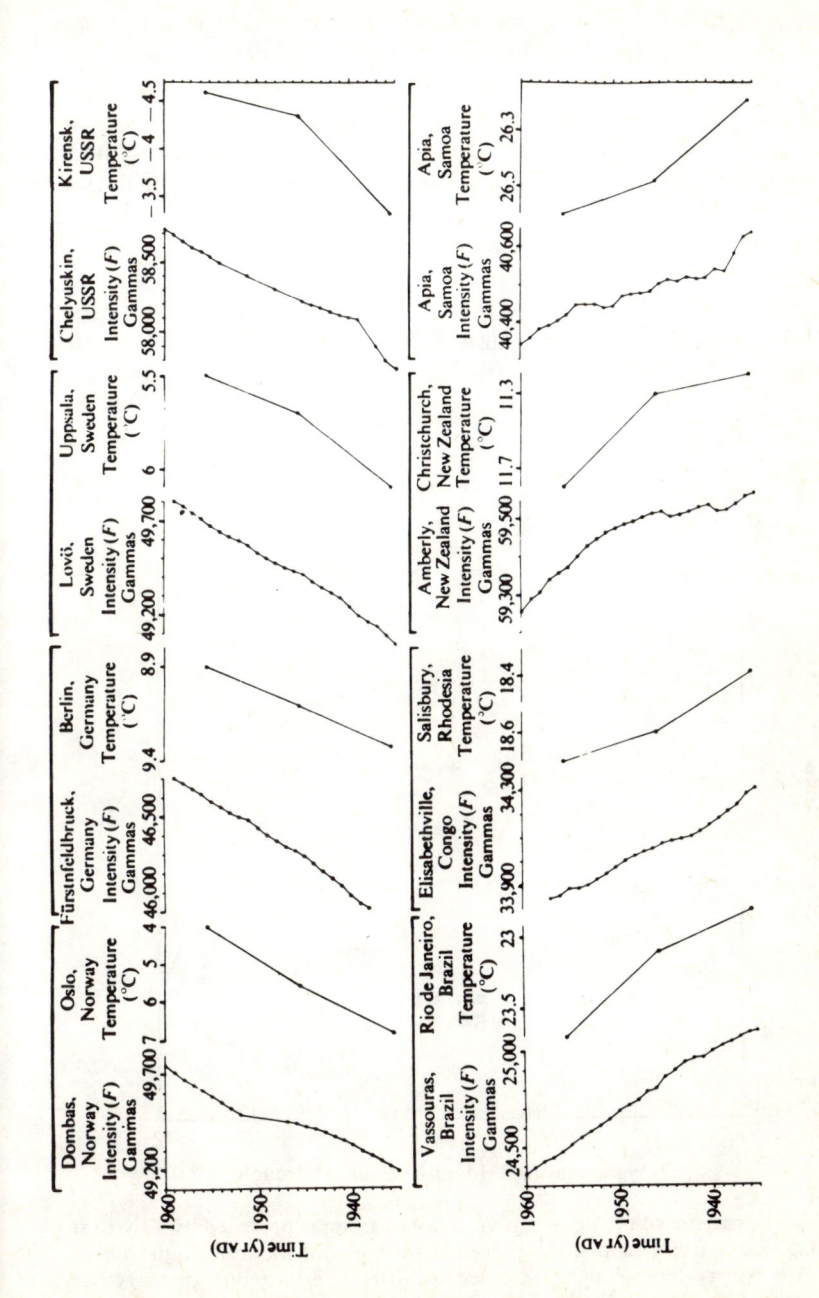

FIG. 28. A comparison of the changing temperature and magnetic intensity at various parts of the world (Wollin et al., 1971).

Certain detailed contemporary considerations throw additional light on the topic. In 1961 MacDonald and Roberts showed that, during the winter, troughs in the westerlies (cyclonic waves) which entered the North Pacific area some 2–4 days after a major magnetic storm were likely to undergo significantly greater deepening than those that entered at other times. Roberts and Olson (1973) then studied an objectively derived index of high positive absolute vorticity for each trough. This was defined as the area of the trough for which the absolute vorticity is $\geq 20 \times 10^{-5}$ s^{-1} plus the area for which it is $\geq 24 \times 10^{-5}$ s^{-1}. Most winter troughs at the 300 mbar level reach a value of vorticity above 20×10^{-5} s^{-1}, and large ones have a substantial region where the vorticity exceeds 24×10^{-5} s^{-1}.

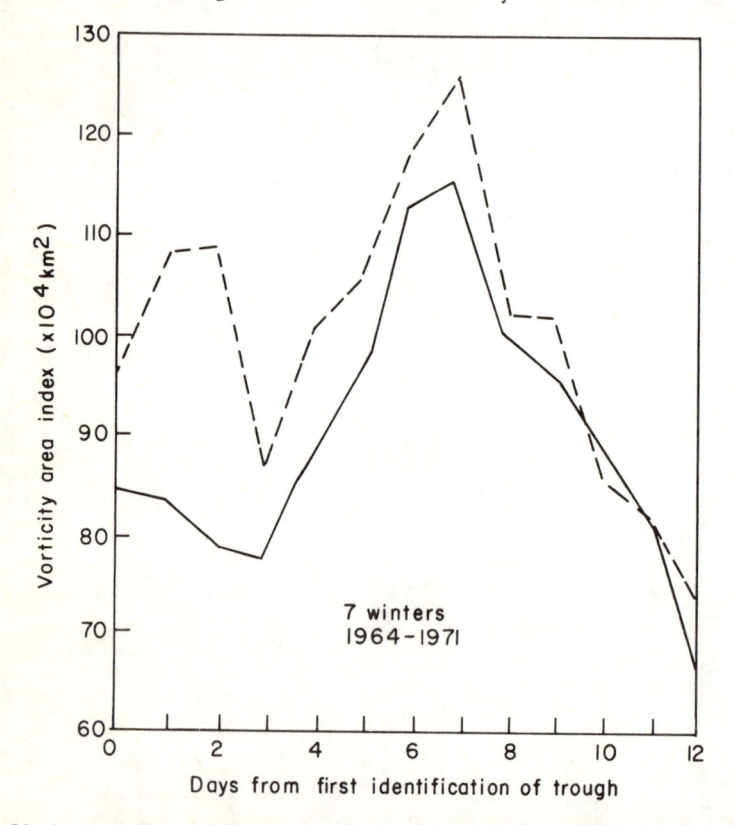

Fig. 29. A comparison of the degree of vorticity of troughs preceded by a sharp rise in geomagnetic activity, and those preceded by a geomagnetically quiet ten-day period. ---, Ninety-four troughs preceded by sharp rise in geomagnetic activity; ——, a hundred and thirty-four troughs preceded by a quiet ten-day geomagnetic period. (Roberts and Olson, 1973.)

In their study any troughs that entered the North Pacific and crossed the 180th meridian from the west, or were formed in that region, 2–4 days after a sharp rise in geomagnetic activity were called key troughs. The subsequent path of a trough can usually be followed for 1–2 weeks by which time it has usually dissipated or has moved into Western Europe in which case it was no longer studied. During this movement across half a hemisphere there are two periods of time when such troughs exhibit a marked rise in vorticity and during which their average vorticity index exceeds the values for troughs whose inception was preceded by magnetic quiet days.

The first rise in vorticity is during the first three days of the trough's existence east of 180° longitude. This is, on average, the 3rd to 5th day after the sharp geomagnetic rise. The contrast between this "behaviour" and that of troughs preceded by quiet days is represented in Fig. 29. This convinced Roberts and Olson that solar corpuscular emissions which are responsible for the geomagnetic changes are also systematically related to the larger sizes of key troughs in the first days of their existence.

The second period during which rises occur is about 9–10 days after the geomagnetic storm by which time the trough has reached the Atlantic coastal region. Troughs that are preceded by a quiet period also exhibit a rise in this time but it is of smaller magnitude. Roberts and Olson suggested that any rises on days 6–7 are a result of the trough's history and are not related to solar activity. However, the second period of regular intensification may reflect the significant pressure fall over the east coast of America that follows 10 days after the geomagnetic storm (Asakura and Katayama, 1958). If the semi-permanent Atlantic coastal trough intensified about 10 days after a magnetic storm, the key troughs coming from the west might lead to

TABLE 4

Numbers of wintertime troughs that attained an average vorticity area index of large, medium or small value during their first three days of existence in the North Pacific east of 180° longitude (Roberts and Olson, 1973)

	Troughs preceded by a sharp geomagnetic rise	Troughs preceded by 10 days of quiet	Total
Large	45	28	73
Medium	27	46	73
Small	22	60	82

increased cyclogenesis at that time. This they called a second-stage solar effect.

Subsequent to Roberts and Olson's paper King (1974) suggested that the regions of low atmospheric pressure that are observed near the magnetic poles occur because these regions, which are linked magnetically to the interior of the magnetoball, are strongly shielded against the incursion of solar particles. Although the mechanisms by which energetic particles may affect the troposphere are not fully known, he described the possible influence of the geomagnetic field on the height of the 500 mbar level in the regions surrounding the north and south magnetic poles. He also concluded that certain features of the "permanent" atmospheric pressure system had moved westwards during some decades of the present century and that this westward drift might well be correlated with the corresponding westward drift of the magnetic field pattern.

Figure 31 shows the average height of the 500 mbar level during January in the northern hemisphere. The contours follow a typical winter pattern of two lows, one near 80°W and the other at 130°E.

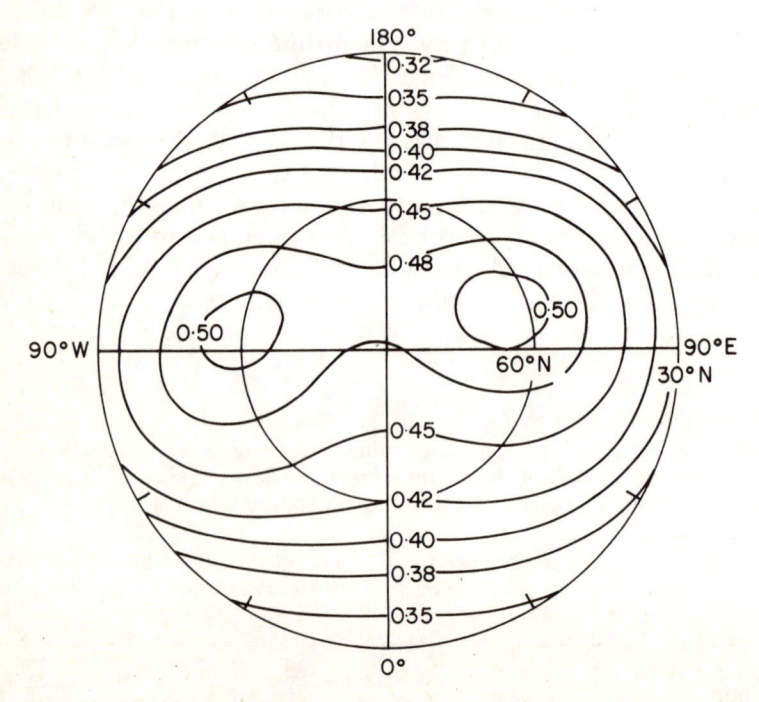

Fig. 30. The distribution of the magnetic field of the earth for the northern hemisphere in 1965 (King, 1974).

Other average pressure maps all show a highly elongated "dumbbell" shaped low at high latitudes. A comparison of this data with Fig. 30 is instructive. Here the magnetic intensity of the northern

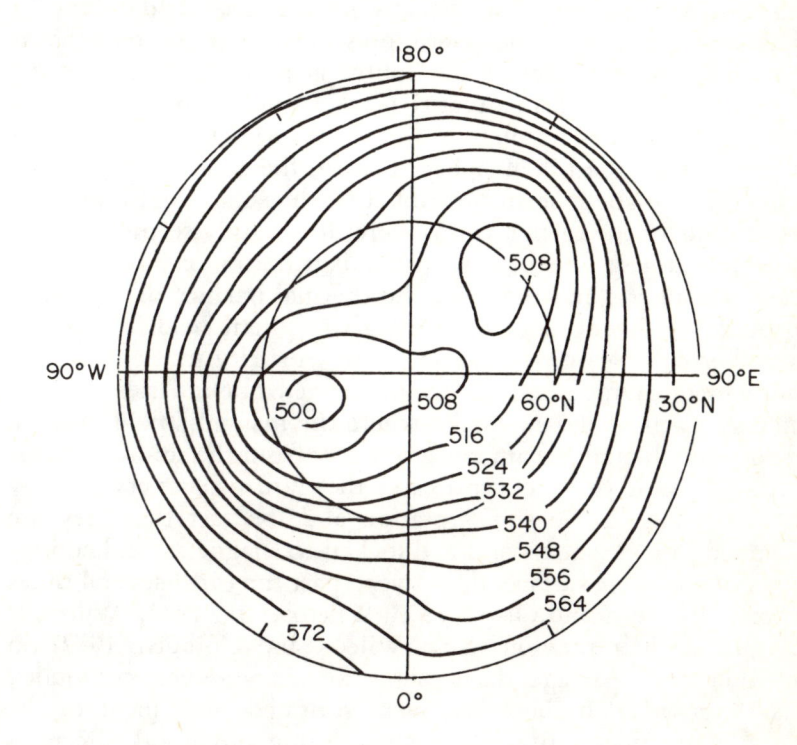

FIG. 31. Distribution of pressure over the northern hemisphere represented as contours of the average height in decametres of the 500 mbar level in the atmosphere (King, 1974).

hemisphere magnetic field at an altitude of 400 km, in 1965, is shown in polar view. Although the meteorological data relate to a different time the fit is striking, apart from the fact that the magnetic data occur some 25° towards the west. As no account was taken of the known westward drift of the magnetic pole a correction of this nature would remove at least part of the difference. Comparisons suggest a drift of $c.$ 3° per decade, although it is by no means uniform. King suggested that remaining phase differences may arise from the complicated relationship between atmospheric pressure and the modulating effects of the magnetic field dependent driving force.

In the southern hemisphere the magnetic invariant pole is situated at longitude 125°E and the geomagnetic contours are much more circular than the elongated ones of the north pole. King concluded, by using data published by Lamb (cf. p. 75), that the height of the 500 mbar level is most reduced where the magnetic field is strong. The resultant conclusion, that some magnetic field dependent mechanism modulates tropospheric pressures by an amount that is greater in the north than in the south, is particularly interesting because it is well established that the intensity of auroral emissions, produced by particles impinging on the atmosphere, is 30 per cent greater in the northern hemisphere than in the southern one. Such considerations made it seem probable that the solar wind influences the behaviour of the earth's atmosphere. It certainly seemed worthwhile to investigate whether the spatial distribution of water vapour in the stratosphere, and therefore the thermal balance of the lower atmosphere, is also dependent on the geomagnetic field.

A further comparison of the 300 mbar vorticity index data with the movement of interplanetary magnetic sector boundaries was also of interest. Each boundary marks where the magnetic field in space reverses sign, changing from a vector away from the sun to a vector towards the sun, or vice versa, and they are often very sharply defined. Owing to the sun's rotation and the fact that they are "embedded" in the solar wind and locked to magnetic field configurations of the solar surface, they sweep past the earth several times per month (Roberts and Olson, 1973; Wilcox *et al.*, 1973). Wilcox *et al.* compared their previous data (Wilcox and Colburn, 1972) on sector boundary passage dates with the average vorticity index values. Even though these last were summed over most of the northern hemisphere, thus seriously diluting any local effects, a clear-cut dip emerged in those values centred about 1 day after the passage of a sector boundary. Figure 32 shows the result of this analysis. The data were subdivided in three ways. The first group separated interplanetary magnetic sector boundaries of opposite sign; the second separated the first half of the winter season from the later half; the third separated the first three relevant winters from the latter four. All sets exhibited essentially identical curves which convincingly demonstrated an effect in the 300 mbar vorticity that is correlated with magnetic field configurations of solar origin and lying far outside the earth's atmosphere. Because of the complexity of the relationships between the interplanetary sector boundary passages and geomagnetic phenomena it was not possible to determine what particular characteristic is the most causally significant in relation to 300 mbar circulation, but when the sector boundaries pass the earth there is a decrease in average geomagnetic activity which reaches minimal levels about one day prior to sector passage. This is then followed, on average, by a sharp rise on the day of sector passage and the two succeeding days. Roberts and Olson were

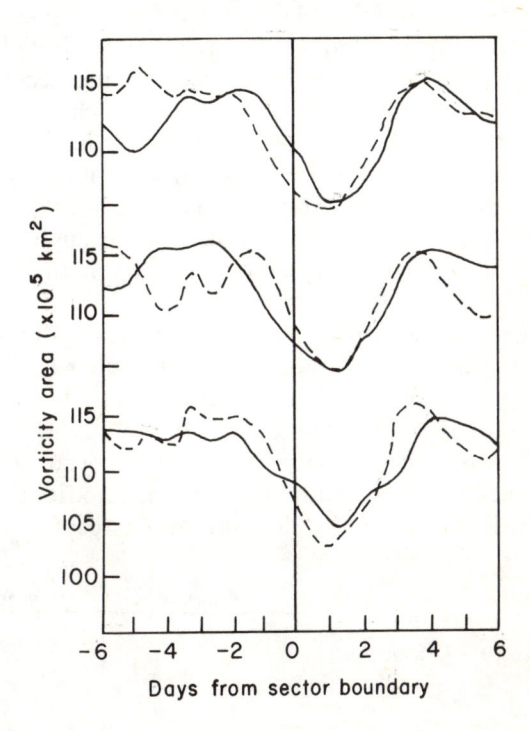

Fig. 32. A comparison of the vorticity indices and the days from the sector boundary (Wilcox *et al.*, 1973). (Copyright American Association for the Advancement of Science.)

therefore tempted to associate the dip in hemisphere vorticity, and its subsequent rise, with the dip in geomagnetic activity before sector passage and the subsequent rise on the following two days. This would clearly provide a markedly self-consistent picture.

6 THE MAGNETISATION OF ROCKS

6.1. *Introduction*

In view of the widespread involvement of the geomagnetic field in atmospheric and climatic events the known occurrence of polarity reversals in the past is clearly of considerable direct significance to any consideration of past climates. Furthermore Reid *et al.* (1976)

have postulated that links between such reversals and faunal extinctions may be the result of catastrophic depletion of the stratospheric ozone as a result of solar proton irradiation in the presence of a reduced geomagnetic field. Harrison (1968) together with the other authors mentioned in Chapter 1, has also concluded that during a reversal organisms living at the equator would receive 14 per cent more radiation, but he concluded that "the ensuing climatic changes would probably be more influential than a mere rise in the overall mutation rate". The fact that various faunal events of the last 12 million years are contemporaneous with geomagnetic reversals, coupled with the climatic effects that are discussed above, clearly necessitates a consideration of such geomagnetic reversals at this point.

Summaries of the principal events can be obtained in many text-books and articles on geophysics (cf. Bullard, 1968; Cox, 1969; 1973; Tarling, 1971; Garland, 1971). As was emphasised above, those periods of the earth's magnetic field which are most crucial to an understanding of the geomagnetic dynamo occur at the ultra-low frequency end of the spectrum. Yet, until the sixties this had received relatively little attention—if for no other reason than because it

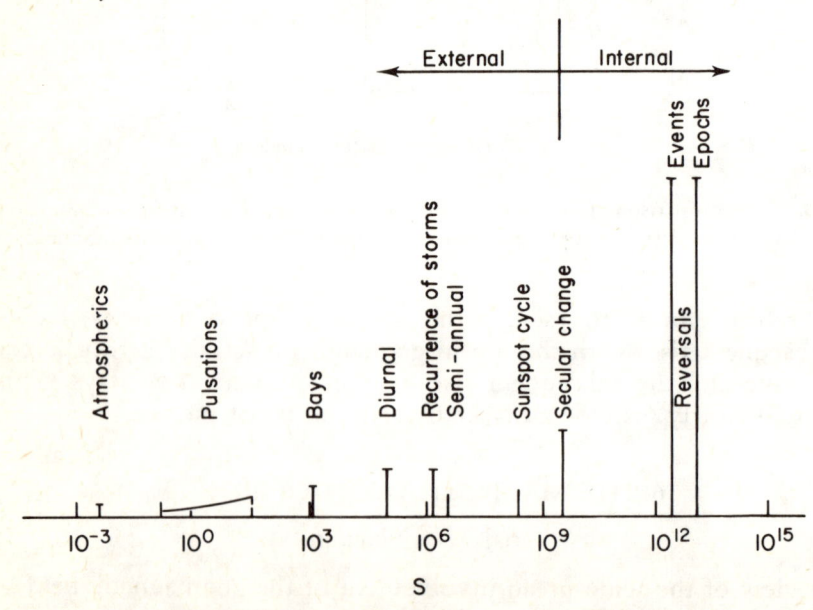

FIG. 33. The spectrum of changes in the earth's magnetic field; only the most important lines are shown, and the amplitudes of the shorter period changes are exaggerated relative to secular change and reversals (Garland, 1971).

extends to periods which exceed the productive life-times of individual scientists. Indeed the longest periods exceed the entire history of science (Fig. 33).

It is somewhat difficult to apply physical theories to rocks because their magnetic components are rarely homogenous at the time of formation and their properties change with time, even in the absence of geological events. As their magnetic remanence is usually only carried by some 5 per cent of the total magnetic material present, and as this is dispersed through the rock, the overall structure corresponds to a weak "solution" of ferromagnetic particles which lies ensconced within a paramagnetic matrix. The magnetisation observed in a rock—the natural remanent magnetisation or NRM—comprises any remaining *primary* magnetisation together with all subsequent or secondary magnetisations. Rocks which have been subjected to either pressures or temperatures of sufficient magnitude to cause physical or mineralogical changes will only rarely retain any of their primary magnetisation so that the magnetisation of metamorphic rocks is more or less entirely secondary. However, if it reflects activities at a distinct identifiable time it is usefully considered as if it were primary (cf. Tarling, 1971). When primary remanence has been isolated it is necessary to determine whether it was acquired exactly parallel to the ancient field and whether heterogeneity prevents true measurements of remanent directions being made.

Igneous rocks have a primary magnetisation which is, for all practical purposes, of thermoremanent origin. As the magma cools from temperatures in excess of 1,000°C it solidifies, and eventually reaches the Curie temperature of its ferromagnetic constituents. This is usually between 400 and 600°C. In detailed studies this thermoremanence is not absolutely reliable as the material undergoes physicochemical interactions. However, the natural primary remanence of igneous rocks is somewhat simplified by their slow cooling rates. Deep intrusive rocks may retain their heat for hundreds, possibly thousands, of years, and the slow acquisition of remanence evens out any short-term fluctuations in the local field that are due to magnetic storms, lightning, etc. It is usually unimportant that the natural remanence is of variable thermal, chemical and high-termperature, viscous origins because most of the magnetisation which is stable over geological time is acquired above 300°C.

Sedimentary rocks differ from the foregoing because they contain magnetised particles which have their origin in pre-existing rocks. As these components fall through the water they assume the alignment of the existing ambient field and this alignment may be preserved within the sediment. The chemical composition of the aligned particles can then change with time and whether or not they do so is dependent upon their nature. As the sediment dries out any titanomagnetites are oxidised and the iron hydroxides are reduced. They thereby give rise to haematite and this is also formed as other iron-bearing silicates, such as clays, olivines and pyroxenes, disintegrate. Most such sediments therefore acquire a chemical remanence as these crystals grow. Since the diagenetic processes which are involved in the conversion of a wet slurry to a compact rock may be exceedingly prolonged, sediments rarely carry a stable remanence that is closely related to that occurring at the time of deposition.

Such materials retain a "magnetic memory" of the earth's field in the past and, if the natural thermal remanence of the rocks is stable, then the ancient field can be determined by reheating the sample and cooling it in a known field. The ancient field intensity is then given by

$$F_o = F_a \frac{J_o}{J_a}$$

where J_o is the natural remanence, and J_a the remanence acquired in the known applied field F_a. Virtual dipole moments obtained in this manner for samples of the same age, but from differing parts of the world, are scattered and have a standard deviation of $c.$ 20 per cent, because the earth's geomagnetic field consists, in part, of an irregular non-dipole component.

6.2 *Geomagnetic reversals*

The first hint of periods that last in excess of a century arose from early observations on changes in field intensity. In 1835, the first year for which Gauss was able to assemble enough world-wide data to subject the field to harmonic analysis, the earth's dipole moment was $8 \cdot 5 \times 10^{25}$ gauss cm^3. By 1965 it had fallen to 8×10^{25}. During the intervening period the dipole field decreased at a remarkably uniform rate; a rate which, if continued, will pass through a zero point in about 2,000 years. It would then presumably reverse its polarity, although alternative explanations would result in oscillations without a change of polarity. The study of the natural magnetism of rocks and baked clay has now increased the length of the available magnetic record by more than 6 orders of magnitude.

The decrease in the dipole moment which has occurred since 1885, reflected by the slanting bar on the left of Fig. 34, is seen to be but the most recent part of a well-defined half cycle, which began *c.* 4,000

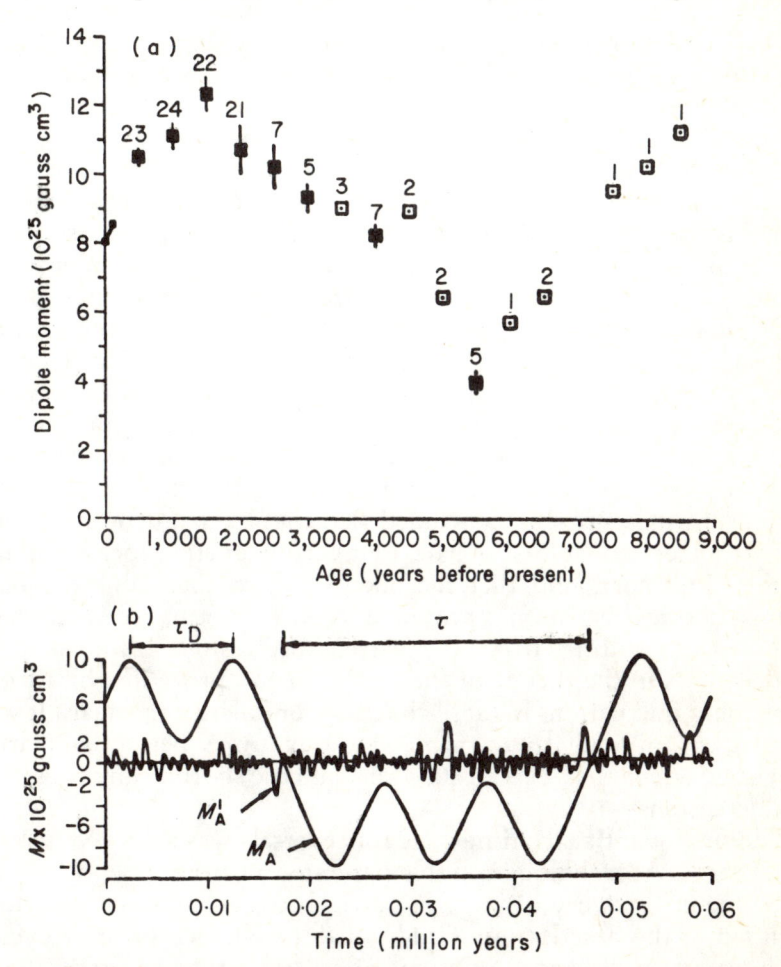

FIG. 34. (a) Variations in geomagnetic dipole moment. Changes during the past 130 years, as determined from observatory measurements, are shown by the slanting bar at left. Other values were determined paleomagnetically. The number of data that were averaged is shown above each point, and the standard error of the mean is indicated by the vertical lines except for points (□) with too few data to provide meaningful statistics. (b) Model for reversals used to derive the distribution function for reversals. τ_D is the period of the dipole field and τ is the length of a polarity interval. A reversal occurs whenever the quantity M'_A, which is a measure of the non-dipole field, becomes sufficiently large relative to the dipole moment M_A. (See Olsson, 1970.)

years ago, and has a maximum of 12×10^{25} gauss cm^3. It has also been established that the earth's dipole moment alternates between two anti-parallel polarity states—a normal state in which the field at the earth's surface is directed northward, and a reversed state in which the field has the opposite direction. In either state the dipole undergoes an irregular wobble about the earth's axis of rotation. The time taken to complete a transition between these polarity states is estimated to be from 10^3 to 10^4 years and, during this time, the field does not decline to zero but undergoes an intensive decrease of from 60 to 80 per cent. Cox concluded that, averaged over long periods, the total amount of time which the dipole spends in the reversed state equals that spent in the normal one, and the average field intensity is also the same suggesting that the two states have equal energy levels. This would imply that the earth's field acts as a remarkably symmetrical oscillator, or bistable flip-flop circuit. The greatest element of irregularity is the length of time that intervenes between two reversals of polarity. Cox drew attention to a long interval of 5×10^7 years; intervals of the order of 10^6 years are common; and short ones of less than 10^5 occur. It is these latter that are the most difficult to measure. He concluded that the geomagnetic field may well be generated, at least in part, by hydromagnetic processes in the earth's fluid core, and that the energy which maintains the field against ohmic dissipation is provided by either thermal convection or turbulence resulting from the earth's precession. Unfortunately inadequacies in the theory of the fluid dynamo prevented him from explaining fluctuations in dipole intensity or polarity reversals. It was particularly difficult to reconcile the long times between polarity reversals, which may exceed 10^6 years, and the shorter time constants of fluctuations—10^4 years.

The first quantitative time scale for reversals was achieved in 1963 using the K-Ar technique and this suggested a pattern of epochs. The subsequent discovery of inconsistencies between ages and polarities then led to the description of additional intra-epoch polarity events with unexpectedly short durations of $c.$ 10^5 years. The first of these to be recognised were the Olduvai event ($1 \cdot 9 \times 10^6$ B.P.) and the Mammoth event ($3 \cdot 1 \times 10^6$ B.P.). Their discovery clearly established the fact that a thorough and complete resolution of the fine structure of reversals would necessitate an immense number of paleomagnetic and radiometric data. A summary of the general results for the last 4·5 m.y. is contained in Fig. 36a which shows the Gilbert and Matuyama reversed epochs together with the Gauss and Brunhes normal ones. Older periods are covered by Fig. 36b. Cox concluded that, on average, 20 fluctuations in intensity occur between successive polarity reversals. Such phenomena are recorded in the sea floor that is constantly being produced (Fig. 35), and making allowance for sea floor spreading he also concluded that the average duration of polarity intervals was greater towards 45×10^6 B.P., and even greater still between $45-75 \times 10^6$ B.P. Further back in time an average length of 10^7 years has been put forward for the polarity intervals of the early Paleozoic with the Kiaman reversed polarity interval of the late Paleozoic having lasted 5×10^7 years. If proven, such changes would reflect changes in the earth's geomagnetic dynamo.

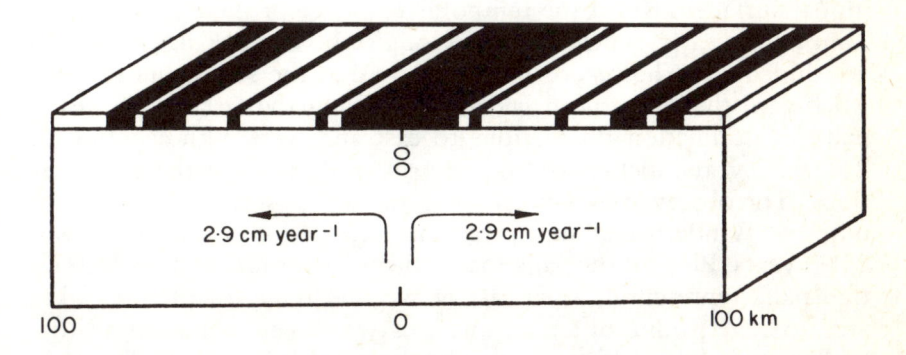

FIG. 35. The Vine–Matthews mechanism for the generation of oceanic magnetic anomalies.

During the Cenozoic the magnetic field reversed in polarity at least 171 times (Hays, 1971; Heirtzler *et al.*, 1968). The average duration of each period of constant polarity seems to have been 0·22 m.y. for the past 10 m.y. and somewhat longer (1·0 m.y.) for the early Tertiary. All the data for the Tertiary support the assumption that the field has spent equal amounts of time in the reversed and normal states. There is, though, substantial evidence that the reversal pattern for the Tertiary is not representative of all geological time and there were several phases of the Phanerozoic when the field maintained constant polarity for long intervals, interrupted only occasionally by short intervals of opposite polarity. As noted above the Kiaman interval persisted for 50 m.y. of the Carboniferous and Permian. The uppermost Permian, like the lower Triassic, had numerous reversals, but Helsley and Steiner (1969) documented long periods of constantly normal polarity in the Upper Cretaceous. The sampling suggested normality from the Upper Albian to the Maastrichtian with a short interval of reversed polarity in the Santonian. The

Maastrichtian itself, like the lower Tertiary, contains intervals of both polarities. Further data are portrayed in Fig. 58 below.

Archeomagnetic investigations (Bucha, 1970) suggest that the curve characterising the field intensity during the last 8,500 years has a maximum around 400 B.C., when the level reached 1·6 times its present value, and a minimum around 4000 B.C., when the intensity dropped to $c.$ 0·5 times its present level. In addition to changes with an 8,000–10,000 year periodicity shorter fluctuations have also occurred which may well reflect an overall westward drift of the dipole field. It is probably as a consequence of this sort of drift that these fluctuations do not occur simultaneously over the whole of the global surface. Instead the temporal sequence of their maxima and minima is clearly dependent upon longitude. Creer *et al.* (1976) also concluded that the record contained within the sediments of Lake Michigan, that have been laid down during the last 11,500 years, exhibits declination fluctuations to east and west with a period of 2,090 ^{14}C years. Inclination and intensity did not show these fluctuations. The observed variations were, in fact, closely similar to those noted in Windermere but, in that case, the period of the cycles was 2,800 years. Plots of the paleomagnetic poles for inclination–declination pairs representing each east or west extreme for the two lakes are, however, quite different, and this was taken as indicating that such geomagnetic effects were not the result of shifts in the main dipole field. Additional data of this nature are contained in Battarbee *et al.* (1975).

6.3 The dating of rocks

The use of paleomagnetic studies enables rocks to be dated at three levels of precision; by secular variations with periodicities of $c.$ 10^3 years, by use of polarity zones or transitions with periodicities of $c.$ 10^3–10^7 years, and by average geomagnetic pole positions exhibiting variations of $c.$ 10^6–10^9 years. Reviews of the geomagnetic time scale occur in Dalrymple (1972), Opdyke (1972) and Watkins (1972). Few secular variation cycles have been studied in detail but they seem to have characteristic patterns that can be used for precise correlations on time scales of 10^2–10^3 years. The irregularity of the sequences of geomagnetic reversals has also enabled the matching of polarity sequences in rocks from a variety of exposures although the irregularity of rock accumulation itself tends to obscure such similarities if the exposures are separated by extensive distances. Once the polarity sequence has been dated the polarity time scale can then be utilised for absolute dating but because of the attendant difficulties this is not well established for ages in excess of 150 m.y. It is, nevertheless, possible to distinguish sequences of Triassic rocks from those of Lower to Middle Permian age and because the rocks are of such great ages the apparent pole positions are increasingly displaced from the earth's present axis of rotation so that it is possible to construct a curve connecting the average geomagnetic pole positions for each continent through geological time. Such curves are now available for the last 300 m.y. and, by referring the apparent pole of an unknown rock to the curve, it is possible to achieve additional dating results.

6.4 Tectonic and structural considerations

The magnetic anomaly strips of the igneous ocean floor mark its growth and this can also be dated by geomagnetic reversals (cf. Figs 35 and 36). These studies demonstrate that most of the ocean floors have been formed during the last 150 m.y. and during this period they have spread gradually away from the oceanic ridges. In combination with seismological studies this has corroborated the hypothesis that the surface of the earth is composed of vast plates, some 60–120 km thick, which include oceanic or continental crust material together with elements of the upper mantle—the lithosphere. Each individual plate moves as a single unit block, and contemporary tectonic activity is concentrated along their margins.

As emphasised above, the average values which have been obtained for the declination and inclination of stable remanence in rocks of comparable age define the location of the geomagnetic pole at that time. When the position of the pole is defined in relation to two separate blocks their own relative latitudes and orientation, although not their absolute longitudinal relationships, can then be determined. If there are sufficient paleomagnetic pole values available to define polar wandering curves from each tectonic block the blocks can be projected on to a map so that their curves coincide, thereby defining their spatial relationships. Determinations of this nature involving data from the last 300 m.y. have broadly confirmed pre-existing suggestions about continental assemblages and Wegener's hypothesis of continental drift has thereby been substantiated.

Most polar wandering curves exhibit pronounced changes of direction within the last 50 m.y. and some of these, although still imprecisely defined, appear to have been simultaneous (cf. Fig. 37). This could clearly reflect interactions of the various plate movements

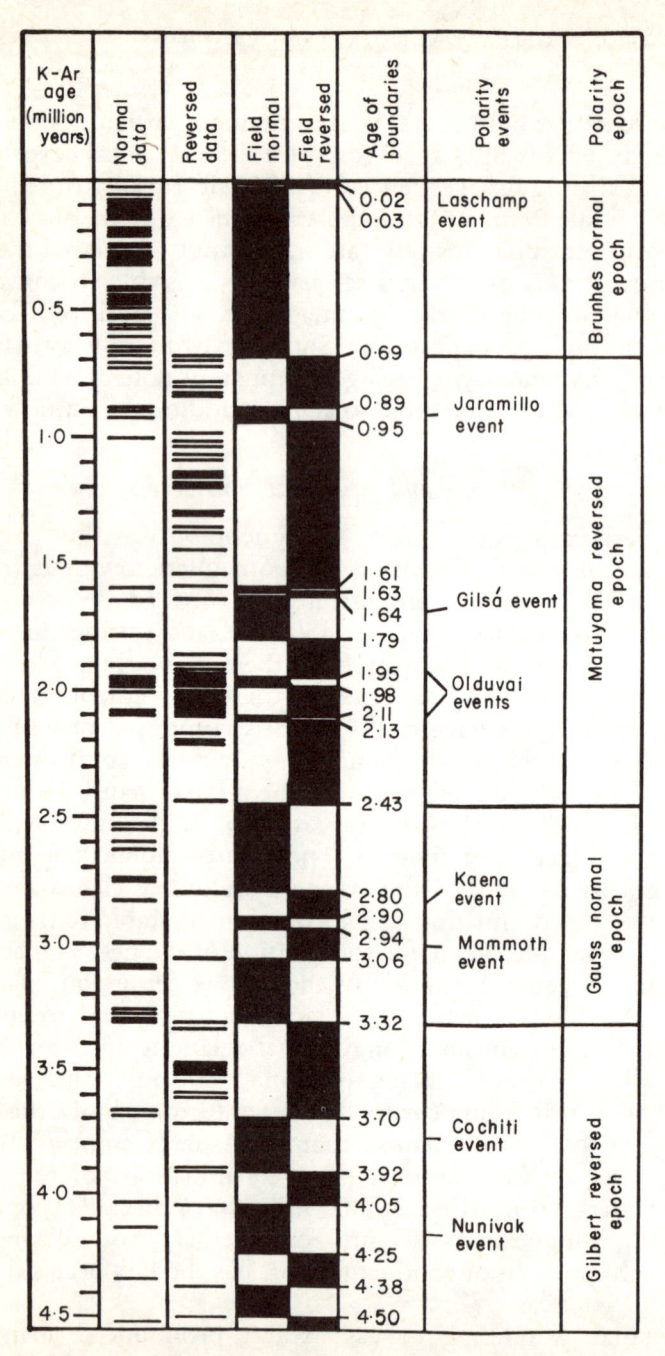

FIG. 36a. Timescale for geomagnetic reversals. Each short horizontal line shows the age as determined by K-Ar dating. Normal polarity intervals are represented by the solid portions of the "field normal" column, and reversed polarity intervals by the solid parts of the "field reversed" column. (Cox, 1969.)

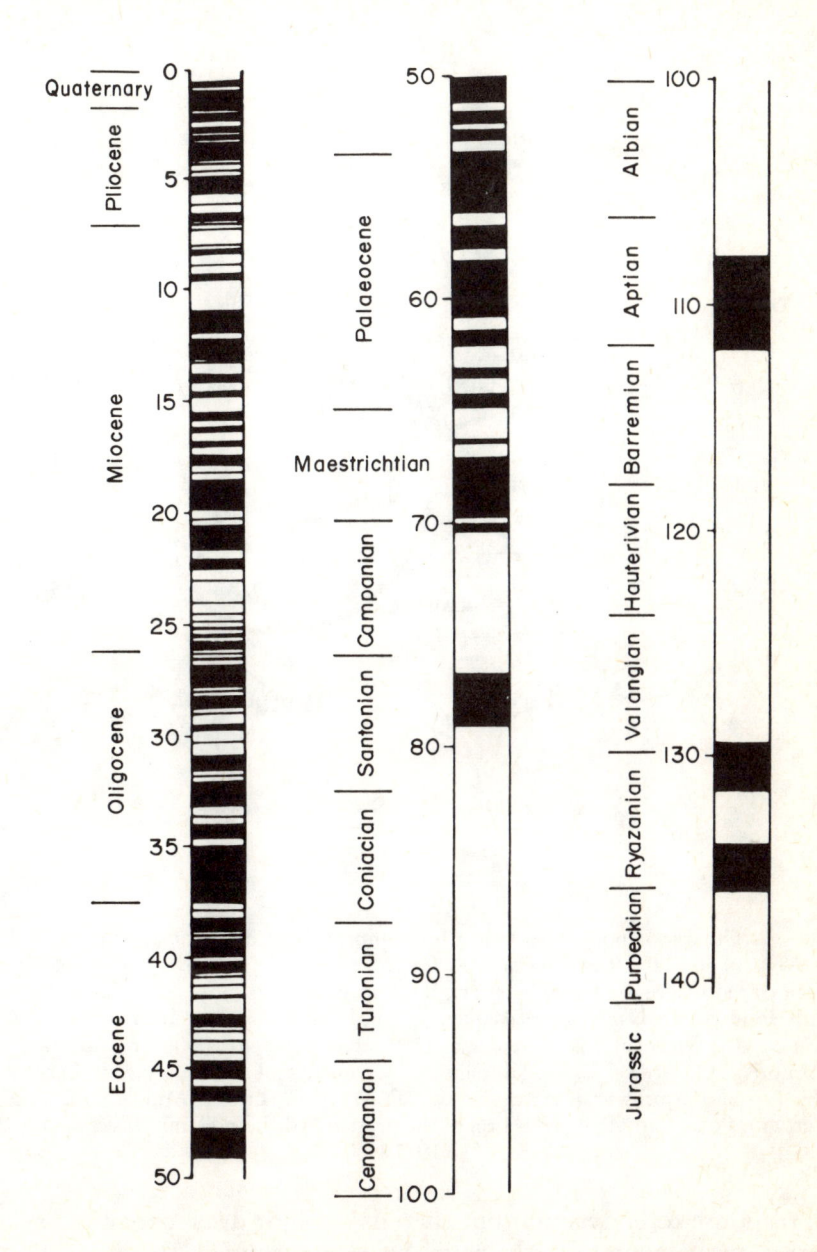

FIG. 36b. Summary scale for the last 140 million years (Tarling, 1971).

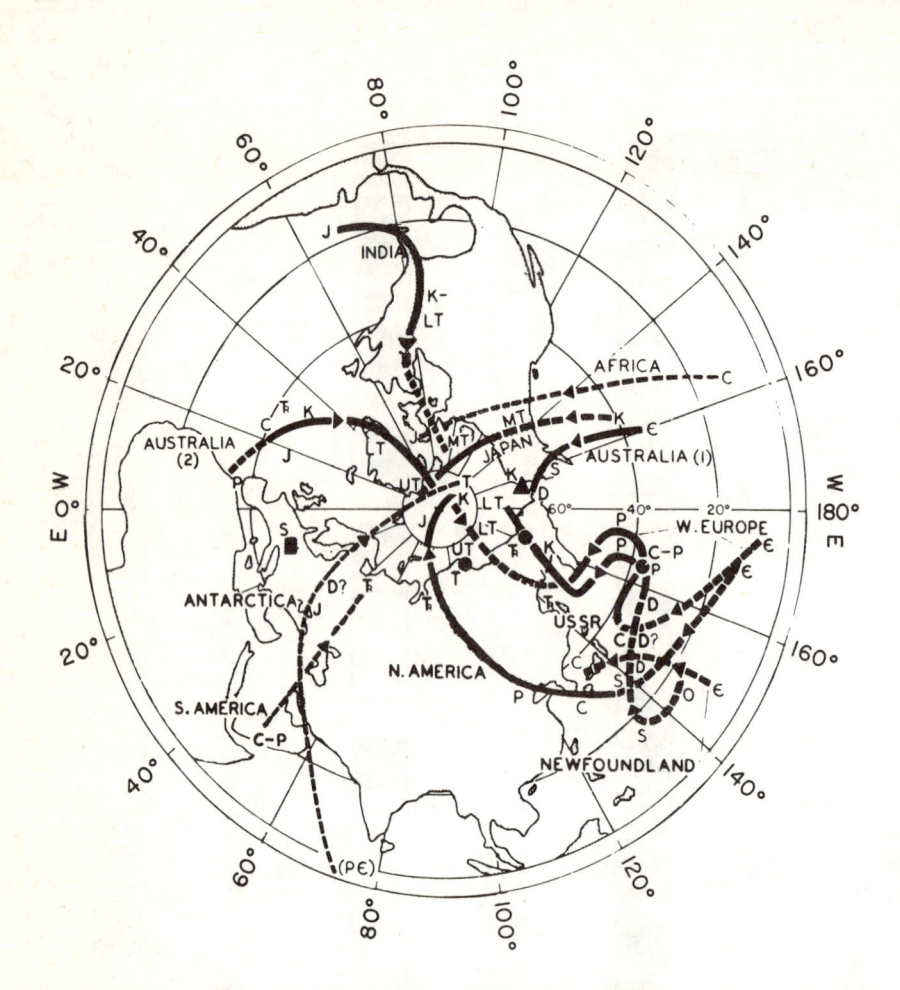

FIG. 37. Curves of polar wandering for samples from different continents. Polar movement since the Precambrian, relative to various land masses. Solid curves have been traced where the palaeomagnetic data from three or more levels in geological time follow a fairly consistent sequence. Single pole positions are relative to: ■, China; ●, Greenland; ▲, Madagascar. Letters refer to: (Pε), Precambrian; ε, Cambrian; O, Ordovician; S, Silurian; D, Devonian; C, Carboniferous; P, Permian; Tr, Triassic; J, Jurassic; K, Cretaceous; LT, MT, UT, Lower, Middle, and Upper Tertiary. Polar azimuthal projection of the present Northern Hemisphere. (Garland, 1971.)

in response to convection but there is a major discrepancy between those movements which have been determined from sea-floor spreading data and those determined by paleomagnetic analysis. Oceanic anomalies and transform faults suggest that, as a result of sea-floor spreading in a northwest–southeast direction, the North Atlantic has been enlarging at some 2 cm year^{-1} during the last 55 m.y. In contrast, paleomagnetic data from Greenland or Europe suggested a predominantly northward movement of Greenland at 5·4 cm year^{-1} and of Europe at 2·6 cm year^{-1}. This implies (Tarling, 1971) that the observed sea-floor spreading has been superimposed upon a net northerly motion of some 2–3 cm year^{-1} which is common to both places and has carried the sea-floor spreading with it.

Various additional hypotheses have been put forward which suggest that the earth has been expanding since its formation and that continental drift may be a result of such expansion. Tarling pointed out that an increase of 1 per cent in the earth's radius would necessitate an increase of 2 per cent in the surface area. If continental drift arose from this cause some two thirds of the earth's surface would have to have been formed during the last 150 m.y. and paleomagnetic evidence demonstrates that this rate of expansion is not possible.

6.5 *Paleomagnetism and paleolatitudes*

A close association between the position of the average geomagnetic pole and that of the rotational pole can be demonstrated for the last 25 m.y. and strong theoretical considerations suggest that the association existed in earlier periods. Paleomagnetically determined paleolatitudes should therefore correspond with other, contemporary, latitude-dependent features. Clearly two such occur—rock types which can only form under certain climatic conditions and, potentially, fossils of species which had precise environmental requirements. As the present rather contracted latitudinal zonation is not easily extrapolated to past times the latter are not easily considered. Nevertheless, in the case of low latitudes, such indicators do frequently conform to the available paleomagnetic data. In the case of the characteristics of high latitudes there are greater difficulties—if for no other reason than because the physical characters of high latitudes are, of course, common to high altitudes of low latitudes.

7 VARIATIONS IN ATMOSPHERIC ^{14}C CONTENT

DeVries (1958) was the first worker to demonstrate the occurrence of fluctuations in the ^{14}C content of tree-rings, and hence, by implication, of the atmosphere. Since then such studies have been widely influential (Willis *et al.*, 1960; Stuiver, 1965; 1971; Suess, 1965; 1967; 1971; Damon *et al.*, 1966). As the variations are only of the order of a few per cent, statistical difficulties rendered the early analyses controversial. However, once such fluctuations had been established their origins were quite clear and both Stuiver (1971) and Suess (1971) emphasised that they must have been caused by changes in the geomagnetic field and in the activity of the sun. During geomagnetic pole reversals the geomagnetic dipole moment is reduced by 60–80 per cent. The cosmic ray flux reaching the atmosphere will therefore be greatly increased, and nearly doubled when the dipole reduction is of the order of 80 per cent. The resulting increase in global ^{14}C production causes the ^{14}C levels in the atmosphere–ocean system to increase, and to do so with a characteristic time of *c*. 8,000 years if the duration of the transition between polarity states is of that order (cf. Cox, 1969; and section 6 above). For shorter transition states, and with a reduction of 80 per cent in the geomagnetic field over only part of that period, the increase in atmospheric ^{14}C is appreciably smaller.

Lingenfelter and Ramaty (1970) concluded that other short-term variations in the ^{14}C content may reflect solar modulated cosmic rays, solar flare particles and, possibly, supernova gamma rays. Longer-term variations may reflect local cosmic ray flux resulting from nearby supernova explosions. Nevertheless, the close correlations between the atmospheric ^{14}C content and solar activity are not unexpectedly also correlated with climatic effects. Cain and Suess (1976) showed that tree-rings from two different continents, and from various altitudes, have similar ^{14}C content. Stuiver (1965) had previously compared the ^{14}C levels in tree-rings dating from the eighteenth and nineteenth centuries with the levels of solar activity as measured by the total number of sunspots seen in each cycle. As the production of ^{14}C is suppressed during sunspot maxima the scale for solar activity is reversed in Fig. 38. The solid part of the curve is based on continuous observations at Zurich whilst the dotted part represents more scattered observations but the close relationship between known levels of sunspot activity and the experimentally determined ^{14}C content confirmed suspicions that had been widely voiced since the pioneer work of DeVries (1958) and Willis *et al.* (1960). The fact that the cold periods of the fifteenth and seventeenth centuries seem to coincide with rising ^{14}C levels was simultaneously emphasised by Suess (1965). Low solar activity seems to coincide with low temperatures and rising ^{14}C levels; high sunspot numbers coincide with relatively high temperatures and a decrease in ^{14}C

levels. Prior to the Little Ice Age the most pronounced concentration of ^{14}C was in the eighth century B.C., when, according to many observations, the climate changed from sub-Boreal to sub-Atlantic.

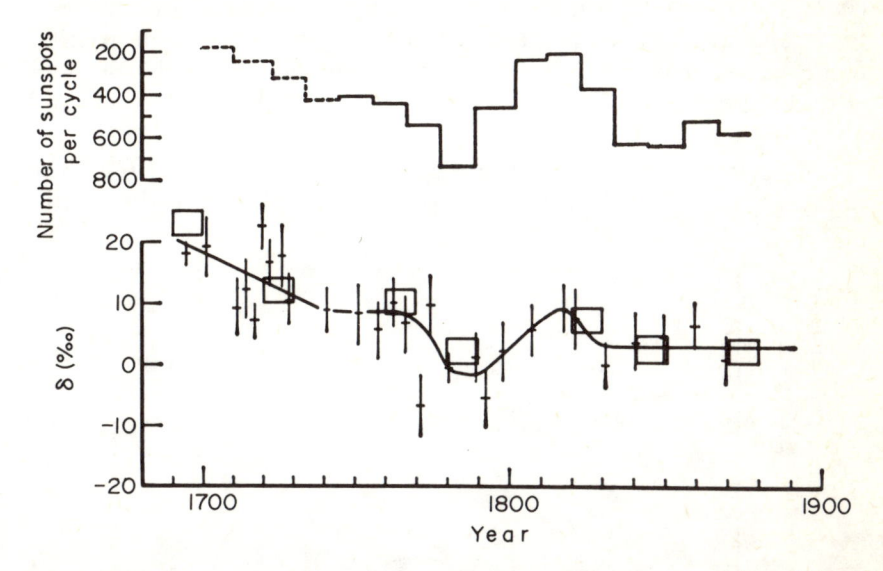

FIG. 38. Carbon-14 activity of tree rings given as per mill deviation of the activity of the samples from the age-corrected oxalic acid standard. The horizontal parts correspond with the number of tree-rings used for analyses and the vertical lines correspond with the standard error. The lower curve is a visual aid only. The blocks represent older results reported by De Vries. The upper curve gives solar activity. (Stuiver, 1965; 1971; Suess, 1965; 1967; 1971.)

Many additional data exist which elucidate short-term oscillations in the atmospheric ^{14}C content—each lasting about 100–200 years. These all correlate well with solar cycle modulation and the periodicities mentioned in Chapter 3 above. In addition Suess (1969; 1971) suggested that the available data intimate the existence of a longer periodicity of *c*. 400 years. This is of particular interest in view of the discussions of folk migrations and history that are contained in Chapter 11.

Analyses of the ^{14}C content of *Agathis australis* and *Dacrydium cupressinum* from New Zealand, together with comparable analyses of *Agathis palmerstoni* and *Athrotaxis selaginoides* from Australia, suggest that the main trends of the secular variation agree well with data from the northern hemisphere but have a depression of 0–20 per cent (Jansen, 1970). Lerman *et al.* (1970) concluded that there is in fact a small but real latitudinal dependence with the material at 42°S containing 4·5 ± 1 per cent less ^{14}C than that at 42°N. This was explained by assuming that a faster absorption of ^{14}C takes place into the southern ocean than into the northern one as a result of its 40 per cent greater surface area; that there is an increased absorption rate due to greater average wind speed between 40°S and 50°S (the roaring forties); and that there is a steeper ^{14}C gradient at high southern latitudes (see also Rafter and O'Brien, 1970; Labeyrie et al., 1970; and Suess, 1970b).

Longer-term considerations are epitomised by Stuiver (1971). The upper curve in Fig. 39 represents the average change in the earth's

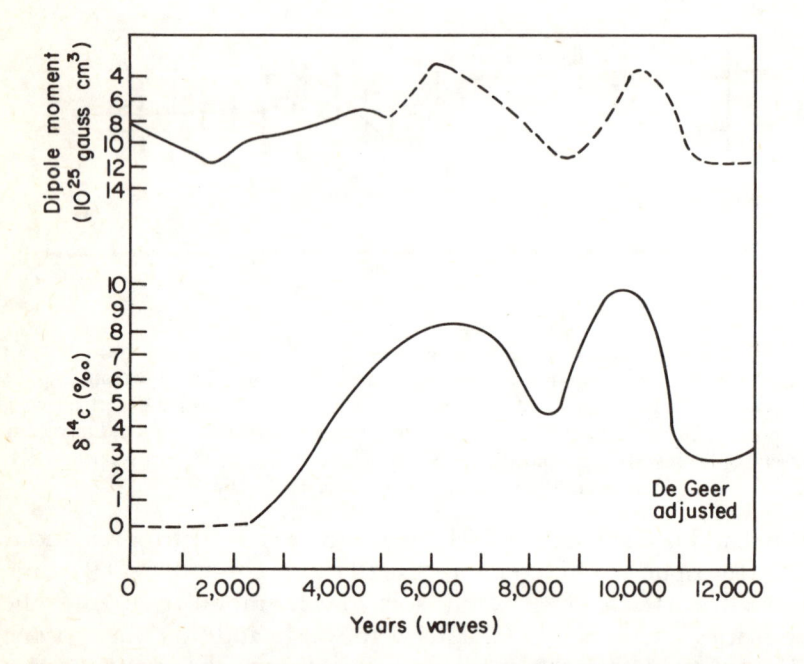

FIG. 39. δ^{14}C as a percentage of the atmospheric ^{14}C content, plotted against Lake of Clouds varve years. The 10,000–12,500 interval is based on an adjusted De Geer chronology. δ^{14}C values are only approximate for this interval. The earth dipole moment is plotted above. (After Stuiver, 1971.)

magnetic dipole moment which certainly seems to be correlated with ^{14}C levels. The moment increases by a factor of at least 1·8 between 6000 and 1500 B.P. This should result in a c. 30 per cent reduction of the ^{14}C production rate and the smaller change reflects a slow response of the large ocean reservoirs to changes in the production rate. The causes of a minimum in the atmospheric ^{14}C around 8,300

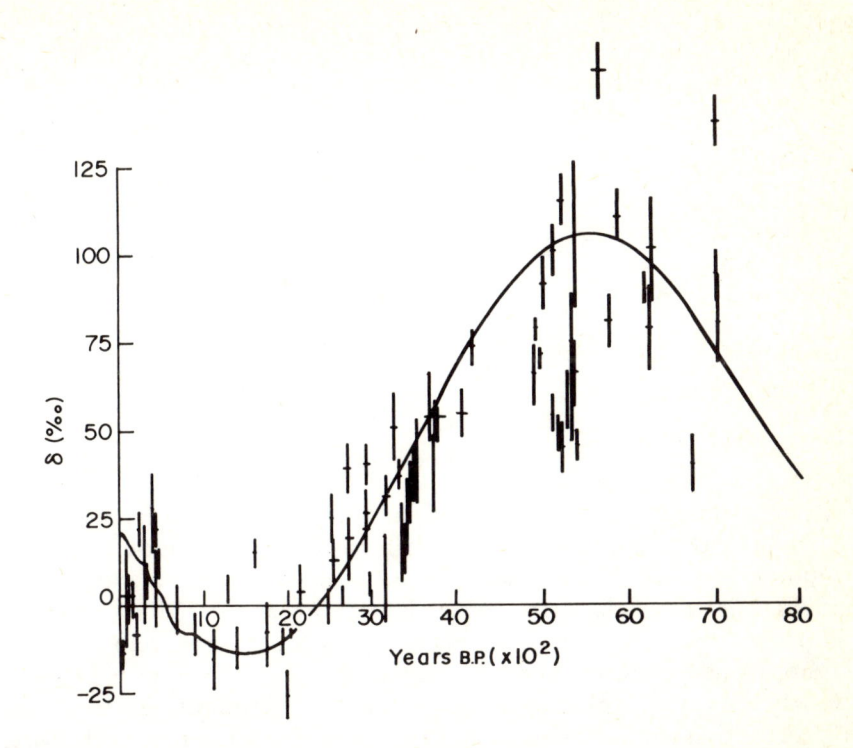

Fig. 40. δ (‰) plotted against tree-ring age. The theoretical curve assumes a sinusoidal geomagnetic field intensity with a period of 8,000 years and peaking at 500 B.C. (Bucha, 1970; cf. Figs 75 and 76.)

varve years ago were by no means clear but it may reflect the well-known rapid change in both ocean temperature and sea level c. 10,000–8,000 years ago (Vogel, 1970). Other ^{14}C analyses of tree stumps dating from c. 6000 and 5000 B.C. also suggest that the ^{14}C level was not at that time decreasing at the rate observed between 3500 B.C. and 1500 B.C., but rather that the rate was rising at about 6000 B.C. and was more or less constant at 5000 B.C. (cf. Fig. 40).

5
Long-Term Considerations

1 ANCIENT ICE AGES

Many compilations of ancient glacial deposits exist (Coleman, 1926; Schwarzbach, 1963; Cahen, 1963; Harland, 1964a, b; Holmes, 1965; Dunn *et al.*, 1971; Steiner and Grillmair, 1973; Harland and Herod, 1975). As such data are an essential prerequisite for the brief consideration of cosmic theories contained in section 2 below a short synopsis is provided here. Some workers have suggested that a nearly continuous glaciation has persisted at high latitudes from late Precambrian times (Crowell and Frakes, 1970; Crawford and Daily, 1971). Others, the majority, consider that glaciation has been episodic, at least in its widespread form. It is the most recent of these episodes which is the best known, and the older ones are more controversial. Certainly in many parts of the world successive deposits which are of obvious, or presumed, glacial origin are separated stratigraphically by rock sequences of considerable and often immense depth. These presumably reflect non-glacial, and probably warm, intervals. Steiner and Grillmair (1973) considered that seven glacial epochs are well documented on several or all continents. These are summarised in Table 5. Harland and Herod (1975), in their more recent synoptic account, gave a slightly different summary classification of Precambrian events and ascribed locality names to the principal features. These are outlined in Table 6. The Paleozoic and late Cenozoic glaciations are considered in subsequent chapters but it is reasonable to give a brief account of the Precambrian ones here.

Steiner and Grillmair (1973) concluded that the late Precambrian glaciogene deposits appear to be grouped into three clusters which they attributed to the three independent late Precambrian glacial epochs that are intimated in the Table 5. A further eight Precambrian

TABLE 5

Epochs of glaciation which are either accurately dated or dated by their stratigraphical position within a dated sequence according to Steiner and Grillmair (1973)

Glacial epoch	Absolute age (m.y.)	Location
Gowganda glaciation	2,288 ± 87	Eastern Canada
		North central USA and Wyoming
Infracambrian II	950 ± 50	Zaire
	950	Tien Shan
	950	China
Infracambrian I	740–750 ± 40	Australia
	750 ± 50	Zaire
	715 (?) 810 (?)	USSR (European)
	747–810	Siberia
	750	China
	800 ± 50	British Columbia
	820	Appalachians
	825	Washington
Eocambrian	650 ± 50	Australia
	600+	Brazil
	600 ± 30	Norway and Sweden
	600 ± 30	Greenland
	600–640	Spitzbergen
	660–680	USSR
	570, 600, 650	China
	560–630	Normandy
	570–600	Newfoundland
	620–650	Algeria
Siluro–Ordovician	410–470	North and South Africa, Argentina, Brazil, Spain, France, USSR?, Nova Scotia?, Yukon
Permo–Carboniferous	255–340	Australia, South Africa, Madagascar, South America, Falkland Isles, Antarctica, India–Pakistan
	235–320	Siberia
Late Cenozoic	0–14	All continents and ocean floor

glacial deposits occur in rocks of even greater age, some of which may be synchronous. Although the IUGS recommended that the terms Eocambrian and Infracambrian should be dropped, Steiner and Grillmair retained them because their galactic model (see below)

TABLE 6

A summary of late Precambrian glacial stratigraphy (Harland and Herod, 1975)

Era	Glaciation	Age at beginning m.y. B.P.	Comments
Vendian	Varangian	? 700±	More severe than Paleozoic glaciations. Two major glaciations with many minor components
Keratan	Sturtian	? 750±	More severe and prolonged in Australia but not so extensive as the Varangian

predicted three late Precambrian glacial phases. The term Infracambrian II was used for possible glacial evidence centred on 940 ± 50 m.y.; Infracambrian I refers to that material which appears to precede the Cambrian by $c.$ 160 m.y. and to date from 760 ± 50 m.y.; the term Eocambrian refers to a glaciation, or glaciations, which seem to have directly preceded the Cambrian which began 600 ± 50 m.y. B.P.

Harland and Herod (1975) considered that the Varangian and Sturtian were the only Precambrian glaciations of which we have an extensive knowledge. Nevertheless, they certainly agreed that the Huronian ($\equiv$ Gowganda) glaciation probably included at least three principal phases which are represented by various horizons within a total thickness of some 12 km. These can be ascribed to the Elliot Lake, Hough Lake, Quirke Lake and Cobalt groups. The same authors also noted that the profound environmental changes which must have been coincident with such climatic deteriorations would surely have had at least some effect on the contemporaneous biological evolution. In particular, the Varangian ice age is restricted in time to a period which is just prior to the emergence of recorded metazoan life. Although it cannot be argued with certainty that it caused this early explosive phase of evolution, our knowledge of the evolutionary events which coincide with Cenozoic climatic deteriorations certainly makes such a correlation likely.

2 POSSIBLE GALACTIC CAUSES OF PERIODIC GLACIATIONS

The majority of the sections of this book refer to the many factual data that have been accumulated about climatic change. There are, however, various very stimulating papers in the literature which refer to largely unverifiable hypotheses. They attempt to incorporate global glacial phases into a galactic framework and, if correct, portray such phases in cosmological perspective. In retrospect many of the early ones now suffer from their dependence upon contemporary astronomical theories that are now considered to be erroneous; however, together they form a slim but continuing thread of interest which any consideration of climatic change can ill afford to ignore.

The first such suggestion that one can reasonably mention is that of Shapley (1921) which was contemporaneous with the closing phases of that great surge of climatic studies that is epitomised by Penck, Brückner and Huntington. The publication of Sir George Simpson's suggestion that a slight increase in the solar flux reaching the earth is needed to initiate an ice age by leading to increased precipitation led Shapley, and then, at a later date, Hoyle and Lyttleton (1939), to suggest that the passage of the solar system through a cloud of interstellar matter could give the increased flux required. Subsequently Umbgrove (1947) also emphasised that the length of a cosmic year approximately corresponds to the cyclic recurrence of late Precambrian and Phanerozoic glaciations together with the major orogenic cycles. Lungershauzen (1957) further emphasised this possible correlation by postulating an Ordovician glaciation for which there was some evidence in the USSR (cf Schwarzbach, 1963). More recently Tamrazjan (1967) attempted to correlate a variety of geological phenomena with the length of the anomalistic cosmic year but deliberately ignored paleoclimatic criteria because his model of the year was foreshortened by the retrograde rotation of the Kepler ellipse of the solar galactic orbit. At the same time Machado (1967) postulated pulsating gravitation with a periodicity similar to that noted by Tamrazjan but proffered no physical explanation, and Steiner (1967) compared major geological phenomena, including glaciations, to a controversial gravitational model of the galaxy for the past 1·25 cosmic years. Schwarzbach then extended this model to 2 cosmic years and was impressed by the results of this extension. Gidon (1970a, b) also discussed the possibility of a correlation between solar galactic revolutions and periodic glaciations but the majority of these hypotheses, apart from those of Steiner and Schwarzbach, were based upon the outdated *c.* 200 m.y. cosmic year. In contrast, other more recent estimates of the cosmic year have been compared with major paleomagnetic polarity epochs by Crain *et al.* (1969) and Crain and Crain (1970); with biological phenomena by Hatfield and Camp (1970); and with the known occurrences of carbonatite by Macintyre (1971).

In the early seventies a renewed interest in such concepts led to the work of Steiner and Grillmair (1973), Lequeux (1972) and McCrea (1975; 1976). Dealing with McCrea's ideas first, one may say that he developed a rather more up-to-date formulation of Hoyle and Lyttleton's type of idea, although he himself has rather belittled their contribution by saying that it was "associated with older astronomical concepts". In approximate terms he concluded that the geological evidence suggests that extensive ice-cover recurs on earth at intervals of 250 m.y. These ice epochs may each last for several million years and involve several distinct ice ages that are separated by warmer interglacial periods. Like earlier writers he pointed out that the period between these ice epochs appears to be just half the time that is envisaged as being necessary for the solar system to orbit the galaxy. So-called spiral arms are a feature of many galaxies and, according to many theories, a concentration of dark gas and dust characterises the permanent spiral feature—a standing "shock wave"—through which stars must pass. When the solar system passes through such a concentration of dust it is suggested that the first effect is that the sun will be warmed up a little by dust falling into it and relinquishing gravitational energy in the form of heat. The solar system, currently on the edge of the Orion spiral arm, has recently (in astronomical terms) passed through the associated lane of dust and gas. According to McCrea it emerged into clear space about 10,000 B.P. Lequeux's data suggest that if the sun enters a dense cloud it is likely to travel a distance of the order of a parsec through it. At, say, 20 km s^{-1} this would take 50,000 years. As the solar system must take a few million years to cross an entire compression lane several consecutive glaciations would reasonably be expected. Earlier passages through such compression lanes might explain the origin of the solar system itself.

McCrea's suggestions have been supported by Lindsay and Srnka (1975) from a rather different standpoint, and by Begelman and Rees (1976). They have also been actively promulgated by Gribbin (1976a, b). Lindsay and Srnka concluded that three, near cyclical, increases in the flux of micrometeorites appear to be represented in lunar cores and that they are separated by $c.$ 10^8 years. McCrea had, of course, pointed to such a time as the interval that would elapse between each traverse of the spiral arms, because the solar system would take 10^6 years to cross the compression lane and would spend a total of $c.$ 10^7 years in each arm. Begelman and Rees suggested that even immersion in less extreme, and more widespread, interstellar matter with a density 10^2–10^3 cm^{-3} could still affect the solar wind reaching the earth. This hypothesis obviates the need for the high concentration of interstellar matter which would be required by the specific accretion mechanism. However, Talbot *et al.* (1976) could see no evidence for the dust grains which they considered should also have accreted on the earth under such circumstances.

Steiner and Grillmair (1973) used a different approach in their paper and it is interesting that they reached analogous conclusions. They, too, assumed that the Milky Way system is a spiral galaxy with a diameter of 30 kiloparsecs (kpc), that the solar system is situated within the spiral arms at 10 kpc from the galactic centre, and that it revolves around the centre in an elliptical orbit that is close to the galactic plane. They extended their calculations back 3 billion years and assumed that the duration of the cosmic year has been decreasing from 400 m.y. in the early Precambrian to 274 m.y. at the present. This was because they assumed that the solar system is spiralling inward within the galaxy at a radial contraction velocity of 1.4 km s^{-1}. The eccentricity of the solar system's orbit was taken to be such that the average galactocentric distance varies from $c.$ 10 kpc to $c.$ 11.7 kpc with one complete cosmic year. The orbital positions which are respectively nearest to, and farthest from, the galactic centre, are, by analogy with lunar and global orbits, known as the peri- and apogalacticum—i.e. apsides. Steiner and Grillmair assumed that the sun is currently approaching the perigalactic position which it will reach in 8 m.y. Astronomical data permitted the construction of several galactic models but, using Occam's razor, they chose the one that compared well with the available data on glacial epochs. In constructing it they ignored the solar orbital motion perpendicular to the galactic plane which might reasonably introduce minor oscillations of $c.$ 40 m.y. which would be superimposed on the overall curve of Fig. 41.

The resultant galactic model predicted that the solar system would have experienced a central galactic force during the last 3 b.y. Seven of their minima correlated well with the midpoint, or mean age, of seven glacial epochs—giving errors which were generally of a few m.y. The degree of clustering of dated glacial evidence around the computed ages for central galactic force minima is shown in Table 7. An average misfit of ±13 m.y. is indicated between the midpoint of the glacial epochs and seven apsides. The poorest correlations were exhibited by Chumakov and Cailleaux's (1971) age assignment for the late Precambrian glaciation of the European regions of the USSR (75 m.y.), and the Australian Egan Marinoan glaciation (55 m.y.). However, those were the only 2, out of some 30 dated glacial localities, that correlated with near maxima of the central galactic force. The model also predicted 5 more Precambrian glaciations at 1,120 m.y., 1,490 m.y., 1,870 m.y., 2,660 m.y. and 3,060 m.y.

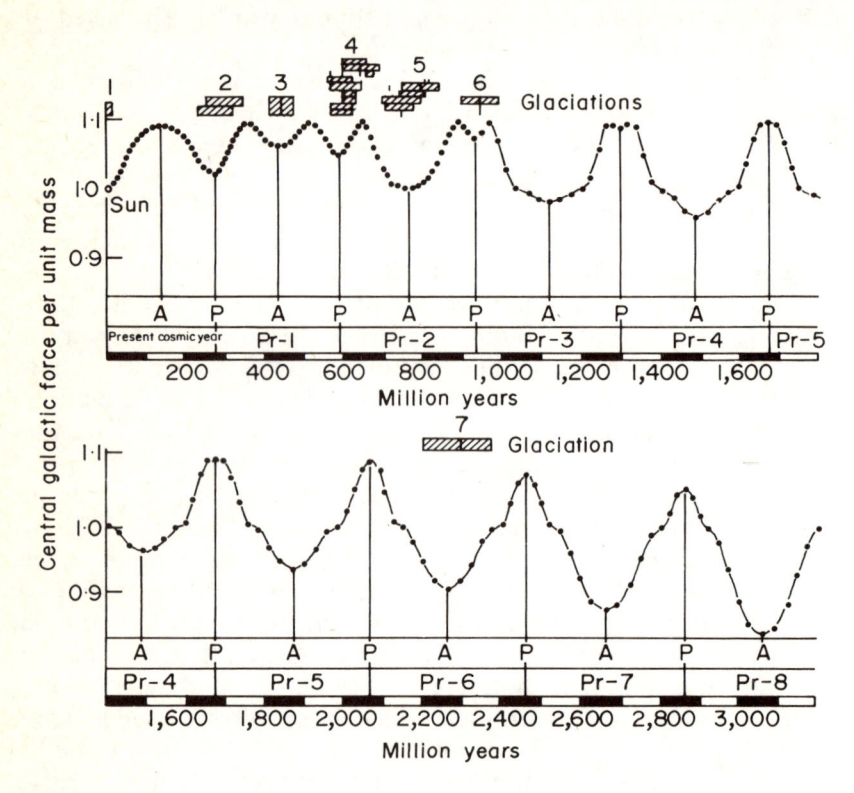

FIG. 41. Comparison of galactic model with well-documented glacial episodes. Central galactic force per unit mass is plotted as a function of time, as experienced by the solar system. A, Apoglacticum; P, Perigalacticum. Cosmic years are designated as Pr (present cosmic year), and Pr-1, Pr-2, and so forth. Glacial Episodes: 1, *Late Cenozoic*; affected all continents and sea-floor sediments. 2, *Permo-Carboniferous*; Australia, South Africa, Madagascar, South America, Falkland Islands, Antarctica, India–Pakistan, Siberia. 3, *Siluro–Ordovician*; Africa, South America, parts of Europe, Northern Canada? 4. *Eocambrian*; Australia, Europe, Greenland, Spitzbergen, Newfoundland, South America, North Africa, China. 5, *Infracambrian I*; Australia, European Russia and Siberia, China, North America, Africa. 6, *Infracambrian II*; Africa, Asiatic Russia, China. 7, Gowganda; North America. (Steiner and Grillmair, 1973.) (By courtesy of The Geological Society of America.)

Both these two groups of suggestions do, then, provide potential, if unproven, galactic rationales for episodic glaciation. The known

TABLE 7

Comparison of established glacial epochs and the central galactic force minima of Steiner and Grillmair (1973)

Glacial epoch	Absolute age (m.y.)	Galactic model (m.y.)	Apsides
Late Cenozoic	0–14	−8 ± 4	Perigalacticum
Permo–Carboniferous	235–340	280	Perigalacticum
Siluro–Ordovician	410–470	437	Apogalacticum
Eocambrian	av. 616 ± 30	595	Perigalacticum
Infracambrian I	av. 777 ± 40	766	Apogalacticum
Infracambrian II	av. 950 ± 50	937	Perigalacticum
		1,119	Apogalacticum
		1,489	Apogalacticum
		1,873	Apogalacticum
Gowganda	2,288 ± 87	2,265	Apogalacticum
		2,660	Apogalacticum
		3,060	Apogalacticum

periodicity of other climatic phenomena and their association with shorter-term, cyclic, astronomical phenomena certainly suggests that some such celestial mechanism is implicated as a causative factor in recurrent climatic changes such as those that are listed in Table 5 above. Steiner and Grillmair concluded that the basic trigger mechanism must have a periodicity of 10^7 to 10^8 years. Galactic variables such as those with which they, Hoyle and Lyttleton, and McCrea are dealing, certainly fulfil this criterion. However, at the moment, an act of faith is required to accept their suggestions. This does not in any way preclude conclusions which see the glacial epochs themselves as influential on life. It merely fails to support an unequivocal philosophical link between chance evolutionary processes on earth and long-term galactic parameters.

3 CONTINENTAL DRIFT

Biologists have long been aware of the concept of continental drift, thanks, in particular, to the enthusiasm with which Jeannel, amongst others, espoused Wegener's original suggestion (see Jeannel, 1942). He put forward immense numbers of data which he supposed supported the theory. Nevertheless the geophysical data which have become available in the last 20 years can be said to have revolutionised the precision of our understanding. The theory of plate tectonics implies differing continental geographies in the past and these geographies can be reconstructed from a variety of geophysical, petrological, structural and stratigraphical investigations. They necessarily involve both differing climatic régimes on the varying continental blocks and an overall variation in global climate in association with differing atmospheric and oceanic circulations. More detailed accounts of continental dispersion at different times are contained in Chapters 6, 7 and 8. Here we may consider some general results.

The general theory of global plate tectonics holds that the outer part of the earth is composed of a series of rigid plates that move on a plastic "aesthenosphere" (cf. Le Pichon, 1968; Vine and Hess, 1970). Oceanic crust is created at mid-oceanic ridges (Fig. 35) and "consumed" in subduction zones that are broadly marginal to continents or island arcs (see Briden and Irving, 1964; Irving, 1964; Maack, 1964; Creer, 1965; Runcorn, 1965). The work of Dewey and Bird (1970), Dewey and Horsfield (1970), Moores (1970) etc. has suggested that alpine-type mountain belts may be the result of collisions or marginal interactions between these blocks, and full intra-continental belts, such as the Urals (Hamilton, 1970) or the Appalachian-Caledonides (Dewey, 1969; Bird and Dewey, 1970; Naylor, 1970), result from the collision of two continental areas which had previously been separated by an ocean. As long as the deformation and metamorphism of major linear belts has been occurring, so such plate tectonics may have been operative. This may reasonably include the period since at least 3×10^9 B.P.—or since Grenvillean times (see Vine and Hess, 1970; Valentine and Moores, 1972).

Although no climatic predictions which relate to land–sea relationships that are very different from those that pertain today can be precise, the effects of such changing situations must have been profound. A few generalisations were made by Valentine and Moores:
1. Any net movement of continents from low to high latitudes will lead to a decrease in the average annual temperatures and an increased seasonality. Net movements from high to low latitudes will have the opposite effect.
2. The exact pattern of continental dispersion can either accentuate, or depress, the extent to which low-latitude oceans are exposed to high-latitude effects, and vice versa.
3. The assembly of continents into super-continents may enhance marine seasonality by, for example, a monsoon-type effect.

Complementarily, fragmentation into smaller land masses, and the continuing separation of such fragments by drift, may increase the overall homogeneity of marine habitats.

Thus continental movements both change the distribution of the continents relative to climatic conditions and also modify these climatic conditions themselves—often drastically. Now, many hypotheses have been formulated to account for species diversity patterns (Pianka, 1966; Sanders, 1968), and those that are best supported by empirical data hold that environmental stability is the key factor (see Chapter 1). In the present oceans the pattern of energy resources within ecosystems, as represented by sunlight and nutrients for plants, and by food for animals, exhibits a good correlation with species diversity patterns. In terms of latitude the gradient of seasonality in solar radiation can be correlated with a diversity gradient on continental shelves and there are also longitudinal correlations—particularly with nutrient supply. Relatively unstable, "continental", marine shelf climates are associated with a rather low species diversity latitude for latitude (Valentine and Moores, 1972), while more stable maritime shelves have a higher diversity. A reasonable working explanation merely involves those populations most able to endure suboptimal conditions being favoured in a fluctuating environment (see also Pearson, 1963). Their numbers might therefore be expected to increase with subsequent improved circumstances. The characteristics which one might expect to be especially useful in these circumstances include broad food tolerances; wide habitat tolerances allowing ubiquitous populations to develop during favourable periods; high reproductive potential allowing rapid utilisation of rising resource levels; and finally a general individual robustness. These broadly conform to Pearson's (1963) prediction that extinction in a fluctuating environment will be likely to affect stenotopic stenotherms first of all, and eurytopic eurytherms last. In contrast, in stable environments successful populations could be expected on *a priori* grounds to have lower reproductive potentials, unless extensively preyed upon; narrower food and habitat preferences; and more limited tolerance of environmental change. Clearly a cyclic succession of stable and unstable environments would maximise the natural selective pressures, the evolutionary "expectations" and the level of extinctions.

4 PERIODIC VULCANISM AND TECTONISM

4.1 Long-term effects

A number of authors have considered the possibility of periodic vulcanism and tectonism. Some of their suggestions conform to the requirements of modern geological theory whilst others do not. Joly (1930) intimated that during the Phanerozoic there had been four major revolutions with the intervening periods only being subject to minor disturbances that resulted from partial "melting" and tidal creep of the substratum. Similarly, Stille (1924; 1940) postulated that Phanerozoic history consisted of *aperiodic*, episodic phases of orogeny, each having a short duration of some 3×10^5 years, which were intercalated between anorogenic periods of very long duration. In their works Umbgrove (1947) and Rutten (1949) envisaged two major periodicities, of 300 m.y. and 60 m.y. respectively, which are superimposed upon a generalised tectonic unrest. In contrast Gilluly (1949; 1963) saw no evidence for any periodicity, but rather viewed Phanerozoic time as exhibiting an essential uniformity of both tectonism and vulcanism and thought that there had been no very great fluctuations in intensity.

In recent years the topic has been reopened by Damon (1971). He concluded that a study of K-Ar dated vulcanism and hypabyssal plutonism suggests that dates for silicic magmatism in the Cretaceous and related times, when plotted as 5 m.y. class intervals, resolve themselves into two quasi-Gaussian distributions with a standard deviation of 7·5 m.y., and peak at the Cretaceous–Paleogene and Paleogene–Neogene boundaries. Umbgrove had suggested that diastrophism accompanied by silicic magmatism results in orogeny and oceanic regression. This then gives a climatic deterioration. Planimetric analyses of Schuchert's paleogeographic maps then suggested to Damon that each of the North American orogenies is represented by a distinct regression of the epicontinental seas. Grasty (1967) had previously concluded that in models involving two continents, one deformed and one undeformed, an orogenic event is necessarily associated with an eustatic fall in sea level. Damon then plotted his planimetric measurements as a histogram with a 10 m.y. class interval and found that, in addition to the Mesozoic and Cenozoic orogenies, the three classical North American orogenies—Taxonian, Accadian and Appalachian—all showed up as distinct regressions. Several other such regressions appeared to correspond to the Caledonian and Hercynian movements of Europe (see Fig. 42). In order to distinguish broad epeirogenic movements

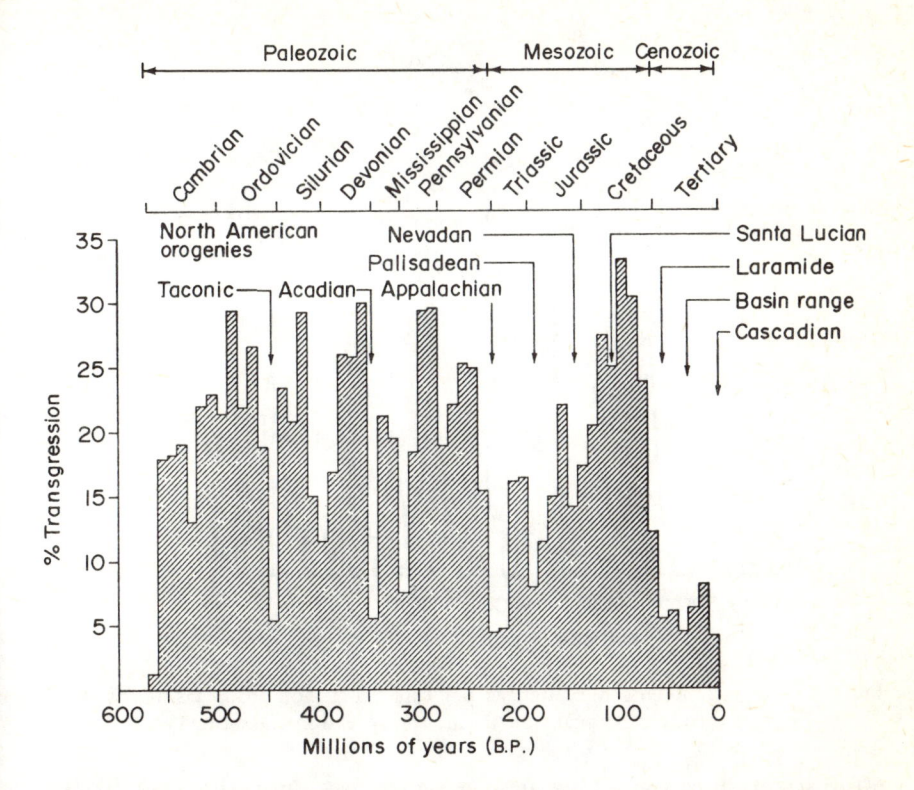

FIG. 42. Extent of epicontinental seas during the Phanerozoic as measured from Schuchert's paleogeographic maps. (Damon, 1971.)

from specific orogenic epochs he then passed a smooth curve through the transgression peaks and measured the extent of regression from a smoothed curve. The results are represented in Fig. 43 where Stille's orogenies are shown as straight vertical lines. Each of the main peaks can be correlated with major orogenies and Stille's orogenies typically appear as minor episodes within the span of more extensive events. If the orogenies are approximated by Gaussian curves the standard deviations are about 9 m.y. which is not too dissimilar to the 7·5 m.y. observed for Laramide or Tertiary magmatism.

Leaving aside the Triassic–Jurassic boundary, which was an exception, the ages of the boundaries between geological periods and the regression minima appeared to show a good correspondence—although once again one has to beware of circular arguments. Where minima do not correspond to geological boundaries in the Cambrian, Ordovician and Cretaceous the geological periods exceed

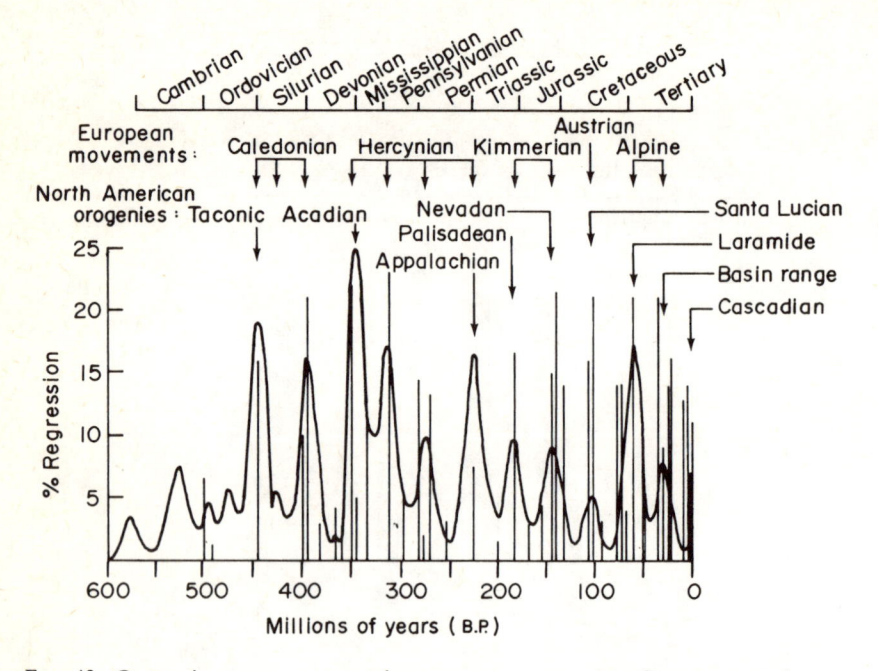

FIG. 43. Orogenic events measured as per cent regression from a smooth curve passed through the peaks of marine transgression (Damon, 1971).

60 m.y. in duration. This was, nevertheless, not the case in the Silurian. In general terms the orogenic periods lasted 36 ± 11 m.y., the geological periods 50 ± 16 m.y., and Damon suggested that, in this respect, the Cretaceous can reasonably be subdivided into two periods.

The upshot of Damon's considerations was that orogenic phases are certainly periodic, that the standard deviation of an orogenic pulse is 8 m.y. and the periodicity of pulses is 36 ± 11 m.y. The apparent intensities of the various individual orogenies vary by an order of magnitude, and the rules which govern geological boundaries have resulted in many of these boundaries having been fixed close to the peak of orogenic pulses.

4.2. Short-term seismic and volcanic cycles

Studies of recent earthquake and volcanic activity suggest that many smaller cycles are superimposed upon the long-term ones of section 4.1 above. Winkless and Browning (1975) have incorporated much of the data into their popular book. Although I consider that their conclusions give too great an emphasis to the part played by volcanism and earthquakes in history, their summary of earthquake data is useful. My disagreement would be with their suggestion that volcanism is a major controlling causative factor in recent climatic change. It certainly has an effect (see below and Chapter 2 above) but it is also itself responding to periodic tidal phenomena that themselves reflect solar characteristics which independently affect climate. Their summary of events runs as follows:

1. Large earthquakes are triggered by the additional "tidal" forces caused by the perihelion configuration of earth and sun ($P < 0.05$).
2. Great earthquakes tend to occur in winter.
3. Great earthquakes occur at perigee ($P < 0.001$).
4. Earthquake triggering is in synchrony with a tidal force beat due to the alignment of perigee and full, or new, moon every 413+ days, and there is a great probability of effects in the northern and southern hemispheres being 180° out of phase. The tidal force beat is reflected in the "sawtooth" frequency of earthquakes since 1900.
5. There is a tidal force beat due to alignment of the perigee with perihelion which happens at 8·85/2 year intervals (i.e. 4·425 years).
6. Great earthquakes occur in synchrony with a tidal beat every 9·3 years—i.e. at the coincidence of perihelion and eclipse nodal alignments.
7. A significant outburst of great volcanic eruptions is synchronous with the approximate coincidence of perigee, perihelion and an eclipse node ($P < 0.05$).

Chinnery and Landers (1975) certainly concluded that seismic activity, even when small, includes significant variations that can be correlated over large distances. They postulated that tectonic plates are subject to a variety of stresses of differing origin whose effects have different amplitudes and different spectral characteristics. When the various factors happen to reinforce one another the triggering stress can be large. One might therefore expect widespread triggering of large events (cf. Anderson, 1967). Tamrazyan (1968) compared the frequency of earthquakes with magnitudes in excess of 7·9 on the Richter scale, with the combined anomalistic and synodic tidal waves. In an analogous study Hamilton (1973) demonstrated that most volcanic eruptions occur when the synodic and anomalistic cycles are either in phase, or 180° out of phase. The frequency, intensity and latitude of occurrence of eruptions certainly seemed to him to vary with the well-known tide cycles. The major peaks in eruption occurred 3·5 days before maximum negative lunar declination ($-\delta_L$ max.) and 2·5 days prior to $+\delta_L$ max. There is also a minor peak in eruption frequency 3 days after $+\delta_L$ max. His study showed that the eruptions certainly vary as the moon moves from perigee to apogee, with peak frequencies 6 days after perigee and 5 days after apogee. The semi-annual variation of solar declination and the earth–sun distance are nearly in phase, and Hamilton found peak eruption frequency in May. There was also a distinct 8·85 year cycle that was presumably generated by the summation of the lunar declinational and the anomalistic cycles. Every 8·85 years the moon is at perigee when it is also farthest south of the equator. The cumulative triggering potential may then enhance the chance of eruptions. Finally there is a 19 year tidal cycle that is the sum of synodic and solar annual cycles. New moon occurs within 1·5 days of perihelion every 19 years. Moreover in years like 1965 the new moon occurs at the winter solstice. Eruption frequency since 1500 reaches peak values 1 year before these times of coincidence.

A further correlation was established by Press and Briggs (1975). They demonstrated that a relationship exists between the seismicity of major earthquake belts and the drift of the eccentric geomagnetic dipole for 1901–1964. This, they suggested, reflects both displacements of the lithospheric plates, and core motions that, besides producing compensatory changes in the rotation of the earth, also perturb the geomagnetic field.

A connecting link between this short-term cycle and the 36 ± 11 m.y. ones of Damon was provided by Stewart (1975). Major tephra eruptions appear to have occurred in the Aleutian and Kuril Island arcs at 10 m.y. B.P. The rate of eruption then averaged less than 1 layer per m.y. until 4 m.y. B.P., when a sporadic increase of up to 20 layers per m.y. occurred and persisted until 1·2 m.y. B.P. There was then a decrease to zero at 0·2–0·4 m.y. B.P., and a dramatic increase to about 100 layers each m.y. at the present time. This gives some idea of the type of smaller perturbations that occur within the longer cycles. Gribbin links these to planetary effects.

5 VOLCANIC ERUPTIONS AND CLIMATE

The foregoing sections clearly intimate that the global environment is subject to periodic volcanic and seismic events. Following the suggestions of Abbot, Fowle, Brooks and Hunt (cf. Chapter 2) a number of recent authors have considered the relationship between such phenomena and climatic events. Lamb (1969) provides the most outstanding recent discussion of the effects of a dust veil in the atmosphere and has given shorter accounts in the context of a number of other papers. Auer (1956; 1958), who was, of course, working prior to Lamb's contribution, considered that his Patagonian data indicated waves of enhanced volcanic activity. Those in the Andes were attributed to the period around 9000 B.P.: 5500–5000 B.P.; 2400–2100 and 500–75 B.P. For his part, Lamb (1971) suggested that elsewhere such phases could be dated from 11,000 to 9000 B.P., 4000–5000 B.P., 2000–2500 B.P., and from A.D. 1550 to 1900, but particularly 1750–1850. He concluded that there seems to be a tendency for the bouts to occur at the end of a long homogeneous climatic era and wondered whether a gradual change in world sea level might be implicated. Like Brooks before him, Lamb also concluded that associations certainly exist between volcanic dust veils, weather and climate. A comparison of the dust veils, wind circulation, prevailing temperatures and Arctic Sea ice conditions during the 3–7 years following a great eruption yields numbers of statistically significant correlations (Lamb, 1971, see also Budyko, 1968). However, despite their simultaneous occurrence, Lamb concluded that volcanism during the period A.D. 1600–1900 was not the cause of either decadel, or century to century climatic differences. The two types of phenomena might, of course, reflect differing terrestrial effects of related astronomical variables such as planetary positions.

Nevertheless workers still produce data on the undoubted climatic effects of atmospheric turbidity. Rasool and Schneider (1971) demonstrated that an increased turbidity reduces global surface temperatures. Roosen *et al.* (1976) calculated the tidal stresses produced on the earth from 1200 to 1970 and concluded that a statistically significant correlation existed between the envelopes of peak tidal stresses at high northern latitudes and the mean temperatures as represented by oxygen isotope ratios of the Greenland ice cap. They again suggested that the tidal stresses caused by the sun and moon caused increased dust from volcanic activity and impaired the atmospheric radiation balance. As the 179·3 year periodicity of tidal stress at high northern latitudes is precisely out of phase with that in southern latitudes they predicted that the 179·3 year cycle in Antarctic ice cores should be exactly out of phase with that in Greenland cores. Gow (1970) found that the volcanic ash in the Byrd core was contained within the cold phase, but pointed out that this might merely reflect particular sedimentary characteristics. However, cation analysis showed that impurities and $\delta^{18}O$ are negatively correlated. Hamilton and Seliga (1972) showed that there was an exponential relationship between the $\delta^{18}O$ and calcium content, which would conform to the suggestion that increased turbidity is at least associated with climatic deterioration. They concluded that suggestions which envisage that a polar temperature decrease can itself give rise to the necessary 10–20-fold increase in turbidity, through strengthened meridional transport, are unlikely. This remains to be proven.

6
The Paleozoic Era

1 INTRODUCTION

Fossils of filamentous blue-green algae occur in rocks dating from 2,000 m.y. ago, and both unicellular eucaryotic green algae and fungi are known from 1,000 m.y. (Banks, 1970). Between 1,000 m.y. ago and the beginning of the Cambrian at 600 m.y. other algae evolved, as did various invertebrate phyla (see Glaessner, 1962). The earliest acceptable fossil evidence of vascular plants containing xylem elements comes from late Silurian deposits in the UK and Czechoslovakia (Arnold, 1968; Chaloner, 1970), whilst plants exhibiting sporangia attached laterally on an axis, and with transverse dehiscence, are evident by the end of the Gedinnian stage (390 m.y. ago). Fusiform terminal sporangia, with narrow attachments and longitudinal dehiscence, appear during the Siegenian (390–374 m.y. ago). There is also an increase in the diversity of form, and in the complexity of the dehiscence mechanism of lateral sporangia. Some of these occur in spikes of associated sporangia and sterile appendages, and others have a regular axillary status with respect to microphyllous leaves. By the Emsian (374–370 m.y. ago) there had been a further elaboration of lateral systems. Although the sizes of the spores obtained from Lower Devonian plants are consistent with a homosporous life cycle, the dispersed spores that are obtained by rock maceration suggest that the trend to heterospory was already under way by the close of the Lower Devonian.

Basal Cambrian faunas are considered by Cowie (1967), and House (1967) emphasised that changes are not easy to document in the Cambrian although the overall rise in generic numbers as the period proceeds has been widely interpreted as reflecting high rates of evolution. Whether or not the Tremadocian is included in the Cambrian it is also probable that the period from the Tremadocian to the mid-Ordovician marks a period of major diversification in the marine invertebrate faunas (cf. Newell, 1963; Stubblefield, 1960). The groups which are particularly affected are those with calcareous skeletal components. These include the tabulate and rugose corals and stromatoporoids; the Bryozoa; Brachiopoda; Crinoidea and Nautiloidea; but comparable changes also characterise Trilobita and Graptolithina.

There is no faunal change at the Ordovician–Silurian boundary which is comparable with that of the Lower Ordovician, nor is there a widespread break within the Silurian (House, 1967). Similarly, the difficulties which attend any attempts to define the Siluro–Devonian boundary emphasise the absence of major changes. Most major early Devonian taxa have their origins in the Ordovician although there is evidence of a burst of evolutionary activity at the generic and familial level during the Devonian.

For many groups an impoverished generic record from the Famennian probably gives a false impression of a rise in the early Carboniferous. Four new rugose coral families occur in the Tournaisian, and the goniatite resurgence is notable. Furthermore the Mississippian is the Paleozoic peak for crinoid species and the number of genera drops from 74 in the lower Carboniferous to less than half that figure in the Permian.

In general terms both the Devonian and the late Carboniferous appear to have been characterised by extensive extinctions. Copper (1977) has suggested that spells of cold climates may have influenced the Frasnian–Famennian mass extinctions, but other workers consider that the evidence demonstrates that the Devonian extinctions, although most marked at the close of the Givettian and Famennian, are gradual. House maintained that this was also true for the late Carboniferous changes and Newell (1963) related these events to marine regressions and the consequent restriction of littoral environments.

On land Devonian insects moved into an almost competition-free habitat, and similar considerations apply to the early tetrapods. Studies of the earliest reptiles suggest that amongst the fundamental factors contributing to their evolution were their small body size and a modification of the jaw mechanism from the kinetic inertial system of amphibians to a static pressure system. Carroll (1969) concluded that all adequately known Paleozoic reptiles could reasonably have had a common ancestry among predecessors of the known gephyrostegids. During the Permian the prevalence of the synapsid lineage, including, as it does, the commonest reptiles at that time suggests that synapsid characteristics were at a premium. As many remains intimate the existence of hair and other homoiothermal characteristics it has long been speculated that this reflects the climatic conditions associated with Carboniferous or Permian glaciation.

2 CONTINENTAL DISPOSITIONS

The probable disposition of continental land masses in the geological past has been reviewed by many authors (see for example Bullard et al., 1965; Sproll and Dietz, 1969; Smith and Hallam, 1970; Tarling, 1971; and Marvin, 1973). As one example one may cite Smith and Hallam. They presented a reconstruction of the southern continents which was produced by using computer matching of the 500-fathom contours and combining the results with the most plausible fit estimated on geological and geophysical grounds. Both India and Australia were adposed to Antarctica and this was placed against Africa with Madagascar and Ceylon fitted into the gaps. Tarling also fitted India to Australia, Australia to Antarctica, and then apposed Antarctica and Africa without moving Madagascar (cf. Fig. 44).

All seem to agree that Pangaea existed in the form of a U-shaped continent by late Paleozoic times, although the intervening Tethys Ocean may occasionally have transgressed over the continents thereby forming two separate land masses at certain times. Houten (1976) thought that bathymetry, paleomagnetic pole positions and regional stratigraphic relationships all suggest a late Paleozoic fit of western Morocco against the north Appalachian province of New England, and western Iberia against the Grand Banks. If this was the case then the major Devonian orogeny, and the Carboniferous rifting in northern New England, appear to be anomalous with respect to Iberia and north Morocco. He thought that these unique events could be most easily explained by assuming a mid-Paleozoic convergence, and a later separation, of north-eastern North America and north-west South America prior to a late Paleozoic collision of Africa with North America that produced the Variscan–Alleghanian orogeny.

All such conclusions clearly imply very different oceanic and atmospheric circulation patterns from those which prevail with the land distributions of today. Sellers and Meadows (1975) certainly concluded that the albedo changes which result from two contrasting continental dispositions are considerable. They computed the probable albedo when the continental land masses are gathered together around equatorial regions and compared it with that occurring when they form a cap around one, or both, poles. The results intimated a

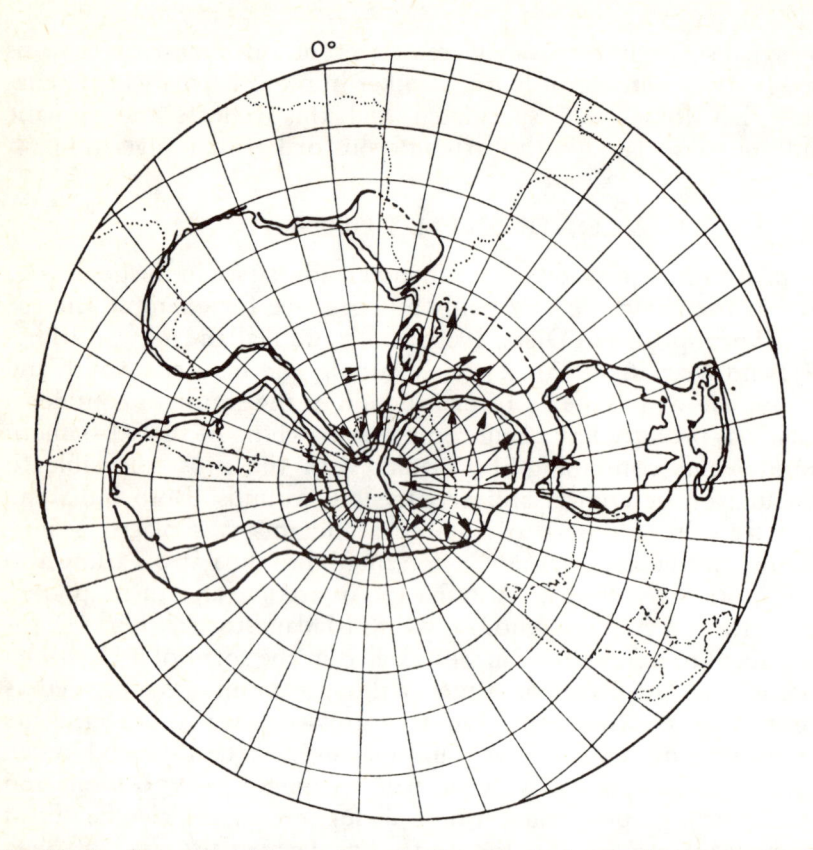

FIG. 44. Configuration of the southern continents in the late Carboniferous (Jordan, 1971). Arrows indicate directions of ice-flow (cf. Fig. 45).

difference of temperature of up to 12°C. As the difference between the average values during glacial and interglacial periods is less than this, it clearly implies very different global heat budgets. Such considerations are, of course, greatly influenced by the particular heat budget concepts which one uses as premises, but they may reasonably be assumed to indicate the possible variations involved. Ewing and Donn (1956; 1958), Donn and Ewing (1966; 1968), Irving and Robertson (1968), and Tanner (1968) certainly all considered that any changes in the distribution of continents and oceans in relation to the earth's rotational axis will modify the circulation patterns. It is therefore possible that a detailed comparison of the land and sea distribution during the Paleozoic and late Cenozoic will, in the future, reveal some common pattern. Actual attempts at reconstructing the Paleozoic climates in terms of continental distribution have been made on a number of occasions, by Robinson (1973) and Termier and Termier (1973) for example.

3 PALEOCLIMATIC CONSIDERATIONS
3.1 *Isotopic data*

Precise data on Paleozoic climates are sparse and, even if available, would be difficult to interprete in view of the lack of precision in our knowledge of exact continental relationships. Compston (1960) published ^{13}C and ^{18}O measurements that had been made on Devonian brachiopods from the Gneudna formation of West Australia. However, the suggested temperatures fell between 33·8°C and 50°C which Bowen (1966) understandably discounted. They are improbable and suggest secondary effects such as the incorporation of calcite.

Lowenstam (1961) then gave temperature values for three Mississippian samples. These were 24·7°C, 28·7°C and 30·0°C, and appear reasonable. Nevertheless analyses of the related magnesium and strontium ratios showed that there had been a progressive diagenetic alteration. In a subsequent publication (1964) he concluded that data from Permian material did not suffer from such inadequacies and were valid indicators of paleotemperature. A single specimen from "glacial" deposits (see below) in the Lyons group of Sakmarian age gave a value of 7·7°C. Four specimens from the Noon Kambah formation, of Upper Artinskian age, gave temperatures of 23°C and 17·4°C. Two others, which were thought to have been deposited in isolated bodies of water, suggested 23·7°C and 18·2°C. In his discussion he added that, if the water chemistry of the Fitzroy Basin during the Permian was comparable with that of Recent Bermuda and Barbados samples, then the true temperature values could be as high as 26°C and 23°C. These four samples suggested a climatic deterioration from tropical to subtropical conditions. Dorman and Gill (1959) had previously obtained values of 19·4°C, 21·5°C and 22·5°C from molluscs in Tasmanian Permian deposits and, as a result, when considering the Western Australian region Lowenstam (1964) pointed out that the sparse paleotemperature data suggest a relatively rapid passage of the 8°C and the 24–26°C isotherms over the same area. This in a region where the lowest Permian deposits comprise 8,800 feet of tillites and therefore themselves suggest a glacial phase.

3.2 Climatic variation

A variety of data contribute to our rather scanty knowledge of cyclic effects during the Paleozoic. Vegetational cycles have been reported from Carboniferous deposits but difficulties arise from the occurrence of cyclothems of local, non-climatic, origin (see Merriam and Sneath, 1967). However, in view of the contents of earlier chapters it is of great interest that Turner (1975) provided evidence for secular variations in the geomagnetic field during Paleozoic time. Studies carried out in Wales also enabled Thomas and Briden (1976) to demonstrate that there may have been an anomalous field for several million years during the late Ordovician. Smith (1976) did, indeed, review the concept of dipolarity with some care but Evans (1976) concluded that the frequency distribution of paleomagnetic inclination angles implies a continuous dipolarity throughout Phanerozoic time.

Cyclic depositional patterns have been reported on a number of occasions in the past. Having established apparent periodicities of c. $2\frac{1}{2}$ years, $5\frac{1}{2}$ years and 11–12 years in Precambrian strata, Anderson (1961) reported analogous $2\frac{1}{2}$, $5\frac{1}{2}$, 7–8 and 10–14 year cycles in Devonian, Carboniferous and Permian deposits. Similar conclusions emerged from Richter-Bernberg's (1964) study of Upper Permian salt deposits in Germany. Within these it was possible to detect 5–6, 10–12, 23, 85–105, 170–210 and 400 year periodicities, all of which compare very closely with the periodicities revealed by long-term studies of world climate during the last two or three hundred years. Anderson was certainly clear that power spectra analysis of the marine varves that occur within the Devonian Ireton shale show a prominent peak corresponding to 22 years. This was not obvious in a simple plot of varve thickness but was apparently responsible for a group of maxima on the smoothed curve. Its similarity to the Hale cycle hardly needs emphasising.

Counts of the growth lines that are exhibited by fossil organisms have also been taken to indicate that the number of days per year has decreased through geological time (Wells, 1963; Runcorn, 1964; Mazullo, 1971). This is thought to reflect a slowing of the axial rotation rate of the earth due to tidal interactions within the earth–moon system (Munk and MacDonald, 1960; Stacey, 1969). Using Mazullo's estimates Lovenburg *et al.* (1972) suggested that the Silurian year comprised 421 days and that a Silurian day lasted 21 hours. Such a daylength, if correct, would have considerable climatic implications. The reduced temperature difference between days and nights might be expected to contribute to an enhanced level of equability and thereby influence biotic diversity.

The possible periodicity of glacial epochs throughout the last 3,000 m.y. was intimated, alongside theoretical explanations of the phenomenon, in Table 5 (p. 99). Mesolella et al. (1969) emphasised that, since orbital perturbations provide a mechanism for climatic change in the Pleistocene, similar effects may have been operative in other geological periods. There are, indeed, indications that the climate, world ice budget, and hence sea level, all fluctuated during other geological periods. When discussing the Pennsylvanian and Permian glaciations of Australia, Wanless (1960) pointed out that detailed sequences at many localities indicate numerous alterations between glacial and non-glacial conditions. The apogee is a 50-stage sequence near Bacchus Marsh, Victoria, but a sequence of Upper Paleozoic deposits in Rhodesia also suggests an oscillating ice margin, with 15,000–20,000 years separating intervals of glacial advance and retreat (Bond and Stocklmayer, 1967).

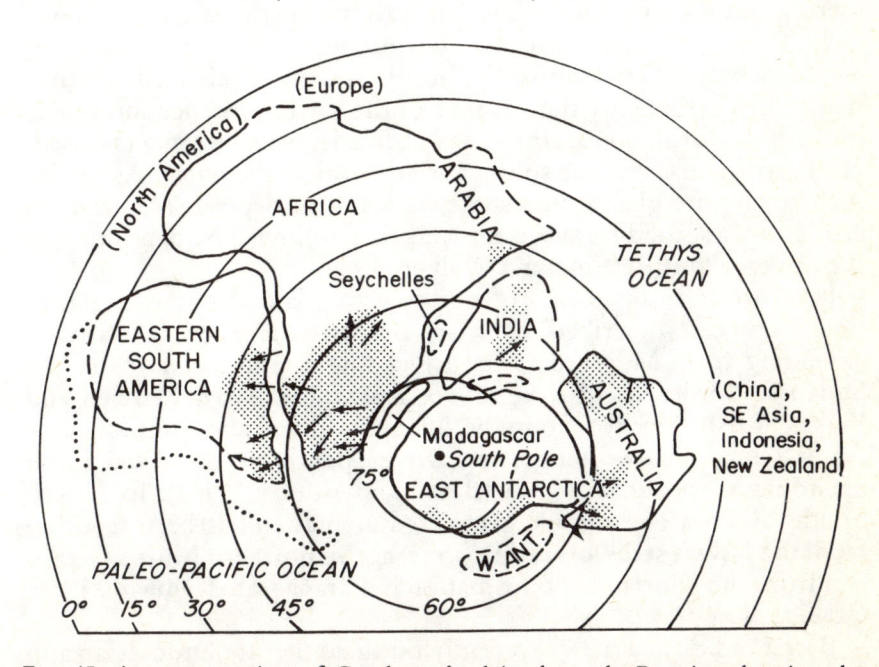

FIG. 45. A reconstruction of Gondwanaland in the early Permian showing the paleolatitudes. Stippling marks the distribution of known tillites and arrows indicate the directions of ice-flow that are suggested by a study of glacial pavements. The dashed lines show margins of continental masses that have been greatly deformed since the Permian. (Hamilton and Krinsley, 1967.)

Hamilton and Krinsley (1967) considered that the total land area involved in glaciation during the late Paleozoic was comparable with that of the Quaternary (cf. Fig. 45). Crowell and Frakes (1970) thought that the Phanerozoic glacial history of the earth, although not yet reconstructed in detail, suggests that, in Gondwanaland, ice caps waxed and waned from time to time throughout the Paleozoic to culminate near to the end of the Carboniferous. On the whole they did not consider that the available evidence permitted any conclusions about cyclical glaciation. In their opinion it did not suddenly sweep across the earth at the end of the Precambrian, at the Carboniferous–Permian transition, or at the end of the Cenozoic. Although no record for Silurian and Devonian times exists, they thought that the climatic conditions during the Paleozoic permitted intermittent continental glaciation for a period of over 400 m.y., followed by about 200 m.y. for which we have no record of widespread ice sheets.

Precambrian glacial phenomena are tabulated in Table 5. One may merely emphasise that, following various, perhaps synchronous, early phases of glaciation, the beginning of the Cambrian was heralded by an "Eocambrian" glaciation. This is reflected in Finnmark, for example, by the advance of the lower tillite ice sheet. The lower tillite formation seems to have been deposited from wet-based, grounded shelf-ice in the south, and icebergs in the north. As the ice melted an interglacial mudstone facies was deposited and, after erosion by a second ice sheet, this was then followed by deposition of the upper tillite (Reading and Walker, 1966).

In North Africa evidence of a widespread, late Ordovician glaciation has been described over an immense area of the Sahara, extending from Morocco to the River Niger, and eastwards to the Sudanese border (Beuf et al., 1966; Fairbridge, 1969; Crowell and Frakes, 1970). Striated floors lie beneath tillites, and Silurian coldwater faunas in overlying strata were apparently deposited in an epeirogenic "postglacial" sea (Berry and Boucot, 1967). In eastern South America comparable glacial sedimentation has been reported from the Lavras series of Cambrian (?) age in northern Minais Gerais, and from the Silurian Lapo formation in Paraña state (Oliviera, 1956; Grabert, 1965).

Berry and Boucot (1973) recently outlined the late Ordovician and early Silurian stratigraphical sequences across the world's platforms and provided evidence for onlapping relationships in the early part of the Silurian. In general the late Ordovician, marine, benthic, faunal communities that are found in the platform rocks differ from those of the early Silurian (Boucot, 1968; Sheehan, 1972; Boucot and Johnson, 1972). Boucot concluded that most brachiopod phyletic lineages seem to have become extinct in the North American region by the close of the Ordovician, and that the early Silurian faunas are derived from a restricted group of ancestors which are represented in northern Europe. Planktonic graptolites are also conspicuously different in early Silurian strata by comparison with those of the late Ordovician. Berry and Boucot (1973) therefore considered that the impressive evidence for late Ordovician and early Silurian glaciation in Africa and South America, together with evidence for only restricted orogenic activity (cf. Chapter 5 above) at that time, suggests that glaciation was the principal *agent of evolutionary change*. The apparent shallowing of marine waters across the late Ordovician platforms was seen as probably related to locking up of oceanic waters during glaciation. Onlapping relationships then ensued as the glaciers melted and the sea level rose. In a different context Dennison and Head (1975), who considered Devonian sea-level variations in the Appalachian basin and compared them with Johnson's (1971) data for western North America and Sloss's (1972) for the Frasnian inundation of the Moscow region, also wondered whether a world-wide sea-level rise was indicated by the data. However, Johnson (1971) had considered that it is during times of orogeny that there is transgression of the epicontinental seas onto continental interiors.

During the early Carboniferous glaciers seem to have radiated from several centres in what is now South Africa. They may also have extended into what is now the Paraña Basin of South America. On the basis of paleo-botanical evidence Plumstead (1969) considered that the base of the Dwyka tillite ranged down into the Lower Carboniferous and probably into the Devonian. In basins that parallel ancient Andean trends glacial marine tongues contain early Carboniferous fossils and the sediments display imprints of glaciation in the striated stones, and dropstones from ice-rafting, which lie in thin-bedded sequences. Such stones may have originated within small, rather than continental, glaciers.

Such evidence suggests that glaciation may have reached its maximal extent during the late Carboniferous when the Gondwana super-continent had moved so that the southern rotational pole lay somewhere in west Antarctica. At that time a lobe of the principal ice mass, which probably covered most of southern Africa, extended through glacial valleys and on, westward, into the Paraña Basin. It probably also covered much of Antarctica and an ice cap occupied

Victoria Land, providing glacial material for Tasmania and the southern region of Australia. Along the Andean belt, and west of the Falkland Islands, glacial centres waxed and waned as they did in India and in the Carboniferous mountains of central eastern Australia. Around an ancient polar embayment, in the vicinity of the junction between Antarctica, Africa and South America, thick deposits containing large, deformed, sandstone bodies, interpreted as remobilised till or outwash, probably accumulated on submarine slopes beneath, or bordering, shelf-ice (Crowell and Frakes, 1970). The Dwyka series within the Lower Karroo rocks of the mid-Zambezi valley also has three cycles of coarse to fine sediments that are thought to reflect periodic advances and retreats of mountain glaciers situated on the east side of an Upper Carboniferous freshwater lake. Associated varves in the lacustrine deposits give an indication of the length of time which elapsed between the various advances and retreats. This amounted to 15,000–20,000 years (Bond and Stocklmayer, 1967), a startlingly interesting detail if it is true.

Early in the Permian period such glacial centres seem to have nearly disappeared although traces do remain in Antarctica, Australia and Namibia. In South Africa the non-glacial beds of the Ecca formation were then being deposited in the Karroo Basin (Haughton, 1963), and *postglacial* beds were being laid down in the Paraña Basin of South America (Rocha-Campos, 1967). Paleomagnetic data suggest that by this time these localities may have approximated to 30° latitude and that the two united continents had moved rapidly away from the south rotational pole (Crowell and Frakes, 1970).

Frakes *et al.* (1975) concluded that comparable evidence for late Paleozoic glaciations is only represented in the northern hemisphere by material from India, although Schwarzbach (1976) drew attention to some possible additional evidence. Siberian deposits comprise rafted structures that probably accumulated in paleolatitudes 50–60°N, and, being Kazanian in age, they post-date most of the Gondwanaland tillite. They were, however, approximately contemporary with the ice-rafted deposits of south-east Australia. This led to the conclusion that the ice sheet of peninsular India was separated from even larger, and possibly contemporaneous, ice bodies in central Africa, Madagascar and west Australia.

4 PALEOZOIC EXTINCTIONS

A very stimulating review of the heterogeneous literature was provided by Tappan (1968) who was concerned to prove that

THE PALEOZOIC ERA 125

fluctuating productivity underlay marine faunal extinctions. The apparent synchroneity of these had been emphasised in the previous decade by Newell (cf. Fig. 46). Tappan concluded from her data that

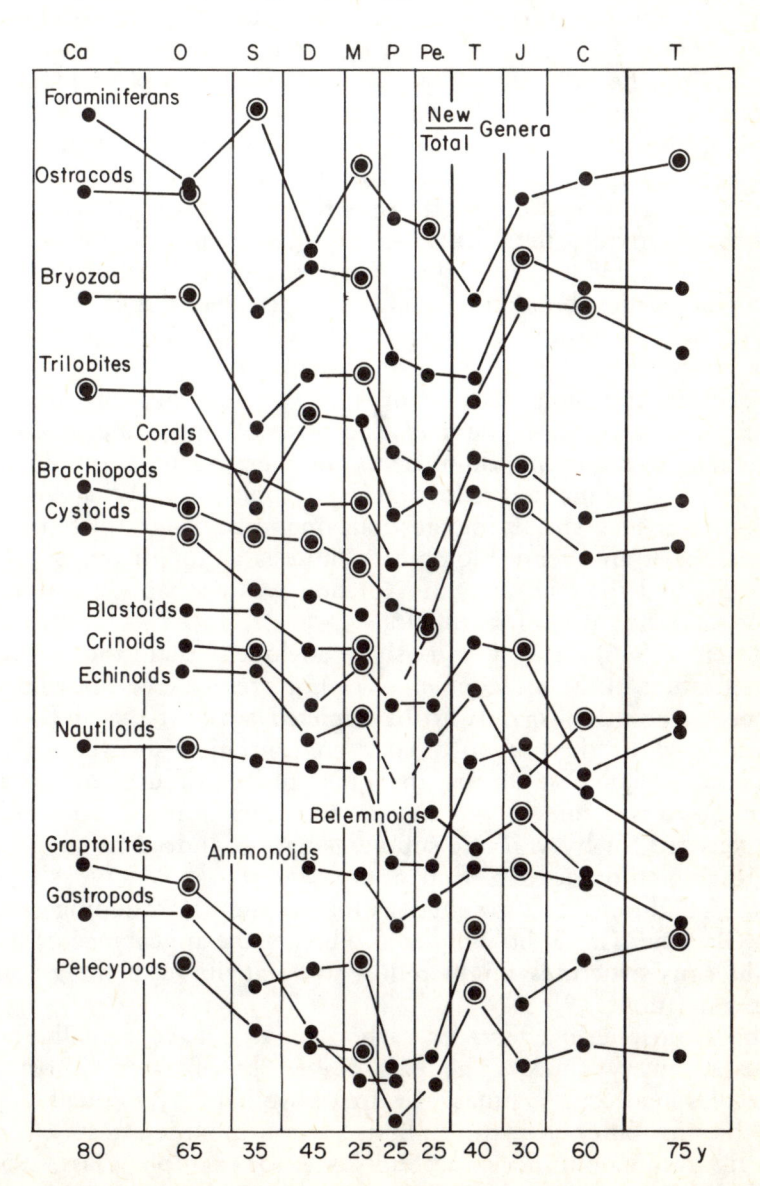

Fig. 46. A compound graph showing the comparative fluctuations in the percentage of new genera in successive faunas (cf. Fig. 1). (Newell, 1952.)

the phytoplankton maxima which are indicated by the geological record coincide with, and may have caused, both biogenic calcareous deposition and also evolutionary diversification of the contemporaneous biota. In contrast, she submitted that the onset of decreased productivity gave rise to a general biotic turnover both on land and in the sea. She suggested that extensive phytoplankton extinctions coincide with similar extinctions of animal taxa, rather than with those of terrestrial plants. She clearly envisaged that during periods of severe reduction in the world's microflora there would be a consequential depletion of atmospheric oxygen, an increased level of carbon dioxide, the formation of ^{12}C-enriched limestone and ^{32}S-enriched sulphates, and submarine dissolution of carbonates. The phytoplanktonic abundance which she detected might, she suggested, have been the product of the contemporary continental physiography through its affect on climate, atmospheric circulation and oceanic upwelling. Low continents, equable climates, reduced efflux of material from the land, and lessened upwelling, could all contribute to the sinking of nutrients and thereby, in her opinion, be the source of the marked reduction in phytoplankton. Whatever one thinks about such specific suggestions one must congratulate her on an attempt at an overall biological synthesis although Lipps (1970) has suggested that the oxygen depletion was probably a result of, rather than the cause of, extinctions.

Rutten (1966) had previously concluded that the oxygen concentration in the atmosphere overshot present levels during the Upper Carboniferous, only to be depleted again at the Hercynian orogeny, whilst the carbon dioxide concentration showed a complementary depletion during the quiet phases of orogenic cycles when the losses due to organic photodissociation were not fully compensated for by volcanic supplementation. Indeed he suggested that carbon dioxide depletion about 600 m.y. B.P. gave alkaline marine conditions that resulted in marine animals building shells. Like Glaessner (1962) he wondered whether the appearance of these fossiliferous structures might reflect some attribute of the Eocambrian glaciation.

The atmospheric effects of carbon dioxide have actually been discussed many times. The part played by infrared absorptive molecules in affecting climate was first postulated by Tyndall (1861) and the possibility that atmospheric carbon dioxide affects climate then figures in a number of accounts (see, for example, Plass, 1956a, b; 1961). Plass considered that quite reasonable variations in the carbon dioxide, ozone and water content of the atmosphere could result in changes of the infrared flux and have a significant effect on global climates. Such effects of CO_2 have now been given a considerable amount of discussion in the context of pollution (cf. Sawyer, 1972). Cheney (1971) suggested that during long periods of geological time an absence of burrowing organisms was one of three non-equilibrium processes that prevent the oxidation of minor amounts of carbon and affect the O_2/CO_2 ratio. Variations of the concentration of carbon dioxide have probably occurred since the Precambrian (Crowell and Frakes, 1970) but there is no evidence of greater fluctuations occurring in association with ice ages. The complex interaction of volcanic carbon dioxide emanation, chemical weathering, biochemical processes, carbonate fixation in rocks, and the concentration in the atmosphere–ocean system as a function of temperature, are all seen as damping effects on climatic change.

Pitrat (1970) made a further detailed study (Figs 47 and 48) of the

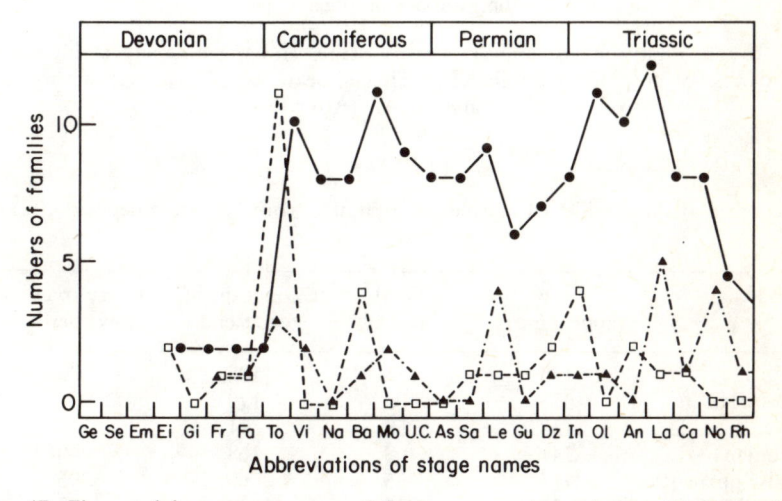

FIG. 47. First and last appearances of freshwater and euryhaline families of the Holostei and Chondrostei. □, First appearance; ▲, last appearance; ●, diversity. (Pitrat, 1973.)

relationship between phytoplankton productivity and abundance. A summary of his data is contained in Table 8. He concluded that a radical decrease in the abundance of phytoplankton, beginning in the late Devonian, cannot logically be regarded as the cause of late Paleozoic extinctions amongst marine invertebrates which, he concluded, was largely a Permian event.

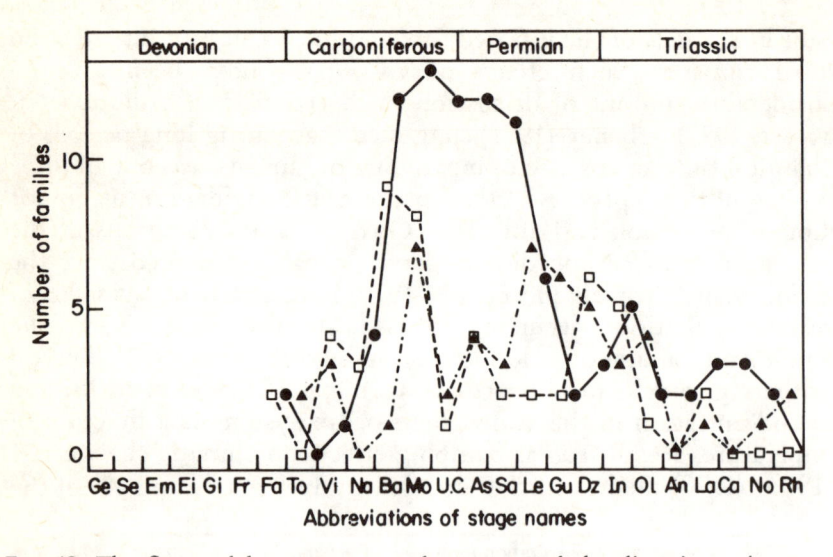

FIG. 48. The first and last appearances by stage, and the diversity at interstage boundaries, of amphibian families. □, First appearance; ▲, last appearance; ●, diversity. Compare Fig. 47. (After Pitrat, 1973.)

TABLE 8

A synopsis of the families of marine invertebrates from Paleozoic deposits (Pitrat, 1970)

Period	New appearances	Total present	Extinct during or at end	Carry over to next period
Cambrian	178	178	108	70
Ordovician	335	405	179	226
Silurian	132	358	91	267
Devonian	141	408	168	240
Mississippian	115	355	60	295
Pennsylvanian	30	325	50	275
Permian	29	304	170	134

Tappen (1970), in reply to Pitrat, expressed his figures as percentages which gave 60 per cent, 44 per cent, 25 per cent, 41 per cent, 17 per cent, 15 per cent and 56 per cent respectively for each of the periods as listed in Table 8. She concluded that a higher percentage of families became extinct during the Cambrian, Ordovician, Devonian and Permian, which lasted 100 m.y., 75 m.y., 55 m.y. and 50 m.y. respectively, than at any later time. Furthermore, the extinction rate in the Silurian and Devonian was comparable with that in the late

Permian. The nature of the organisms passing into extinction during the first of these periods was particularly interesting. The highest extinction rates typified animals that appear to have been sessile suspension feeders or occupied the upper trophic levels. This included one-fifth to one-third of the bryozoans, corals, brachiopods and crinoids, and, amongst the carnivores, 88 per cent of ammonites, 90 per cent of fish and 66 per cent of amphibians. The invertebrates with the lowest extinction rates were detritus feeders—only 9 per cent of gastropods and 15 per cent of bivalves. During the Permian the extinctions were of a similar nature with 70–75 per cent of the Bryozoa, corals, Brachiopoda, ammonites and Amphibia disappearing. In contrast bivalves remained little affected. She concluded that offshore communities with the putative lowest productivity underwent rapid changes and that the direction of evolution supported her initial thesis as phytoplankton is most abundant near shores and decreases in quantity offshore and in the open sea.

On the whole the record of marine fishes is similar to that of marine invertebrates with a pronounced minimum in diversity at the end of the Permian. On the other hand freshwater and possibly euryhaline fishes, together with Amphibia, have their minimal diversity at an earlier stage in the Permian. They were apparently on the increase at the Permo–Triassic boundary (Pitrat, 1973). The major peculiarity in the reptilian record is a great burst of both first appearances and apparent extinctions in the Dzhulfian stage of Africa

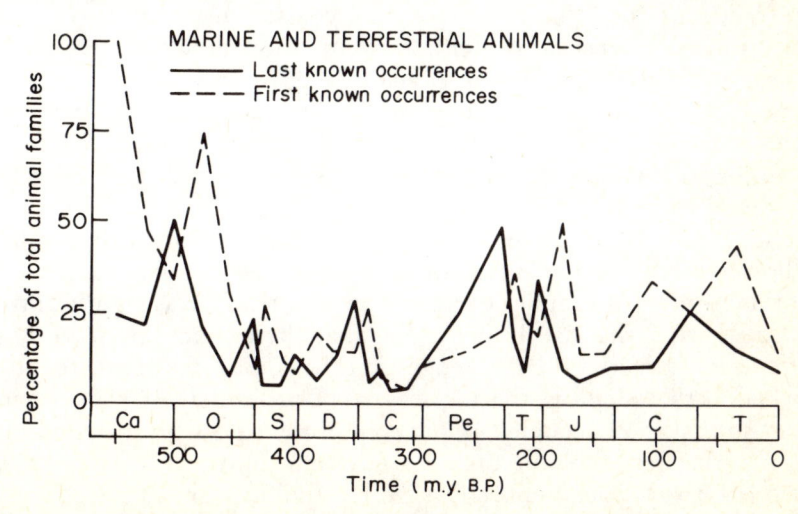

Fig. 49. Animal extinctions and radiations during the Phanerozoic (after Newell, 1967).

for which local causes were suggested. He suggested that the Permo–Triassic faunal crisis was mainly a marine event.

In some parallel studies Valentine and Moores (1970; 1972) discussed evolutionary rates in terms of taxonomic level. Valentine (1973) concluded that the rapidity of evolution at lower taxonomic levels makes the standing diversity at these levels more "volatile" than at higher ones. He suggested that whilst it is possible for enormous numbers of species to evolve rapidly during periods when barriers to gene flow are arising, this may produce few new families. The higher the taxonomic category the more stable is the diversity. His compilation intimated that there is one drop in diversity at the phyletic level in the Cambrian due to the extinction of the Archeocyathida. Complementarily, there is a single diversity rise in early Ordovician time reflecting the appearance of the Ectoprocta. Classes display a great increase in diversity during Cambro–Ordovician times and suffer significant declines in the Devonian and Permian. Orders have a similar diversity increase in the Cambro–Ordovician, a Devonian decline that persists into the early Carboniferous, and a Permian decline. Having discussed the possible causes of such changes he concluded (1973) that a reduction in the number of marine climatic zones reduces diversity and causes extinction of the biota adapted to a vanished climate. This might reflect either polar warming or equatorial cooling. Alternatively longitudinal provinciality is reduced by continental collision or the appearance of intercontinental or intercoastal dispersal corridors. Extinctions then ensue from either competition between analogous species or from predation (see also Bretzky and Lorenz, 1970). Extraordinary events that cause radical alterations in the environment seemed less likely and all these global changes could, he felt, be accounted for by tectonic processes such as those which are currently considered to be likely.

Schopf (1974), Simberloff (1974) and Boucot (1975) made similar studies. Schopf, who analysed the Permo–Triassic fauna, suggested that the number of families of marine invertebrates was significantly reduced during the last 32 m.y., and that the extinctions were not particularly selective. Paleogeographical studies led him to the conclusion that shallow marine seas were progressively reduced in extent so that they occupied 40 per cent of their possible distribution in the early Permian but only 15 per cent at its end. They then expanded to 34 per cent coverage in the Lower Triassic. This apparent late Permian marine regression was attributed to water withdrawing into a deepening ocean basin so that shallow epiconti-

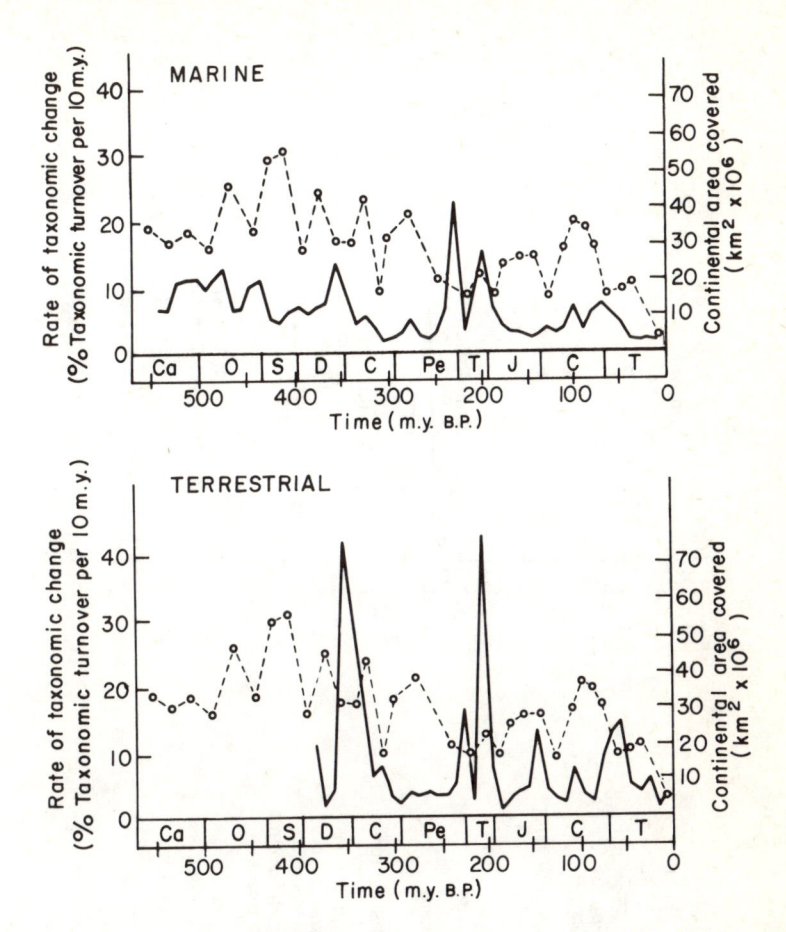

Fig. 50. A comparison between the rates of taxonomic change and the areas of shallow seas. ——, Rate of taxonomic changes; O, continental area covered. (Flessa and Imbrie, 1973.)

nental seas became limited to continental margins. The geographical ranges of shallow-water species were therefore reduced and the probability of extinctions increased. Schopf again concluded that no extraordinary biological process, atmospheric change or astronomical event is needed to account for paleontology's outstanding dilemma.

An interesting parallel approach involving both plant and animal taxa is that of Flessa and Imbrie (1973). They followed Valentine's analysis of family diversity through geological time and explained the diversity fluctuations of 59 marine taxa by reference to ten

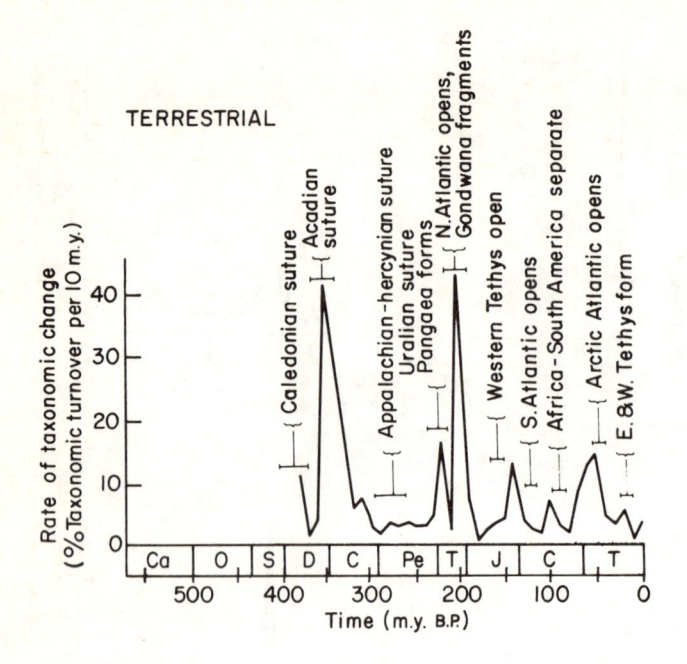

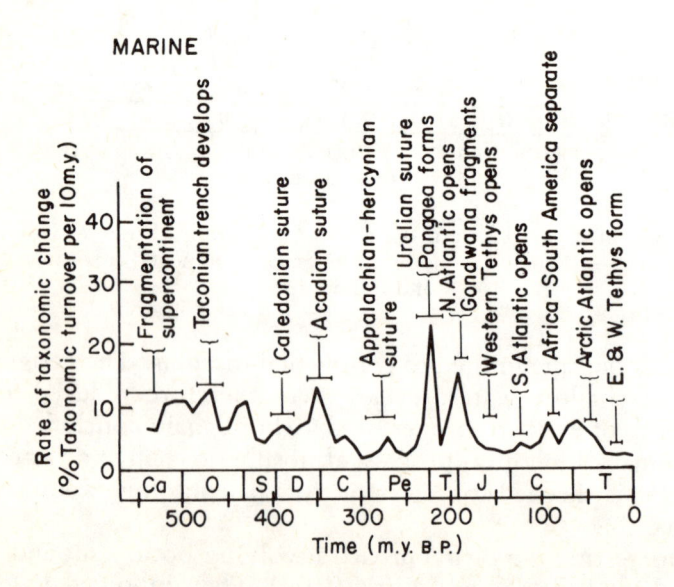

FIG. 51. Comparison between rates of taxonomic change and major plate tectonic events through the Phanerozoic (Flessa and Imbrie, 1973).

diversity associations (Figs 49–52). Peaks in the curves indicate maximum development of the diversity association. The trilobite–archeocyathid association understandably peaked in the Cambrian and this was attributed to marine factor 1. The graptolite–orthid association peaked slightly later, at the beginning of the Ordovician, and this was attributed to a second marine factor. An association involving Cryptostomata and Tabulata had a longer-lasting maximum that extended from the Ordovician to the Permian. Proceeding in this way they epitomised both Paleozoic and Mesozoic faunas in a series of contemporary associations. A comparison of their marine curves with comparable ones that were based upon

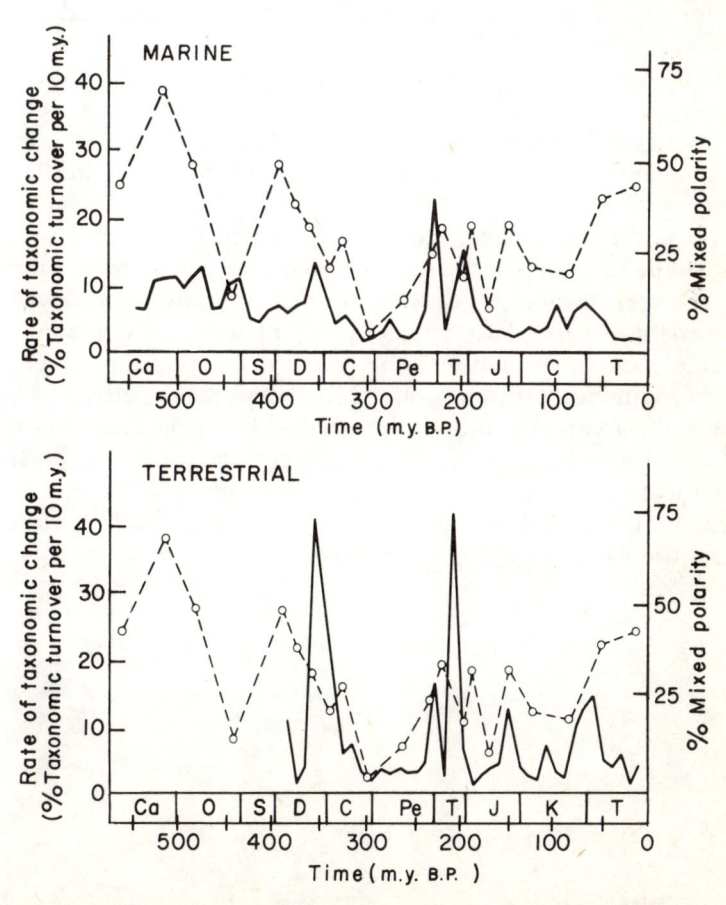

Fig. 52. A comparison between the rates of taxonomic change and the percentage of mixed polarity measurements through time. ——, Rate of taxonomic change; O, per cent mixed polarity. (Flessa and Imbrie, 1973.)

terrestrial biota showed an interesting difference. Whilst the majority of the marine associations exhibited a gradual rise and fall in their relative dominance, the terrestrial ones were characterised by much sharper increases and decreases. This clearly seems to indicate a more rapid biotic turnover amongst terrestrial taxa. In either case widespread extinctions permit diversification of opportunistic species taking the places of disappearing taxa.

They then compared their data with that for various factors such as magnetic polarity reversals (Crain, 1971) and continental movements. Crain had found a correlation of 0·912 between the mixed polarity measurements of McElhinny (1971) and animal extinctions. They concluded that a possible relationship was suggested by their data (Fig. 52) although the correlation was not as good as Crain's. Cambrian–Ordovician, Siluro–Devonian, Middle Carboniferous and Permo–Triassic marine association changes all corresponded with high estimates for reversal rate. In the terrestrial record a similar correspondence characterised the Lower Devonian, Middle Carboniferous, Permo–Triassic and, indeed, late Jurassic reversals. Flessa and Imbrie therefore concluded that geomagnetic polarity reversals continued to be good candidates for the major role of triggering past biotic changes. However, they developed a predictive model based on continent–ocean relationships due to plate movements and, like Valentine, gave prominence to this as the main source of diversification and extinctions. In fact, one would expect two effects. Clearly continental movements must have affected biotal associations and be correlated with changes. As polarity reversals appear to be linked with climatic fluctuations they may also have contributed to the changes that mark the international boundaries both within and between the various geological periods.

7
The Mesozoic Era

1 INTRODUCTION

Further immense changes characterise the history of biota during the Mesozoic Era. The fact that this era has long been distinguished from both the foregoing Paleozoic, and the subsequent Cenozoic, emphasises its relative unity in global terms but the question of the Permo–Triassic boundary has remained extremely difficult. Continuous deposition has frequently seemed the exception rather than the rule (cf. Neaverson, 1955) and the early Triassic biota exhibit affinities with those of the Permian. Furthermore, when considering various rather tenuous suggestions about the effects of diastrophism on oceanic circulation, coupled with the known effects of late Cenozoic climatic changes, Rhodes (1967) concluded that the biological consequences of the latter were of a different order of magnitude to those at the Permo–Triassic transition. This is, however, clearly difficult to quantify. He also, understandably, deemed insupportable those suggestions (Pavlov, 1924; Ivanova, 1955) which see extinction at that time as a product of volcanic poisoning or isotopic effects.

Cox (1967) suggested that the South African record indicates that after the Carboniferous Dwyka glaciation the climate became successively hotter and drier until it led to the deserts of the Upper Triassic. The earliest Triassic fauna was a swamp facies which retained elements of conservative synapsid lineages. During the remainder of the Triassic these were then replaced by the evolving diapsids which were themselves replaced by more "progressive" forms during the Jurassic. Although it was, indeed, the diapsid and parapsid lineages that dominated the Mesozoic, in contrast to the synapsid dominance of the Permian, this latter lineage persisted and Triassic forms such as the tritylodonts and ictidosaurs provide us with documentary evidence of skeletal characteristics that were closely similar to those of mammals. Cox suggested that these Triassic near-mammals, together with the Jurassic mammals such as triconodonts, symmetrodonts and pantotheres, were probably homoiothermal but not viviparous.

Another Mesozoic event which was of immense significance in evolution was the emergence of flowering plants as a dominant component of world floras. Floral remains figure in an immense number of papers and books (see Manten, 1967; or Penny, 1969, for example). It has been suggested that palynological data imply a single major radiation of flowering plants which started in the Upper Jurassic, developed slowly in the Lower Cretaceous, and gradually

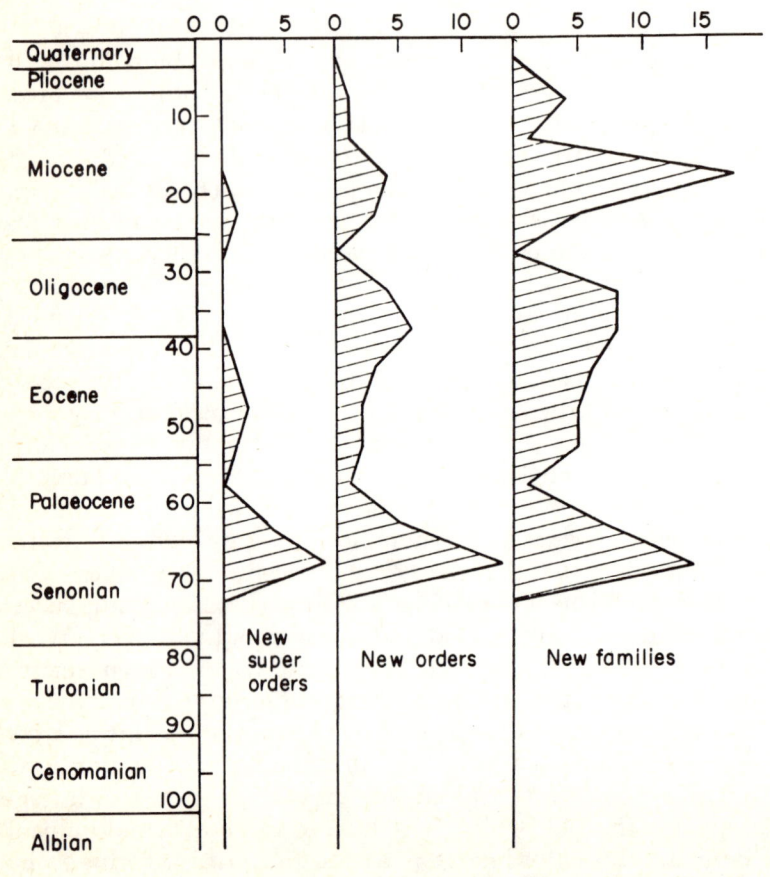

Fig. 53. A summary of the palynological evidence for the appearance of new taxa (Muller, 1970). Age in millions of years B.P.

accelerated in the Upper Cretaceous. However, little acceptable evidence of definitive angiosperms occurs prior to the Cretaceous and all those characteristic attributes of flowering plants that might be expected to persist as fossils appear during or close to the Aptian–Albian (Hughes, 1976). Muller (1970) intimated that a primary radiation in the Lower Cretaceous comprised a restricted number of small, simply built taxa of uncertain affinities. An increase in morphological diversity then occurred in the Cenomanian, and angiosperms finally achieved large-scale diversification, geographical differentiation and dominance in the Turonian and Senonian. It is from this stage that one can first find forms that correlate with extant families or genera (Fig. 53).

Such data pinpoint various critical points at the beginning and end of the Triassic, Jurassic and Cretaceous, at which otherwise continuous gradual trends are emphasised. This is, of course, no more than was originally recognised when the respective periods of geological time were separately designated within the stratigraphical column. Numerous geographical data also exist that suggest latitudinal differentiation of climates, habitats and taxa at such times. Drewry *et al.* (1974) and Khudoley (1974) reviewed this information from a variety of standpoints. The first-named considered that paleolatitude studies of tillites and evaporites intimate the persistence of a geocentric dipole paralleling the earth's spin axis. They also suggested that the distribution of Mesozoic, and indeed Tertiary, cherts implies the existence of trade-winds. From this they concluded that subtropical high pressures were unlikely to have extended as far as 50–60° latitude. Khudoley, who considered that the continents retain similar dispositions to those in the Mesozoic, concluded that the width of the carbonate belt has changed with time and that its northerly extent decreased from the Triassic to the Cretaceous. In both the Paleozoic and Triassic the distribution of labyrinthodonts certainly seems to vary with latitude—80 per cent, and the greatest morphological diversity, occurring in paleolatitudes of less than 30°. Despite the difficulties of interpretation that are inherent in varying continental dispositions it has been suggested that this latitudinal effect is more marked in the case of Permian remains than in the case of Triassic ones. In a paper published a decade earlier Irving and Brown (1964) took such data to indicate much stronger latitudinal differentiation of temperature gradients during the Upper Paleozoic than in the Triassic. Khudoley also suggested that the boreal ammonoid zone failed to extend further south than 38°N during the Triassic, Jurassic and early Cretaceous. This southern boundary was, however, inconstant. Complementarily he concluded that the number of Tethyan realm genera was greatest in the equatorial belt and decreased polewards. Such ammonoid diversity gradients were, he thought, in both cases symmetrical with respect to the present thermal equator.

2 CONTINENTAL DRIFT

Discussing the bearing of Mesozoic geology on the time of opening of the North Atlantic Hallam (1971) concluded that, although some tension and subsidence occurred in the late Triassic, the continental fragments did not begin to move apart until the Jurassic. Basing his conclusions upon the collapse of the Mediterranean carbonate platform, the contemporary faunal divergence between Europe and Africa, and igneous episodes in the Atlantic region, he inferred that the earliest likely date of opening was the late Lower Jurassic. Rifting subsequently extended northward in the Cretaceous and separated

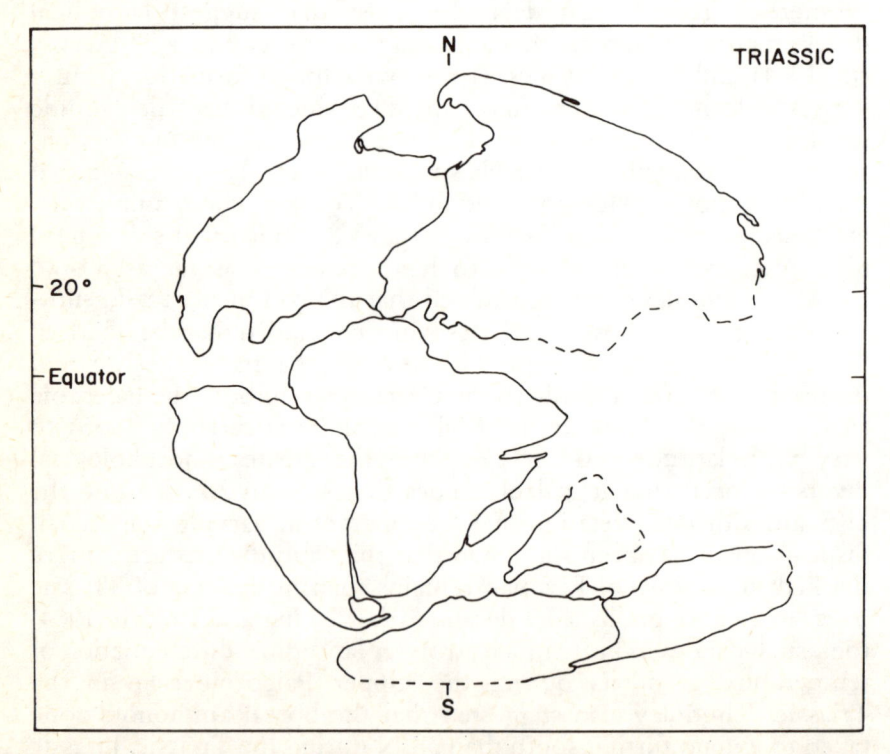

Fig. 54. A reconstruction of Pangaea at the end of the Triassic (Smiley, 1974).

the Rockall bank from the British Isles, whilst an accelerated rate of sea-floor spreading in the Upper Cretaceous was associated with the collapse, and consequent detachment, of the continental margins.

According to Phillips and Forsyth (1972), the Central Atlantic, Caribbean and Gulf of Mexico began to form in Triassic time (*c.* 200 m.y. B.P.) as a result of the drift of Africa and South America away from North America. The South Atlantic then opened up about 150 m.y. B.P. when South America separated from Africa. In the North Atlantic they thought that the initial opening of the Rockall trough began between 200–150 m.y. ago; the Bay of Biscay formed during the period 150–80 m.y. ago, and the Labrador Sea opened between 80–45 m.y. B.P. Linden (1975) suggested that this sea actually opened in two stages. A primary phase took place in the late Jurassic to early Cretaceous, and a secondary one during 60–47 m.y. B.P.

Eastern Gondwanaland appears to have begun to split up in the mid-Jurassic when marine incursions spread along the coasts of India and Africa. Paleomagnetic data (see Bullard *et al.*, 1965; Sproll and

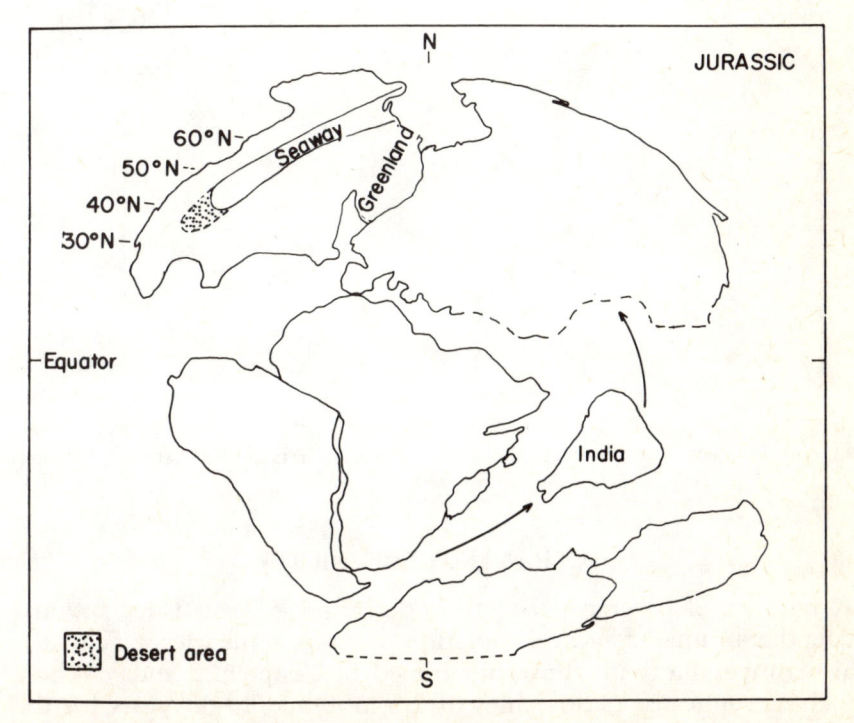

FIG. 55. Pangaea: a reconstruction at the end of the Jurassic (Smiley, 1974).

Dietz, 1969; Smith and Hallam, 1970; Tarling, 1971) suggest some contemporaneous separation of India from Australia but Antarctica is widely presumed to have remained connected to Australia as this is still indicated in the Paleocene. According to Sclater and Fisher (1974), India began to separate from Antarctica around the early Cretaceous to late Cretaceous boundary and was separated from Australia–Antarctica around 80 m.y. B.P. (see Figs 54–56). All these conclusions help to elucidate the paleoclimatic data referred to in section 5 below.

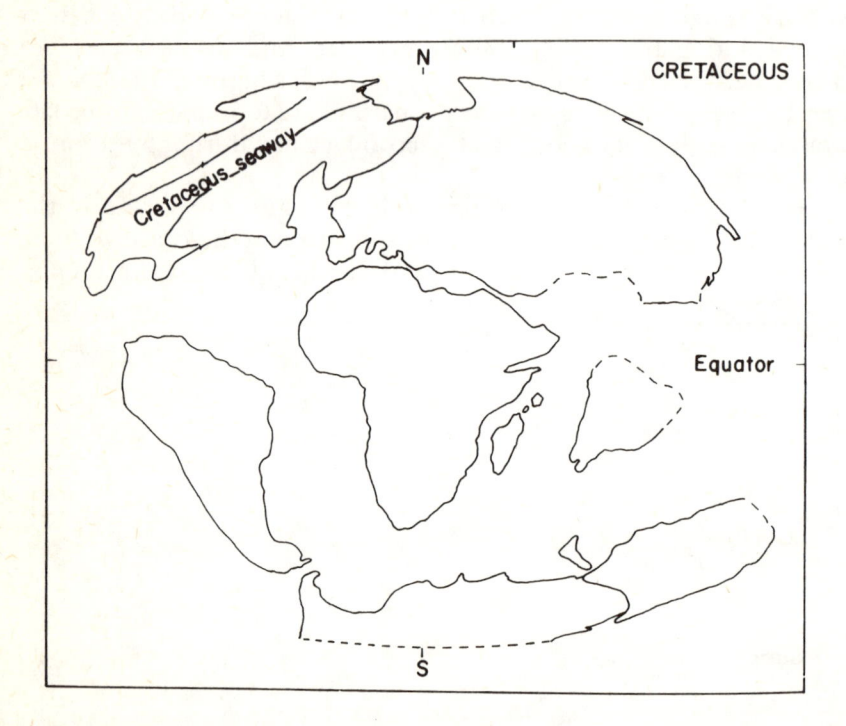

FIG. 56. Pangaea: a reconstruction at the end of the Cretaceous (Dietz and Holden, 1970).

3 CLIMATIC PERIODICITY

A number of older papers (cf. Anderson, 1961) cited depositional data that intimated cyclical climatic variations in the Mesozoic which are comparable with those mentioned in Chapters 2 and 3. These include suggested periodicities of 2·5, 6, 8 and 10–13 years for the Jurassic and Cretaceous. An interpretation of Jurassic and Miocene deposits has also given peaks at 8–9 or 12–14 years, and a sequence representing 1,592 years provided evidence for a 180 year cycle.

Various reviews of longer-term periodicity have been produced on a number of occasions (cf. Vella, 1965; Bock and Glenie, 1965). Another exceedingly interesting and influential account is that of van der Hammen (1961). Very few examples of continuous floral records that extend through large parts of the Mesozoic and Cenozoic exist (see, however, Zaklinskaia, 1967; and Srivastava, 1967). For this reason van der Hammen's Colombian data were of immense importance. He produced a composite pollen diagram that encompassed sites stretching from the uppermost Cretaceous to the Miocene and included data for the pollen of palms and other angiosperms together with pteridophyte spores. These all fell into one of eight ecological groupings, several of which exhibited synchronous maxima and minima at rather regular intervals.

The outstanding fluctuations were associated with the *Monocolpites medius* palm pollen but these could be correlated with those of a number of other assemblages. Both short- and long-term fluctuations occurred, and using indices derived from the sedimentation van der Hammen calculated the probable times involved. A glance at Fig. 57 will show that during the Maestrichtian, Paleocene and Lower Eocene the intervals between the peaks then seem to be surprisingly constant. Furthermore, every third maximum is greater than the foregoing two. As he suggested that these third maxima correspond

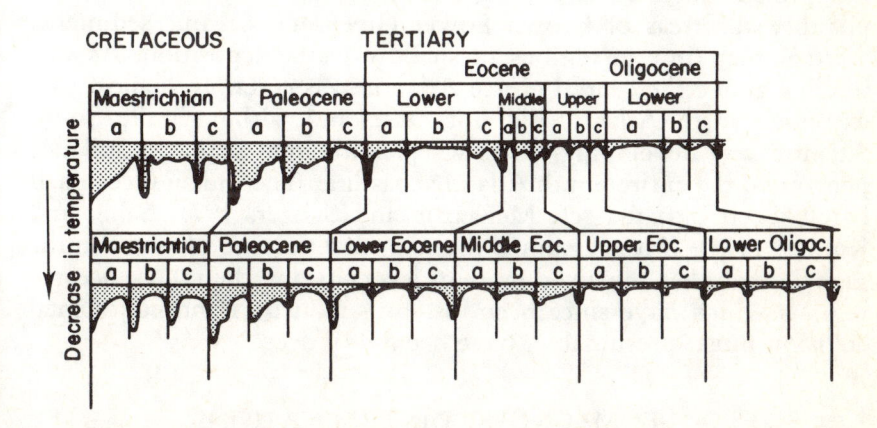

Fig. 57. Diagram showing the curve of the representation of the pollen of the *Monocolpites medius* group of palms in the deposits of Colombia. Below the same curve is shown redrawn on a time scale and somewhat simplified. Peaks are shown downwards. (From Pearson, 1964, after van der Hammen, 1961.)

to the bases of the international geological units, and that the *Monocolpites* peaks corresponded to climatic deterioration, their potential importance was clearly immense (see Pearson, 1964).

Other cyclic features emerge as a result of sedimentary studies. For example Talbot (1973), considering the corallian beds of southern England, concluded that these consist of four asymmetrical upward shallowing cycles with each one separated from the next by a non-sequence—usually an erosion surface—that marks a marine transgression. These transgressions were apparently the result of sudden rises in sea level over a period of 7,000 years. As there is evidence for similar non-sequences elsewhere in Britain, and abroad, it was suggested that the transgressions resulted from world-wide eustatic changes. Each provided small increments to a general Jurassic transgression that reached its acme in the Lower Kimmeridgian (Hallam, 1969a, b). The basic cause of this may have been a progressive displacement of water by the growth of mid-oceanic rises and Brookfield (1970) invoked variations in such rises as the underlying factor providing world-wide sea-level fluctuations.

In a complementary manner a major micropaleontological non-sequence in the British Cenomanian can be correlated with comparable features elsewhere in Europe and North America. A comparison of such results with the facies in deep-sea cores indicated that the effect is widespread and probably reflects the long known, major eustatic episode in the mid-Cenomanian. The evidence has been interpreted by Hart and Tarling (1974) as suggesting that most, and possibly all, areas of known Lower Greensand oceanic sediments were at that time in regions of shallow-water deposition. As was implied above the central North Atlantic was certainly shallow, the extreme North Atlantic did not exist, and, although the South Atlantic was developing, shallow epicontinental seas had still not penetrated the entire South Atlantic coastline. The Indian Ocean had barely been initiated (cf. McKenzie and Sclater, 1971; Sahni and Kumar, 1974). If it is assumed that the total volume of water in the global oceans has remained more or less constant, then those oceanic regions which have since been lost by subduction and continental collision must, presumably, have been very deep.

4 GEOMAGNETIC DETERMINATIONS

Before turning to temperature determinations it is of interest to cite work on paleomagnetic determinations. Larson and Pitman (1972) extended the time scale of geomagnetic reversals back to the base of the Lower Jurassic and the intervals of reversed polarity between 110 and 150 m.y. ago are contained in Table 9 and Fig. 58. The latter

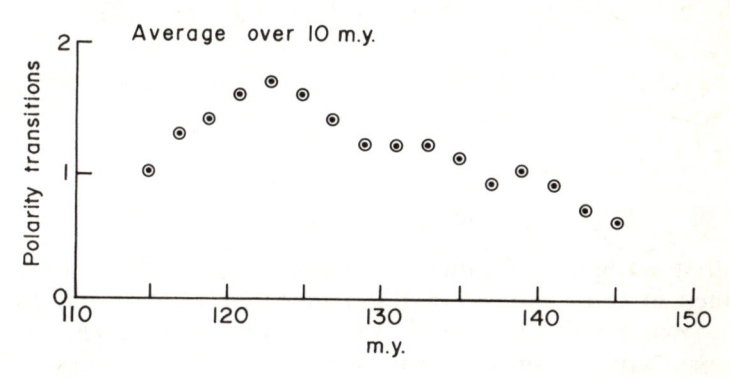

FIG. 58. A representation of the average number of reversals (polarity transitions) per million years, from 115 to 145 m.y. B.P. (Larson and Pitman, 1972). (By courtesy of The Geological Society of America.)

TABLE 9

Late Jurassic to early Cretaceous intervals of reversed magnetic polarity expressed in millions of years (Larson and Pitman, 1972)

111·50–112·25	128·10–128·70
113·25–115·90	129·15–130·00
117·75–118·25	130·60–131·20
118·50–118·75	133·15–133·80
119·00–119·80	134·60–136·15
120·33–120·66	136·85–137·45
121·00–121·60	138·90–139·50
122·10–122·50	141·15–142·20
123·65–125·25	143·35–144·00
125·80–125·95	146·70–148·10
126·30–127·20	

Figure permits a comparison of the frequency with which such reversals appear to have taken place at different times. If averages are made over a sliding 10 m.y. window, then the average reversal frequency is between 0·5 and 2 reversals per million years for the whole period. Larson and Pitman noted that the frequency of reversals appears to show an increase from the beginning of their Mesozoic interval and to decrease towards its end; longer polarity periods, or, to put it the other way, fewer reversals characterise the initial and closing phases. The average reversal frequency is approximately similar to that observed by Heirtzler *et al.* (1968) for the period 75–50 m.y. B.P. On present evidence the period between 50 m.y. B.P. and the present has had a greater average reversal frequency of between 2–4 reversals per million years.

5 PALEOTEMPERATURE DATA

5.1. *Jurassic Paleotemperatures*

The first isotopic determination of Jurassic paleotemperatures was included in Urey *et al.* (1951) and involved a belemnoid rostrum from Skye. Analyses of both ^{13}C and ^{18}O were carried out on carbonate samples ground from each side of a disc cut from the specimen. This provided right and left values for two ratios—$^{13}C/^{12}C$ and $^{18}O/^{16}O$. Although the right and left samples of the outermost ring failed to agree, and the check for the two samples from the second ring was bad, the remainder had an agreement of within 0·2 per cent. Radial variation occurred in the case of both elements with that of the carbon failing to correlate with any other variable. However, in the case of oxygen the variations were attributed to seasonal fluctuations. It was thought that three summers and four winters were represented and that the animal had died at four years of age. On such grounds the maximal seasonal temperature variation appeared to have been 6°C. The original temperature scale used was subsequently corrected by Bowen (1966) who concluded that the results reflected an average environmental temperature of 20·8°C.

Subsequent investigations provided data on both the Lower and Upper Jurassic (Bowen, 1961a, b, c; 1962; 1963a, b; 1964a, b). Four temperature determinations on Liassic material from the Northampton and Yorkshire regions gave values of 23·8°C, 25·7°C, 29·6°C and 31·7°C. The last value was thought to possibly represent material of littoral origin and reflect the $\delta^{18}O$ values of freshwater influxes. Two French Pliensbachian specimens of *Hastites umbilicatus* gave 24·3°C and 24·6°C respectively. Bowen concluded that during the Lias and Middle Jurassic the German area comprised deep water, with the nearest shores sufficiently distant to prevent such a freshwater dilution effect. For this reason the data obtained from German specimens of *Passaloteuthis*, *Nannobelus* and *Acrocoelites*, were thought to provide a more accurate picture of surface water temperatures. These appear to have ranged from 18·8°C to 23·6°C for the Lower

Pliensbachian (Lias γ); 16·5–20·2°C for the Upper Pliensbachian (Lias δ); and 27–32·9°C for the Toarcian. This clearly suggested that Schwarzbach's (1961) suggestion, that the Liassic was cooler than the Upper Jurassic, was inappropriate (see below). In contrast it corroborated Arkell's (1956) recording of a rich temperate Liassic flora as far north as Greenland. Bowen (1966) cited additional corroborative values of 24·2°C, 27°C and 28·4°C for Toarcian belemnoids, whilst Bowen and Fritz (1963) obtained a value of 29°C from Lower Bajocian *Acrocoelites* sp., which suggested that the high temperatures were maintained in the German arena after the Toarcian but were abruptly succeeded by low temperatures in the Upper Bajocian. Values of 14–18·1°C were obtained for *Belemnopsis*

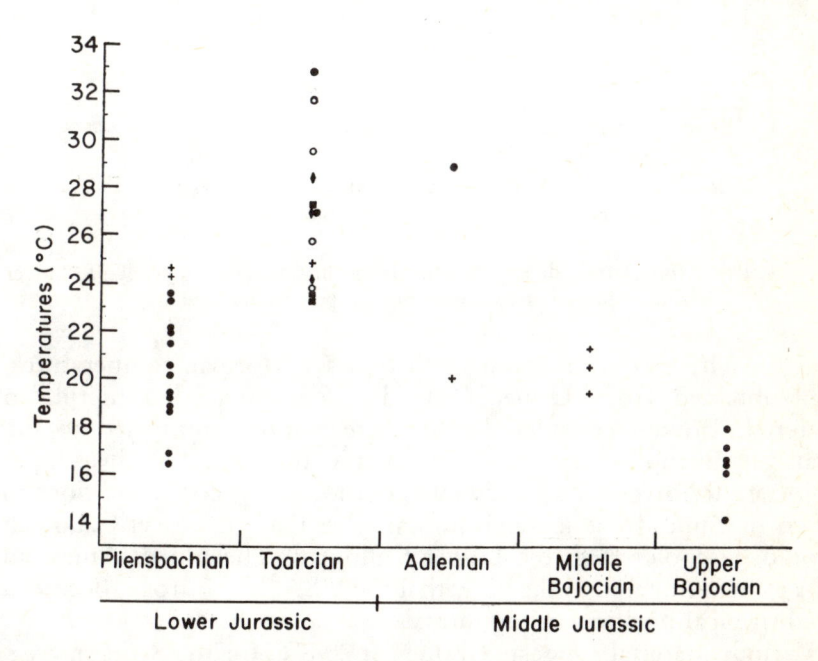

Fig. 59. Data on paleotemperatures from the European region. ●, Data from Pliensbach, Germany; ◆, data from Bamberg, Germany; +, data from France; ■, data from Switzerland; ○, data from England. (Bowen, 1966.)

canaliculatus and *Megateuthis giganteus* that date from that time. Three temperatures of Bajocian age obtained from Normandy ranged from 19·5°C to 21·4°C and were therefore again different from the German data (see Figs 59–60). Latitudinal variation was suggested by data derived from Alaska and Canada (Bowen, 1966). A reliable value of 24·2°C was obtained from the Callovian of Alberta, and

146   CLIMATE AND EVOLUTION

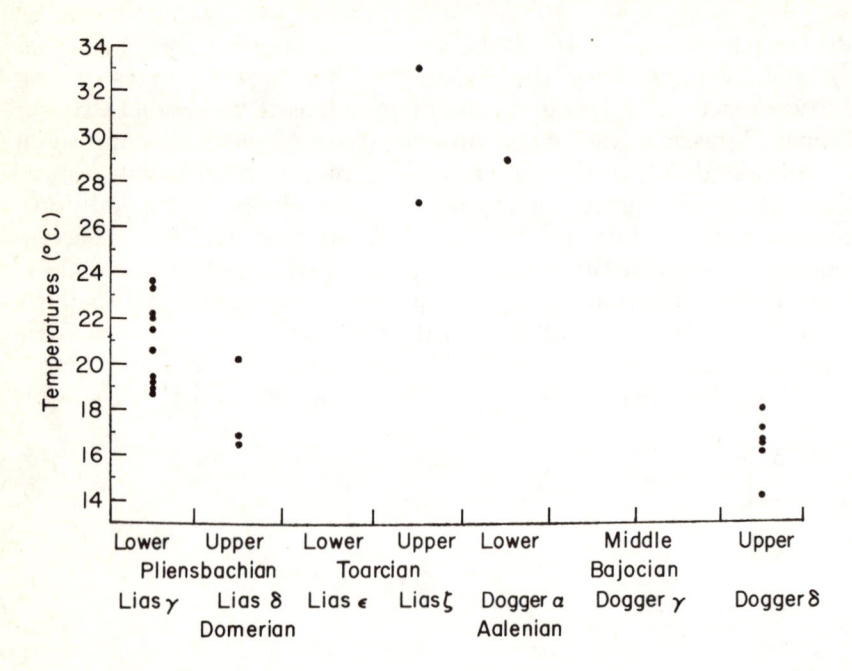

FIG. 60. Paleotemperature determinations from material of Upper Lias, Lower Middle Jurassic from western Europe (Bowen, 1966).

25·7°C, which is comparable with Swiss Oxfordian temperatures, was obtained from Upper Oxfordian or Lower Kimmeridgian material. Bowen considered that these results conformed to the available European data since a climatic minimum in the Upper Bajocian, followed by a steady amelioration of the cool conditions to attain an Upper Jurassic maximum, implies that the Lower Callovian should be cooler than the Upper Callovian. The North American data also conformed to the view that the USA, like Europe, occupied a subtropical position in the Jurassic.

Various material suggested values of 20·8°C for the Scottish area, and 21·4°C was obtained from English Oxfordian specimens of *Cylindroteuthis puzosiana*. A slightly higher value of 23·9°C typified another specimen and this conformed with data from a specimen of *Belemnites hastatus* that derived from the upper levels of the Oxfordian at Arc in France. Bowen (1966) considered that these higher values reflected the warmer Tethyan region and he cited in corroboration of this a value of 26·7°C for another *B. hastatus* originating from Vaud, Switzerland; and 24·4°C for one at Aargau. Lower temperatures, more nearly comparable with those from the UK, were obtained from German Kimmeridgian material. This appeared to confirm the southward retreat of coral reefs by the Kimmeridgian because reef building species habitually inhabit areas with a temperature of 25–29°C at the present time, and the minimum temperature which they can endure is 22°C. All such temperatures were, at that time, used to corroborate both Arkell's suggestion of a boreal spread in the mid-Upper Jurassic, and also the cooling effects detectable between the Oxfordian and Kimmeridgian. An Oxfordian specimen from Greenland gave a value of 19·6°C.

5.2. Cretaceous paleotemperatures

On the basis of biological data, such as macro-remains of plants, the climate of the late Cretaceous has generally been interpreted as subtropical or warm (see Axelrod, 1966; Hall and Norton, 1967). As far as isotopic determinations are concerned Bowen (1966) emphasised that temperatures derived from the ^{18}O composition of oysters and brachiopods do not agree with those from the associated chalks. These last gave temperature values of 18·3–25·8°C for English Upper Cretaceous strata. The belemnoid data were different again. Oysters and brachiopods that were of comparable age to the belemnoid which gave the highest value gave 27·9°C and 26·1°C respectively, but data derived from *Belemnitella americana* originating in the south-east of the USA suggested a range of 16·5–21°C. Clearly such divergences can arise from a number of ecological causes but Bowen evinced reasons to conclude that whereas belemnoid rostra were formed throughout the year, other organisms tended to restrict their skeletogenous activity to certain seasonal periods. For example *Chama macerophylla* was shown by Urey *et al.* (1951) to only lay down shell after the surface water had reached 24°C. On this basis the belemnoid data are better indicators of the mean annual temperature of their environment. Urey *et al.* also attributed a northern, cooler habitat preference to the genus *Belemnitella*.

Material from early Cretaceous horizons clearly established a temperature maximum in the Albian. This then declined during the Cenomanian only to be followed by a further maximum in the Coniacian–Santonian interval. The Maastrichtian was then characterised by declining temperatures. Such overall trends are illustrated by Fig. 61. Although some imprecision existed in the ascription of Cenomanian–Turonian data, it was difficult to escape the conclusions that both the Cenomanian and the Lower Turonian were cool.

Rising temperatures in the Upper Turonian then led to the Coniacian–Santonian climax.

Different data were obtained from the Crimea by Teis *et al.* (1957).

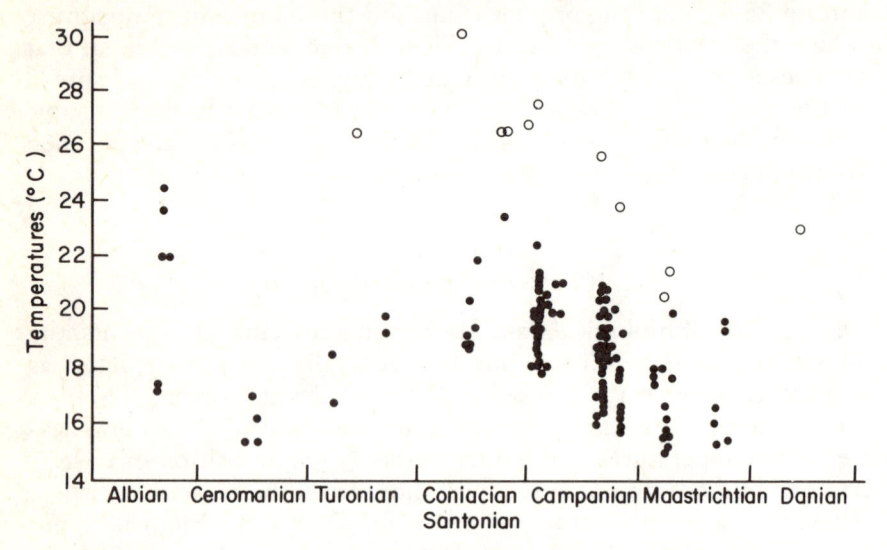

FIG. 61. Mean temperature data obtained from belemnoid and brachiopod material originating between the Albian and Danian in western Europe. ●, Belemnites; ○, brachiopods. (Bowen, 1966.)

A climatic low for the Valangian–Aptian interval was followed by an Albian maximum and this persisted into the early Cenomanian. A warm phase then characterised the Santonian and the early Campanian which was itself followed by a climatic minimum in the late Campanian. The Maastrichtian was notable for a slight rise in temperature. However, as these data were all based upon an inorganic scale of temperature they are not comparable with those of other workers.

Bowen concluded that, in global terms, the Aptian was cool relative to an Albian high, whilst Australian and African material suggest that there may have been a greater latitudinal variation than was the case during the Jurassic. Bowen suggested that, at that time, the pole to equator temperature range may have spanned 15–20°C, whereas during the Cretaceous there appeared to have been a range of 30°C, or substantially in excess of that in the Jurassic. This he interpreted as representing much less equable conditions in the Cretaceous than in the foregoing periods of the Mesozoic. Although it is not easy to correct for the effects of continental drift at a particular locality Fig. 62 gives curves for the latitudinal climatic profiles of the Lower Maastrichtian, Cenomanian, Albian and Santonian times (Lowenstam, 1964). On these grounds average tempera-

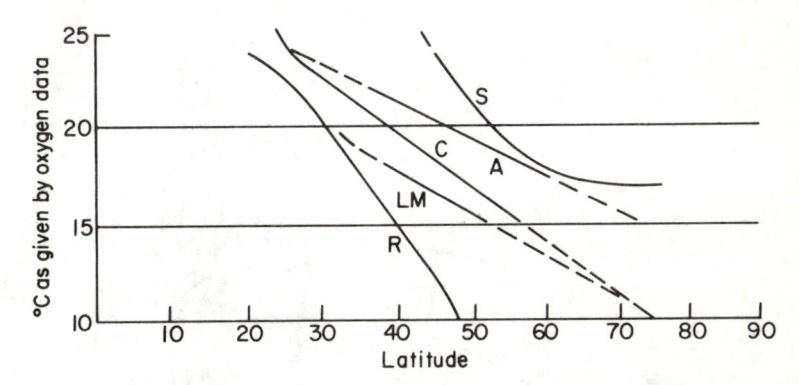

FIG. 62. Cretaceous climatic profiles. R, Recent; LM, lower Maastrichtian; C, Cenomanian; A, Albian; S, Santonian. (Bowen, 1966.)

tures at 70°N lay around 16–17°C during the Santonian. A comparable value was obtained for a Jurassic Callovian temperature at sites about equally distant from the pole. It is difficult to make precise statements but the poleward shift of the 15°C, 18°C and 20°C isotherms for the warmer Albian may have been more pronounced than for the cooler Cenomanian and approximated to that of the Santonian.

6 MESOZOIC CLIMATES

Following a discussion of the effects that differing continental dispositions have upon climates Robinson (1973) attempted to reconstruct the climatic regions of the Triassic continental aggregation. A paleogeographic analysis of Upper Triassic times was achieved by utilising Triassic paleomagnetic data, the pre-Cretaceous relationships of the continents and geological data. The reconstruction obtained in this way was then plotted on to an oblique Mollweide projection (see Robinson, 1971). The equator bisected the landmass into roughly equal halves—a northern Laurasia and southern Gondwanaland. Figure 63 presents the postulated July conditions. A high-pressure maximum in the interior of the southern continental component has an outward flow of winds bringing a dry winter season, and the trade winds from this high-pressure centre

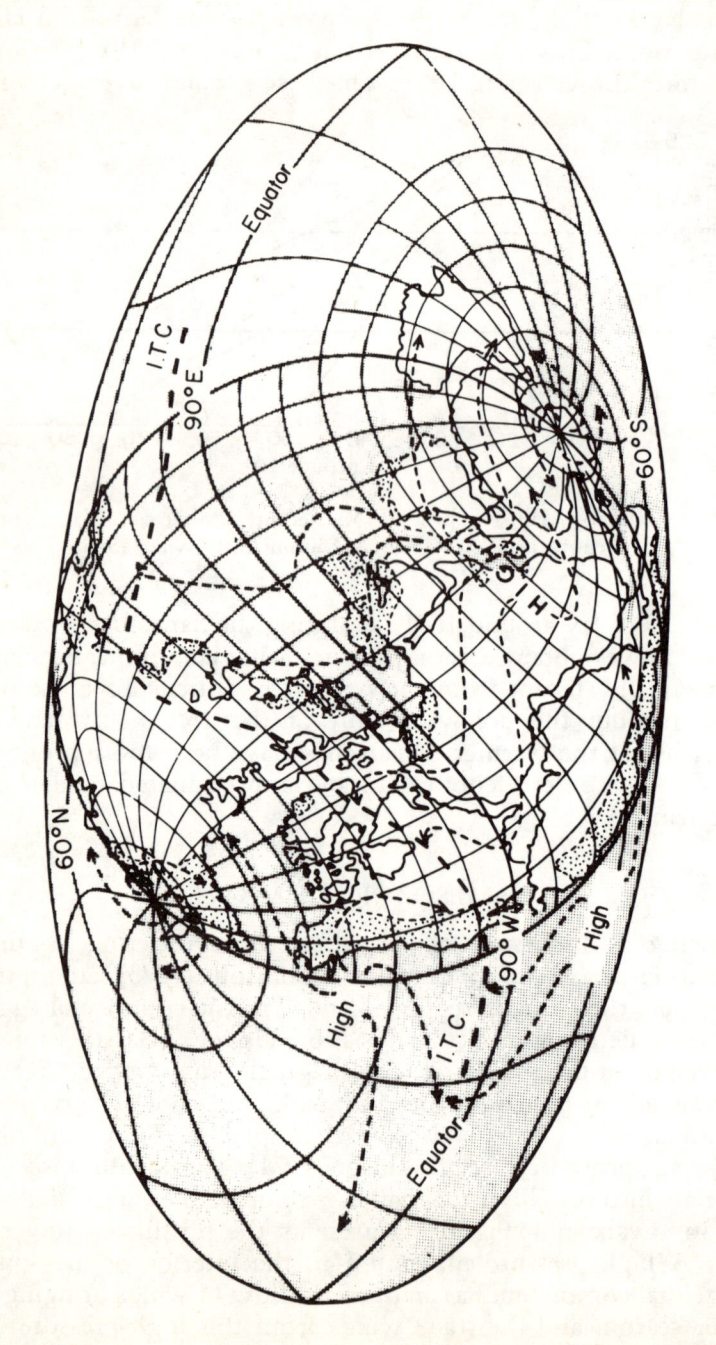

FIG. 63. A diagrammatic sketch of the major high-pressure maxima, winds and intertropical convergence zone (heavy dashed line) for July in the Upper Triassic (Robinson, 1971; 1973).

cross the paleoequator by virtue of the northward deflection of the intertropical convergence zone. Those blowing to eastern south Laurasia cross the Tethyan ocean to bring summer monsoon rainfall to the coastal regions. In contrast, those blowing to the western region cross land and result in a dry summer. The January map would reveal a mirror image situation with a high-pressure centre in north-east Laurasia and a deflection of the intertropical convergence zone into Gondwanaland. As a result January trades would carry summer monsoon rains into eastern North Gondwanaland, whilst the west and central part would have a dry summer season under the influence of landbound winds. Thus in latitudes lying between the two tropics the western and central components of the landmass would tend to have dry climates in summer and winter. Dry conditions would also predominate in those western coastal areas dominated by horse latitude high-pressure centres, whilst the annual cycle of these high-pressure maxima would bring seasonal rainfall to those areas lying a little to the south and north of their mean distribution.

High-latitude regions of both hemispheres would be dominated by the belt of westerlies and polar easterlies with associated systems of travelling cyclones and stormier, wetter climates. The absence of any record of glaciation suggests that the high latitudes probably lacked permanent ice fields. Three principal continental regions thus emerge. There are those that are mainly dry at all seasons; those with alternating wet and dry seasons; and those with more continuous precipitation. Clearly the effect of oceanic currents and differential relief would greatly increase the total number of local climates. Nevertheless this notional map does conform to the known distribution of fossil evaporites, aeolianites, Red-beds and coals (Fig. 64). Fossil sand-dunes occur in two areas—in the dry western and central intertropical zone; and in the dry, southern, continental interior. Coals do occur as minor deposits in monsoon coastal districts but they are mainly within the belt of westerlies and polar easterlies of higher latitudes.

Luyenduyk *et al* (1972) approached the problem from a different angle and used planetary vorticity models, that were based on the ancient configuration of the continents, to consider the northern hemisphere circulation patterns from the Middle Cretaceous to the onset of Cenozoic glaciation. The parameters which they considered included lithospheric plate motions (sea-floor spreading and orogeny), the location of the earth's spin axis, the zonal paleowind profile and, finally, the effects of glaciation. These factors suggested

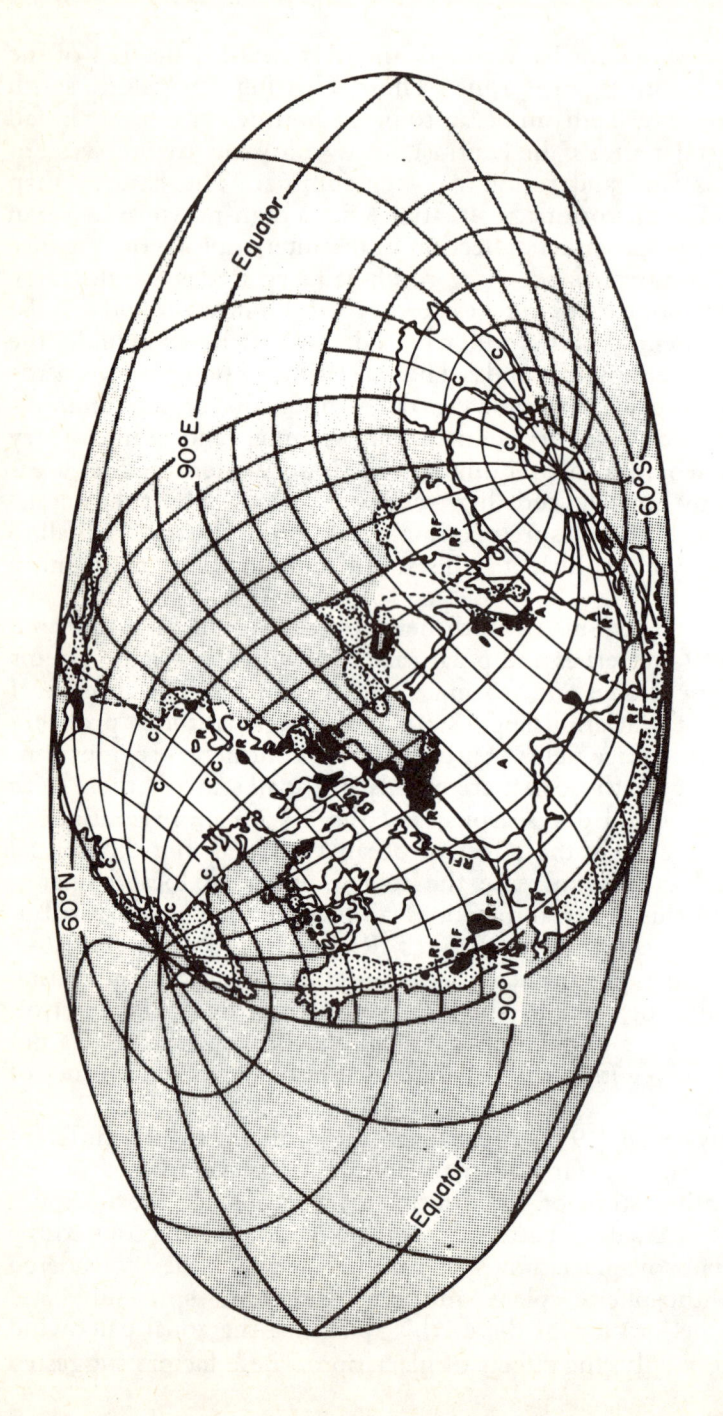

FIG. 64. Distribution of certain Upper Triassic "climate-sensitive" sedimentary rocks. Arrows indicate wind direction obtained from aeolianites; evaporites in black. A, aeolian; C, coals; F, fluviatile; L, lacustrine; R, Red-beds. A short horizontal bar divides two members of a sequence of Upper Triassic deposits at any one locality. (Robinson, 1973.)

that, in the Middle Cretaceous, the Tethys current circled the northern hemisphere, the Gulf Stream (*sic*) flowed up to Newfoundland, and the North Atlantic circulation was mainly above 20°N. On their hypothesis the greatest changes in subsequent periods resulted from tectonic action since the wind profiles remain constant prior to the onset of arctic glaciation in the late Cenozoic.

An attempt to reconstruct ocean currents was made by Gordon (1973) using modern ocean currents as analogies. The principal constraints on his system were imposed by the known distribution of

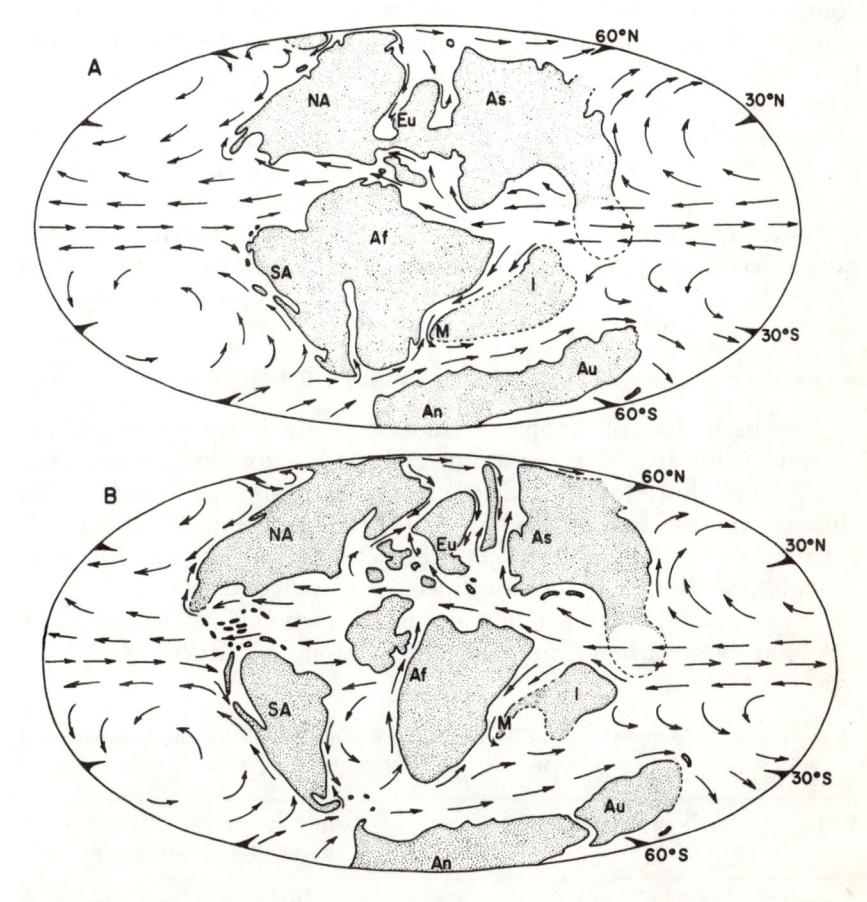

Fig. 65. A. Inferred Early Cretaceous oceanic circulation. Coastlines drawn for Valanginian time. Af, Africa; An, Antarctica; As, Asia; Au, Australia; Eu, Europe; I, India; M, Madagascar; NA, North America; SA, South America. B. Inferred later Late Cretaceous oceanic circulation. Coastlines drawn for Maastrichtian time. (Gordon, 1973.) (By courtesy of the University of Chicago Press.)

stenothermal organisms which served as indicators of cool or warm water. He concluded that, as at the present time, the planetary wind systems must have exerted powerful influences and that the outstanding feature of Cretaceous oceanic circulation was an equatorial current system flowing through the Tethys Sea and across the central Pacific Ocean in a circumglobal band of warm water with its own characteristic fauna (Fig. 65). He thought that the West Wind Drift probably existed at high latitudes in both the northern and southern hemispheres. The putative existence of cold currents that were comparable with today's Californian and Peruvian Currents, and of warm currents comparable with the Mozambique Current or the Kuroshio, suggest that current gyres existed then, as now. The Africa–Arabia landmass also seems to have diverted warm tropical water into the Northern Hemisphere so producing a sharper climatic gradient between the Tethyan and Arctic regions than between the Tethys and more southerly regions. Among fossil organisms the clear latitudinal distribution of both rudist lamellibranchs and large Foraminifera in Cretaceous deposits certainly indicates an important temperature effect—as do the Tethyan and Boreal assemblages of ammonoids and belemnoids.

7 SOME FAUNAL CONSIDERATIONS

In the discussion of Tappan's suggestion that was mentioned in Chapter 6 Pitrat (1970) gave figures for Mesozoic extinctions etc., that parallel those for the Paleozoic. These are summarised in Table 10, were summarised by Tappan (1970) as 37 per cent, 21 per cent, 31 per cent, 8 per cent and 3 per cent respectively, and elicit comparable thoughts to those already outlined. A detailed discussion of the events in a single taxonomic grouping is provided by Wiedmann's (1969) account of heteromorphs and ammonoid extinctions.

TABLE 10

A summary of the appearance and disappearance of *families* during the Mesozoic and Cenozoic eras (Pitrat, 1970)

Period	New appearances	Present	Extinct during or at end	Carry over to next period
Triassic	144	278	103	175
Jurassic	237	412	87	325
Cretaceous	302	627	198	429
Paleogene	134	563	45	518
Neogene	49	567	19	548

Noting that the arguments about the extinctions range from the biological–ecological through diastrophic–geological to the catastrophic–cosmic, he concluded that it was scarcely possible to bring forward new suggestions. However, he thought that suggestions which see competition as responsible for the extinctions of the ammonoids at the Cretaceous–Tertiary transition (Simpson *et al.*, 1957; Nicol, 1961; Newell, 1962) are, from the outset, unpromising. The investigations carried out by Herm (1965) on the globotruncanids of the late Cretaceous, suggest that a unique catastrophic event occurred just prior to the Maastrichtian–Danian boundary where heteromorph and dwarfed forms of these pelagic Foraminifera appear. A quite different picture is shown by the ammonoids. Although dwarf forms also appear just before the Danian boundary a quantitative statistical analysis of the genera (Fig. 66) shows that

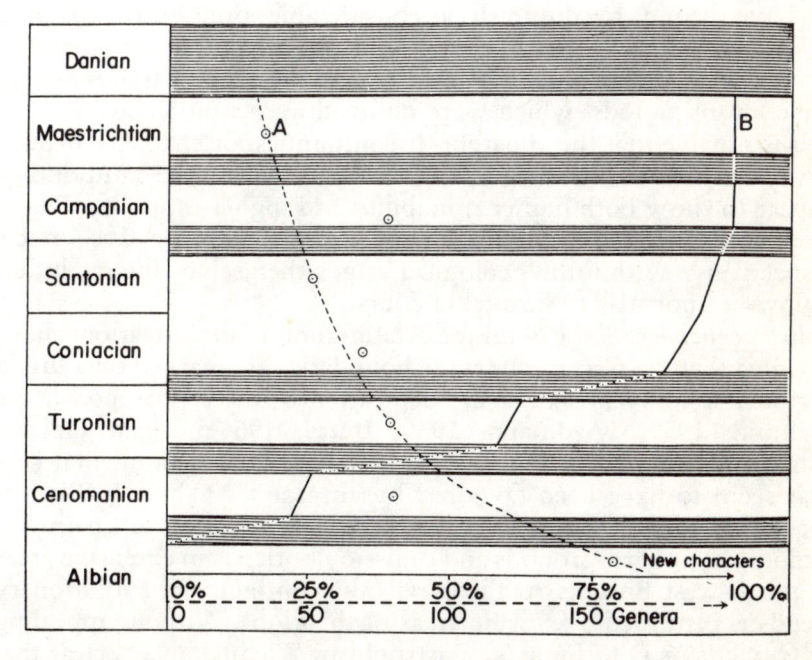

Fig. 66. The continuous decline of the number of genera of Cretaceous ammonites (A), and the appearance of new characters (B), in relation to marine transgressions (lined areas) (Wiedmann, 1969).

extinction of the group can in no way be tied to a unique catastrophic occurrence at the end of the Cretaceous. The reduction in the number of genera, and the final demise of the ammonoids, begins at the base of the Upper Cretaceous and progresses continuously in a paraboloid curve to zero at the base of the Danian. If one rejects the existence of inherent endogenous factors this regressive tendency, obvious from the Cenomanian onwards, can only be understood as a symptom of continuously effective, detrimental, environmental influences.

A second curve was then constructed in a different manner but expressed on the same time scale. The character breaks which are recognisable at the base of each new ammonite family are a measure of evolution and produce a similar broken paraboloid curve which exhibits a clear progression in the Cenomanian and Turonian. An evolutionary deceleration and stagnation, detectable in the Coniacian, reaches a climax in the Campanian. Qualitatively new characters of family rank are not observable in either this last-named stage or the subsequent Maastrichtian. Thus, on these grounds, the "mutability" and "evolutionary capability" of the ammonites seems to have begun to diminish a considerable time prior to their extinction—the crisis that they experienced was not sudden but drawn out. One can only draw attention to the climatic trends during the relevant periods, which were outlined in section 5 above.

It is notable that the apparent discontinuities, or character breaks, always coincide with stage boundaries at which the ammonoids appear to show both higher mutability and higher mortality. These were interpreted by Wiedmann as positive and negative effects respectively. Within the geological stages themselves the evolution follows a "normal" (? horotelic) course.

In recent decades careful biostratigraphical investigations have revealed that the Cretaceous stage boundaries are marked on a broad regional scale by breaks in the deposition of the cephalopod facies (Schmid, 1959; Wiedmann, 1959; Burgl, 1964), which indicate "rhythmic" regressions in just those shelf and epicontinental seas that seem to have been favoured by ammonites. These breaks are represented by the sandy detritus and "Grenzkalke" of Spain and Colombia, or hard-grounds and omission horizons in extensive areas of north-west Europe. At the breaks the continuity of evolutionary trends is disturbed over wide areas of the globe. Without appealing to Cuvier's or D'Orbigny's catastrophism Wiedmann was clear that it was exceedingly probable that a causal connexion existed between the sedimentary disjunctions and the evolutionary discontinuities. Only the exact nature of the interrelationship was in question.

It is possible, indeed plausible, that repetitive retreats of the oceans resulted in ammonoids vacating the previously favoured shelf environments and "emigrating" to deep-ocean regions. With the return

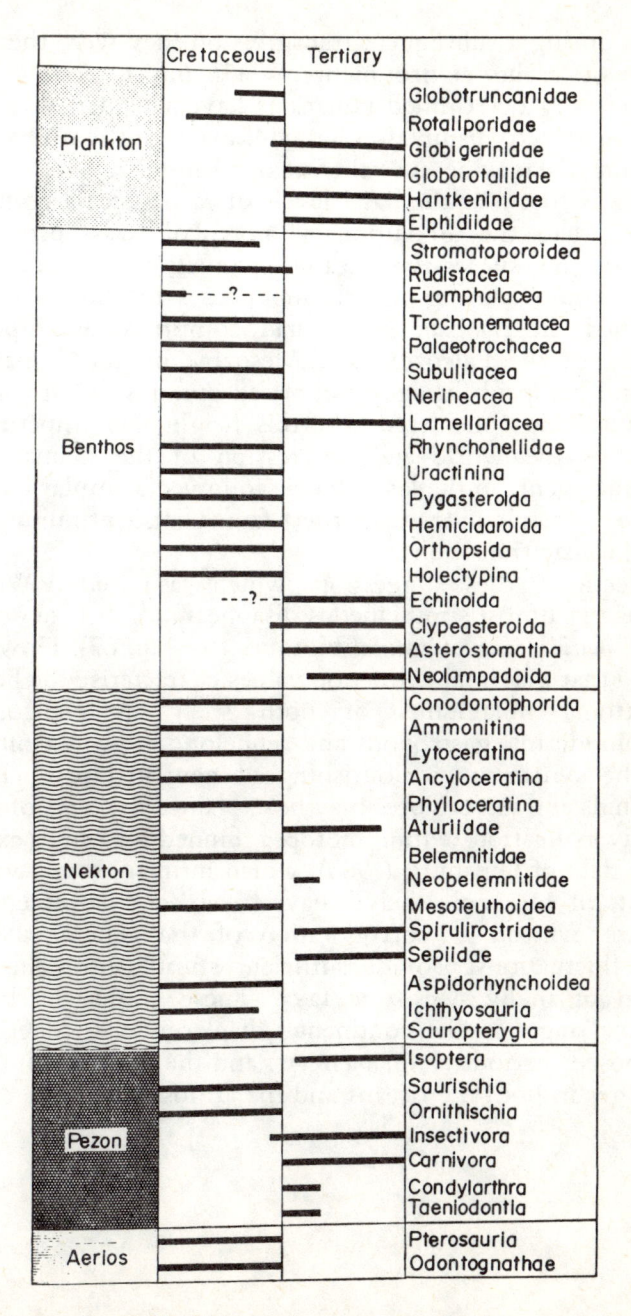

	Cretaceous	Tertiary	
Plankton	▬▬▬▬	▬▬▬▬▬▬	Globotruncanidae
	▬▬▬ -?- - -	▬▬▬▬▬▬	Rotaliporidae
		▬▬▬▬▬▬	Globigerinidae
		▬▬▬▬▬▬	Globorotaliidae
		▬▬▬▬▬▬	Hantkeninidae
		▬▬▬▬▬▬	Elphidiidae
Benthos	▬▬▬▬		Stromatoporoidea
	▬▬▬▬		Rudistacea
	▬▬-?-▬		Euomphalacea
	▬▬▬▬		Trochonematacea
	▬▬▬▬		Palaeotrochacea
	▬▬▬▬		Subulitacea
	▬▬▬▬		Nerineacea
	▬▬▬▬	▬▬▬▬▬	Lamellariacea
	▬▬▬▬		Rhynchonellidae
	▬▬▬▬		Uractinina
	▬▬▬▬		Pygasteroida
	▬▬▬▬		Hemicidaroida
	▬▬▬▬		Orthopsida
	▬▬▬▬		Holectypina
	▬▬-?-▬	▬▬▬▬▬	Echinoida
		▬▬▬▬▬	Clypeasteroida
		▬▬▬▬▬	Asterostomatina
	▬▬	▬▬▬▬▬	Neolampadoida
Nekton	▬▬▬▬		Conodontophorida
	▬▬▬▬		Ammonitina
	▬▬▬▬		Lytoceratina
	▬▬▬▬		Ancyloceratina
	▬▬▬▬		Phylloceratina
	▬▬▬▬	▬▬▬▬	Aturiidae
	▬▬▬▬		Belemnitidae
		▬	Neobelemnitidae
	▬▬▬▬		Mesoteuthoidea
	▬▬▬▬	▬▬▬	Spirulirostridae
	▬▬▬▬	▬▬▬▬	Sepiidae
	▬▬▬▬		Aspidorhynchoidea
	▬▬▬▬		Ichthyosauria
	▬▬		Sauropterygia
Pezon	▬▬▬▬	▬▬▬▬	Isoptera
	▬▬▬▬		Saurischia
	▬▬▬▬		Ornithischia
	▬▬▬▬	▬▬▬▬	Insectivora
		▬▬▬▬	Carnivora
		▬▬	Condylarthra
		▬▬	Taeniodontia
Aerios	▬▬▬▬		Pterosauria
	▬▬▬		Odontognathae

Fig. 67. "Mass extinctions" of biota at the Cretaceous–Tertiary transition in terms of their biotopes (Wiedmann, 1969).

of the sea during a subsequent transgression they were then able to recolonise the earlier environments. Wiedmann suggested that such environmentally determined radiations have a tendency to weaken from disjunction to disjunction, but still manifest themselves within the individual stages because the maximal number, and variety, of the species is found at the basal levels of each successive stage. He concluded that the evolutionary potential was progressively "weakened" by successive oceanic fluctuations so that a small external stimulus during the closing phases of the Maastrichtian extinguished the *Bauplan* which had comprised as important a component of the Paleozoic and Mesozoic marine faunas as the diapsid and parapsid lineages comprised amongst Mesozoic vertebrate faunas. He considered that this heightened impetus was a reflection of the world-wide regression of the Danian oceans. Epeirogenic events in the late Triassic followed a similar course and may have precipitated the earlier faunal discontinuities at the Triassic–Jurassic transition.

An objection to these suggestions, which was raised by Wiedmann himself, is the almost simultaneous disappearance of taxa occupying almost all *marine* and *continental* biotopes (see Fig. 67). However, he concluded that maximal extinction values characterise the benthonic and nektonic inhabitants of both shelf and epicontinental seas—echinoderms, gastropods and cephalopods. As Valentine suggested, the synchronous flourishing of new groups such as the globigerinids and insectivores may be explained in terms of invasion of, and diversification within, biotopes thinned by a high extinction rate. The data of Ginsburg (1965), which intimate that a variety of inhabitants of Mesozoic shelves have survived at continental margins, were evinced as corroboration of the general thesis that sea-level fluctuations provide sufficient stimulus for the gradual extinction of many Mesozoic taxa. These could clearly reflect progressive stages in the continental displacements, together with superimposed, periodical solar effects, and the concomitant circulation changes in both the oceans and the atmosphere.

8
The Tertiary Period

1 INTRODUCTION

The boundary between the Mesozoic and Cenozoic eras has long had an especial place in the lay imagination. This is epitomised by the disappearance of the dinosaurs and the factors that perhaps led to this faunal change have been discussed by many authors. Vegetational and climatic changes in association with the early phases of an orogeny have often taken pride of place in such discussions. The vegetation changes may themselves, of course, reflect climatic variations in Aptian and Albian times. However the actual extinctions were rarely sudden and, as shown for ammonoids in Chapter 7, many lineages exhibit a "decline" for long periods prior to their disappearance. Nevertheless the parapsid stocks had become extinct by the end of the Cretaceous and the diapsid ones had been reduced to a number which is more closely comparable with that today than with those of earlier Mesozoic time. These events necessarily left immense numbers of ecological niches unoccupied and explain the widespread tachytelic phases that characterise the mammals during the early Tertiary. There then arises the question of what factors led to the replacement of these early forms, and to the establishment of the faunal associations that typify the ensuing periods.

The Tertiary comprised the Paleocene, Eocene, Oligocene, Miocene and Pliocene periods and was followed by the Quaternary or Pleistocene period during which ice advances brought arctic glaciers well to the south of their present limits. During the Paleocene and Eocene rather archaic mammalian lineages were predominant. These include the carnivorous Deltatheridea; the herbivorous condylarths; the Plesiadapidae and Apatemyidae amongst the Strepsirhine Primates; and the Microchoeridae amongst the Tarsioidea. Hippomorph perissodactyls included the extinct chalicotheres and brontotheres, whilst in South America herbivorous genera gave rise to the indigenous fauna of notoungulates, litopterns and pyrotheres. In regions other than South America the present-day genera derive from lineages that began to assume forms similar to those extant today around the Oligocene and Miocene. Camels perhaps reflect an independent artiodactyl lineage that dates from the Eocene, but the Cervoidea (deer), Giraffoidea and Bovoidea, although probably originating from an Upper Eocene hypertragulid ancestry, are essentially the herbivores par excellence of the late Tertiary and Quaternary. Indeed during the Miocene and Pliocene many extinct genera, such as *Sivatherium* amongst the giraffids or *Dromomeryx* amongst the near-deer, flourished at the time that the dryopithecines were apparently adapting to changing habitats and giving rise to early hominids. Like the large cursorial ruminants and protoruminants man's evolution and pre-eminence seems to essentially reflect the changing environmental conditions that characterise post-Miocene time.

2 TERTIARY FLORAS

There are, of course, an immense number of articles in existence which list, and discuss, plant remains from these periods. Many of these papers also include considerations of the foregoing Upper Cretaceous floras, comparisons with the modern flora of the regions concerned, or discussions of the present distribution of related taxa. One may cite Chandler (1961), Chaney and Sanborn (1933), Sanborn (1935), Potbury (1935), MacGinitie (1937; 1953), Chaney and Axelrod (1959), Axelrod (1937), Szafer (1946) who gave details of the London Clay, Goshen, Comstock, La Porte, Weaverville, Florissant, Mascall, Blue Mountains, Stinking Water, Mount Eden and Krościenko floras respectively. Very wide-ranging reviews of these and other works relating to sites throughout the globe were then provided by Penny (1969) and Leopold (1969). Analogous detailed discussions of the problems associated with isotopic dating of such material were provided by Axelrod (1966), and some 40 floras were actually dated using the K-Ar method by Evernden and James (1964).

However, relatively few of the available data refer to the Paleocene, and those that do are frequently of questionable provenance. Significant faunal changes occur at the Maastrichtian–Danian transition and, wherever it is drawn, the Mesozoic–Cenozoic transition encompasses a major faunal discontinuity even if the characters of the break are incipient at earlier stages. In contrast the paleobotanical record has been widely conceived as showing few such discontinuities. Data from Bigarella and Ab'Saber (1964) and Mabesoone (1966) reveal that the climate in the Brazilian region was rather humid at the end of the Cretaceous and became drier in the early Tertiary. The typical semi-arid climate of north-eastern Brazil then appears to have been subject to oscillations from dry to more humid conditions in the period intervening between the Cretaceous–Tertiary transition and the present time. At the same time the Cretaceous climate of mid-continental North America seems, on the basis of macroscopic plant remains, to have been subtropical or warm temperate (Axelrod, 1966b). The dicotyledons were already a dominant feature of the Cretaceous floras but there is a notable decline in the number of fern remains as the Tertiary proceeds.

In his study of the Cretaceous and Tertiary floras of Colombia van der Hammen (1961) drew attention to the rise of *Monocolpites medius* pollen relative to the pollen and spores of definitive Cretaceous taxa at the Mesozoic–Cenozoic transition. He compared this with the parallel changes that had been habitually observed in relation to the climatic deteriorations of the Neogene and Quaternary. In Central Europe Krutsch (1957) had also noted that, at the same time, Normapolles were relegated to a less prominent position by the genera that dominate the Paleogene. Our knowledge of such changes is, nevertheless, in stark contrast to that epitomised by the disappearance of diapsid and parapsid genera from the world tetrapod faunas.

Macroscopic remains from widely scattered localities in the northern hemisphere suggest that, at that time, there were extensive temperate forests of *Populus*, *Platanus*, *Metasequoia* and *Ginkgo*, with elements of *Cercidiphyllum*, *Trochodendron*, *Viburnum*, *Alnus*, *Aralia* and *Vitis* extending well into the present arctic regions. In the southern hemisphere vast areas were covered by *Nothofagus* and podocarp forests that are analogous to those of New Zealand and South America. Needless to say, our relatively scanty information gives little indication of the degree of heterogeneity involved.

In contrast the Eocene fossil record gives clear evidence of the rather modern, and largely tropical to subtropical, aspect of the vegetation. In the palynological record certain major morphological groups of pollen grains, perhaps absent prior to the Tertiary, are fully evolved by the Eocene (Penny, 1969). Chaney (1947) and Axelrod (1960) summarised much of the available literature, and emphasised that a widespread tropical zone, ranging between 45–50°N and S, was probably associated with continuously moist, temperate climates extending into the present polar regions. Daley (1972), reflecting the conclusions of Reid and Chandler (1933), concluded that the London Clay flora indicated a seasonal climate which was frostless but had a rather high rainfall. The temperature was elevated but was not, perhaps, as high as the values customarily met in tropical rain forest today—this in view of the increased precipitation. He suggested that during the Oligocene the climate then became comparable with eastern margin warm temperate conditions today. If true, the occurrence of such conditions on the *western* margin of a continent presumably reflected rainfall distributed throughout the entire year and introduced by a second belt of westerlies, or moisture-bearing winds, from the Tethys. Arid conditions that are apparently necessitated by the Paris gypsum were unlikely to occur alongside the foregoing and he therefore postulated alternating pluvial and dry periods.

Like so many Tertiary floras those from the Eocene period are frequently indicative of lowland habitats but palynological studies confirm one's *a priori* expectations and demonstrate the existence of extensive upland forests. The available data have frequently been interpreted as showing that climates remained broadly zoned throughout most of the Paleogene but then subsequently diversified further with the cooling and, in certain cases, drying, of the Neogene. Early megafossils from holarctic sites indicate forests of mixed deciduous hardwoods and temperate conifers.

Numerous component genera are known and include *Acer, Carpinus, Juglans, Pterocarya, Quercus, Ulmus, Zelkova, Fagus, Nyssa, Liquidambar, Engelhardtia, Castanea, Carya, Ilex* and *Ailanthus*. Complementarily in the neotropical province the long-established common families include the Lauraceae, Leguminosae, Moraceae, Rhamnaceae, Sapindaceae, Juglandaceae, Araliaceae, Apocynaceae, Celastraceae and Palmae.

The Oligocene period is more difficult—because of its transitional character that is intermediate between the Upper Eocene and Lower Miocene. In Europe both faunal and floral evidence points to at least two major biotic provinces, the Northern and Mediterranean. The plant associations which have been reconstructed from spore and pollen analyses indicate a general decrease in Palmae and Sapotaceae, an increase in the representation of conifers, and a gradual increase in Betulaceae, Fagaceae, Juglandaceae and herbaceous genera of the Gramineae, Polygonaceae and Chenopodiaceae. However, on palynological grounds there is little or no evidence for a significant floral change until mid-Oligocene times and the boundary between the Paleogene and Neogene, the Oligocene–Miocene transition, is quite arbitrary (cf. Barbashinova, 1962). In Central Europe the floral character of the Neogene is first evident in the Rupelian or Middle Oligocene period. In Antarctica palynological studies of the Ross Sea area suggest that vegetation persisted there until the late Oligocene, when ice-rafting of clastic debris began, but the floral assemblages are much less diverse than those from early Tertiary sequences in Australia and New Zealand, and are dominated by *Nothofagus*-type pollen although that of the Proteaceae is also well represented. Among gymnosperms *Microcachrydites* and *Podosporites* are most common.

In any given area of the middle to high latitudes progressively younger Cenozoic floras tend to include fewer taxa. This has long been explained as reflecting the overall climatic deterioration of the Tertiary in which the tropical floras of the Eocene gradually gave way to an extended temperate vegetation. Neogene changes in the relative abundance of pollen types in the German brown coals include a general increase in the abundance and diversity of saccate conifer pollen, mostly attributable to the Pinaceae, and a general increase of types like the Ulmaceae, *Alnus* and *Fagus*. Analogous changes typify the Polish Miocene. The overall variations during the Miocene, Pliocene and Quaternary periods were summarised by Szafer (1946; 1961, see Fig. 68). By late Miocene times the vegetation

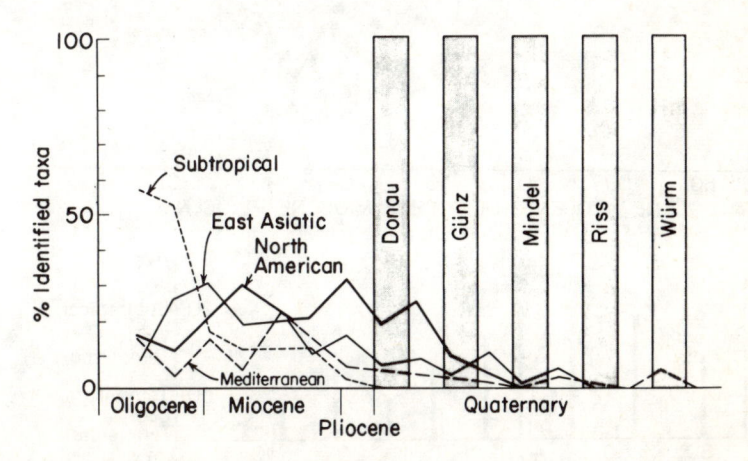

FIG. 68. Decreasing geographic elements in late Cenozoic floras of southern Poland (modified from Szafer, 1961; Leopold, 1968); the data include generic as well as specific identifications. The present distributions of the nearest living relatives of the fossils are the basis for classifying the geographic elements. (The vertical bars mark the times of European glaciations.)

of the USSR was quite definitely temperate in character (cf. Pokrovskaya, 1956; Petrov, 1963; 1967 etc.) and lacked strictly subtropical taxa. In all such areas the known floras of late Miocene origin are much less diverse than early Miocene ones (cf. Leopold, 1969), and contain fewer hardwood species. Pinaceae increase in importance whilst, on the contrary, the Podocarpaceae and Taxodiaceae, previously important, are rare. The early Miocene subtropical associations of the Black Sea region are similarly replaced by temperate hardwoods, pine forest and steppe associations. In Siberia, from the Urals to Lake Baikal, the vegetation became cool temperate in character with spruce, fir, hemlock or pine the predominant elements, and *Betula* or *Alnus* fulfilling an important role in northern regions. By the end of the Pliocene the hardwoods have disappeared from northern Siberia apart from some small relict areas.

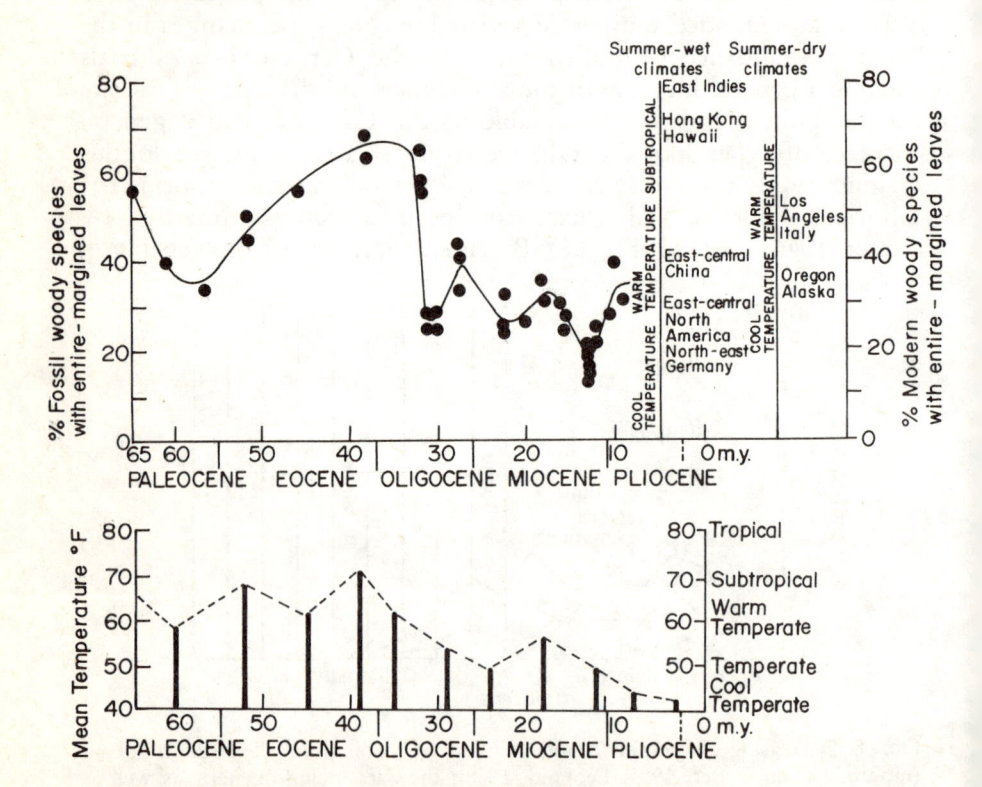

FIG. 69. Synoptic diagrams showing the climatic conclusions drawn by various paleobotanists as a result of their studies on Tertiary plant fossils (Axelrod and Bailey, 1969).

3 THEORETICAL CONSIDERATIONS OF CLIMATE

Indirect data on the world's climates during the Tertiary have, for many years, been derived from studies of biological material. A relatively recent example of such works is provided by Strauch (1968), who suggested values for the yearly extremes of temperature in the southern North Sea Basin during the Oligocene, Miocene and Pliocene, as the result of studying the shell parameters of *Hiatella arctica*. His values for the late Oligocene lay in the range 20–27°C, and for a Dutch Miocene locality 24–27°C. A summary of the available botanical conclusions was provided by Axelrod and Bailey (1969) and is represented in Fig. 69. Like many earlier workers they suggested a gradual trend towards lower annual temperatures, and an increased overall range, at least in the western USA. Comparable considerations for Australia are contained in Gill (1961). The cyclical effects noted by van der Hammen (1961) then have to be seen as superimposed upon such a general trend.

In broad terms the changes appear to have been more marked in the interior of continents than at their coastal margins, and a mid-Miocene warming in some maritime regions perhaps reflected changed relationships between land and sea. Expanding maritime conditions may have brought a temporary increase in warmth and equability. When interpreting a diatom flora from an Upper Miocene section in California Barron (1973) suggested that temperatures declined sharply in the region at that time to reach a winter minimum of 10°C. Thereafter a gradual and fluctuating rise characterised the minimal seasonal temperatures of the latest Miocene so that 17°C was approached by the early Pliocene. At such times it seems probable that south and west Africa enjoyed a wet climate which became progressively drier until, in the late Pliocene, it was not unduly dissimilar to that which is prevalent today (Gill, 1961). In New Zealand and southern South America there are complications that reflect local orogenies but again various data suggest a warmer and wetter régime.

Periodic variations in the Pliocene climatic characteristics of Europe emerged from the palynological work of Zagwijn (1960). Different data lead to similar conclusions elsewhere. The Miocene and Pliocene climatic and glacial history of Antarctica was summarised by Blank and Margolis (1975) who were of the opinion that the development of ice shelves during the Middle to late Gilbert time may mark the initiation of extensive, late Cenozoic, Antarctic glaciation. Fluctuating quantities of ice-rafted quartz grains, which are contained in sediments of Pliocene age, are indications of the probable oscillations of this glaciation which continued through the Quaternary until today.

Mesolella *et al.* (1969) emphasised that for earlier periods such as the Eocene, when global ice accumulations were restricted, it is far less likely that one will obtain any direct evidence of fluctuating ice budgets in the form of interbedded glacial and non-glacial deposits. They felt that the most probable evidence is likely to be cyclical deposition of sediments comparable with those recorded by Bradley (1929) who interpreted his data in terms of a climatic oscillation that approximated in duration to the precession cycle of 21,000 years.

Changes in average relief would, of course, have made influential contributions to climatic variation. Hallam (1963) contended that the world's surface has undergone a progressive increase in relief since the end of the Cretaceous as it has been exposed to a series of epeirogenic movements of opposing sense in the oceans and on the continents. He attributed the discernible transgressions and regressions in the Tertiary record to successive, eustatic rises and falls of the ocean levels. These, he thought, were consequential upon changes in the cubic capacity of the extant oceanic basins. A gradual overall regression of the seas, that resulted from oceanic subsidence, was seen as being superimposed upon these fluctuating transgressions and regressions which he summarised as:

a. Upper Cretaceous—a time of extensive transgression which is often regarded as beginning in the Cenomanian but perhaps started in the Albian or even earlier times;
b. Lower Paleocene—a period in which the seas were rather restricted but in which local Danian and Montian transgressions are evident;
c. Upper Paleocene—with both a transgression and a subsequent regression;
d. Lower Eocene—generally transgressive;
e. Middle Eocene—major world-wide transgression;
f. Upper Eocene—regressive in global terms;
g. Lower Oligocene—some evidence of a transgression;
h. Middle Oligocene—a minor regression followed by a transgression in the European and Caribbean regions;
i. Upper Oligocene—a general and comparatively sudden retreat of the epicontinental seas.

He thought that, broadly speaking, the seas have never subsequently extended as far as they did in the Lower Tertiary, although an important transgression did occur in the Lower Miocene. This was then followed by a general withdrawal of the oceans from the continents that was only interrupted by rather minor transgressions.

Local effects can, of course, be of paramount importance in particular areas. Colquhoun and Johnson (1968) concluded that in South Carolina a rise in sea level during the Cretaceous led to relatively stable conditions throughout the early phases of the Tertiary. A fall in the pre-Claiborne, and a rise in the Claiborne, were followed by relative stability in the late Eocene, Oligocene and early, or possibly, Middle Miocene. There was also evidence of a change from warm pre-Oligocene waters to cooler ones during the Oligocene–Middle Miocene interval, and a fall in the sea level was then followed by a rise to at least 190 ft O.D. in the warm climate of the late Miocene.

More recently Frakes and Kemp (1972) attempted to derive a semi-quantitative model of global climates in the Paleocene, the later half of the Eocene, and the earlier part of the Oligocene (30–37 m.y.), which they considered was an interval of very marked climatic change. Using available oxygen isotope data (see further in section 4 below) they calculated warming rates for the probable oceanic currents. The Paleocene isotherms which they deduced intimated that there were interrelationships between evaporation and precipitation. Evaporation was possibly maximal in those areas where warm oceanic segments came into contact with colder air. In their models they followed Lamb's (1961) suggestion that, on an ice-free globe, the trade winds would be expanded polewards at the expense of high-latitude westerlies. Monsoon conditions were then assumed to have existed on those coastal regions that both faced the equator and were within the range of the seasonally varying inter-tropical convergence zone. Like so many before them they took the innumerable records of fossil plants and climatically significant rock types as corroboration of the prevalence of warm, wet climates in high latitudes.

Circulation patterns during Oligocene times were then assumed to differ from those in the intervening Eocene as a result of the initial segmentation of the Indo-Pacific and the northward movement of Australo-New Guinea. Furthermore, as South America was by then detached from Antarctica, a circumpolar current encircled the globe in the southern oceans. In their construct an important climatic effect of the supposed cooling of Oligocene waters was a restriction of the high latitude wet belts to latitudes below 60°. The greater warmth of high latitude regions during the Eocene could be at least partially explained by the long periods which surface water would have to spend in equatorial regions. Frakes and Kemp envisaged that equatorial transport in the oceanic gyrals of the Pacific became rather more restricted in the Oligocene and colder surface waters in high latitudes, then led to lowered evaporation, decreased precipitation and cooler air temperatures.

4 ISOTOPE DATA ON TERTIARY MARINE PALEOTEMPERATURES

Various authors have demonstrated that, except in the highest latitudes of the North Atlantic and in the Arctic Ocean, the deep, oceanic bottom waters originate at the surface along the coast of Antarctica (see Savin et al., 1975). Emiliani (1954) recognised that paleotemperature measurements of material formed on the deep sea floor could thus yield a close approximation to the coldest temperature to which contemporaneous surface waters were exposed. He further intimated that the thermal inertia of the mass of deep-sea ocean waters might be expected to modulate short-term climatic shifts and thereby enhance the possibility of our detecting long-term trends. Once these have been determined short-term phenomena become of interest—particularly the possible existence of records reflecting cyclical variations. He reported bottom temperatures of c. 10·5°C for the Middle Oligocene; c. 7·0°C for the early Miocene; and c. 2·2°C for the latest Pliocene; thus providing a non-biological documentation of the climatic deterioration during the later Tertiary. These early studies were then followed by those of Dorf (1964), Devereux (1967), Dorman (1966), Wolfe and Hopkins (1967) and Tanai and Huzioka (1967) which dealt with Europe, New Zealand, Australia, the USA and Japan respectively.

Oxygen isotope determinations from deep-sea drilling projects now provide an even more effective, general picture of low latitude, marine temperatures during the period intervening between the Maastrichtian and the present (Figs 70 and 71). The rather sparse late Cretaceous analyses indicate that, at that time, the high-latitude surface waters were warm and did not fall much below 10–20°C, even at the coldest season. Prior to the beginning of Middle Miocene times the high- and low-latitude temperatures then seem to have changed in parallel (Savin et al., 1975). Following an apparently small and short-lived drop in temperature close to the Cretaceous–Tertiary boundary, temperatures remained warm and relatively constant through the Paleocene, and up to mid-Eocene time when bottom temperatures seem to have been of the order of 12°C. A sharp drop in temperature during the Upper Eocene was then followed by a rather more gradual lowering that culminated in late Oligocene high-latitude minima of around 4°C. A subsequent rise during the early

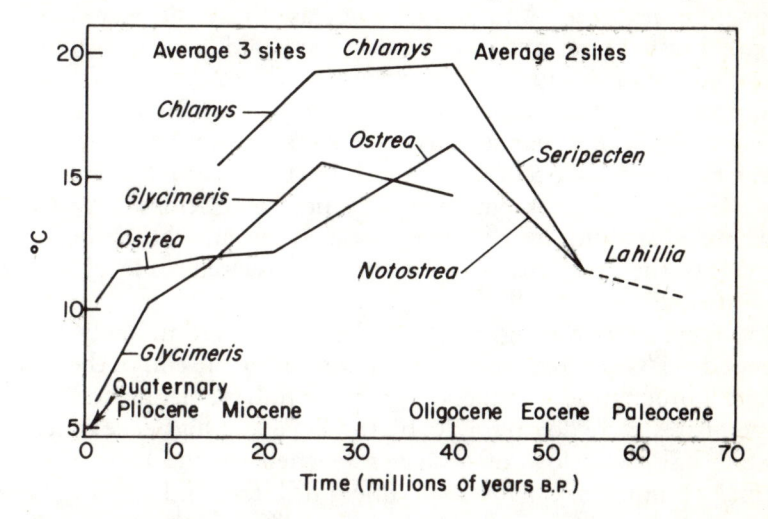

Fig. 70. Temperature distributions through the Tertiary in Australia (Bowen, 1966, after Dorman and Gill, 1959).

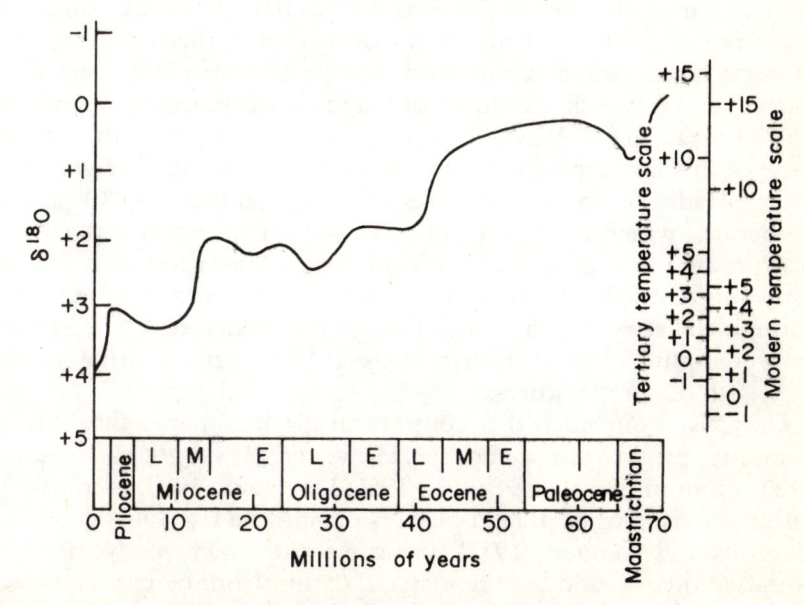

Fig. 71. Isotopic temperatures determined from deep-sea drilling projects (Savin *et al.*, 1975). (By courtesy of the Geological Society of America.)

Miocene was followed, in the Middle Miocene, by a divergence of the trends in high and low latitudes. The high-latitude values dropped dramatically, perhaps in concert with the initiation of a major glaciation in Antarctica, whereas those of low latitudes remained rather constant and possibly increased. This uncoupling of the trends was suggested by Savin *et al.* to be related to the establishment of the circum-Antarctic circulation. Bandy (1968a, b) certainly concluded that the first major expansion of polar foraminiferal associations occurred around $10–11 \times 10^6$ B.P.—during the later Miocene. There seem to be definite correlations between the expanded distributions of these associations and both the glacial intervals of the Quaternary and periods of lowered sea level since the late Miocene.

Cooling effects during much of the Eocene are unlikely to have exceeded $0.1°C$ per 1 m.y., but some time after the end of the Middle Eocene a much more rapid cooling seems to have begun and bottom temperatures were down to 7°C by the Eocene–Oligocene transition. As stated above a low of 4°C was reached by the late Oligocene thermal minimum. From this time until the end of the Lower Miocene such temperatures rose by about 3°C and the most dramatic cooling then occurred after the Middle Miocene. During a period of some 2–3 m.y. the temperatures appear to have fallen by about 3°C or at a rate of $1.0°C$ per 1 m.y. Little overt change then occurred until Pliocene times, when the derived isotope temperatures again drop sharply, and it was this decline that led to the deep oceanic conditions which prevail today. However, it has to be borne in mind that at least some of this last apparent decline in temperature, together with that in the Middle Miocene, may reflect a change in the $^{18}O/^{16}O$ ratio of the oceans, which resulted from increased quantities of water being incorporated into growing continental ice caps, rather than a direct temperature effect. Although the available data do not permit us to distinguish between such possibilities (see Shackleton, 1967), Savin *et al.* were quite clear that there was a 10°C net lowering of the high-latitude temperatures.

They also concluded that continental glaciation was absent from Antarctica prior to the late Eocene. However, the Oligocene temperature minimum (see also Dorman, 1966; Devereux, 1967) is consistent with the existence of upland glaciers during the late Oligocene, and Margolis and Kennett (1971), using electron microscopy, detected ice-rafted quartz sand in core material dating from before the Lower Miocene. They concluded that both this, and the low planktonic foraminiferal diversity, were associated with periodic, major cooling phases of the southern ocean during the early Eocene, late Middle Eocene and early Oligocene. Increased species diversity, the presence of re-worked sand grains, and the absence of definitive ice-rafted sand, were, they thought, indicative of a warming trend in the late Miocene. They were, nevertheless, of the opinion that glaciation may have persisted within the Antarctic region for much of the Cenozoic. In contrast, Savin *et al.* considered that values of 4°C for the temperature of the bottom waters were too warm for this to have been possible and preclude the development of either major sea-level ice-cover or the formation of sea ice itself.

Kennett *et al.* (1971) established a paleomagnetic chronology for the Pliocene and early Pleistocene sediments in New Zealand within which major temperature fluctuations are detectable from the Upper Gauss (Mid-Pliocene) to the Middle Matuyama (early Pleistocene). They concluded that the first observed cooling in the austral seas spans the Gauss–Matuyama boundary and that pronounced cold phases occur in the Middle Pliocene Waipipian, the late Pliocene Mangapanian, and the early Pleistocene Lower Hautawan stages. These authors were amongst the first to explicitly suggest a relationship between paleoclimatic and paleomagnetic changes on the grounds that cooling trends commonly become apparent at, or shortly after, geomagnetic polarity changes, e.g. at the end of the *Kaena* event (2·8 m.y. ago); near the base of the *Reunion* event (1·98 m.y.) and near the base of the *Gilsa* (=*Olduvai*, 1·79 m.y.). Cooling maxima also coincide with magnetic reversals at the Gauss–Matuyama transition, *c.* 2·43 m.y. ago, and climatic changes have been detected at, or close to, 6 of the 8 late Neogene polarity changes (cf. Heirtzler, 1968; Kennett and Watkins, 1970; and Chapter 9 below).

Various biological data corroborate the generalised conclusions about temperature changes. Data from 59 Antarctic piston cores that date from the Middle Gauss suggest that *Spongopyle osculosus*, *Cenosphaera nagata*, *Chromyechinus antarctica*, *Stylatractus neptunus*, *Diploplegma banzare*, *Prunopyle titan* and *Desmospyris spongiosa* have persistently required water that is slightly warmer than that in the Ross Sea. Their occurrence at intervals in the cores has therefore been used as a paleoclimatic indicator (Fleming, 1973), and the resulting curves suggest that the early Gauss was warmer than the late Gauss, the Matuyama and the Brunhes. Warm and cold periods during the Matuyama and Brunhes seem to have been of equal amplitude, and temperatures since the Middle Gauss never seem to have exceeded those of today by more than 3°C.

Additional interesting data have been obtained in the Caribbean region. Analysis of a piston core that had been taken from the eastern edge of the Blake Plateau revealed increasing "sediment starvation" and sorting, together with increasing ocean surface temperatures beginning at 5·7 m.y. ago (Emiliani *et al.*, 1972). This could result from three principal causes: uplift of the plateau; an increased strength of oceanic circulation in association with the development of glaciation in Antarctica; or, more probably, the closing of the communication between the Atlantic and Pacific oceans across Central America. The Central American passage, broad during the early Miocene, became progressively narrower during the later Miocene and was finally interrupted by early Pliocene times (Lloyd, 1963). This restricted the Gulf Loop Current to the Straits of Florida and accelerated current flow.

Today the surface water on the two sides of the isthmus is of generally similar temperature (26–28°C) but exhibits a salinity difference of 2–3 per million, or more. Removal of the isthmus would lead at least part of the Pacific counter current ($26 \cdot 10^6$ m^3 s^{-1}) into the Caribbean, and at least part of the more saline Caribbean current would flow into the Pacific. Because of the salinity difference the deep colder Pacific water would cross into the Caribbean riding over the counterflow of warmer more saline Atlantic water. As a result of this a situation comparable with that at the Straits of Gibraltar would be established, with the major difference being a vastly increased water transport. Under the conditions of the Miocene the bi-directional flow would probably have been less but still significant. Colder, less saline, Pacific water would enter the Caribbean region and flow north-eastward off the eastern border of North America. Studies on Ostracoda, Foraminifera and Mollusca from Virginia and North Carolina (Gibson, 1967) complement isotopic temperature determinations and confirm that lower surface water temperatures did exist at that time.

In contrast Asano *et al.* (1974) drew attention to two distinct biological assemblages in the late Neogene of Japan. A tropical-subtropical one typified the eastern side, and a cool temperate one the western. These, they concluded, suggest that the Pacific current systems in the area were comparable with the extant ones, although on the Japan Sea side the cool water forms were more significant during the late Neogene than they are today.

Various authors have detected short-term cyclical effects that must be seen as superimposed upon the gross, climatic trends. Fluctuations during Middle Eocene times appear to have been slight, but data derived from very closely spaced early Miocene samples exhibit some more prominent variations, and these would have been missed if the spacing used for many Eocene samples had been used. Isotopic analyses of *Globoquadrina altispira* from one core demonstrated a total variation of *c*. 1 per million over a period of some 3 m.y., and periodicities of several hundred thousand years also emerge (cf. Savin *et al.*, 1975). Analyses of *Spherodinellopsis seminulina* provide data that seem to exhibit parallel variations. Less data are available for the Middle Miocene but those that do exist intimate analogous periodicities.

5 NEOGENE PLANKTONIC BIOSTRATIGRAPHY

The last decade has seen the development of an immense interest in the zonation of marine cores obtained from both the equatorial and polar regions; its relation to a radiometric time scale; and its relation to global polarity reversals. An excellent summary of such work was provided by Berggren and Couvering (1974) whose paper contains a wealth of relevant references. Various other articles evaluate the available radiometric data (e.g. Evernden *et al.*, 1964; Funnell, 1964; Bodelle *et al.*, 1969; Evernden and Evernden, 1970; Turner, 1970; Couvering, 1972; Gill and McDougall, 1973; and McDougall and Page, 1974). Foster and Opdyke (1970) extended the paleomagnetic record back beyond 5 m.y. and erected a late Miocene sequence of seven paleomagnetic epochs (numbers 5–11), with the bottom one correlated with sea-floor spreading anomaly 5 at 9·5 m.y. Relationships between the entire geomagnetic polarity time scale and various faunal and floral datum levels were demonstrated by Opdyke *et al.* (1966), Berggren *et al.* (1967), Hays *et al.* (1969), Hays and Berggren (1971), Berggren (1972), Burckle (1972), etc. A synthesis of such data with continental mammalian stratigraphies was then subsequently provided by Berggren and Couvering (1974).

From 0–5 m.y. B.P., the polarity time scale is based upon that of Cox (1969) and the biostratigraphical calibration is thought to have a high degree of reliability. Data on the Pliocene–Pleistocene boundary are varied and widespread and Stipp *et al.* (1967) dated it at 2·5 m.y. on the West coast of the Auckland region. The various correlations within the earlier 10 m.y. are more tentative. In correlating paleomagnetic epochs 6–11 with the magnetic anomaly patterns Foster and Opdyke (1970), together with Opdyke (1972), relied upon a correlation of paleomagnetic epoch 11 with magnetic anomaly 5. According to Talwani *et al.* (1971) the limits of this last-named anomaly are 8·71 and 9·94 m.y. An alternative interpretation would expand the paleomagnetic epochs and displace them downwards (Dreyfus and Ryan, see Berggren and Couvering, 1974) relative to the magnetic anomaly pattern so that epoch 9, rather than epoch 11, corresponds to anomaly 5.

Miocene and Pliocene chronostratigraphical terminology has been subject to much controversy. In particular, in marine deposits the problem of the transition between these two periods has suffered from the widespread regression that occurred in the Mediterranean region (Berggren and Couvering, 1974). First evident in the Caspian Sea and in the Vienna Basin of the Paratethys north of the Alpine–Dinaride–Tauride orogenic belt in the east, it was influential several million years later in the oceanic basin of the western Tethys (cf Couvering and Miller, 1971). Ultimately the western Tethys was cut off from the Atlantic and a series of gypsum anhydrite beds, which alternate with marine fossils, was laid down over large areas of the basin. This gives a complex stratigraphy, and complex geographical relationships between marine and non-marine areas. Many of the terms that have been used to denote periods of time may therefore reflect little more than local depositional effects.

The age of the Miocene–Pliocene boundary has been variously estimated to be as young as 2·7–3·0 m.y. (Bandy and Casey, 1969; Bandy, 1968; 1971; Bandy *et al.*, 1971; 1972), or as old as 15 m.y. (Trevisan, 1958). Vertebrate paleontologists classically ascribed to it an age of 10–12 m.y. Recent determinations within the marine succession of the Mediterranean basin support a date that is younger than 6 m.y. but older than 4·5 m.y. (Couvering, 1972; Selli, 1970; Hays *et al.*, 1969), and a date of 5 m.y. was indeed suggested by Berggren (1969; 1972; 1973), Cita (1973; 1974), Gill and McDougall (1973) and Saito *et al.* (1974).

In deep-water deposits the *Sphaeroidinella dehiscens dehiscens* datum is selected as the Miocene–Pliocene boundary and it was dated by Berggren and Amdurer (1973) and Saito *et al.* (1974) at c. 4–8 m.y. This level is at the upper limit of the *Globoquadrina dehiscens dehiscens* assemblage and at the base of the *S. dehiscens dehiscens* and *Globorotalia truncatulinoides* section. *Pullieniatina obliquiloculata*, which is relatively rare in the upper part of the Miocene, becomes both abundant and predominantly sinistrally coiled above the datum. There is then an abrupt reversal to dextral coiling which persists for the remainder of its range in time.

The pioneering investigations of Riedel (1957) and Riedel and Funnell (1964) laid the basis for a radiolarian zonation of Neogene

TABLE 11

Antarctic–subantarctic radiolarian zonation (after Berggren and Couvering, 1974)

Radiolarian zone after Hays, Opdyke etc. loc. cit.	Age according to Paleomagnetic time scale m.y. B.P.	Subdivision by Bandy et al. (1971)
ω		a. Modern *Spongoplema antarcticum* complex plus warm water *Theoconus zancleus*
		b. Modern *Spongoplema antarcticum* complex lacking warm water forms
	0·4	
ψ		*Acanthosphaera* group (Middle Brunhes)
	0·7	
χ		*Saturnulus planetes* and *Pterocanium trilobum* (Upper Matuyama boundary)
	1·8	
φ		*Eucyrtidium calvertense* (Gilsa event)
	2·4	
		a. *Desmospyris spongiosa* and *Helotholus vema* (Lower Matuyama)
	2·7	
		b. *Prunopyle titan* and *Lychnocanium grande* (Upper Gauss)
ν	3·4	
		c. Oroscena (digitate) and *Oroscene carolae* (Upper Gilbert)
	3·6	
		d. *Cyrtocapsella tetrapera* and *Theocyrtis redondoensis* (Upper Gilbert)
	4·2	
		a. *Triceraspyris* sp. (Gilbert b)
τ	4·5	
		b. *Ommatocampe hughesi* and *Cannartiscus marylandicus*

sediments in the equatorial Pacific. Radiolarian zonations for Antarctic regions figure in Hays (1965), or Hays and Opdyke (1967), and high-latitude schemes based upon Foraminifera were formulated for the Pliocene of New Zealand by Jenkins (1971) and Kennett et al. (1971). The general radiolarian scheme as modified by Bandy et al. (1971) is contained in Table 11.

These data can be compared with the probable ages of various other boundary definitions. That between the Serravallian and Tortonian, Middle and Upper Miocene, is between 10·5–10·7 m.y. B.P. In the Mediterranean region the initiation of relatively cool summers in temperate areas (early Turolian) lies around 10 m.y. The Messinian–Zanclian or Miocene–Pliocene transition is at c. 5·0 m.y., and the Zanclian–Piacenzian, or early to late Pliocene, is at c. 3·3 m.y. The base of the Calabrian has been widely ascribed an age of 1·6–1·8 m.y. Microtine rodents appear in south-west Europe during the mid-Ruscinian, about 4 m.y. ago, and Elephantidae appear in the early Villafranchian at c. 2·5 m.y. ago.

The reduction in the time scale which encompasses the period from the Miocene to the Quaternary, coupled with the demonstration that the climatic changes which led to the Quaternary were *initiated* in the Miocene, renews the speculation that man's evolution was a result of these environmental changes. There seems little doubt that the evolution of bipedal, ground-living hominids took place prior to the Quaternary, but the demonstration of climatic deterioration in the late Tertiary sustains the arguments previously applied to the evolution of man in the early Quaternary.

9
The Quaternary Succession

1 INTRODUCTION

The Quaternary period must be pre-eminent in any discussion of the evolution of modern faunas. During its early phases a number of rather archaic genera still continued to flourish—only to become extinct in more recent times. For example, amongst the mastodon lineage both trilophodont and tetralophodont genera were still extant, although the stegomastodons were already in existence, as were elephantids. These, like the members of many other orders, then exhibit a sequence of genera in successive interglacials. It is only during the last decade that the part played by man, and *Pleistocene Overkill*, in the extinction of many such genera has been fully appreciated.

This contribution of man to the extermination of species may well date back to his earliest tool-using existence. *Homo erectus* remains are associated with both implements and giant antelope remains in Africa, and the disappearance of the North American megafauna coincides with the invasion of that continent by proto-amerindians. Although some considerable controversy must still surround the relative parts played by man and climate in such extinctions, one may reasonably assume that any trend towards extinction that was caused by climatic change would be greatly enhanced by man's activities. As Martin has pointed out, it is indeed significant that the chances of extinction were maximised by large body size, and it was this, amongst other things, that led him to postulate an early *Overkill*, which was analogous to the extinction of birds like the Moa and Dodo in more recent time (see Table 12).

2 THE PERIOD INVOLVED

Numerous papers have been produced on the world Quaternary

TABLE 12

Examples of the extinction of large African mammals. Where an extant genus is cited the reference is to an extinct species (cf. Martin and Wright, 1967; Boughey, 1975)

Order	Villafranchian and Early Middle Pleistocene (1·0–2·0 m.y.)	Late Middle Pleistocene extinction (last 100,000 years)
Primates	*Gorgopithecus* *Dinopithecus* *Cercopithecoides* *Australopithecus* *Paranthropus* *Telanthropus* *Parapapio*	*Simopithecus*
Carnivora	*Lycyaena* *Meganteron* *Homotherium*	*Machairodus*
Proboscidea	*Anancus* *Stegodon* *Deinotherium*	*Archidiskodon* *Gomphotherium*
Perissodactyla	*Metaschizogherium* *Serengeticeros*	*Stylohipparion* *Eurygnathohippus*
Artiodactyla (Suidae)	*Potamochoerops* *Omochoerus*	*Potamochoeroides* *Mesochoerus* *Notochoerus* *Tapinochoerus* *Stylochoerus* *Metridiochoerus* "*Kolpochoerus*" *Orthostonyx*
Camelidae		*Camelus*
Cervidae		*Megaceroides*
Giraffidae		*Libytherium*
Bovidae	*Pultiphagonides* *Numidocapra* *Megalotragus* *Makapania* *Phenacotragus*	*Homoioceras* *Bularchus* *Pelorovis* *Lunatoceras* *Syncerus* *Cephalophus* *Kobus* *Redunca* *Hippotragus*

		Oryx
		Addax
		Damaliscus
		Alcelaphus
		Beatragus
		Connochaetus
		Aepyceros
		Litocranius
		Gazella
		Capra
		Ammotragus
Total	22	37

deposits since Penck and Brückner (1909) first enunciated their five glacial stages on the basis of alpine geomorphology. Their glacial stages, the Donau, Gunz, Mindel, Riss and Würm, formed a complex series in which the Donau, for example, included three cool stadia that were separated by warmer interstadia. Dutch workers were subsequently able to demonstrate a comparable series of glacial and interglacial deposits in Holland in the absence of widespread surface phenomena of glacial origin. These Dutch deposits were summarised at different times by van der Vlerk and Florschutz (1950), Pannekoek et al. (1956), van der Vlerk (1959) and Zagwijn (1957; 1960). They eventually provided a sequence representing some six major phases of climatic deterioration that were initially all referred to as glacial periods although, in recent years, there has been a growing tendency to acknowledge that the earlier ones were merely cool and that it is the last 4 that are perhaps representative of definitive glaciation. Such papers led to a widespread flowering of analogous studies all over the globe. Wide-ranging reviews of the British succession were provided by West (1968; 1970) and Stuart (1974), information on North America is contained in Flint's books, whilst a global synthesis is presented in works such as Rankama (1967) and John (1977).

It was implicit in the last chapter that workers using different criteria have ascribed varying dates to the Pliocene–Pleistocene boundary. The international congress of 1949 defined the boundary at the base of the Upper Villafranchian phase of the Mediterranean series and Pliocene–Pleistocene boundary faunas in central and western Europe were summarised by Tobien (1970). The late Villafranchian faunas of Italy figure in Azzaroli and Ambrosetti (1970), the Tiraspol complex in Gromov (1970) and its Siberian equivalent in Vangengeim and Sher (1970). Overall synoptic pictures are also provided by Kurten (1971) and the boundary in marine

sediments was epitomised by Ericson *et al.* (1963) and Riedel *et al.* (1963) in the following terms:
1. Extinction of discoasters.
2. A change in the predominant coiling direction of the planktonic foraminiferan aggregation *Globotoralia menardii* from 95 per cent dextral, at lower levels, to 95 per cent sinistral above.
3. A reduction in the *G. menardii* aggregate to a single fairly uniform group above the boundary.
4. An increase in the thecal diameter of *G. menardii* above the boundary.
5. The appearance of *G. truncatulinoides* in abundance above the boundary.
6. The disappearance of *G. triloba sacculifera* (*G. fistulosa auctt*) at the boundary.

Emiliani *et al.* (1961) suggested that in southern Italy the general cooling trend across this boundary was from an average summer surface-water temperature of 23–25°C to one of 15°C.

Once again the marine sequence actually contains features that are not easily correlated and expressed as a single chronology. As a result of this no single correlative system is universally acceptable and, in particular, the relationships of continental glacial episodes to the cycles that are discernible in deep-sea sediments remain controversial. Much of such controversy reflects the characteristics of the material surveyed. Terrestrial records of glacial events are, by their very nature, essentially discontinuous, disparate and discordant, although exceptions to this statement would be lacustrine sequences, and continuous, stratified loess deposits. In contrast, marine sequences are essentially continuous and frequently provide very sensitive records of relatively minor climatic variations.

The basic glacial–deglacial cycles each involve a series of minor cycles during which there was a gradual overall deterioration of climate lasting up to 90,000 years. These are offset in the deglacial phase by sharp rises of climate, that are reflected by rapid ice-melt and can be accomplished in rather less than one tenth of the time. This gives the saw-toothed curves of Broecker and Donk (1970). The underlying curve is therefore yet again the summated effect of numerous, perhaps irregular, secondary, tertiary or quaternary oscillations. The application of ^{14}C dating to widely separated deposits enables the most recent ones to be correlated with an inaccuracy of only a few hundred years (cf. Flint, 1971). Although the earlier ones are much more difficult to interrelate the overall pattern is clear, and it is known that a definite correlation exists between the cooling effects and paleomagnetic events.

Berggren and Couvering (1974) suggested that major continental glaciation was perhaps initiated in European sub-polar regions at 0·6 m.y. B.P.—at the end of the Biharian. This event they equate with the Mindel glaciation of the classical sequence. Extensive montane glaciation preceded this by, perhaps, a million years. Clark (1971) certainly concluded that the Arctic Ocean has been continuously frozen at least since the Middle Pliocene, and that, since that time, the most significant changes have involved the thickness of the ice-cover. There are at least two abundance peaks of Foraminifera in the Brunhes interval, one representing conditions in the uppermost part of the cores and the other lying near to the Brunhes–Matuyama boundary. As studies of Pliocene cores suggest that foraminiferans have never been more abundant in the Arctic than they are today, the extant ice-cover has been taken as the warmest conditions that are necessary to explain the older peaks. However, such peaks show no easy correlation with the classical, continental, glacial stages, and continental glaciers presumably advanced and retreated whilst the Arctic ice-cover remained relatively stable.

Some difficulties also attend attempted synonymies between events in the North Pacific and North Atlantic arenas (cf. Connolly and Ewing, 1970; Kent *et al.*, 1971; Briskin and Berggren, 1975) but, by analogy with present ice limits, the expansion of iceberg limits in the Pacific could have been slower than in the North Atlantic (cf. Berggren and Couvering, 1974). Transported glacial debris appears in North Pacific cores around 2·5 m.y. B.P. In both oceanic arenas renewed climatic deterioration occurred at about 1·3–1·2 m.y. B.P., and then at 0·9 and 0·8 m.y. in the North Pacific and North Atlantic respectively. Smaller amplitude peaks of ice-rafted material occur at 1·2, 1·1 and 0·95 m.y. in the North Pacific, with parallel temperature minima detectable in the North Atlantic. Ice rafting in the Pacific around 0·85–0·75 m.y. B.P. may correspond to a cooling trend around 0·8 m.y. in Atlantic cores.

Kent *et al.* (1971) concluded that at least 11 periods of ice-rafting are detectable in cores representing the last 1·2 m.y., whereas only 4 could be identified in the period 1·2–2·5 m.y. B.P. Their studies of detritus indicated a cooling phase that began around 1·2 m.y. B.P. and became very intense between the Jaramillo event and the Brunhes–Matuyama boundary. At least six zones of ice-rafted debris occur in the Brunhes normal polarity series and correlations with carbonate fluctuations of the central Pacific are good. There was evidence for a very well-marked interglacial period between

0·53–0·46 m.y. B.P. Erosional disconformities in the deep oceanic basins, that were created by a general increase in the velocities of Antarctic bottom water, also demonstrate major pulses during the Brunhes epoch (0·69 m.y. to the present) and during part of the Matuyama epoch of 2·43–0·69 m.y. (see Kennett and Watkins, 1976).

It is quite clear from all such data that the overall cooling trend of the later Tertiary ultimately culminated in the extreme climatic oscillations of the Quaternary—whose total duration only corresponds to that of one of the minor oscillations in van der Hammen's data for the Cretaceous and early Tertiary. The dates ascribed to this Quaternary climatic nadir vary from Emiliani's suggestion of 0·6 m.y. B.P., to other values of 3·5–4·0 m.y. B.P. for the age of the earliest Villafranchian faunas. However, these last are generally agreed to date from the Pliocene and, if the Calabrian is taken as the basal Pleistocene level, this gives an overall period of $c.$ 1·8 m.y. (Berggren *et al.*, 1967; Glass *et al.*, 1967; Berggren, 1968; Briskin and Berggren, 1974). The successive cyclical variations that are indicated by oxygen isotope determinations appear to have a periodicity of $c.$ 100,000 years and have been numbered so that each warm half-cycle has an odd number and each cold one an even one. Their incorporation into an absolute chronology was discussed by Rosholt *et al.* (1961) using the ^{231}Pa/^{230}Th method. Broecker and Donk (1970) reviewed all such contributions to chronology and suggested that, beyond the range of ^{14}C dating, Emiliani's original chronology should be expanded by 25 per cent. Hence the age of 295,000 years that he put forward for the U/V boundary of Ericson *et al.* would become $c.$ 400,000 years. Briskin and Berggren (1974) actually date this particular level at $c.$ 430,000 years and oxygen isotope determinations on Pacific cores confirm this (Shackleton and Opdyke, 1973). On *a priori* grounds such a correction might be expected to increase in magnitude as one proceeds further back in time and Hays and Berggren (1971) did provide evidence that Emiliani's chronology may need a correction of 2 below the Brunhes–Matuyama transition.

As an overall synthesis Berggren and Couvering (1974) suggested the following:

1. Early Blancan cold climate = Pretiglian of Holland: begins $c.$ 2·5–3 m.y. B.P.
2. Blancan warm climate = Tiglian interglacial.
3. Nebraskan = (? later) Donau = Eburonian: begins $c.$ 1·6 m.y. B.P.
4. Aftonian = Waalian interglacial.
5. Kansan = Gunz = Menapian: begins $c.$ 0·9 m.y. B.P.

6. Yarmouthian interglacial.
7. Illinoian = Mindel = Elster: begins 0·6 m.y. B.P.
8. Sangamonian = Holstein interglacial.
9. Wisconsian = Riss–Würm = Saal–Weichsel: begins 0·35 m.y. B.P.

Elsewhere in the world the conditions seem to have paralleled these. Thus in New Zealand the Gunz, Mindel and Riss glacial stages are represented by the Porikan, Waimaungan and Waimean glaciations.

In recent years some additional and exciting correlations have emerged! Zagwijn (1976) concluded that the Brunhes–Matuyama boundary (0·7 m.y. B.P.) is between middle Pleistocene interglacials I and II, and that the transition from the Waalian to the Menapian coincides with the Jaramillo event at about 0·9 m.y. B.P. (see also Zagwijn et al., 1971). Furthermore the top of the Tiglian corresponds to the Gilsa event—about 1·7 m.y. B.P. In each case a cold, or glacial phase, is correlated with a paleomagnetic event. Again, the frequency of oscillations exhibits an increase upwards, especially after 0·9 m.y. (the Jaramillo event), and, although temperatures of the warm or temperate phases remained similar throughout the Pleistocene, the colder temperatures became lower.

TABLE 13

British Pleistocene succession (Shotton and West, 1969; West, 1972). See Figs 72 and 73. Zagwijn (1976) concluded that a hiatus between the Baventian and Pastonian encompassed the Dutch Waalian, Menapian, Taxandrian complex

	Stage	Climate	Principal strata
Upper	Flandrian	temperate	Glacial and
	Devensian	cold/glacial	interglacial
	Ipswichian	temperate	succession
	Wolstonian	cold/glacial	
Middle	Hoxnian	temperate	Weybourn Crag
	Anglian	cold/glacial	and Cromer
	Cromerian	temperate	Forest bed
	Beestonian	cold	series
	Pastonian	temperate	
Lower	Baventian	cold	Red Crag and
	Antian	temperate	Norwich Crag
	Thurnian	cold	
	Ludhamian	temperate	
	Pre-Ludhamian	cool	

3 THE UNITED KINGDOM SUCCESSION

The sequence of deposits in the southern and eastern parts of England has enabled West (1968; 1970) to summarise the British Pleistocene succession. A brief synopsis is contained in Table 13.

Each temperate stage from the Pastonian to the Ipswichian can be divided into four, major, pollen assemblage zones (Turner and West, 1968). The Flandrian, or most recent of these sequences, only reaches as yet to zone III, the present day. The zones are as follows:

ZONE I   The pre-temperate zone characterised by the presence of boreal trees, *Betula* and *Pinus*, accompanied by heliophilous shrubs and herbs.

ZONE II The early temperate zone that is dominated by the mixed-oak forest association.

ZONE III The late-temperate zone that is characterised by the

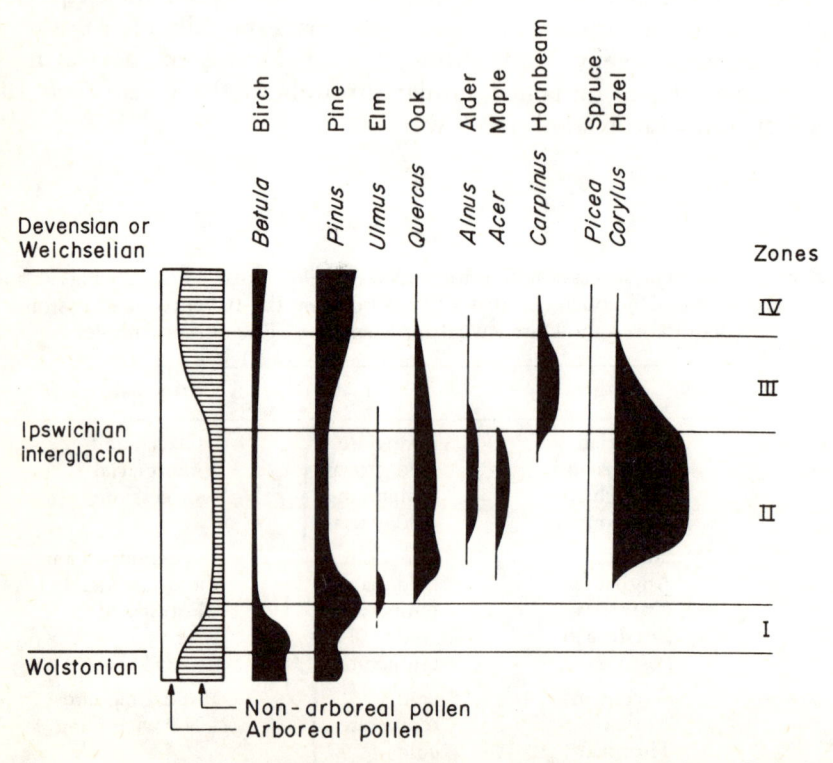

FIG. 72. A pollen diagram showing how certain trees varied in abundance during an interglacial period. In this particular case, the Ipswichian interglacial. (After West, 1968.)

expansion of forest trees which are not abundant in earlier phases—*Carpinus, Picea, Abies*—at the expense of the Quercetum mixtum.

ZONE IV The post-temperate zone with *Betula, Pinus* and *Picea* as the dominant trees, and non-tree pollen frequent—particularly that of the Ericales associated with damp heathland.

The Lower Pleistocene includes three cold stages and two temperate stages but their regional vegetation is difficult to determine as they are predominantly represented by the shelly marine sands and gravels of the Red and Norwich Crags of East Anglia. The effects of pollen deposition under marine conditions are imperfectly known. However *Tsuga* was present in the temperate phases and this recalls its presence alongside other exotic genera in the early Pleistocene of the Netherlands. The pre-Ludhamian assemblage is suggestive of boreal forest (Beck *et al.*, 1972). The overall global climatic conditions are intimated by the sea levels which, in spite of Pleistocene sinking, seem to have been higher than that at the present time and reached at least 45 m O.D. during Red Crag times (West, 1972).

The Weybourne Crag and Cromer Forest Bed series are found at numerous localities, with the former including Baventian and Pastonian marine sands and gravels. The Cromer Forest Bed series includes both marine and freshwater sediments and covers the Pastonian, Beestonian, Cromerian and early Anglian phases. During the Pastonian and Cromerian temperate stages the climate was probably much as it is today. In the Baventian, Beestonian and Anglian cold phases the climate became much colder, sub-arctic or even arctic, and there is evidence of permafrost. *Tsuga* made its final appearance in the Pastonian.

The Middle and Upper Pleistocene glacial–interglacial succession includes three definitive glacial stages—the Anglian, Wolstonian and Devensian—during which ice sheets covered much of Britain and periglacial conditions characterised the southern regions. During the intervening Hoxnian and Ipswichian interglacial periods temperate environments intervened and this is also true of the postglacial, or Flandrian, period, which includes the present day.

More and more investigations throughout the world are now providing corroborative evidence of such contemporaneous climatic and vegetational cycles on a global scale. Ronai (1970) described some 25 climatic phases in Hungary; Tsukada (1967) found a Pre-Tiglian analogue in Taiwan; whilst Leopold (1969) summarised the rather sparse data for North America.

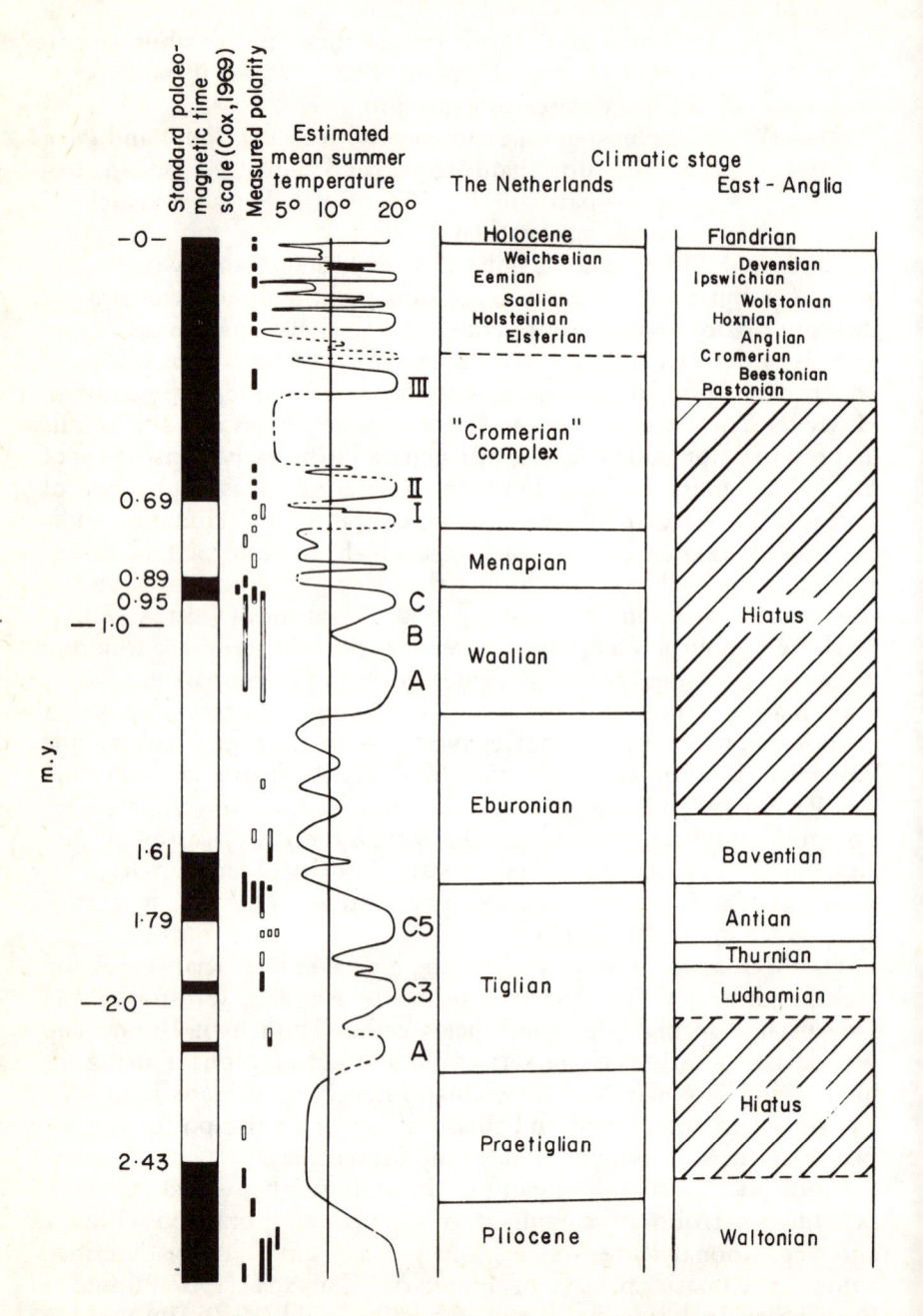

FIG. 73. Paleomagnetic measurements, climatic curve and the stratigraphic subdivisions of the Quaternary in the Netherlands and East Anglia (Zagwijn, 1976).

4 SEA-LEVEL VARIATIONS

During the periods of climatic deterioration the amount of water locked up in ice caps was much greater than during interglacial periods. Estimations of the changes in the Antarctic ice sheet during pleniglacial periods suggest that the mass might have exceeded that at the present time by 40–50 per cent (Voronov, 1960). Hollin (1962) intimated that this might equal a volume increase of between 2·5–8·5 × 10⁶ km³. However, pulsations of the Antarctic ice sheet, eustatically controlled by the waxing and waning of northern ice sheets, are not clear in sediments around the continent. This is, perhaps, because such changes in the mass budget of the area were small, or because they are masked by other large fluctuations (Warnke, 1970: cf. Denton *et al.*, 1969; 1970).

Nevertheless, sea-level fluctuations are widely represented by raised shore-lines throughout the world and these figured large in Zeuner's (1945) syncretic account of global climatic changes. The glacio-eustatic factors that were probably involved were also discussed by Miller (1964) and Russell (1964), whilst sea-level rises in general have been reviewed by Zeuner (1945), Disney (1955), Fairbridge (1960; 1961), Bruun *et al.* (1962), Fairbridge and Krebs (1962), Donn and Shaw (1963), Harris (1963) and Schwartz (1967). Complementary low stands have also been documented by, for example, Froget *et al.* (1972) who demonstrated that in the western Mediterranean *Arctica arctica*, *Chlamys septemradiata* and *Modiolus* occurred when the sea level was 80 metres below the present level. ^{14}C analyses gave dates of 31,500 ± 300 to 9,800 ± 200 years for such components—with the most frequent ages lying between 13,000 ± 300 and 9800 B.P. The recovery of the sea level from this late or pleniglacial low, was first documented by de Vries and Barendsen (1954) and then by Godwin *et al.* (1958). These workers undertook ^{14}C analyses of organic material associated with sea levels of different Flandrian (Postglacial) age and provided an absolute chronology for the global eustatic rise. More recent work has given added precision to these initial results.

Many workers recognise one or more eustatic high stands of sea level during the Wisconsin, Würm or Weichselian glaciation (cf. Guilcher, 1969). Curray (1965) speculated that the sea level rose to slightly below its present level between 35,000 and 22,000 B.P., whilst Milliman and Emery (1968) believed that it was close to its present position around 30,000–35,000 B.P. Hoyt *et al.* have inferred that it was slightly above the present level at 30,000–25,0000 B.P., and

48,000–40,000 B.P. Schnable and Goodell (1968) also suggested that it was close to, or above, its present position between 40,000 and 24,000 B.P., whilst Osmond *et al.* (1970) and McClure (1976) reported a high stand *c.* 30,000 B.P. In the New Guinea region data which were provided by Veeh and Chappell (1970) indicate that a mid-Wisconsian high stand may have been 100 ft below the present. In California there certainly seem to have been 2–3 eustatic high stands between about 150,000 and 75,000 B.P. (Birkeland, 1972). These would corroborate the Ipswichian high in the UK.

Data derived from 54 offshore profiles also indicate four, major, low sea-level still-stands between sea level and −100 m (Flemming, 1972). These lie at −5 to −10, −27, −55 and −96 m. Superimposed upon these major terraces there is also a further sequence of minor terraces and solution notches at −4, −10, −15, −20, −25, −35, −46, −52, −67, −72/79 and −91 m. The majority of these features probably relate to oscillations during the Flandrian rise in sea level, but those at −46, −52 and −67 may belong to a previous major cycle of sea-level changes.

Other data are available elsewhere. Barbados was an area of tectonic emergence during the Quaternary and, as it was uplifted, reef tracts formed around the island. The interaction of this gradual tectonic uplift and glacio-eustatic sea-level changes has resulted in a complex terraced coral cap. Radiometric dating of successive terraces suggest periods of high sea level at 125,000, 105,000 and 85,000 years B.P. (see also Steinen *et al.*, 1973). The next higher group of terraces includes ones at 170,000 and 230,000 B.P. Marked interruptions to the

TABLE 14

A comparison of high sea-level stands and calculated solar radiation maxima
(Steinen *et al.*, 1973)

High sea stands	Radiation maxima of Milankovic and also Broecker (1966)
—	33,000 (weak)
—	60,000 (weak)
82,000	82,000
105,000	106,000
125,000	127,000
—	151,000 (weak)
170,000	176,000
to	198,000
230,000	220,000

formation of well-defined reef terraces from the Recent period to 80,000 B.P., and from 130,000 to 170,000, apparently record prolonged periods of maximum solar radiation in the northern hemisphere and lend strong support to the astronomical theory of climatic change (see Table 14).

More recently Marshall and Thom (1976) obtained $^{230}Th/^{234}U$ dates for coral terraces of the last interglacial and concluded that, at that time, the sea level was 2–9 m above the present. They considered that it had returned to about the same level for each interglacial of the last 700,000 years but that the Ipswichian interglacial was "somewhat unusual" in its great ocean water volume and warm sea temperatures.

5 THE LAST GLACIATION

Our most detailed knowledge about past glacial climates relates to the last glaciation and this has sparked off many theoretical considerations (see Climap, 1973). Differences between the northern and southern hemispheres have led Derbyshire to postulate that the simpler synoptic pattern of atmospheric circulation that characterises the middle latitudes of the southern hemisphere may have suffered less change in the last pleniglacial than did that of the comparable regions of the northern hemisphere. He thought that, given a mean annual temperature at least 6°C below that of today, much of the Pleistocene geological and geomorphological record of Australia appears to be consistent with an atmospheric circulation similar to that existing today. The ground evidence, including the notable contrast in both the extent and style of the glaciation and periglaciation on either side of the Bass Strait, can be accommodated by a model circulation that has a more stable Australian winter high, and a rather greater baroclinicity to the south so that the relative frequency and duration of a stormy westerly pattern is increased.

Data from ice cores suggest that the temperature gradient of the northern hemisphere increased more than that of the southern. Newell (1973) suggested that, if this was the case, then the mean temperatures at 77°N may have been about 20°C lower in 20,000 B.P., whilst those in the 80s were only 13·5°C lower. He considered that this implied that the intertropical convergence zone might have been south of the equator. Indeed, he suggested that the invasion of the savanna by dunes across a broad belt from the Atlantic coast to the Nile valley during the last glacial period might reflect such a southerly position for the zone. Nevertheless, the conditions varied with longitude and, prior to 21,000 B.P., Lake Chad was much more extensive than at present (Butzer, 1971b).

Arrhenius (1952) attempted the first description of trade wind variations. Parkin and Shackleton (1973), who recently found a good antiphase correlation between the coarseness exponent of sediments and isotope deviations in cores, concluded that strong trade winds are a general feature of glacial periods and probably result from an enhanced temperature gradient between the poles and the equator. They also emphasised that the limits within which wind vigour varies have probably remained fairly constant, as have the limits of ice volume and sea temperature variation. The relative synchroneity of the various types of fluctuation does, however, vary. Newell (1974) suggested that the end of a glacial period is first marked by a decrease in the rate of formation of, or even stagnation of, bottom waters. This would lead to an increase in the dissolved carbon dioxide and hence to increased carbonate dissolution. A comparison of the carbonate and silicate accumulation rate curves with the ^{18}O composition of foraminiferal thecae suggested that climatic and oceanographic changes were not synchronous (Pisias *et al.*, 1975). The curves are similar but the carbonate levels change first, and a lag of 2,600 years separates them from the silicate effects. Bonatti and Gartner (1973) also found that, in some cycles, kaolinite to quartz ratios are displaced upwards by a few centimetres relative to the $\delta^{18}O$ maxima, and concluded that there was a lag of a few thousand years between warm temperature peaks and the degree of chemical weathering that is required for the kaolinite to quartz effects.

A recent synoptic view of both the circulation régimes and the climate during the last glaciation was provided by Lamb (1971) using assumed values for climatic parameters that he had derived from biological and geomorphological data. He concluded that at the onset of the last glaciation, between 70–60 × 10^3 years B.P., a rapid fall in temperature took it to near the lowest levels attained during the ice age. These cold conditions were then interrupted by interstadia that lasted for some centuries, or even 2,000 years, and during which the recovery brought conditions close to those at present. A long period of low temperature lasted from 60,000 to 50,000 years ago, and was followed by a period of relatively temperate conditions during the 50,000–30,000 B.P. period. A subsequent cold stadium then persisted for about 10,000 years with the temperatures reaching their lowest levels and the ice sheets perhaps attaining their maximum extent (see also Coope *et al.*, 1971). This phase culminated between 20,000 and 15,000 years ago and the end of the last glaciation, together with the attainment of the postglacial (Flandrian) climatic optimum, followed between 15,000 and 8000 B.P. (Fig. 74).

Lamb assumed that the rate of glacier growth during the early cold stadium, sufficient to enable them to survive the renewed summer

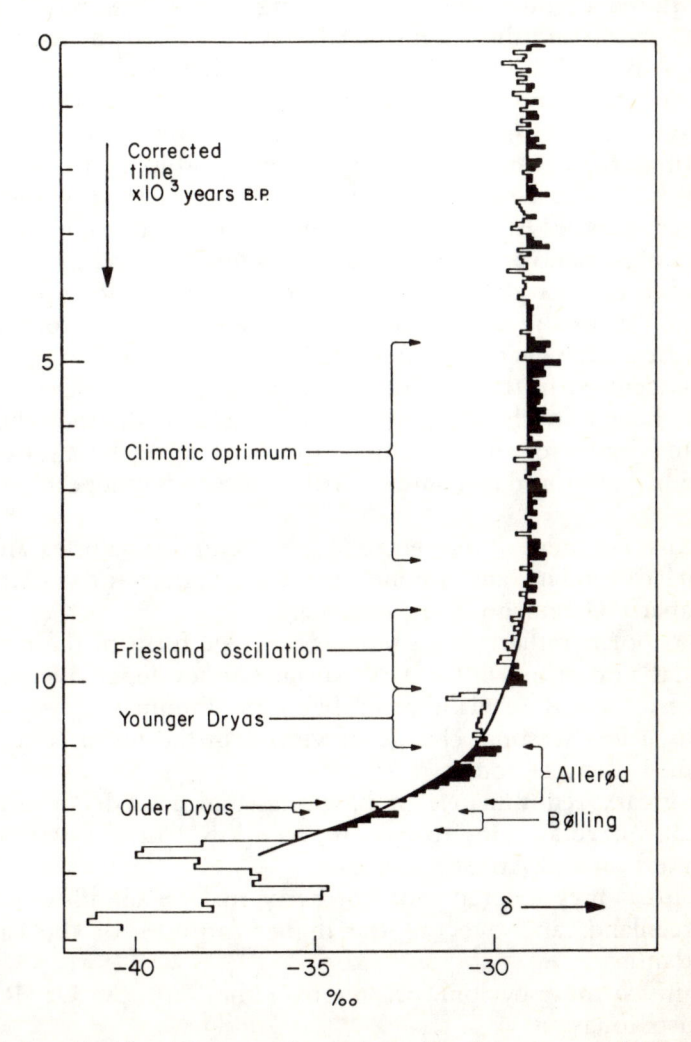

FIG. 74. Late glacial and Holocene δ variations plotted on a corrected time scale. All δs exceeding a smoothed curve are set off in black. Climatic oscillations during the transition period fit the European sequence; they are superimposed on a general increase in δ (14,000–10,000 B.P.), part of which might be due to the gradual opening of Davis Strait and Baffin Bay, or to a changing meteorological circulation pattern connected with the extinction of the large ice sheets. (Dansgaard et al., 1971.)

warmth of the early warm phase, necessitated a highly meridional circulation, with the main moisture supply coming from warm southern seas, and a prevalence of southerly and northerly winds in neighbouring sections of the northern hemisphere. It would also have required a reduced level of incoming solar radiation during the summer period and this might, itself, have favoured the meridional and low-latitude westerly circulation required above.

Mercer (1970) considered that the apparent similarities between the present Arctic Ocean and the former sea now occupied by the West Antarctic ice sheet suggest that, under prolonged pleniglacial conditions, a cold ice cover of the West Antarctic type would have developed in the Arctic Ocean. This would have comprised a complex of ice shelves and ice grounded below sea level. He thought that during the last glaciation the ice cover probably comprised ice shelves only, except for a ground ice sheet in the epicontinental Barents Sea. However, during an earlier glacial period an ice sheet that was centred in the American sector of the Arctic Ocean may have extended onto the adjacent land. In general, Lamb thought that, at the maximum of the glaciation, the main characteristics of the circulation patterns that contrast with those today appear to have been:

1. A displacement of the centre of the circumpolar vortex and the surface polar anticyclone to the region of north-east Canada–Greenland in the summer.
2. A tripolar, rather than a bipolar, average form of the circumpolar vortex in winter, with surface anticyclones over north-east Canada–Greenland again being predominant.
3. Much less seasonal change of vigour in the mean circulation than is the case today.
4. A great predominance of blocking, and a tendency for any progressive systems to pass in very low latitudes within the American and Atlantic sectors.
5. A great preponderance of northerly surface windflow east of Greenland, and over all the higher latitudes of the eastern Atlantic.
6. A much more cyclonic régime over the European USSR than exists today.
7. The mean surface wind (and water?) circulation over the polar basin may have been more cyclonic than today.
8. The warm air that penetrated the Arctic came in largely from the Pacific side, traversing Alaska, and in part from north-east Asia.

A variety of data from all over the world have to be seen against this theoretical background. Palynological studies in central Taiwan (Tsukada, 1967) demonstrate an early Tali glacial stage dating from prior to 60,000 B.P. which was characterised by *Symplocos, Tsuga chinensis* and *Pinus* that were taken to indicate a temperature some 5–9°C cooler than today. The maximal Tali glacial stage, dating from sometime between 60,000 and 50,000 B.P., had a predominance of boreal conifers and pine, very low percentages of temperate elements, and plentiful aquatics such as *Trapa, Nuphar* and *Persicaria*. According to Tsukada this was the coldest phase of the late Pleistocene, and had a temperature some 8–11°C lower than the present, but it nevertheless still supported *Trapa*. The last Tali glacial phase lasted from 50,000 to 10,000 B.P., and was dominated by the cool temperate *Cunninghamia konishii, Quercus, Ulmus, Zelkova, Juglans cathayensis, Ligustrum* and *Salix*. After an increase in temperature from 45,000 to 40,000 B.P. a short cooling phase began around 35,000 B.P. From 10,000 B.P. onwards the cool temperate species were then replaced by such subtropical and thermophilous species as *Mallotus paniculatus, Trema* cf. *orientalis, Liquidambar formosa* and *Castanopsis* sp. This seems to reflect earlier conclusions about European conditions that have been considerably modified in view of data obtained in the last decade.

The chrono-stratigraphical sequence of the eastern Cordillera in Colombia was also correlated with known European and American stages by van Geel and van der Hammen (1973). Their most important conclusions were that after a humid lower and middle pleniglacial phase the period between 20,000 and 13,000 B.P. was extremely dry. This was then followed by a wet phase during 13,000–11,000 B.P., and a short dry phase around the Allerød and Upper Dryas times of Europe, 11,000–9500 B.P. Such South American data provide an interesting comparison with those from equatorial America and equatorial Africa (Kendall, 1969; Livingstone, 1975). Prior to 30,000 B.P. the climate in the Sahara region seems to have been moist. For a subsequent period of from 10,000 to 25,000 years, centred on 20,000 B.P., it was then dry, and at a time that varies from place to place but is commonly close to 13,000 B.P., it became wet. It stayed wet, with a minor transitory dry phase between 7000 and 5000 B.P., until about 3,000 years ago. Furthermore, in the lowland forest areas of Africa conditions seem to have been dry during the late Pleistocene hypothermal periods. Street and Grove (1976), basing their argument on ^{14}C-dated lake levels, concluded that during the period 21,000–12,000 B.P. desert and semi-desert conditions expanded over large areas of tropical Africa. Independent biogeographical evidence also suggests that equatorial lowland forest was drastically reduced in extent at that time and restricted to refuges in West Africa. In the Sudan desert conditions penetrated up to 450 km further south into the present semi-desert grasslands, scrub and savanna areas. In northern and southern Africa there are also limited indications of an opposing trend with Mediterranean parkland intermittently invading steppelands. South African data certainly imply that montane grass veldt displaced semi-desert scrub prior to 17,000 B.P., and from 13,200 to 12,600 B.P. There was then a general restoration of forest vegetation across central Africa during the period 12,500–10,000 B.P.

Deglaciation in the Kashmir region of the Himalayas was in progress around 15,000–14,000 B.P. (Singh and Agrawal, 1976). However the history of late Quaternary climates in low latitudes is still controversial. Studies of the Timor Sea region that are supplemented by ^{14}C dates certainly indicate that it was considerably more arid than the adjacent land today. The area was largely above sea level during the lowest sea-level stand and a shallow-water environment occurred near the edge of the Sahul shelf at 17,000 B.P. The subsequent marine transgression that submerged the area was rapid, and isolated numerous small islands which may have trapped terrestrial vertebrates. The available evidence (Andel *et al.*, 1967) appears to support Fairbridge's earlier contentions (1964; 1965), based on observations in Africa and the Mediterranean, that during the hypothermal glacial periods the west wind belts and their associated rainfall were displaced northward by some 5–10° of latitude. The equatorial pluvial zone was compressed rather than extended and a 5–10° northward shift of the west wind belts would bring the Sahul shelf into a region of reduced rainfall. The northward shift of the west wind drift would also divert 15–25°C water into the Timor current and similar displacements of mid-latitude water during the last glaciation had previously been reported in the south-east Pacific by Blackman and Somayajulu (1966).

Circulation of near surface water in the extensively studied Gulf of Mexico was also significantly different from that today around 18,000 B.P. Surface temperatures were 1–2°C cooler, and the salinity was 0·4–0·5 ‰ higher than today. In the present gulf climate the isotherms trend north-easterly but Brunner and Cooley (1976) suggest that at that time they exhibited a northerly trend. In a similar manner the isohalines parallel the basin edge today and the gradient decreases coastward. In the pleniglacial period the isohalines still followed the coastline but the gradient increased coastward. When they were all taken together these patterns were suggested to reflect an anticyclonic system in the western gulf.

Elsewhere a progressively increasing quantity of diverse data relate to North America and the history in arctic areas was reviewed by Nichols (1974). Other data abound. The net advance of the Woodfordian glacier in Illinois around 23,000–20,000 B.P. was 62 m per ^{14}C year, which falls within the 25–106 m range that was recorded from Ohio (Kempton and Gross, 1971). The Sidney–Fayette ^{14}C dates indicate that Fayette ice entered Ohio around 23,000 B.P., and reached its southernmost limits at *c.* 21,000 B.P. Wood from the top of the Sidney paleosol has been dated at 23,000 ± 800 and 22,480 ± 800. This was then overridden by ice.

Two marshes in north-east Kansas provided a vegetational record back to 25,000 B.P. (Gruger, 1973). The earliest spectra are comparable with extant ones in south Saskatchewan and may reflect a rather open vegetation with some pine, spruce and birch, together with local stands of alder and willow. This picture seems to have changed about 23,000 years ago and spruce forest prevailed until 15,000 B.P., during the period of maximum ice extent in the UK. Because of a hiatus the vegetation changes that resulted in the immigration of mixed deciduous forest and prairie—present by 11,000 B.P.—are unknown. However, Heusser (1973) has documented a pronounced climatic amelioration elsewhere that lasted from 18,000 to 17,500 B.P. and preceded the classical Bølling or Allerød phases of late Weichselian time. This was the Evans Creek–Vashon interstadial. It is particularly interesting that at this period the cooling effects are again contemporary with polarity events and it is difficult to escape the conclusion that the two types of event have a close, if not causal, relationship.

10
Late Weichselian and Flandrian Time

1 INTRODUCTION

The vast number of investigations that have been carried out upon organic material laid down since the maximum of the last glaciation have now gone a long way towards elucidating the complex climatic and vegetational changes that have occurred during this period. The resultant data provide the most complete picture available to us about the changes that occur during a period of climatic amelioration and during the early phases of a subsequent climatic deterioration. They therefore form a coherent and reliable model of the events before, and just after, an interglacial hypsithermal period. Furthermore, the initial contribution of Godwin, Walker and Willis (1957) has led to an accurate evaluation of these changes in terms of an absolute chronology based on ^{14}C analysis.

Early workers in the field of pollen analysis were quick to see its potential for a study of the world's climatic history (see Godwin's 1973 summary). This has resulted in a progressive increase in the number of palynological studies that are carried out throughout the world. Synoptic reviews of early work in the European region, which have served as a reference against which data from elsewhere are compared, were provided by Firbas (1949) and Godwin (1956). These, too, served to stimulate yet greater levels of research. More recent surveys include those of Pearson (1964), West (1968) and Leopold (1969), whilst a plethora of papers deal with the individual continents or island groups. An introduction to this vast and still expanding literature can be obtained from Bryson *et al.* (1970) and from works referred to in the previous chapter such as Nichols (1974), who dealt with North America; van Geel and van der

Hammen (1973), who worked in Colombia; Tsukada (1967), who presented a preliminary account of pollen analytical studies in Japan; and Livingstone (1975), who summarised our knowledge of African events. All such works established that the principal features of the record in individual regions corroborate the overall picture which was originally derived from studies in Central Europe, Fennoscandia and the British Isles.

Until relatively recently the period of time involved in the climatic changes since the last glaciation, roughly the last 13,000 years, was divided into two principal phases—the Late-glacial and Postglacial periods. Of these the first comprised the Older and Younger Dryas Periods and interpolated phases of climatic amelioration comprising the Bølling and Allerød periods. In the scheme of Godwin (1940a, b; 1949; 1956) this involved zones I–III with the material of zone I including additional minor periods of climatic amelioration such as the Bølling. It is, of course, now quite clear that during the overall period of deglaciation these additional short-term periods of climatic amelioration, which are less extensively reflected by organic material, involved considerable climatic changes. One such period is represented by the Colney Heath erratics that were dated by ^{14}C analysis at 13,600 B.P. (cf. Pearson, 1962; Godwin, 1961), or the material at Nazeing (Allison et al., 1952). The fact that this material is frequently erratic in nature, consisting of large blocks of organic detritus mud interbedded in gravels, itself suggests the reason for its earlier paucity. Organic deposition took place in pools or hollows that were subsequently exposed to melt-water in the later, definitive, deglaciation.

Numerous investigations in the Fennoscandian region long ago provided evidence that the older *Dryas* period, zone I in the British scheme of Godwin, is broadly comparable with the Daniglacial stage of ice-retreat together with the early part of the Gotiglacial stage; and that zone III, the upper Dryas time, is approximately synonymous with the period of deposition of the Norwegian Raa, the Central Swedish and the Finnish Salpausselka moraines. On the basis of the varve chronology of de Geer these periods were originally envisaged as lasting from 15,000 to 10,000 B.P.—a general conclusion which was broadly justified by the early applications of ^{14}C analysis. In order to bring the nomenclature into line with other usages the whole of this period of cyclical climatic amelioration and deterioration has, in recent years, been ascribed to the late *Weichselian*. The Holocene commission of the International Quaternary Association then suggested using 10,000 B.P. as the Pleistocene–

Holocene boundary.

The Postglacial period of older authors comprises the period from the end of Godwin's zone III up until the present day. In Godwin's scheme it consisted of a further five pollen zones, IV–VIII, that were characterised by the changing values for the percentage representation of various tree species. These zones, whose broad synchrony at different locations was established following Dr Willis's analysis of material from Scaleby Moss (cf. Godwin *et al.*, 1957), were originally erected on the hypothesis that they reflected discrete climatic phases. The subsequent revision of the value for the half-life of radiocarbon, coupled with the realisation that the atmospheric ^{14}C content varies, subsequently led to a revision of the suggested dates—on the basis of bristle cone pine chronology. Nevertheless, it is fair to say that the numerous other investigations which followed this primary paper have confirmed the broad synchrony of many of the climatic changes that underlie the Postglacial sequence—this in regions as widely separated as New Zealand, Australia, America etc. It is this period, the Postglacial, that is now referred to as the *Flandrian*, for reasons which are analogous to those that led to the Late-glacial being assigned the name *late Weichselian*. Furthermore, the zonation of Godwin has been revised by Hibbert *et al.* (1971) to bring it into line with the synoptic zonation of earlier interglacial deposits that was referred to in the foregoing chapter.

2 THE LATE WEICHSELIAN PERIOD

As originally conceived, Late-glacial deposits typically comprised two layers of relatively inorganic material with an intervening layer of more organic material between them. Since remains of *Dryas octopetala* occurred within the upper and lower inorganic strata the names early and late Dryas times were ascribed to their periods of deposition. A further depositional phase was then found which divided the early Dryas. These two phases of climatic amelioration were given the names Allerød and Bølling respectively, after the sites at which they were first described (Hartz and Milthers, 1901). The favourable conditions of the Allerød period were subsequently summarised by Schutrumpf and again by Godwin (1956 etc.). The salient points of their summaries include the colonisation of the lake and sedge peat formation; recession of non-tree pollen; attainment of high values for the percentage representation of *Pinus* pollen; and the absence of macroscopic remains of *Betula nana* or other dwarf species. Complementarily, the evidence for a deterioration of climate leading to the upper Dryas time is provided by the rise in non-tree pollen coupled with the recurrence of remains of *Betula nana*; a rise in the percentage representation of *Betula* at the expense of Pinus; a rise in that of *Salix*; a return of the spores of *Selaginella*, the pollen of *Empetrum* and other members of the Ericaceae, and that of *Hippophae*, the sea buckthorn. The results of a wide variety of investigations (summarised in Godwin, 1973) suggested that a grass–sedge tundra with scattered stands of birch was widespread over southern Sweden, Norway and much of Denmark. The presence of *Artemisia*, *Rumex*, *Thalictrum* and *Hippophae* within this vegetation, alongside arctic species of *Dryas*, *Oxyria*, *Armeria*, *Empetrum* and *Selaginella*, led Iversen (1947) to suggest comparisons with central European alpine, rather than northern arctic conditions, and he proposed the term "park-tundra" for the vegetation. It was in an environment provided by this park-tundra that the final European phase of the paleolithic took place. This cultural phase, recorded in the cave paintings of the Franco–Calabrian region, ended with the disappearance of many large ungulates at the beginning of the Flandrian.

In their consideration of iodine in lake sediments Pennington and Lishman (1971) concluded that indications of a major environmental change actually precede the Allerød period or tree birch pollen zone. Pre-Allerød interstadial conditions are indicated by a change to a more organic sediment, greatly increased values of juniper pollen, and a tenfold increase in the numbers of pollen grains deposited per year, or at least preserved in the sediments. From such evidence they concluded that the onset of interstadial conditions in north-west UK, preceded the immigration of *Betula* into the lowland vegetation.

Data on the Coleoptera preserved in the sites corroborate this conclusion. Henriksen (1933) and Pearson (1963) summarised the available data on the late Weichselian coleopteran remains and concluded that, in broad terms, they suggested analogous conclusions to those drawn by palynologists. Pearson also drew attention to the presence of markedly continental species that are not particularly northern in their distribution but fail to penetrate the British Isles today. More recently Coope (1975) has summarised data derived from Coleoptera of zone I of Godwin's scheme and concluded that, following an arctic phase prior to 13,000 B.P., the climate ameliorated and included a warm spell prior to the Allerød. During this phase beetles which do not today extend as far north as the UK lived in the area—implying a very considerable warming.

Lamb (1971) concluded that during the Allerød oscillation, and the post-Allerød cold centuries, the atmospheric circulation patterns still differed from those that prevail today. However, with the disappearance of much of the north European ice sheet, and of the Atlantic floating ice, he thought that the circulation weakened over Europe while remaining strong over North America. This would have resulted in an enhanced local radiation budget. The only effect of the sharp decline in temperature around 9000 B.C. comes out meteorologically as slight shifts of minor features in the surface isobar and wind patterns, which would conform with a shortening of the wavelength in the upper westerlies and a slight southerly movement. Lamb suggested that a "quasi-flickering" of the radiation input, with a $c.$ 2,000 year periodicity due to the tidal force of the planets, could have had an extremely critical effect when much of the ice sheet, although retreating, was still present. Other suggestions draw attention to the effects of a wave of volcanic activity—giving an enhanced atmospheric dust veil.

As noted above it was during this late Weichselian period that the final phase of the Upper Paleolithic occurred in the Old World, and is there associated with numerous remains of the larger herbivores. In the British Isles the remains of the Irish Elk have been accurately assigned to this period and one may conclude that the onset of the Flandrian afforestation, coupled with increased depredation by man, led to its disappearance (cf. Blackburn, 1952). As is so often the case, the available data intimate that the extinction of these large herbivores represents the combined effects of a changing environment, which reduced the total numbers that could be sustained by a diminishing food supply, and a critical contribution by a, perhaps increasingly numerous, predator—Man.

3 THE FLANDRIAN PERIOD

Godwin summarised the floristic elements of interglacial periods into successive cryocratic, protocratic, mesocratic and telocratic groupings. West (1970) emphasised that, since the first pollen diagrams were described by von Post, palynological investigations throughout the world have added considerably to the complexity of our knowledge. Jessen (1935) and Godwin (1940; 1956) originally described a definite sequence of pollen zones for the postglacial deposits of Jutland and England. In this context a pollen zone is usually an assemblage zone, and reflects a vegetation unit, but at the type site these biostratigraphical zones correspond to chronozones.

The five classical zones of the Flandrian (Postglacial) period, as defined by Godwin, were in the past referred to as zones IV, V, VI,

VII and VIII. Zone IV comprised the Pre-boreal period of Blytt and Sernander and its lower boundary was characterised by a rapid increase in the percentage representation of birch pollen. This was generally interpreted as reflecting the replacement of a pre-existing "park-tundra" by close, but according to Godwin (1956), not dense, woodland. Zones V and VI then represent the Boreal period of Blytt and Sernander and the boundary between zones IV and V was set by Godwin at the level where hazel pollen suddenly achieves high values. Alongside these *Corylus* stands *Pinus* seemed to predominate over *Betula* in the south and east of Britain, although birch was dominant in the north and west. The eventual replacement of this residual birch marked the boundary separating zones V and VI. It is at this point that the pollen record indicates the appearance of the elements of mixed oak forest.

A forest consisting of a Quercetum mixtum together with *Alnus* persisted for a long time. This comprised zone VII of Godwin's scheme and he equated the sub-zones VIIa and VIIb, differentiated on the basis of the elm decline, with the Atlantic and Sub-boreal periods of Blytt and Sernander. Following the early phase of climatic amelioration, which took place in pollen zones IV and V, there appears to have been a period of optimum conditions during zone VII. This is the so-called Postglacial, or Flandrian, climatic optimum, otherwise referred to as the hypsithermal period. During this phase the forest belts of Europe moved north to occupy higher latitudes than they do today and macro-remains of *Corylus*, *Trapa natans*, *Cladium mariscus* and *Emys orbicularis* occur at positions to the north of their present species limits.

Zone VIII of the general British scheme of Godwin is the so-called alder-birch-oak-beech period of Flandrian vegetational history. There was a pronounced shift in the forest composition and where *Tilia* had persisted into VIIb it disappears. The period is characterised by two principal effects. The first is an overall climatic deterioration, whilst the second is a marked and progressive deforestation by man. One general effect was a resumption of bog growth and it is within these bogs that the various recurrence layers provide an accurate record of successive climatic fluctuations.

These pollen zones that were established by Godwin, and tied by him to the climatic succession of Blytt and Sernander, have now been expressed by West (1970) in terms of chronozones that are comparable with those of earlier interglacials. In broad terms three such chronozones seem to have elapsed during the Flandrian; the fourth and final one having yet to occur. A succinct summary of both

West's chronozones and the assemblage zones of Godwin is provided by Table 15 and their ^{14}C ages by Table 17.

TABLE 15

The relationship between the pollen assemblage zones of Godwin (1940; 1956) and the chronozones of West (1970)

Pollen assemblage	Assemblage zone of Godwin (1940)	Flandrian chronozone of West (1970)
Alder-birch-oak-beech	VIII	F III
Alder-oak	VIIb	
Alder-oak-elm-lime	VIIa	F II
Pine-hazel	VI	c
Hazel-birch-pine	V	F I b
Birch-pine	IV	a
		Late Weichselian III

4 ^{14}C AGE DETERMINATIONS

In 1955 a pit dug through deposits at Scaleby Moss, Cumbria, enabled Dr Willis to date, by the ^{14}C method, the organic material laid down since the late Weichselian (Godwin et al., 1957). In this study they concentrated on the boundaries between the zones of the general British scheme and noted some striking similarities with other datings on the European continent. Subsequently Willis et al. (1960) confirmed that atmospheric ^{14}C levels vary with time, the value of the ^{14}C half-life was corrected, and then the bristle cone pine corrections were introduced. This has necessarily led to reviews of the original conclusions. In addition there has been the switch to Flandrian zonation (West, 1970). Comparisons of varve dates, and the ^{14}C dates that were obtained by using both the old and new values for the ^{14}C half-life, are presented in Table 16. In addition the assemblage zones for the Flandrian are dated in Table 17. Curves derived from the data of the former Table suggested an increased atmospheric ^{14}C activity in the time interval 6000–1000 B.C., with a maximum c. 4000 B.C. This corresponds to a significant deviation between the ^{14}C dates and the real dates of that time. Deviations of the same magnitude have been deduced using American dendrochronology (Damon et al., 1966; Suess, 1967; Ralph and Michael, 1967). Average ice recession values for southern Sweden during the early part of this time are (Nilsson, 1968):

7–10 km per 100 years from 10,500 to 10,300 B.C.
16–35 km per 100 years from 10,200 to 10,000 B.C.
14 km per 100 years from 9900 to 9800 B.C.
11–16 km per 100 years from 9700 to 9000 B.C.
2–8 km per 100 years from 8900 to 8200 B.C.
24–32 km per 100 years from 8000 to 7900 B.C.

TABLE 16

The conventional and corrected varve dates for the late Weichselian and early Flandrian, together with the conventional ($T_{\frac{1}{2}} = 5{,}570$) and corrected ($T_{\frac{1}{2}} = 5{,}730$) ^{14}C dates (Tauber, 1970; Stuiver, 1970)

Characteristics	Conventional varve years B.C.	Corrected varve years B.C.	Conventional ^{14}C years B.C.	Corrected ^{14}C years B.C.
Yoldia Sea/Ancylus lake	7000	7200	7100	7350
Younger Dryas/Preboreal	8100	8300	8200	8500
Allerød/Younger Dryas	8900	9100	9000	9350
Older Dryas/Allerød	9700	9900	9800	10,150
Bølling/Older Dryas	9900	10,100	10,000	10,350
Oldest Dryas/Bølling	10,200	10,400	10,400	10,750

Additional considerations relate to the rise in sea level which accompanied the period of climatic amelioration. Once again it is far and away the most accurately dated event of this nature. Godwin *et al.* (1958) surveyed the ^{14}C dates which had accumulated for material associated with differing late Weichselian and Flandrian shore-lines. These included data relating to the Mississippi Basin, New Zealand, the continent of Europe and the British Isles. Using the old half-life value for ^{14}C they concluded that there had been a progressive eustatic rise in sea level between 12,000 and 5500 B.P. Several other workers then prepared comparable curves. Broecker *et al.* (1960) provided evidence for an abrupt change around 11,000 B.P. and the longer-term trends were discussed by Jelgersma and Pannekoek (1960), Shepard (1960), Fairbridge (1961), Jelgersma (1960), Upson *et al.* (1964), Broecker and von Donk (1970), Curray *et al.* (1970) and Buddemeier *et al.* (1975). Amongst recent works that of Emiliani *et al.* (1975) identified an episode of rapid ice melting and sea-level rise in the Gulf of Mexico at 11,600 B.P. that roughly corresponds to the Valders re-advance.

TABLE 17

The characteristics and ¹⁴C ages of assemblage zones in Flandrian material at Red Moss, Lancashire (Hibbert et al., 1971)

Assemblage zone	Date B.P. from beginning	Chronozone
Quercus-Alnus zone	5010 ± 80	F III
Quercus-Ulmus-Alnus zone	7107 ± 120	F II
Pinus-Corylus-Ulmus zone	8196 ± 150	F Id
Corylus-Pinus zone	8880 ± 170	F Ic
Betula-Pinus-Corylus zone	9798 ± 200	F Ib
Betula-Pinus-Juniperus zone	9508 ± 200	F Ia

Geomorphological and radiometric data from New Zealand also indicate an abrupt increase in the rate of sea-level rise about 11,000 B.P. (Cullen, 1967). In fact two somewhat conflicting points of view have been adopted in regard to late Weichselian and Flandrian changes. Broecker *et al.* advocated a very abrupt climatic warming with an associated abrupt sea-level rise at that time, whilst Curray (1965) favoured a gradual temperature increase spanning the period 15,000–7000 B.P. According to Golik (1968) the rise of sea level at the beginning of the Holocene which caused a transgression in the Gulf of Panama because of the low relief of the area, represents an overall rise of 0·66 m per 100 years between 11,500 and 8500 B.P. The eustatic curves of Curray *et al.* (1970) indicate that Holocene sea levels rose at a rate in excess of 10 mm per year after 4000 B.P. In contrast Buddemeier *et al.* (1975) concluded that there has in fact been a drop in level from a highstand at 4000 B.P. They detected a rapid growth of coral reefs until 3500–3000 B.P.; a sea level that reached its present height no later than 4000 B.P. and was significantly more than 1 m above its present height during the period 3500–2000 B.P.; and finally a drop to present sea level, accompanied by extensive reef erosion, in the period 2000–1000 B.P. Easton and Olson (1976) found that Hanauma Reef in Hawaii started growing at *c.* 7000 B.P., and that most of its vertical growth was accomplished 5,800–3,500 radio-carbon years ago. They concluded that during the last 3,500 years the sea level has *risen* to its present position at a decreasing rate and that it is unlikely that it has stood at an appreciably higher level during the last 3,500 years.

Willis (1961) pointed out that the marine transgression which occurred in the east of the British Isles at 3000 B.C. was due to sinking of the Fenland Basin. However, the transgression of Romano–British times was, in contrast, certainly of eustatic origin because it can be detected in both stable and unstable areas. The various historic sea-level changes which were mentioned in Chapter 3 presumably reflect further eustatic perturbations that are related to climatic variations which gave rise to the recurrence surfaces which occur in peat bogs. Besides the original *Grenz-horizont* of Weber, others occur at 2200 B.C., 1600 B.C., 1200 B.C., at approximately 1,980 years ago, at A.D. 600, and one or two between 800 and 400 B.P. They often fit well with the wriggles of the ^{14}C curve and in this respect it is extremely interesting that one of the steepest portions of the eustatic rise during Flandrian time is between 10,000 and 7000 B.P. which coincides with a peak in the ^{14}C-anomaly curve (Willis and Tauber, 1970).

Other dates obtained in various ways but of comparable significance are those relating to ice-advance. One may cite a few. Many others have been used by historians of climate to identify the climatic conditions during historic time (cf. Chapter 11 below). The Kaskawulsh glacier in Yukon exhibited a maximal retreat between 12,000 and 9000 B.P., and a marked neoglacial advance some 2,600–3,000 years ago (Borns and Goldthwait, 1966). It reached its terminal position, where it left a prominent loop moraine, by *c.* 300 years ago and was still there as recently as 145 years ago. Following a recession, and indeed a disappearance of many residual Wisconsin age alpine glaciers during the warmest part of the hypsithermal, there was, in fact, a widespread neoglacial advance around 4600 B.P., and major re-advances culminating 2,800–2,600 years ago (Porter and Denton, 1967). Recent moraines of the Gulkana and College glaciers of Alaska have been dated using lichenometry and provided dates of 1580(?), 1650, 1830 and 1875. The 1650 and 1830 advances can also be correlated with those of the nearby Black Rapids, Castner and Canwell glaciers (Reger, 1968). Other workers have also described similar advances in the Brooks range. In Chilean Patagonia the ice on the east side of the Cordillera receded into the mountains prior to 12,500 B.P. and, on the west coast, the glaciers were smaller than they are today by 11,000 B.P. Three posthypsithermal neoglacial re-advances subsequently culminated respectively prior to 4200 B.P.; between 2700 and 2200 B.P.; and in the late eighteenth century A.D. Between these re-advances the retreat phases took them back to within their present limits. All these data correlate well with those of Europe (cf. Ladurie, 1971) and with the world-wide cold epoch of meteorologists.

Biological effects all parallel such data. For example the growth rates of *Mya truncata* and *M. pseudoarenaria* in the Canadian arctic and sub-arctic reached maximal values c. 3500 B.P. and have since declined (Andrews, 1973). The oxygen and carbon isotopic composition of *Mya, Hiatella* and *Mytilus* shells suggests that the arctic waters reached a salinity c. 1–2 per cent greater than at present some 3,500 years ago. However, the surface and near-surface waters of Baffin Island also seem to have been more saline than at present during the early Wisconsin advance and Andrews (1973) suggested that such effects may represent low levels of melt-water discharge.

5 CLIMATE DURING THE FLANDRIAN PERIOD

In his consideration of late Weichselian and Flandrian climatology Lamb (1971) concluded that the beginning of the Boreal warm period of Blytt and Sernander corresponds to a dramatically anomalous geographical situation. Glacial conditions still covered much of North America whilst European glaciation had, to all intents and purposes, disappeared. This would have induced a strong thermal wind pattern that might be expected to have steered warm air north-east over the Atlantic and probably favoured dry, anticyclonic conditions over Europe. In Europe, apart from Scandinavia, a warm, or even very warm summer, was coupled with cold winters. Climatic maps generated on the basis of the available biological and geomorphological data readily explained the rapid opening up of both Iceland and Greenland to biota approaching from the European side where the habitats were moving north.

In a similar context Manley (1971) considered that the instability of North American climates, as exhibited in the varying lengths and intensities of known oscillations (Nichols, 1969), may have been emphasised by changes in the circulation of the upper air which can be both amplified and damped by oceanic events. He wondered whether the occurrence of large amounts of drift ice, and melt-water from, for example, the Barents Sea, would affect the climate of Europe in the absence of an associated effect in North America. His thoughts certainly emphasised the need for much further study of the effects that oceanic events, such as the break up of shelf-ice, have on atmospheric behaviour.

The long period of warm climates that followed this early Flandrian period was accompanied by the gradual disappearance of the North American ice sheets. Lamb (1971) considered that channels resulting from the earlier ice load probably connected the Atlantic and Arctic oceans in Canada until around 4000 B.P. The corresponding hemispheric circulation that was suggested by his studies became more westerly (zonal), and therefore moister in Europe, than was the case during Boreal times. However, he considered that it was probably a rather high latitude westerly circulation. The maps generated from available data suggested that by 4000 B.P. the European climate was once again becoming more continental, due to a shortening of the prevailing wavelength of the upper westerlies which was perhaps itself due to weakening of the circulation as the warm era gradually reduced the south–north temperature gradients.

Comparable studies of the prevailing situation during the period around 500 B.C.—at the beginning of what was classically called Sub-Atlantic time—point to a renewed increase of wavelength associated with both cooling in high latitudes and a stronger zonal circulation. The main flow was possibly at lower latitudes than during the foregoing warm phases, and the westerlies and storm tracks would have begun to penetrate Europe to a greater extent than in the earlier Flandrian periods that Lamb considered. The thermal distribution suggested that prominent, cool, north-westerly surface winds in the European summers around *c.* 500 B.C. were accompanied by westerly winds in winter. A suggestive prevalence of cyclonicity within the Scandinavian sector during both seasons further intimated that this period, which marked the onset of the cooler recent climates, was characterised by a very heavy precipitation in Europe.

The circulation and climatic development since the onset of the Flandrian climatic optimum appeared to have both periodic and aperiodic components. The warmest eras—A.D. 950–1300, and to a lesser extent around A.D. 400 and A.D. 1900 to A.D. 1950—all seem to have been associated with a poleward shift of the middle latitude westerlies and their associated depressions (cf. Chapter 3). The coldest periods have been marked by the occurrence of these phenomena further south and their more frequent interruption by blocking and meridional circulation. The shortening of the wavelength in the upper westerlies that accompanies expansion of the circumpolar vortex, and the displacement of the main stream of the upper westerlies to lower latitudes, seem to cause most climatic deteriorations to be accompanied by an increased incidence of upper cold troughs over Europe, and northerly surface winds in the east Greenland–Norwegian Sea area. Traces of such effects are particularly clear in the recorded details of those cooler climatic regimes that set in around 500 B.C. and A.D. 1560, 1690, 1750 and 1950. They are also suspected around 1190, and from 1315 to 1350. Lamb (1969) noted the *c.* 200 year quasi-periodicity that affects the westerly type of circulation over the British Isles and other factors which are probably reflected in fluctuations of the zonal index. This quasi-periodicity may be associated with many of the lesser climatic fluctuations of the last 2,000 years.

As would be expected from the discussion in Chapters 2 and 3 the variations at temperate or arctic latitudes are accompanied by comparable changes in more southerly regions. A statistical assay of the frequency distribution of all the available ^{14}C dates for the Sahara region led Geyh and Jäkel (1974) to suggest that a climate which was able to support vegetation may have prevailed in the Sahara region from 12,500 B.P. Between 11,700 and 10,500 B.P. the climate was dry but it later became humid, and a phase of relatively high humidity was ascribed to 10,000 B.P. Around 8700 B.P. the overall climate then became more balanced and was still able to support vegetation. At *c.* 6000 B.P. there was a slightly more humid phase which was succeeded by an arid one from 4700 to 3700 B.P. After this, relatively humid and arid phases alternated with each other every 700 to 800 years.

Comparable data can be derived from the available palynological data elsewhere. Tsukada (1967), who provided a first approximation to a Flandrian climatic curve in Japan, concluded that material from Lake Nojiri, and the Tsubogakure and Mi-ike bogs, demonstrated a late Weichselian phase of pine and boreal species. This was followed by an early Flandrian boreal forest. A rapid decrease of boreal pollen occurs around 9500 B.P., and the subsequent levels have maximal values for mesophytic broad-leaved species. Converted into annual mean temperatures these suggested values for 11,000 B.P. which were 7–9°C lower than today at an altitude of 650 m, and 3–5° lower at 1,500 m. He suggested that a 5°C rise in temperature occurred around 10,000 B.P., whilst 9,800 years ago the mean annual temperature was 1–3·5°C below today's at the 1,500 m contour. The temperature at the hypsithermal period was *c.* 2·0°C higher than today's. Once again this reflects European conclusions.

6 RADIOCARBON VARIATIONS IN THE ATMOSPHERE

Damon (1970) concluded that, as indicated in Chapter 4 above, the long-term trend of the atmospheric ^{14}C content during the last eight millennia is dominated by a geomagnetic effect (Figs 75 and 76), whereas short-term fluctuations are dominated by a heliocentric modulation. A comparison between the ^{14}C fluctuation curve and

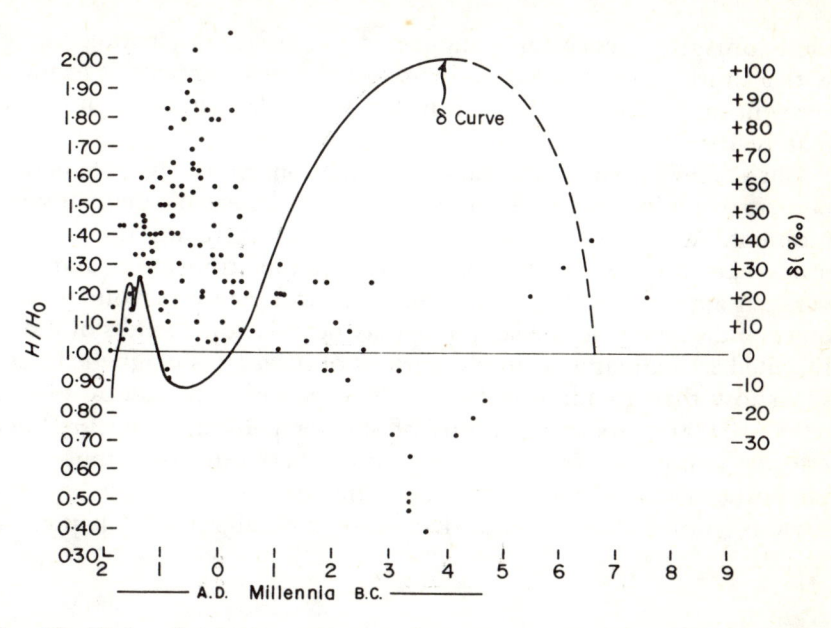

FIG. 75. Ratio of ancient to modern equatorial geomagnetic field intensities compared with an idealised δ curve. The time scale for the δ curve is dendrochronologic years, whereas the B.C. time scale for the geomagnetic data (points) is in radiocarbon years. (Damon, 1970.)

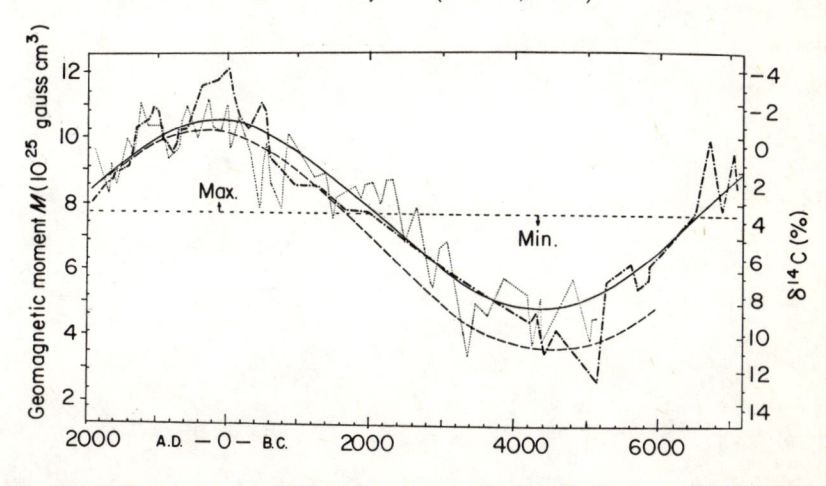

FIG. 76. A comparison of the geomagnetic moment changes (−·−·) with ^{14}C deviations for the half-life 5,730 years (····). The smoothed sinusoidal curve for both geomagnetic moment changes and ^{14}C deviations has a period of c. 8,900 years. Its maximum value is at A.D. 130 and its minimum value at 4320 B.C. (Bucha, 1970.)

the geomagnetic curve also suggested that a ^{14}C fluctuation model with a short lag time of approximately 10^2 years is preferable to more conventional models which indicate longer lag times of approximately 10^3 years.

Bucha (1970) concluded that the fluctuations in the ^{14}C production rate correlate inversely with the changes in the earth's geomagnetic moment. When the value of the moment increases there is an immediate decrease in the ^{14}C content of the atmosphere and vice versa. It appears that the mixing between different reservoirs is very quick and, as a result, the lag phase may be only some tenths of years. Detailed archeomagnetic investigations of the earth's magnetic intensity show that, in addition to the changes with a period of around 8,000–10,000 years, fluctuations of shorter periodicity occur. Such effects comprise a connecting link between the long-term phenomena considered in this and the foregoing chapter and the various shorter-term events that were the subject of Chapters 2 and 3.

11
Climate and History

1 INTRODUCTION

The foregoing chapters briefly survey many of the periods in which critical evolutionary events appear to have been contemporaneous with both climatic changes and their causative geophysical events. However, climatic changes of small magnitude continue to the present day and might be expected, on *a priori* grounds alone, to have influenced man's history, but this has proved to be a very contentious subject. In any discussion of the literature the names of Huntington, Toynbee, Markham and Claiborne remain pre-eminent although, with the hindsight of fifty years, the contributions of Huntington now read somewhat naïvely.

Following Brückner's climatic work at the end of the last century Huntington and his co-workers made a massive contribution to our knowledge of historical climatology and, especially, the impact of climate on man and his societies. This was then carried to its apogee in Toynbee's (1934) consideration of nomadic incursions on to settled societies; fundamentally influenced the same author's theory of "stimulus and response"; and was a basic ingredient of the suggestions made by Brooks (loc. cit.), Markham (1942) and Peattie (1940). Nevertheless it would be quite unfair to portray Huntington as explaining all of history in terms of climate. He was well aware that "the ordinary events of the historical record are due to the differing traits of races, the force of economic pressures, the ambition of kings, the intrigues of statesmen, the zeal of religion, the jealousy of races, the rise of men of genius, the evolution of new political or social institutions, and other similar circumstances" (Huntington and Visher, 1923).

Markham (1942) suggested that civilisations have emerged in regions where the 70°F, or closely related isotherms, coincide with moderate humidities and cultivable areas. Huntington had used a similar conclusion to explain the rise and fall of civilisations when climate changed over the centuries. He and Toynbee also drew attention to the synchrony of many historical events which they saw as common responses to widespread climatic change. Much more recently Winkless and Browning (1975) came to similar conclusions in a somewhat different context.

Lamb (1974) is one of the recent authors to provide a synoptic account of recent climatic history, basing his conclusions on those of Godwin (1940; 1956), Jessen (1949), Mitchell (1956), Overbeck *et al.* (1957), Godwin and Willis (1959) and Frenzel (1966). He considered these in terms of the calibration curves provided by Ralph and Michael (1967), and Suess (1970). The principal conclusions for Central Europe and the British Isles can be succinctly summarised as follows. In Central Europe a relatively cold phase detectable from 3400 to 3000 B.C. contrasts with the earlier climatic optimum. A wet phase is detectable from 1250 to 1200 B.C., and other wet phases begin at 900 B.C., 600 B.C., 400 B.C. and 150 to 100 B.C. Further indications of the initiation of wetter conditions leading to bog growth occur in North Germany around A.D. 565–595 and A.D. 690–770. Studies on the Fernau glacier also suggest it may have been colder between 900 B.C. and 300 B.C. (Gimpel, 1977). In Ireland comparable data suggest more humid conditions beginning at 2800, 2400, 2200, 1500, and 800 B.C., together with A.D. 500. During the period 60 B.C.–A.D. 50 English data intimate a markedly drier period. There is evidence for the drying out of surface peat at various points in late Sub-boreal time (cf. Chapter 10), and, in general terms, the recurrence surfaces recognised by Granlund date from 2300 B.C., 1200 B.C., 500 B.C., A.D. 400, and A.D. 1200. It is the one at 500 B.C. that was classically given the name *Grenz-horizont* all over Europe. As a result of such widely discussed information Lamb concluded, like others before him, that it was safe to assume that wet, cloudy weather certainly characterised the climate of northern Europe around 2200, 1200 and 500 B.C., and during the period A.D. 1250–1300. On the other hand relatively dry periods persisted for several centuries between 1800 and 1400 B.C. and from 80 or 60 B.C. until A.D. 550.

It is important to bear these dates in mind when considering what follows. In the past very precisely stated conclusions about the effects that climate has had on history have been subjected to searching or even scornful critiques that have effectively stifled them. It is as well to be aware of the content of such criticisms and to state quite clearly that such climatic effects have to be seen as having essentially synergistic actions alongside man's decisions. For example, overgrazing can have disastrous results under any circumstances but it is clearly more likely to do so during a period of climatic deterioration which reduces even further the population of ungulates that a given area can support.

Grousset (1941) devoted a page to refuting the idea that the Turco-Mongol invasions of China were due to periodic droughts in Mongolian territory—an idea that he wrongly attributed to Lattimore. Complementarily Lattimore himself (1938), having previously been considerably influenced by Huntington, concluded from his own personal experience of the Manchurians that rigidly mechanistic concepts of geographical determinism are untenable. Indeed he has given (1941; 1950) extensive accounts of the dynamic interactions that characterise relationships between nomadic and settled people—what Toynbee epitomised as the "Desert and the Sown". A similar, although perhaps conciliatory, critique was contributed by Hudson to Toynbee's appendix. Clearly any historical interpretations that deny the potential of individuals, or groups of individuals, to influence history are grotesque. Nevertheless, such influences occur within the context of geography and climate, and any denial of the consequences of this are also insupportable. Many of the older criticisms of "climatic determinism" were, indeed, inspired by doubts about the validity of climatic data, and more particularly about their possible periodicity. In as much as they encouraged further definitive factual investigations, as opposed to speculation, they were undoubtedly of great importance (cf. Godwin, 1956; 1973). However, whilst the foregoing chapters certainly demonstrate that climatic fluctuations during the last 5,000 years have to be seen as often rather minor perturbations on a continuing downward curve, they do demonstrate that such perturbations occurred. What is more important in the present context is that they occurred at historically "significant" times.

2 NOMADIC INCURSIONS

A relatively superficial knowledge suffices to emphasise the impact that nomadic hordes have had upon the civilisations with which they came into contact. Complementarily, eruptions of nomads alternate with the encroachments made by settled peoples upon the steppes. In his consideration of nomadic incursions Toynbee emphasised that the most important aspect was the widespread synchronism. In this

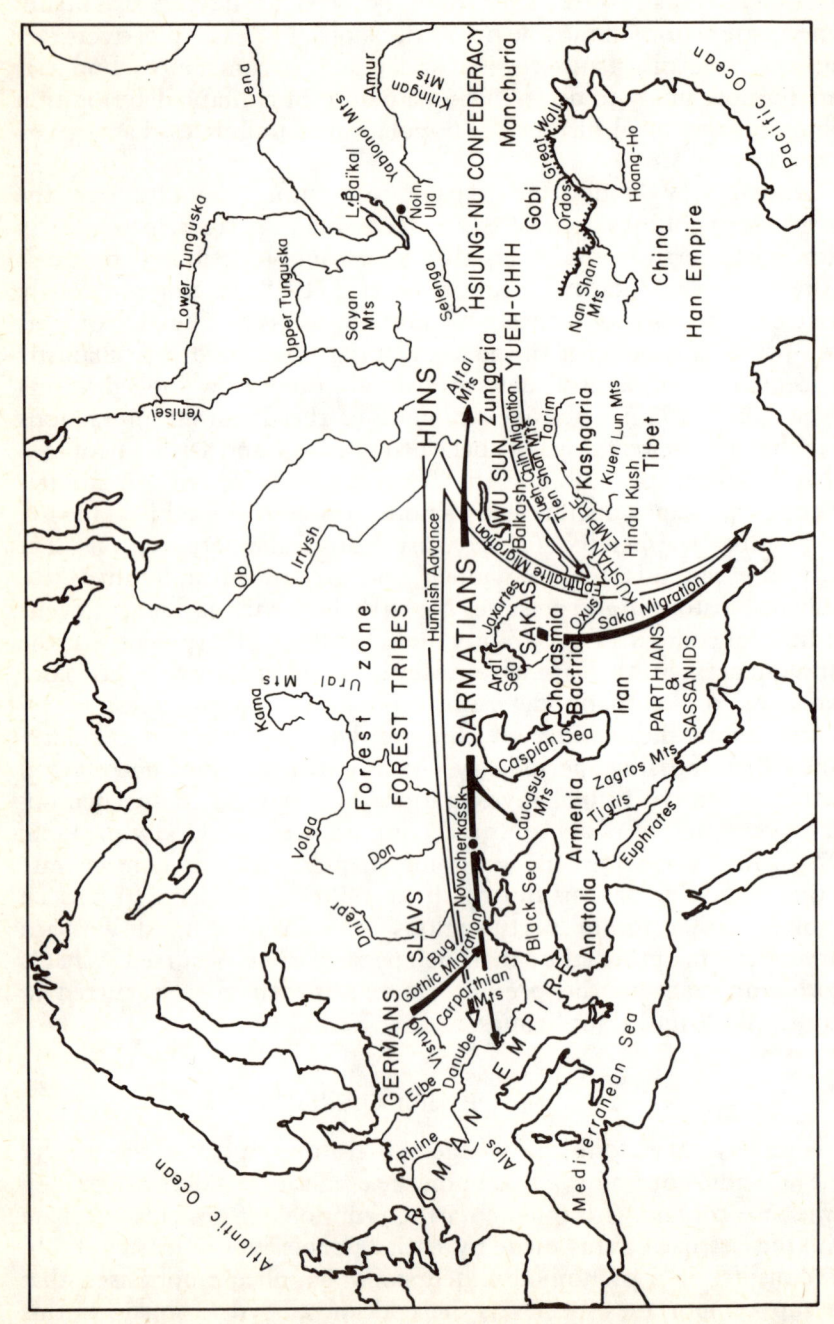

FIG. 77. Map of the Sarmatian, Saka and Hunnish movements of the fourth century B.C. to the fifth century A.D. (Phillips, 1965).

he has recently been supported by Claiborne (1970), Winkless and Browning (1975). For convenience he considered six vents from the Eurasian Steppe and nine from Afrasian regions. Each of these he further subdivided into four thresholds (see Table 18) because, as he remarked, our extant records of nomadic eruptions are almost all derived from the sedentary peoples into whose domains they burst (cf. Fig. 77). Sensational eruptions of this nature have often been preceded by a long "seepage", as in the case of the Arabs whose presence on the borderlands of the Roman and Sassanian empires gave rise, prior to Mohammad's birth, to the Ghassanid and Lahmid Arab Principalities. This preceded the flood of Arabs over the Roman and Sassanid empires in the seventh century A.D. In contrast, the advance of the Avars, Magyars and Mongols on to European territory was as with a bolt from the blue.

The most striking synchronisms are those which involve all the regions. As an example of this Toynbee cited the period around 700 B.C. (see also Phillips, 1965). At that time the Cimmerians and Scythians had arrived at their third threshold in the course of their eruption between the Pamirs and the Caspian, and the Arabs were pressing on the Upper Euphrates from the opposite direction. Again, at the turn of the fourth and fifth centuries A.D., when the Juan Juan were breaking upon China between the Khingan and the Tien Shan, and the Huns were erupting simultaneously between both the Pamirs and the Caspian and the Caspian and the Urals, the Arabs were once more pressing upon the Euphrates and Syria, whilst the Berbers were invading the Roman dominions in Cyrenaica and north-west Africa. Similarly when, in the eleventh century A.D., the Saljuqs were erupting between the Pamirs and the Caspian, and the Cumans between the Caspian and the Urals, the Banu Hilal were, at the same time, breaking out of Arabia across Syria and Egypt into the Maghrib, and the Murabits were emerging from the west Sahara into the Sudan in one direction and into Morocco and Andalusia in the other.

Other synchronisms have also long been known although they do not involve both the Afrasian and Eurasian regions—Winkless and Browning also noted American parallels. Toynbee noted that on the Afrasian Steppe, during the fourteenth, thirteenth and twelfth centuries B.C., the Libyans were pressing from the west bank of the Nile, and the Aramaeans were moving out of the North Arabian steppe into Syria. On the Eurasian steppe at the turn of the third and second centuries B.C. the Hsiung Nu were pressing upon China whilst, at the other extreme, the Sarmatians were crossing the Don. Again, about

TABLE 18

Toynbee's summary of the successive thresholds in the vents from the Steppes through which nomadic eruptions occurred
(Toynbee, 1934)

The vents from the Steppes	I	II	III	IV
Eurasian region				
1. Between Korea and Khingan	Liaotung Pale	Shanhaikuan	Huang Ho–Yangtze Watershed	
2. Between Khingan and Tien Shan	Great Wall	Eastern Plain, Tibet, Tarim Basin	Huang Ho–Yangtze Watershed	Indochina and Burma
3. Between Pamirs and Caspian	Jaxartes	Iran	Punjab, Iraq, Anatolia,	Ganges Basin, Maharashtra, Syria, Egypt
4. Between Caspian and Urals	Emba	Volga and Don, Lower Volga, Kama	Crimea, Lower Danube, Hungary	Thrace and Thessaly
5. Between Urals and Altai	West-Siberian Steppes			
6. Between Altai and Khingan	Baikal Basin			
Afrasian region				
1. Lower Euphrates	Iraq	Iran	Oxus–Jaxartes Basin	

2. Upper Euphrates	Jazirah		
3. Syria	Syria	Anatolia, Egypt	
4. Nile front from the Libyan side	Egypt and Nubia	Syria	
5. Cyrenaica	Cyrenaica		
6. Maghrib	Maghrib	Andalusia	
7. Sudan	West Sudan		Maghrib, East Sudan
8. Yemen	Yemen	Abyssinia	
9. East African front	Somaliland		Andalusia

the middle of the sixth century A.D., when the Avars, with the Khazars at their heels, were sweeping out of the Steppe and across the Emba, Volga and Don, into the Hungarian Alföld, the Khitan were pressing on China. Finally, in the first half of the thirteenth century the Mongols erupted out of the Eurasian Steppe on almost every front simultaneously.

Indo-European nomads seem to have been pre-eminent on the Steppes from the fifth millennium B.P. to around the fifth century B.C. It is not until around the fourth and third centuries B.C. that the Turkic Hsiung Nu become prominent. Thereafter Finno-Ugrian, Turkic, or Mongol nomads emerge in waves. One can only speculate as to whether this reflects a rough latitudinal racial distribution which was first established at the climatic optimum and then displaced southwards by gradual, pulsing, climatic deterioration.

In their summary Winkless and Browning (1975) envisaged some seven bouts of activity. The first they dated at 3500 B.C., when they thought the settled Tripolytes became nomadic. Around 2000 B.C. there was an outburst of activity in the Sahara region at the same time as Indo-Europeans spread out from the southern parts of the USSR into Iran, India, Greece, etc. The Hyksos in Egypt were viewed as a secondary effect of this. The fourth round of events was in the period around 1200 B.C., when Eurasian migrations coincided with the conquest of the Shang dynasty in China by the Chou—long recalled in the Chinese classics—with the emergence of the Chavin culture in Peru, and the Nok iron-age culture in Nigeria. The fifth round they attribute to $c.$ 500 B.C. when they draw attention to a possible synchrony between incursions of mounted insurgents from the Steppes on to western Europe and the end of the Chavin culture. During the fourth century continuing expansion from the east led the Sarmatians to increase the Scythian pressure on the west, and contemporary activities on the periphery of the Middle Kingdom led to consolidation of the early segments of the Great Wall. Recurrent activity of this nature was, subsequently, to have more profound effects on Chinese social, political and dynastic history.

The period from 200 B.C. to A.D. 200 saw increased stability within the confines of both the Hellenic and Chinese worlds. Indeed in the latter location this was the time of the early and later Han, which together stretched from 202 B.C. to A.D. 220, and were only interrupted by the transitory usurpation of Wang Mang between A.D. 9 and 23. Comparable stability was adduced by Winkless and Browning for the Amerindian cultures such as the White Dog. In contrast between A.D. 220 and 589 the Chinese dynastic history was disrupted, first by the establishment of the San Kuo or Three Kingdoms; then by the Ts'in dynasty; and finally by the Northern and Southern Kingdoms. The period of 400 years that separates the Han from the Sui dynasties is, indeed, frequently viewed as the nearest Sinic equivalent to the European Dark Ages. The collapse of the Han was followed by nomadic invasions. In the South, which escaped occupation by alien groups, the culture of the Han survived. In the north the empire, distracted by internal squabbles and having called upon the assistance of a nomad tribe, was overrun in A.D. 311. In A.D. 386 the northern dynasty of the Toba tartars was established and lasted for some 250 years.

In America the Paracas culture of the southern Peruvian desert may have ended around A.D. 400, to be replaced by the Nasca Ica culture. The Sinagua people appear in Little Colorado Valley and the Basket Makers spread over south-western USA. In the fourth and fifth centuries the Maya culture passed through a significant phase whilst, elsewhere, as cited above, the Huns were on the move and penetrated northern India. Between 450 and 560 the eastern Slavs moved from the Don valley to the Danube, Aegean and Adriatic, and were viewed as secondary effects. In the fifth century Frisians, Angles and Saxons invaded England. The scene then switches to the twelfth century. China had a series of catastrophes and in 1132 the Nuchen Tartars conquered all of northern China. Around 1150 the Sinagua people left the Arizona highlands and moved into the river valleys. In 1168 the Aztecs arrived in Mexico, and in 1174 the Almohades conquered and dominated northern Africa. Perhaps the best known effects at such times are, however, the conquests of the Mongols. Between 1220 and 1227 Ghenghiz Khan conquered north China, Turkestan, Afghanistan, Persia and the southern USSR, leading, in 1278, to the final establishment of the Yuan dynasty in China.

It would be out of place to list all the effects of such nomadic invasions. Toynbee (loc. cit.), Fitzgerald (1961), Needham (1954), and others have discussed the role of such peoples in the diffusion of ideas. Suffice it to say that the introduction of Buddhism to China, and hence to Japan, together with all the attendant modifications of the indigenous Taoism and Confucianism, were given great momentum by the fact that the nomadic dynasties intervening between the Han and the Sui were Lamaistic Buddhists. The encouragement of technology in the Northern Sung was also, in no small part, a reflection of the non-Chinese origins of the dynasty.

3 CHINESE HISTORY

Passing references to the history of China have already been made above in the context of nomadic incursions from the Eurasian Steppe, and a synoptic review is contained in Table 19. Broadly

TABLE 19

The dynastic history of China with the generally accepted dates for establishment of unification within the relevant areas

Shang	1500–1027 B.C.
Chou	1027–256 B.C.
Warring States	403–221 B.C.
Ch'in dynasty	221–207 B.C.
Han dynasty	202 B.C.–A.D. 220
(Usurpation of Wang Mang A.D. 9–23)	
San Kuo	A.D. 221–265
Ts'in dynasty	A.D. 265–316
Northern and Southern dynasties	A.D. 316–589
Sui dynasty	A.D. 589–618
T'ang dynasty	A.D. 618–907
Five dynasties	A.D. 907–960
Northern Sung	A.D. 960–1126
Southern Sung	A.D. 1127–1279
Yuan dynasty	A.D. 1279–1368

speaking one may say that those periods of relative stability, that are characterised by dynastic continuity, are separated by phases of rapid dynastic succession which often involve dynasties of alien origin. These factors have long preoccupied the Chinese dynastic historians, if for no other reason than that those employed by a newly established dynasty have felt it incumbent upon themselves to demonstrate that the foregoing dynasty had lost the "Mandate of Heaven". The socio-political background to such changes has also, of course, preoccupied Western historians of the Sinic world and panoramic accounts figure in Fitzgerald (1961), Elvin (1973) and Cotterell and Morgan (1975) amongst others. Synopses of more specific subjects, such as the part played by nomads, merchants, priests, generals and explorers in the transmission of ideas between east and west, and between China, Korea and Japan, figure in the works referred to above.

The significance of the climatic data contained within the Chinese classics was appreciated by Brooks (1949), and has recently been reviewed by Gribbin (1976) who drew on the account of Chu

Ko-chen. The keeping of official records dates back at least to the inauguration of the Chou dynasty and these are supplemented by allusions to natural phenomena which occur in poems or other literary works. At the inception of the Chou the climate seems to have enabled bamboo to grow extensively in the valley of the Yellow River. However, the Han River, a tributary of the Yangtze, froze in 903 and 897 B.C., and this has been taken as indicative of a transient climatic deterioration. Great droughts then followed but, by the mid-Chou, the conditions seem to have improved. From about the ninth century B.C. until the time of Confucius (557–479 B.C.) the Yellow River area appears to have experienced warmer weather. The next cold period began about 200 B.C. and six very severe winters, with frost and snow in late spring, followed in the space of a century. From the first century B.C. to the first century A.D. the climate seems to have been better but between A.D. 155 and 220 attempts to cultivate oranges at Loyang failed. This in spite of their successful cultivation at a date some 300 years earlier during the Han. In A.D. 225 naval activity at Kuangling had to be broken off when the Huai River froze for the first time "on record".

Gribbin considered that it was reasonable to argue that during the eighth and ninth centuries A.D. the temperature and rainfall belts in eastern China were somewhat north of their present positions. A dramatic change occurred in the twelfth century. In China it seems that the climatic deterioration of the medieval Little Ice Age occurred in the twelfth century, somewhat earlier than in the west. A long cold period functionally extended from the tenth to the fourteenth centuries (Arakawa, 1966) and Gribbin thought that its full impact did not reach the west until the sixteenth century.

A glance at Table 19 will certainly show that the periods of climatic deterioration, resulting as they must in marked changes in a peasant, or indeed aristocratic, standard of living, can be correlated with increased strife in the Middle Kingdom, and increased pressure from nomads outside the Pale. Coupled with the complacency of a long-established dynasty they must surely underlie the loss of the "Mandate of Heaven". What is more they had influences further afield. It has been observed by modern historians (see Fitzgerald, 1966) that there is a striking relationship between the rise of strong states in south-east Asia and the decline of strong dynasties in China. This begins to appear in the Vietnam, Laos and Khmer Rouge regions as early as the T'ang dynasty. As T'ang China slowly declined Cambodia grew strong on the continent, and Shrivajaya (=Sumatra) grew strong amongst the islands. When the Sung were

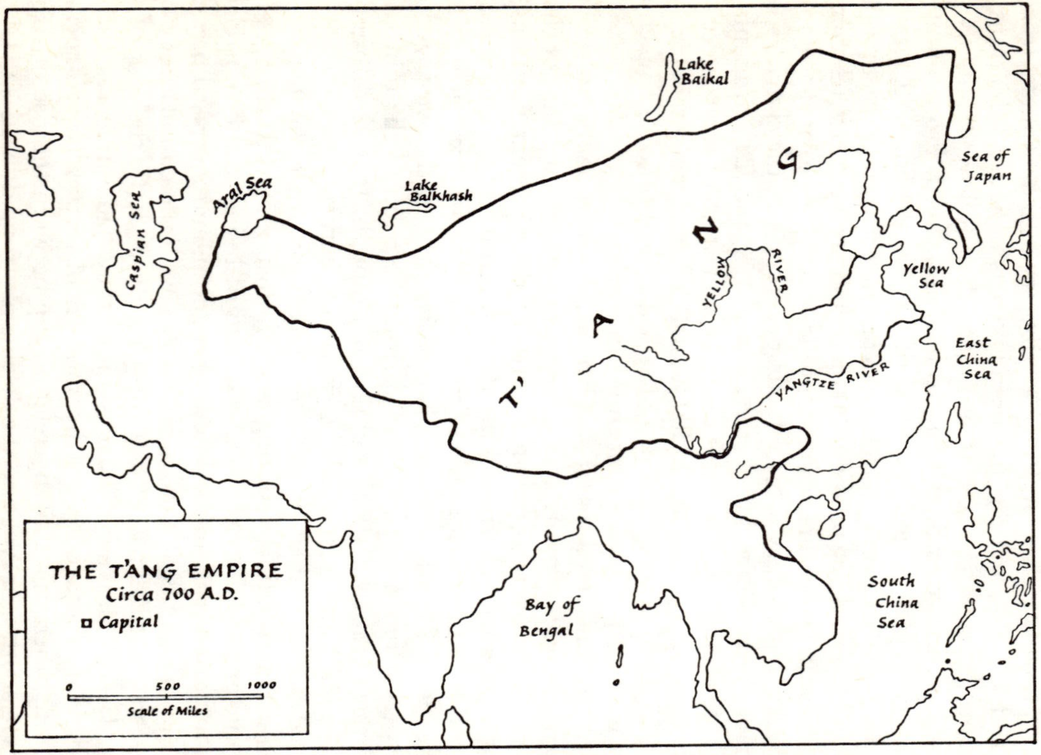
THE T'ANG EMPIRE
Circa 700 A.D.
Capital
0
500
1000
Scale of Miles
T' A N G
Lake Baikal
Lake Balkhash
Aral Sea
Caspian Sea
Sea of Japan
Yellow Sea
East China Sea
South China Sea
Bay of Bengal
YELLOW RIVER
YANGTZE RIVER

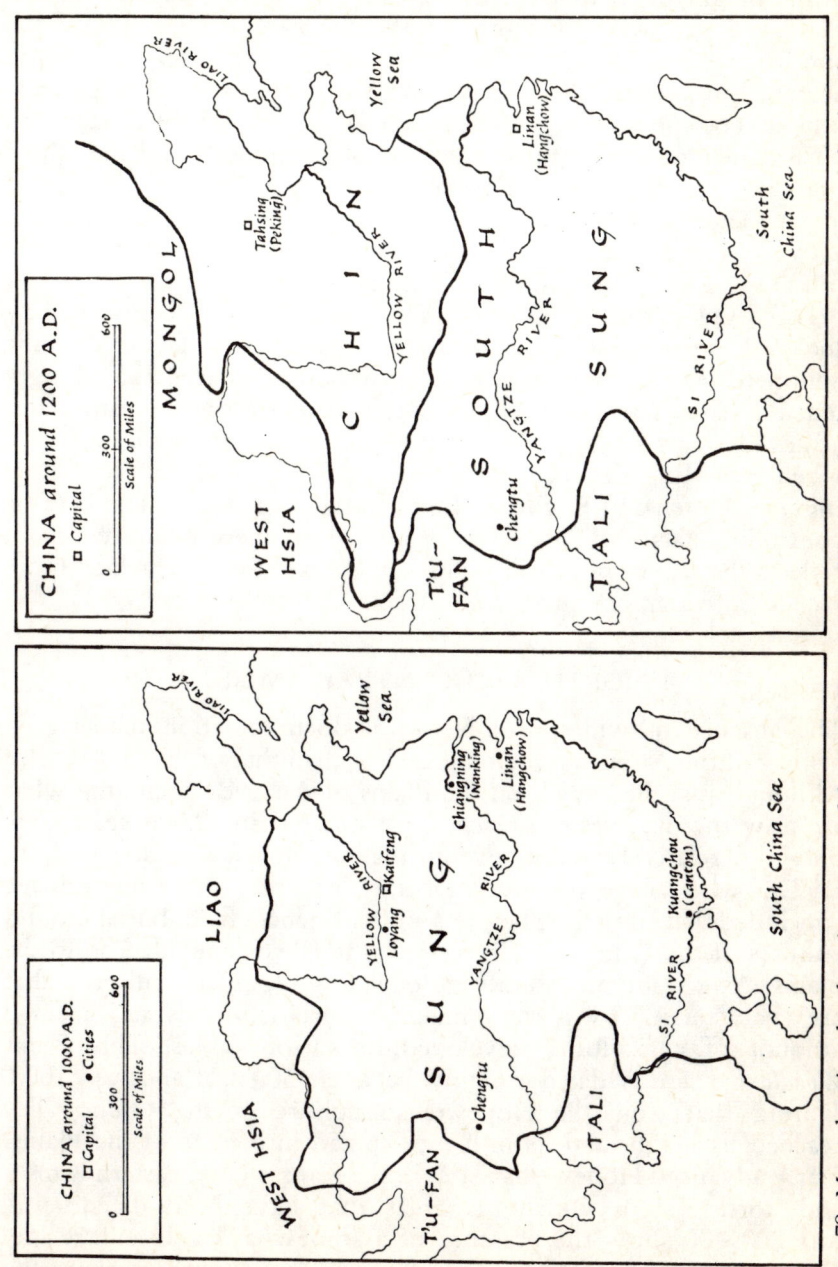

FIG. 78. Maps showing the changing extent of the "Middle Kingdom" around the first millennium A.D. and the distribution of neighbouring peoples.

at the height of their influence in China they encouraged rivals to these strong powers—Champa on the one hand against Cambodia, and Java against Shrivijaya. With the decline of the Sung Cambodia achieved importance once again, and Shrivijaya attained its greatest power. The subsequent reunification of China under the Mongols in 1278 coincides with a further decline of Cambodia, and the fall of both the kingdom of Shrivijaya and the new Burmese power of Pagan. There is clear evidence that the Mongol emperor Kublai Khan actively sought these results and it would appear that he was following a well-established Chinese policy.

After Kublai the decline of the Yuan dynasty was accompanied by the gradual rise of Java (Majapahit) in the islands and Thailand on the continent. When the Chinese Ming dynasty replaced the Mongol Yuan dynasty direct interference in the affairs of neighbouring states achieved a new strength. In the sixteenth and seventeenth centuries, when the Ming declined, it was newcomers from the west, Portuguese, Dutch and English, who penetrated the region and became controlling factors. This series is clearly no mere coincidence but reflects the reality of power politics in South East Asia, which more recent European conquests long obscured.

4 NORTH AND CENTRAL AMERICA

The absence of widespread historical documentation renders the history of the American region less clear than that of the Old World. Although man has dwelt on the Plains of America, including what are now the dry western reaches, for more than 12,000 years, it is only the relatively recent events that are known to us. Josephy (1972), who surveyed much of the literature on Amerindians, concluded that sometime before A.D. 0 influences from burial mound cultures of the Ohio and Mississippi watersheds extended on to the plains. As a result an assemblage of Plains Woodland cultures, that are characterised by pottery making, burial mounds and a small amount of agriculture, developed in various areas. This *Plains Woodland phase* is dated roughly between 500 B.C. and A.D. 1000. During that time the Hopewellian culture of the Ohio valley reached its height and its influence spread into parts of the Plains. Fairly advanced Hopewellian sites in the Kansas City, eastern Kansas and north-eastern Oklahoma areas that have been dated at *c.* A.D. 200–400 show the presence of a somewhat stable village life. Beginning perhaps around A.D. 800, if not slightly earlier, the woodland cultures were then succeeded by others which had more reliance upon agriculture, a more settled way of life, and seem to have been influenced by the Mississippian culture. In the north Woodland Siouan speakers, with strong Mississippian influences, moved into the Middle Missouri Valley, whilst Caddoan speakers from the south-east moved into the Central Plains and, farther south, a third stream also advanced westwards.

In the period after A.D. 700 Mississippian temple mounds began appearing in the south-east. In the lower Mississippi basin these grew in both numbers and complexity, and flourished until at least A.D. 1600. In southern Arkansas, northern Louisiana, eastern Texas and Oklahoma, the new Caddoan culture had been developing. By A.D. 500 influences from the lower Mississippi, and also perhaps from Mexico via Texas, speeded development. As the Mississippian culture spread, carried into parts of the south-east by what may have been large migrant groups, it was accompanied, after about A.D. 1200, by the diffusion of elements of the southern cult symbolised by the long-nosed God. This is believed to have originated with the Caddoan culture and became widespread at that time.

Between A.D. 500 and 1500 the growth of population in the Californian region, the adaptation to different environments, and the independence of the various groups, led to a variety of differing cultures. Nearby, and occupying a large part of the north-eastern Arizona as well as north-western Mexico and a strip of south-eastern Utah, was the largest tribe—the Athapascan Navahos. They had broken away from the related peoples farther north and migrated south between A.D. 1000 and 1500. Other related groups comprised the Apaches; the Jicarillas of north-eastern New Mexico; the Mescaleros of the south central part; the Chiricahuas of south-eastern Arizona; and the Western Apaches of east Arizona. Additional Apache groups—the Lipans and Kiowa Apaches—settled further east because they followed the life of plains indians.

Centred in the mountainous country of south-east Arizona and south-west New Mexico the Mogollon culture persisted with relatively few changes, except for pottery styles, until A.D. 1100 when it was fundamentally influenced by another south-west group, the Anasazi, who lived further north. A second south-east culture, the Hohokam, was also influential during the period A.D. 900–1100, and one group expanded northward through Arizona's Verde Valley, thereby coming into contact with another agricultural people—the Sinagua. About A.D. 1100 Anasazi influences swept over the Sinagua and, some 50 years later, the latter moved south pushing back the Hohokam and bringing Anasazi traits into Hohokam territory. About A.D. 1300 another Anasazi grouping, the Saladoans from the mountainous regions of east central Arizona, migrated into the Hohokam country of the lower Gila.

Pueblo culture reached its zenith in the south-west during the Great Pueblo period from A.D. 1100 to 1300. However, Anasazi influences began to decline and disappear latterly and their accelerated disappearance has been attributed to a 23 year drought from 1276 to 1299; to a change in rainfall patterns and a consequential acceleration in the rate of erosion which lowered the water table and made agriculture more difficult; to an epidemic; to pressure from hostile nomadic invaders from the Great Basin, or from newly arrived Athapascan speakers; to intra-pueblo factionalism amongst the great clans; or to a depletion of wood supply. In view of the events elsewhere any climatic change would be expected to induce most of these effects. The Pueblos dispersed to new areas where they experienced a Golden Age until the appearance of the Spaniards in 1540. However, after about 1450 new large-scale withdrawals occurred, more settlements and entire districts were abandoned as abruptly as before, and, when the Spaniards reached the area, the Pueblo people were no longer living in the south-west except in, and near, the Rio Grande, and in the Zuni and Hopi areas further west.

Finally, in northern Mexico urban and ceremonial centres flourished in agricultural areas along the eastern and western sides of the Sierra Madre Occidental between A.D. 900 and 1200. A great stirring of peoples, and a predominantly southward movement, seems to have begun in the twelfth century. It has long been thought that this may reflect climatic changes and, in particular, a prolonged drought. Various former agricultural areas were abandoned by highly developed cultures and nomadic groups were also involved. The pressures were experienced all the way to the Valley of Mexico, into which waves of immigrants flowed from the north. These comprised groups of marauding newcomers who were mostly "farmers" from the northern Mexico cultural area, but included nomads who the Mesoamericans referred to as Chichimecs—dog people. Tula, the capital of the Toltecs, fell to them in 1200, and their arrival was associated with many socio-political upheavals. The warlike Mixtecs seem to have expanded into the Zapotec country of Oaxaca, and the Tarascans to have established dominance over a large agricultural population in Michoacan. Other comparable events occurred elsewhere in Central America and the Caribbean region. Chorotegas had entered the area around A.D. 800, and Nicaraos around A.D. 1100, whilst in the Andes the Incas traced their origin to

Quechua-speaking indians of the Cuzco basin. These were epitomised by the semi-mythical Manco Capac who was dated in legend to A.D. 1200. By 1438 they had established their rule over a large area around Cuzco.

5 BRITISH HISTORY

Cunliffe (1974) has reviewed our knowledge of the millennium preceding the Roman invasion of Britain. Many of his cultural theses conform to the known history of climate. For example the change that occurred from the fifth century to first century B.C., that implies a progressive isolation of Britain from the mainland, occurs at a time when paleobotanical data imply more humid, perhaps stormier, conditions. At that time Britain seems to have lacked the close contacts with the continent that typify the seventh and sixth centuries B.C. This lull in continental trading contacts seems to have ended by 100 B.C. and, after that date, trading seems to have become intensified once again. Other changes also occur alongside these varying levels of contact with the continent, and society, as reflected in archaeological finds, began to exhibit more pronounced evidence of aggression from the fifth century B.C. onwards. Cunliffe concluded that this reflected competition for resources as the result of a population increase. Such a population increase may clearly reflect the foregoing mild climate, with resource competition being intensified by a climatic deterioration around 500 B.C.

The climate then ameliorated again and, during Roman times, was probably not dissimilar to that today although, in view of a marine transgression, it may have been rather warmer. Later the general temperature rose further and the seas became less stormy. As a result in late Saxon times, and during the Viking age, there was a more genial climate than we experience today. This was the time of North Atlantic exploration and the establishment of vineyards in southern England. It seems probable that, at that time, this latter region enjoyed a climate which was more closely akin to that of northern France today—with summer temperatures perhaps a degree centigrade warmer than in the sixties of the present century.

There was, indeed, a dry period in the latter half of the seventh century which ended around A.D. 682, but was followed, between A.D. 713 and 775, by fifteen severe droughts—nearly one out of every four years (Brooks and Glasspoole, 1928). In contrast the ninth century produced only one notable drought, that of 822–823. There then follows a gap of 165 years before the next series which began in

987 and was notable for the great heat which accompanied the dryness. The summers of 987, 988, 989, 992, 993 and 994 were so hot that "the corn and fruit dried up". In 1022 the heat was so excessive that "men and animals died". The next group of droughts began in 1102. The winter of 1113–1114, and the greater part of the latter year, were so dry that the "Thames was almost without water", and the summer was so dry that "corn and forests caught fire". The summers of 1129–1131 were all hot and dry and continued to be so until 1137. In between these dry years occur groups of wet ones. For example, between 1087 and 1124 great rains were recorded in 1087, 1093, 1098, 1099, 1100, 1103, 1105, 1116 and 1117 (cf. Lamb, 1972).

Variations of climate, particularly of prevailing temperature and storminess, since 1300 have been of great importance. The effects of the deterioration from 1300 to the sixteenth century have, as Lamb emphasised, commonly been overlooked because of the overwhelming concern with the Black Death. Moreover England, unlike more northern lands, was in the fortunate position that the full range of temperature variation that occurred left her within an optimal European region. To some extent her commerce and fisheries actually benefitted from the deterioration. However, Gimpel (1977) concluded that, in agriculture, the period after 1300 saw a reduction in the cultivation of both fruit and grain, particularly in mountain districts. The plough had reached its highest levels during the twelfth and thirteenth centuries—*beyond the limits of the wartime emergency campaign of 1940–1944*. All such considerations necessarily affected economics and the standards of living. The particularly abrupt chilling from about 1530–1560 also seems to coincide with the general introduction of glass in windows, which had previously been of lattice and wicker.

The late 1500s and 1600s were probably the worst time and it was the 1690s which saw the last serious famine on the mainland of the UK with a run of harvest failures in Scotland producing as many deaths as the plague. Bad harvests occurred in, for example, 1586–1587, and from 1590–1597 harvests were bad, production low and prices crippling. Such conditions were both persistant (cf. Fig. 79) and widespread. The first half of the seventeenth century saw uprisings in Hungary, Russia, France etc., but it was 1648 that was the crisis year. In the British Isles bad harvests occurred from 1646 to 1649; the winter 1647–1648 was a particularly wet one and in London 1647–1649 saw the highest level of wheat prices in the seventeenth century prior to 1661. Elsewhere rains in Andalusia led to bread shortages in 1647–1648. In southern Italy and Sicily the rains of

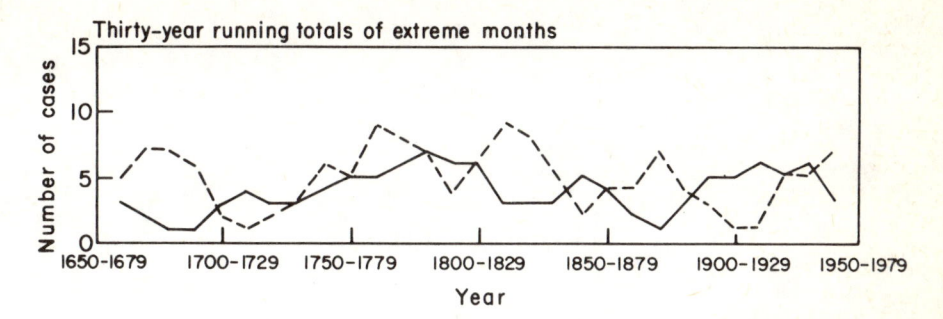

Fig. 79. The frequency of very warm and very cold months in England shown as continuous and broken lines respectively (after Lamb, 1975).

February 1647 were followed by a drought and therefore by famine conditions. In England the Leveller movement under Lilburne, Overton and Walwyn made its first effective appearance in July 1646. At the same time (1648) major revolts occurred in Naples and Palermo; in Granada; in Muscovy; and there was the revolt of the Frondes in France. These all occurred, of course, some 300 years ago, and the periodicities mentioned in earlier chapters involve several of 300–400 years!

Clearly folk migrations, famines, and their attendant strife or social reorganisation, can follow both extreme drought or extreme rain. That this is the case should certainly not lead one to ignore the effect of climatic change on the affairs of men. Pressures resulting from resource competition are maximised at such times but, complementarily, man's ingenuity and initiative may also be maximised. The lessons of the past should give us an intimation of the problems of the future. The twentieth century has already seen far too much human tragedy. Let us hope that the world community will sustain programmes that will prevent future disasters arising from climatic change.

References

ABBOTT, C. G. and FOWLE, F. E. (1913). Volcanoes and climate. *Smithson. misc. Collns*, **60** (29), 24.

ABBOT, C. G. (1963). Solar variation and weather. *Smithson. misc. Collns*, **146,** 99. (See also *ibid* (1967). **151** (5), 32.)

AGER, D. V. (1973). "The Nature of the Stratigraphical Record". Macmillan, London.

AKASOFU, S. I. and CHAPMAN, S. (1961). The ring current geomagnetic disturbance and the Van Allen radiation belts. *J. Geophys. Res.* **66,** 1321.

ALDREDGE, L. R. (1975). A hypothesis for the source of impulses in geomagnetic secular variations. *J. Geophys. Res.* **80,** 1571–1578.

ALDREDGE, L. R. (1976). Effects of solar activity on annual means of geomagnetic components. *J. Geophys. Res.* **81,** 2990–2996.

ALLISON, J., GODWIN, H. and WARREN, S. H. (1952). Late-glacial deposits at Nazeing in the Lea Valley. *Phil. Trans. R. Soc. Ser. B.* **236,** 169–240.

AMERIGIAN, C. (1974). Sea-floor dynamic processes as the possible cause of correlations between paleoclimatic and paleomagnetic indices. *Earth Planet. Sci. Lett.* **21,** 31.

ANDEL, T. H. van, HEATH, G. R., MOORE, T. C. and MCGEARY, D. F. R. (1967). Late Quaternary history, climate and oceanography of the Timor Sea. *Am. J. Sci.* **265,** 737–758.

ANDERSON, D. L. (1967). Accelerated plate tectonics. *Science*, **187,** 1077.

ANDERSON, R. Y. (1961). Solar–terrestrial climatic patterns in varved sediments. *Ann. N.Y. Acad. Sci.* **95,** 424–439.

ANDREWS, J. T. (1973). Late Quaternary variations in oxygen and carbon isotopic compositions in Canadian arctic marine bivalves. *Paleogeog. Paleoclim. Paleoecol.* **14,** 187–192.

ARAI, Y. (1958). Characteristics of long waves in westerlies related to solar activity. *J. Met. Soc. Jap.* **36,** 46–54.

ARAKAWA, H. (1966). Addenda to climatic change as revealed by the data from the Far East. *In* "Pleistocene and Post-Pleistocene Climatic Variations in the Pacific Area" (Blumenstock, D. I., Ed.), pp. 95–101. Bishop Museum Press, Honolulu.

ARKELL, W. J. (1956). "Jurassic Geology of the World". Oliver and Boyd, Edinburgh.

ARNASON, B. (1969). The exchange of hydrogen isotopes between ice and water in temperate glaciers. *Earth. Planet. Sci. Lett.* **6,** 423–430.

REFERENCES

ARNOLD, C. A. (1968). Current trends in paleobotany. *Earth Sci. Rev.* **4**, 283–309.
ARRHENIUS, G. (1952). Sediment cores from the East Pacific. *Rep. Swed. Deep Sea Exped.* (1947–48), **5**, 1–89.
ASANO, K., TAKAYANAGI, Y. and TAKAYAMA, T. (1974). Late Neogene epoch boundaries in Japan. In "Late Neogene Epoch Boundaries" (Saito, T. and Burckle, L., Eds), pp. 115–123. American Museum of Natural History.
AUER, V. (1956). The Pleistocene of Fuego-Patagonia. I. The iceage and interglacial ages. *Suomal. Tideakat. Toim. Helsinki Sarja. A III Geologica. Geographica*, **45**, 266.
AUER, V. (1958). The Pleistocene of Fuego-Patagonia. II. History of the flora and vegetation. *Suomal. Tideakat. Toim. Helsinki Sarja. A III. Geologica. Geographica*, **50**, 239.
AXELROD, D. I. (1937). A Pliocene flora from the Mount Eden beds, Southern California. *Carnegie Inst. Washington Publ.* **476**, 125–183.
AXELROD, D. I. (1960). The evolution of flowering plants. In "The Evolution of Life" (Sol Tax, Ed.), pp. 227–305. Chicago.
AXELROD, D. I. (1966a). Potassium-Argon ages of some western Tertiary floras. *Am. J. Sci.* **264**, 497–506.
AXELROD, D. I. (1966b). Origin of deciduous and evergreen habits in temperate forests. *Evolution*, Lancaster, Pa. **20**, 1–15.
AXELROD, D. I. and BAILEY, H. P. (1969). Paleotemperature analysis of Tertiary floras. *Paleogeog. Paleoclim. Paleoecol.* **6**, 163–195.
AZZAROLI, A. and AMBROSETTI, P. (1970) Late Villafranchian and early Mid-Pleistocene faunas in Italy. *Paleogeog. Paleoclim. Paleoecol.* **8**, 107–112.
BAILEY, H. P. (1960). A method of determining the warmth and temperateness of climate. *Geog. Annal.* **42**, 1–16.
BALFOUR STEWART (1882). Terrestrial magnetism. *Encyclo. Brit.* 9th Ed.
BANDY, O. L. (1968a). Paleoclimatology and Neogene planktonic foraminiferal zonation. *G. Geol.* **35**, 277–290.
BANDY, O. L. (1968b). Cycles in Neogene paleoceanography and eustatic changes. *Paleogeog. Paleoclim. Paleoecol.* **5**, 63–75.
BANDY, O. L. (1971). Recognition of Upper Miocene Neogene Zone N18, Experimental Mohole, Guadeloup site. *Nature, Lond.* **233**, 476–487.
BANDY, O. L. and CASEY, K. E. (1969). Epoch boundaries and paleotemperature cycles of the late Cenozoic. *Geol. Soc. Am. Abstr. Prog.* 1969, part 7, 252–254.
BANDY, O. L., CASEY, R. E. and WRIGHT, R. C. (1971). Late Neogene planktonic zonation, magnetic reversals and radiometric dates, Antarctic to the Tropics. *Am. Geophys. Union. Antarct. Res. Ser.* (Antarctic oceanology 1), **15**, 1–26.
BANDY, O. L., CASEY, R. E. and THEYER, F. (1972). Planktonic events, Upper Gilbert-Gauss magnetic epochs. *Geol. Soc. Am. Abst. Prog.* **4**, 442.
BANKS, H. P. (1970). Summary and time scale to symposium on geological record of plants. *Biol. Rev.* **45**, 451–454.
BANTELMANN, A. (1960). Forschungsergebnisse der Marschenarchäologie zur Frage der Niveauveranderung an der Schleswig-Holsteinischen Westkuste. *Kuste*, **8**, 46–65.
BARBASHINOVA, V. N. (1962). Main features of Miocene flora in the Soviet Far East. *Pollen et spores.* **4**, 2 (abstract).

BARRON, J. A. (1973). Late Miocene–early Pliocene paleotemperatures for California from marine diatom evidence. *Paleogeog. Paleoclim. Paleoecol.* **14,** 277–291.
BARRY, R. G. and CHORLEY, R. J. (1971). "Atmosphere, Weather and Climate". Methuen, London.
BATTARBEE, R. W., OLDFIELD, F., O'SULLIVAN, P. E. and THOMPSON, R. (1975). Magnetic susceptibility of lake sediments. *Limnol. Oceanogr.* **20,** 687–698.
BAUR, F. (1956). "Physikalisch-statistische Regeln als Grundlagen für Wetter und Witterungsvorhersagen" (Vol. I, 1956; Vol. II, 1959). Akad. Verlag., Frankfurt.
BÉ, A. W. H. (1960). Ecology of Recent planktonic Foraminifera. *Micropaleontology,* **6,** 373–392.
BECK, R. B., FUNNELL, B. M. and LORD, A. R. (1972). Correlation of Lower Pleistocene Crag at depth in Suffolk. *Geol. Mag.* **109,** 137–139.
BEGELMAN, M. C. and REES, M. J. (1976). Can cosmic clouds cause climatic catastrophes? *Nature, Lond.* **261,** 298–299.
BELROSE, J. S., BURKE, M. J. and COYNE, T. N. R. (1975). Mesospheric and lower thermospheric wind changes over Canada during the January 1975 warming. *Nature, Lond.* **258,** 62–64.
BERGGREN, W. A. (1968). Micropaleontology and the Pliocene–Pleistocene boundary in a deep-sea core from the south central North Atlantic. *J. Geol. Ser.* 2, **35,** 291–312.
BERGGREN, W. A. (1969). Cenozoic chronostratigraphy, planktonic foraminiferal zonation and the radiometric time scale. *Nature, Lond.* **224,** 1072–1075.
BERGGREN, W. A. (1972). A Cenozoic time scale, some implications for regional geology and paleobiogeography. *Lethaia,* **5,** 195–215.
BERGGREN, W. A. (1973). The Pliocene time-scale, calibration of planktonic foraminiferal and calcareous nannoplankton zones. *Nature, Lond.* **243,** 391–397.
BERGGREN, W. A. and AMDURER, M. (1973). Late Paleogene and Neogene planktonic foraminiferal biostratigraphy of the Atlantic ocean. *Riv. Ital. Paleont.* **79,** 337–392.
BERGGREN, W. A. and COUVERING, J. A. VAN (1974). The Late Neogene. *Paleogeog. Paleoclim. Paleoecol.* **16,** 1–216.
BERGGREN, W. A., PHILLIPS, J. D., BERTELS, A. and WALL, D. (1967). Late Pliocene–Pleistocene stratigraphy in deep-sea cores from the North Atlantic. *Nature, Lond.* **216,** 253–254.
BERKNER, C. V. and MARSHALL, L. C. (1964). The history of the growth of oxygen in the earth's atmosphere. *In* "The Origin and Evolution of Atmospheres and Oceans" (Brancuzi, C. J. and Cameron, A. G. W., Eds), pp. 102–126. John Wiley, New York.
BERLAGE, H. P. (1961). Variations in the general atmospheric and hydrospheric circulation of periods of a few years duration affected by variations of solar activity. *Ann. N.Y. Acad. Sci.* **95,** 354–367.
BERNARD, E. A. (1962a). Le caractère tropicale des paleoclimats a cycles conjoints de 11 et 21,000 ans et ses causes. *Acad. R. Sci. d'Outremer,* **13,** fasc. 6. Brussels.
BERNARD, E. A. (1962b). Théorie astronomique des pluviaux et interp-

luviaux du Quaternaire Africain. *Acad. R. Sci. d'Outremer*, fasc. 1. Brussels.

BERRY, W. B. N. and BOUCOT, A. J. (1967). Pelecypod-graptolite association in the Old World Silurian. *Bull. Geol. Soc. Am.* **78,** 1515–1521.

BERRY, W. B. N. and BOUCOT, A. J. (1973). Glacio-eustatic control of late Ordovician–early Silurian platform sedimentation and faunal changes. *Bull. Geol. Soc. Am.* **84,** 275–284.

BEUF, S., BIJU-DUVAL, B., STEVAUX, J. and KULBICKI, G. (1966). Ampleur des glaciations Siluriennes au Sahara. *Rev. Inst. France petrole.* **21,** 363–381.

BEURLEN, K. (1956). Der Faunenschnitt an der Perm-Trias grenze. *Z. dt. Geol. Ges.* **108,** 88–99.

BIGARELLA, J. J. and AB'SABER, A. N. (1964). Paläogeographische und paläoklimatische Aspekte des Kanozoikums in Sudbrasilien. *Z. Geomorph.* **8,** 286–312.

BIRD, J. M. and DEWEY, J. F. (1970). Lithosphere plate—continental margin tectonics and the evolution of the Appalachian orogen. *Bull. Geol. Soc. Am.* **81,** 1031–1060.

BIRKELAND, P. W. (1972). Late Quaternary eustatic sea-level changes along the Malibu coast, Los Angeles County, California. *J. Geol.* **80,** 432–448.

BLACKBURN, K. B. (1952). The dating of a deposit containing an elk skeleton at Neasham, County Durham. *New Phytol.* **51,** 364.

BLACKMAN, A. and SOMAYUJULU, B. L. K. (1966). Pacific Pleistocene cores; faunal analyses and geochronology. *Science,* **154,** 886–889.

BLANK, R. G. and MARGOLIS, S. V. (1975). Pliocene climatic and glacial history of Antarctica as revealed by southeast Indian Ocean deep sea cores. *Bull. Geol. Soc. Am.* **86,** 1058–1066.

BLOCH, M. R. (1965). A hypothesis for the change of ocean levels depending on the albedo of the polar ice caps. *Paleogeog. Paleoclim. Paleoecol.* **1,** 127–142.

BOCK, P. E. and GLENIE, R. C. (1965). Late Cretaceous and Tertiary depositional cycles in south western Victoria. *Proc. R. Soc. Victoria,* **79,** 153–163.

BODELLE, J., LAY, C. and ODIN, G. S. (1969). Détermination d'âge par le méthode géochronologie K-Ar. *C.r. Acad. Séanc. Acad. Sci., Paris,* **268,** 1474–1477.

BODMER, W. F. and CAVALLI-SFORZA, L. L. (1976). "Genetics, Evolution and Man". Freeman & Company, San Francisco.

BONATTI, E. and GARTNER, S. Jr. (1973). Caribbean climate during Pleistocene ice ages. *Nature, Lond.* **244,** 563–564.

BOND, G. and STOCKLMAYER, V. R. C. (1967). Possible ice margin fluctuations in the Dwyka series of Rhodesia. *Paleogeog. Paleoclim. Paleoecol.* **3,** 433–446.

BORNS, H. W. Jr. and GOLDTHWAIT, R. P. (1966). Late Pleistocene fluctuations of Kaskawulsh glacier, southwestern Yukon. *Am. J. Sci.* **264,** 600–619.

BOUCOT, A. J. (1968). Origins of the Silurian fauna. *Geol. Soc. Am., spec. paper,* **121,** 33–34.

BOUCOT, A. J. (1974). Early Paleozoic evidence of continental drift. *In* "Plate Tectonics—Assessments and Reassessments" (Kahle, C. F., Ed.),

pp. 273–294. Amer. Ass. Petrol. geol. Tulsa, Oklahoma.
BOUCOT, A. J. (1975). Evolution and extinction rate controls. *In* "Developments in Paleontology and Stratigraphy", Vol. 1. Elsevier, Amsterdam, Oxford.
BOUCOT, A. J. and JOHNSON, J. G. (1972). Silurian brachiopods. *In* "Atlas of Paleobiogeography" (Hallam, A., Ed.), pp. 59–66. Elsevier, Amsterdam.
BOUGHEY, A. S. (1975). "Man and the Environment". Collier-MacMillan, London.
BOWEN, R. (1961a). Paleotemperature analyses of Mesozoic Belemnoidea from Germany and Poland. *J. Geol.* **69**, 75–83.
BOWEN, R. (1961b). Paleotemperature analyses of Mesozoic Belemnoidea from Australia and New Guinea. *Bull. Geol. Soc. Am.* **72**, 769–774.
BOWEN, R. (1961c). Paleotemperature analyses of Belemnoidea and Jurassic paleoclimatology. *J. Geol.* **69**, 309–320.
BOWEN, R. (1962). Paleotemperature analyses of Jurassic Belemnoidea from East Greenland. *Experientia*, **18**, 438–441.
BOWEN, R. (1963a). $^{18}O/^{16}O$ paleotemperature measurements on Mesozoic Belemnoidea from Neuquen and Santa Cruz provinces, Argentina. *J. Paleont.* **37**, 714–718.
BOWEN, R. (1963b). Oxygen isotope paleotemperature measurements on Lower Jurassic Belemnoidea from Bamberg, Germany. *Experientia*, **19**, 401–403.
BOWEN, R. (1964a). Faunal realms in Jurassic and Cretaceous Belemnites. *Geol. Mag.* **101**, 374–376.
BOWEN, R. (1964b). Oxygen isotope paleotemperature measurements on Mesozoic Belemnoidea and their importance in paleoclimatic studies. *In* "Advances in Geochemistry" (Columbo, U., Ed.), pp. 1–13. Pergamon Press, Oxford.
BOWEN, R. (1966). "Paleotemperature Analysis". Elsevier, Amsterdam and London.
BOWEN, R. and FRITZ, P. (1963). Oxygen isotope paleotemperature analyses of Lower and Middle Jurassic fossils from Pliensbach, Württemberg. *Experientia*, **19**, 268–275.
BRADLEY, R. S. and MILLER, G. H. (1972). Recent climatic change and increased glacierization in the eastern Canadian Arctic. *Nature, Lond.* **237**, 385–387.
BRADLEY, W. H. (1929). The varves and climate of the Green River epoch. *U.S. Geol. Survey. Prof. Paper*, **158**, 87–110.
BRADSHAW, A. D. (1965). Evolutionary significance of phenotypic plasticity in plants. *Adv. Genet.* **13**, 115–155.
BRADSHAW, A. D., MCNEILLY, T. S. and GREGORY, R. P. G. (1965). Industrialisation, evolution and the development of heavy metal tolerance in plants. *5th Symp. Brit. Ecol. Soc.*, pp. 327–343.
BRAMLETTE, M. N. (1965). Problem of the massive extinctions in the biota at the end of Mesozoic time. *Science*, **148**, 1696–1699.
BRAY, J. R. (1967). Variation in atmospheric ^{14}C activity relative to a sunspot-auroral solar index. *Science*, **156**, 640–642.
BRAY, J. R. (1968). Glaciation and solar activity since the fifth century B.C., and the solar cycle. *Nature, Lond.* **220**, 672–674.
BRAY, J. R. (1972). Cyclic temperature oscillations from 0–20,300 B.P.

Nature, Lond. **237,** 277–279.
BRETSKY, P. W. and LORENZ, D. M. (1969). Adaptive response to environmental stability: a unifying concept in paleoecology. *North American Paleontology Convention Chicago Proc., part E.*, pp. 522–550.
BRIDEN, J. C. and IRVING, E. (1964). Paleolatitude spectra of sedimentary climatic indicators. *In* "Problems of Paleoclimatology" (Nairn, A. E. M., Ed.), pp. 199–224. Wiley Interscience, London.
BRIER, G. W. (1961). Some statistical aspects of long-term fluctuations in solar and atmospheric phenomena. *Ann. N.Y. Acad. Sci.* **95,** 173–187.
BRISKIN, M. and BERGGREN, W. A. (1975). Pleistocene stratigraphy and quantitative paleooceanography of tropical north Atlantic core V16-205. *In* "Late Neogene Epoch Boundaries" (Saito, T. and Burckle, L. Eds), pp. 167–198. American Museum of Natural History.
BROECKER, W. S. (1966). Absolute dating and the astronomical theory of glaciation. *Science*, **151,** 299–304.
BROECKER, W. S. and DONK, J. VAN, (1970). Insolation changes, ice volumes, and the O^{18} record in deep sea cores. *Rev. Geophys. Space Phys.* **8,** 169–198.
BROECKER, W. S., EWING, M. and HEEZEN, B. C. (1960). Evidence for an abrupt change in climate close to 11,000 B.P. *Am. J. Sci.* **258,** 429–448.
BROOKFIELD, M. E. (1970). Eustatic changes of sea level and orogeny in the Jurassic. *Tectonophysics*, **9,** 347–363.
BROOKS, C. E. P. (1934). Variation of the annual frequency of thunderstorms in relation to sunspots. *Q. Jl R. met. Soc.* **60,** 153–165.
BROOKS, C. E. P. (1949). "Climate Through the Ages" (2nd ed.). Ernest Benn, London.
BROOKS, C. E. P. (1954). The climatic changes of the past thousand years. *Experientia*, **10,** 153–192.
BROOKS, C. E. P. and GLASSPOOLE, J. (1928). "British Floods and Droughts". Ernest Benn, London. 199 pp.
BROOKS, C. E. P. and HUNT, T. M. (1929). The influence of explosive volcanic eruptions on the subsequent pressure distribution over western Europe. *Met. Mag. Lond.* **64,** 226.
BRUNNER, C. A. and COOLEY, J. F. (1976). Circulation in the gulf of Mexico during the last glacial maximum. *Bull. Geol. Soc. Am.* **87,** 681–686.
BRUNT, D. (1925). Periodicities in European weather. *Phil. Trans. R. Soc. Ser. A.* **225,** 247–302.
BRUUN, P., MORGAN, W. H. and PURPURA, J. A. (1962). Review of beach erosion and storm tide conditions in Florida. *Florida Eng. Indus. Exp. Stat. Rep.* **13,** 104.
BRYSON, R. A., BAERREIS, D. A. and WENDLAND, W. M. (1970). The character of late-glacial and post-glacial climatic changes. *In* "Pleistocene and Recent Environments of the Central Great Plains" (Dort, W. Jr., and Knox Jones, J. Jr., Eds), pp. 53–76. University Press of Kansas, Lawrence.
BRYSON, R. A. and DUTTON, J. A. (1961). Some aspects of the variance spectra of tree rings and varves. *Ann. N.Y. Acad. Sci.* **95,** 580–604.
BUCHA, V. (1970). Influence of the earth's magnetic field on radiocarbon dating. *In* "Radiocarbon Variations and Absolute Chronology", Nobel Symposium 12 (Olsson, I. U., Ed.), pp. 501–511. Wiley Interscience and Almqvist and Wiksell, Uppsala.

BUCHA, V., HORAČEK, J., KOČI, A. and KUKLA, J. (1969). *In* "Periglacialzone, Löss und Paleolithicum der Tschechoslowaken", p. 123. Czech. Acad. Sci. Inst. Geog. Brno.
BUDDEMEIER, R. W., SMITH, S. V. and KINZIE, R. A. (1975). Holocene Windward reef-flat history. *Bull. Geol. Soc. Am.* **86,** 1581–1584.
BUDYKO, M. I. (1968). On the causes of climatic variations. *Sveriges. Meteorol., och. Hydr. Inst. Medd. Ser. B.* **28,** 6–13.
BUDYKO, M. I. (1974). "Climate and Life". Academic Press, London and New York.
BULLARD, E. C. (1968). Reversals of the earth's magnetic field. *Phil. Trans. R. Soc. Ser. A.* **263,** 481–524.
BULLARD, E. C., EVERETT, J. E. and SMITH, A. G. (1965). The fit of continents around the Atlantic. *Phil. Trans. R. Soc. Ser. A.* **258,** 41–51.
BURCKLE, L. H. (1972). Late Cenozoic planktonic diatom zones from the eastern equatorial Pacific. *Beih. Nova Hedwigia.* **39,** 217–246.
BÜRGL, H. (1964). Die rhythmischen Bewegungen der Kreidegeosynklinale der Ostkordillere Kolumbiens. *Geol. Rundsch.* **53,** 706–731.
BURTON, R. K., MCPHERRON, R. L. and RUSSELL, C. T. (1975). The terrestrial magnetosphere: a half wave rectifier of the interplanetary electric field. *Science,* **189,** 717–718.
BUTZER, K. W. (1958). Studien zum vor- und fruhgeschichtlichen Landschäftswardel der Sahara. *Akad. Wiss. Lit. (Mainz). Abh. Math. Nat. Kl.* **1,** 1–49.
BUTZER, K. W. (1971a). Recent history of an Ethiopian delta. *Dep. Geog. Univ. Publ. Res. Pap.* **136,** 1–184.
BUTZER, K. W. (1971b). "Environment and Archeology." Aldine, Chicago.
CAHEN, L. (1963). Glaciations anciènnes et dérivé des continents. *Ann. Soc. Geol. Belg.* **86,** 21–30.
CAIN, A. J. (1953). Visual selection by tone in *Cepaea nemoralis. J. Conchol.* **23,** 333–336.
CAIN, A. J. and CURREY, J. D. (1968). Climate and selection of banding morphs in *Cepaea* from the climate optimum to the present day. *Phil. Trans. R. Soc. Ser. B.* **253,** 483–498.
CAIN, A. J. and SHEPPARD, P. M. (1950). Selection in the polymorphic land snail *Cepaea nemoralis* (L.). *Heredity,* **4,** 275–294.
CAIN, A. J. and SHEPPARD, P. M. (1952). The effects of natural selection on body colour in the land snail *Cepaea nemoralis. Heredity,* **6,** 217–231.
CAIN, A. J. and SHEPPARD, P. M. (1954). Natural selection in *Cepaea. Genetics,* **39,** 89–116.
CAIN, W. F. and SUESS, H. E. (1976). C^{14} in tree rings. *J. Geophys. Res.* **81,** 3688–3694.
CALDER, N. (1974). "The Weather Machine". BBC publications, London.
CARROLL, R. L. (1969). Problem of the origin of reptiles. *Biol. Rev.* **44,** 393–432.
CARTER, G. S. (1954). "Animal Evolution". Sidgwick and Jackson, London.
CHALONER, W. G. (1970). The rise of the first land plants. *Biol. Rev.* **45,** 353–379.
CHANDLER, M. E. J. (1961). "The Lower Tertiary Floras of Southern England" (2 volumes). British Museum of Natural History, London.
CHANEY, R. W. (1947). Tertiary centres and migration routes. *Ecol. Monogr.* **17,** 139–148.

CHANEY, R. W. and AXELROD, D. I. (1959). Miocene floras of the Columbia plateau. *Carnegie Inst. Washington Publ.* **617**, 237 pp.

CHANEY, R. W. and SANBORN, E. I. (1933). The Goshen flora of west central Oregon. *Carnegie Inst. Washington Publ.* **439**, 103 pp.

CHAPMAN, S. (1919). The solar and lunar diurnal variations of terrestrial magnetism. *Phil. Trans. R. Soc. Ser. A.* **218**, 1.

CHAPMAN, S. and BARTELS, J. (1940). "Geomagnetism" (2 volumes). Clarendon Press, Oxford.

CHAPPELL, J. E. Jr. (1971). Climatic pulsations in inner Asia and correlations between sunspots and weather. *Paleogeog. Paleoclim. Paleoecol.* **10**, 177–197.

CHARD, C. S. and GIDDINGS, J. L. (1962). *In* "Proceedings of the Conference on Climates of the 11th and 16th Centuries." Natl. Centre. Atmos. Res., Boulder Colorado Tech. notes 63, 1.

CHENEY, E. S. (1971). Coelomates, subduction and the history of atmospheric oxygen. *Bull. Geol. Soc. Am.* **82**, 3227–3230.

CHINNERY, M. A. and LANDERS, T. E. (1975). Evidence for earthquake triggering stress. *Nature, Lond.* **258**, 490–493.

CHUMAKOV, N. M. and CAILLEUX, A. (1971). Glaciation et éolisation dans l'est et le nord de l'Europe a l'éocambrian. *Revue Géomorph. dyn.* **20**, 1–4.

CITA, M. B. (1973). Pliocene biostratigraphy and chronostratigraphy. *In* "Initial Reports of the Deep Sea Drilling Project XIII" (Ryan, W. E. B. and Hsu, K. H., Eds), pp. 1343–1379. Government Printing Office, Washington.

CITA, M. B. (1974). The Miocene/Pliocene boundary. *In* "Late Neogene Epoch Boundaries" (Saito, T. and Burckle, L. H., Eds), pp. 1–30. American Museum of Natural History.

CLAIBORNE, R. (1970). "Climate, Man and History". Angus and Robertson, London. 444 pp.

CLARK, D. L. (1971). Arctic ice cover and its late Cenozoic history. *Bull. Geol. Soc. Am.* **82**, 3313–3324.

CLIMAP (1973). Mapping the atmospheric and oceanic circulations and other climatic parameters at the time of the last glacial maximum about 17,000 years ago. Climatic Research Unit, University of East Anglia, Publ. 2.

CLOUD, P. E. Jr. (1959). Paleoecology—Retrospect and prospect. *J. Paleont.* **33**, 926–962.

CLOUGH, H. W. (1933). The 11 year sunspot cycle, secular periods of sunspot activity and synchronous variations in terrestrial phenomena. *Mon. Weather. Rev.* April.

COHEN, T. J. and SWEETSER, E. I. (1975). The "spectra" of the solar cycle and of data for Atlantic tropical cyclones. *Nature, Lond.* **256**, 295–296.

COLEMAN, A. P. (1926). "Ice Ages: Recent and Ancient". Macmillan, London.

COLQUHOUN, D. J. and JOHNSON, H. S. Jr. (1968). Tertiary sea-level fluctuation in South Carolina. *Paleogeog. Paleoclim. Paleoecol.* **5**, 105–126.

COMPSTON, W. (1960). The carbon isotopic composition of certain marine invertebrates and coals from the Australian Permian. *Geochim. Cosmochim. Acta*, **18**, 1–22.

Connolly, A. and Dahl, E. (1970). Maximum summer temperatures in relation to modern and Quaternary distributions of certain arctic montane species in the British Isles. In "Studies in the Vegetational History of the British Isles" (Walker, D. and West, R. G., Eds), pp. 159–223. Cambridge University Press, London.

Connolly, J. R. and Ewing, M. (1970). Ice-rafted debris in north west Pacific deep sea cores. *Mem. Geol. Soc. Am.* **126**, 219–231.

Cook, L. M., Askew, R. R. and Bishop, J. A. (1970). Increasing frequency of the typical form of the peppered moth in Manchester. *Nature, Lond.* **227**, 1155.

Coon, C. S. (1966). The taxonomy of human variation. *Ann. N.Y. Acad. Sci.* **134**, 516–523.

Coope, G. R. (1975). Climatic fluctuations in northwest Europe since the last interglacial, indicated by fossil assemblages of Coleoptera. In "Ice Ages; Ancient and Modern" (Wright, A. E. and Moseley, F., Eds), pp. 153–168. Seel House Press, Liverpool.

Coope, G. R., Morgan, A. and Osborne, P. J. (1971). Fossil Coleoptera as indicators of climatic fluctuations during the last glaciation. *Paleogeog. Paleoclim. Paleoecol.* **10**, 87–101.

Copper, P. (1977). Paleolatitudes in the Devonian of Brazil and the Frasnian–Fammenian mass extinction. *Paleogeog. Paleoclim. Paleoecol.* **21**, 165–207.

Cotterell, A. and Morgan, D. (1975). "China; an Integrated Study". Harrap, London.

Courtillot, V. and Le Mouel, J-L. (1976). On the long period variations of the earth's magnetic field from 2 months to 2 years. *J. Geophys. Res.* **81**, 2941–2950.

Couvering, J. A. van, (1972). Radiometric calibration of the European Neogene. In "Calibration of Hominoid Evolution" (Bishop, W. W. and Miller, J., Eds), pp. 247–271. Scottish Academic Press, Edinburgh.

Couvering, J. A. and Miller, J. A. (1971). Late Miocene marine and non-marine time scale in Europe. *Nature, Lond.* **230**, 559–563.

Cowie, J. W. (1967). Life in Pre-Cambrian and early Cambrian times. In "The Fossil Record" (Harland, W. B. et al., Eds), pp. 17–35. Geological Society of London.

Cox, A. (1968). Lengths of the geomagnetic polarity intervals. *J. Geophys. Res.* **73**, 3247–3260.

Cox, A. (1969). Geomagnetic reversals. *Science*, **163**, 237–245.

Cox, A. (1973). "Plate Tectonics and Geomagnetic Reversals". Freeman, Reading.

Cox, C. B. (1967). Changes in terrestrial vertebrate faunas during the Mesozoic. In "The Fossil Record" (Harland, W. B. et al., Eds), pp. 76–89. Geological Society of London.

Crain, I. K. (1971). Possible direct causal relation between geomagnetic reversals and biological extinctions. *Bull. Geol. Soc. Am.* **82**, 2603–2606.

Crain, I. K. and Crain, P. L. (1970). New stochastic model for geomagnetic reversals. *Nature, Lond.* **228**, 39.

Crain, I. K., Crain, P. L. and Plant, M. G. (1969). Long period Fourier spectrum of geomagnetic reversals. *Nature, Lond.* **223**, 283.

Crawford, A. R. and Daily, B. (1971). Probable non-synchroneity of late Precambrian glaciations. *Nature, Lond.* **230**, 111–112.

Creer, K. M. (1965). Paleomagnetic data from the Gondwanaland continents. *Phil. Trans. R. Soc. Ser. A.* **258**, 27–40.

CREER, K. M., GROSS, D. L. and LINEBACK, J. A. (1976). Origin of regional geomagnetic variations recorded by Wisconsinian and Holocene sediments from lake Michigan, U.S.A. and Lake Windermere, England. *Bull. Geol. Soc. Am.* **87,** 531–540.

CROLL, J. (1875 and 1890). "Climate and Time in their Geological Relations; a Theory of Secular Change of the Earth's Climate" (4th ed. 1890). Edward Stanford, London.

CROWELL, J. C. and FRAKES, L. A. (1970). Phanerozoic glaciation and the causes of ice ages. *Am. J. Sci.* **268,** 193–224.

CULLEN, D. J. (1967). Submarine evidence from New Zealand of a rapid rise in sea-level about 11,000 B.P. *Paleogeog. Paleoclim. Paleoecol.* **3,** 289–298.

CUNLIFFE, B. (1974). "Iron Age Communities in Britain." Routledge and Kegan Paul, London.

CURRAY, J. R. (1965). Continental shelves of the U.S. *In* "The Quaternary of the U.S." (Wright, H. E. and Frey, D. G., Eds), pp. 723–735. Princeton University Press, Princeton.

CURRAY, J. R., SHEPARD, F. P. and VEEH, H. Y. (1970). Late Quaternary Sea-level studies in Micronesia. *Bull. Geol. Soc. Am.* **81,** 1865–1880.

DAHL, E. (1952). On the relation between summer temperature and the distribution of alpine vascular plants in Fennoscandia. *Oikos*, **3,** 21–52.

DALEY, B. (1972). Some problems concerning the early Tertiary climate of southern Britain. *Paleogeog. Paleoclim. Paleoecol.* **11,** 177–190.

DALRYMPLE, G. B. (1972). K-Ar dating of geomagnetic reversals and North American glaciations. *In* "Calibration of Hominoid Evolution" (Bishop, W. W. and Miller, J., Eds), pp. 107–134. Scottish Academic Press, Edinburgh.

DAMON, P. E. (1968). Radiocarbon and climate. *Meteorol. Monog.* **8,** 151–154.

DAMON, P. E. (1970). Climatic versus magnetic perturbation of the atmospheric ^{14}C reservoir. *In* "Radiocarbon Variations and Absolute Chronology" (Olsson, I. V., Ed.), pp. 571–593. Almqvist and Wiksells, Uppsala.

DAMON, P. E. (1971). The relationship between late Cenozoic volcanism and tectonism and orogenic—epeirogenic periodicity. *In* "Late Cenozoic Glacial Ages" (Turekian, K. K., Ed.), pp. 15–36. Yale University Press, New Haven, Connecticut.

DAMON, P. E., LONG, A. and GREY, D. C. (1966). Fluctuations of atmospheric C^{14} during the last six millenia. *J. Geophys. Res.* **71,** 1055–1063.

DANSGAARD, W., JOHNSEN, S. J., MØLLER, J. and LANGWAY, C. C. Jr. (1969). One thousand centuries of climatic record from Camp Century on the Greenland ice sheet. *Science*, **166,** 372.

DANSGAARD, W., JOHNSEN, S. J., CLAUSEN, H. B. and LANGWAY, C. C. Jr. (1971). Climatic record revealed by the Camp Century ice core. *In* "Late Cenozoic Glacial Ages" (Turekian, K. L., Ed.), pp. 37–56. Yale University Press, New Haven, Connecticut.

DANSGAARD, W., JOHNSEN, S. J., REEH, N., GUNDESTRUP, N., CLAUSEN, H. B. and HAMMER, C. U. (1975). Climatic changes, Norsemen and modern man. *Nature, Lond.* **255,** 24–28.

DARLINGTON, C. D. (1959). The origins of Darwinism. *Scient. Am.* **200,** 60–83.

DEFANT, A. (1924). Die Schwankungen der atmosphärischen Zirkulation über dem nord-atlantischen Ozean im 25-jahrigen Zeitraum. *Geog. Ann. Stockholm*, **6,** 13.

DENNISON, J. M. and HEAD, J. W. (1975). Sealevel variations interpreted from the Appalachian Basin Silurian and Devonian. *Am. J. Sci.* **275**, 1089–1120.

DENTON, G. H., ARMSTRONG, R. L. and STUIVER, M. (1969). Histoire glaciaire et chronologie de la région du Detroit de McMurdo. *Revue geog. phys. geol. dyn.* **11**, 265–278.

DENTON, G. H., ARMSTRONG, R. L. and STUIVER, M. (1970). Late Cenozoic glaciation in the McMurdo Sound region. *Antarct. J. (U.S.)*, **5**, 15–21.

DEVEREUX, I. (1967). Oxygen isotope paleotemperature measurements on New Zealand Tertiary fossils. *N.Z. Jl Sci.* **10**, 988.

DEVRIES, H. (1958). Variation in concentration of radiocarbon with time and location in earth. *Kon. Ned. Akad. Wet. Proc. Ser. B.* **61**, 94.

DEVRIES, H. and BARENDSON, G. W. (1954). Measurements of age by the C^{14} technique. *Nature, Lond.* **174**, 1138.

DEWEY, J. F. (1969). Evolution of the Appalachian–Caledonian orogen. *Nature, Lond.* **222**, 124–129.

DEWEY, J. F. and BIRD, J. M. (1970). Mountain belts and the new global tectonics. *J. Geophys. Res.* **75**, 2625–2647.

DEWEY, J. F. and HORSFIELD, B. (1970). Plate tectonics, orogeny and continental growth. *Nature, Lond.* **225**, 521–525.

DIETZ, R. S. and HOLDEN, J. C. (1970). Reconstruction of Pangaea; breakup and dispersion of the continents, Permian to the present day. *J. Geophys. Res.* **75**, 4939–4956.

DISNEY, L. P. (1955). Tide heights along the coasts of the United States. *Proc. Am. Soc. Civil. Engineers*, **81** (666), 9.

DONN, W. L. and EWING, M. (1966). A theory of ice ages III. *Science*, **152**, 1706–1712.

DONN, W. L. and EWING, M. (1968). The theory of an ice-free Arctic ocean. *In* "Causes of Climatic Change" (Mitchell, J. M. Jr., Ed.). *Am. Met. Soc. Meteorol. Mon.* **8**, 100–105.

DONN, W. L. and SHAW, D. M. (1963). Sea-level and climate of the past century. *Science*, **142**, 1166–1167.

DORF, E. (1964). The use of fossil plants in paleoclimatic interpretations. *In* "Problems in Paleoclimatology" (Nairn, A. E. M., Ed.), pp. 13–31. Wiley Interscience, New York.

DORMAN, F. H. (1966). Australian Tertiary paleotemperatures. *J. Geol.* **74**, 49–61.

DORMAN, F. H. and GILL, E. D. (1959). Oxygen isotope paleotemperature measurements on Australian fossils. *Proc. R. Soc. Victoria*, **71**, 73–98.

DREWRY, G. E., RAMSAY, A. T. S. and SMITH, A. G. (1974). Climatically controlled sediments, the geomagnetic field, and trade wind belts in phanerozoic time. *J. Geol.* **82**, 531–553.

DUNN, P. R., THOMSON, B. P. and RANKAMA, K. (1971). Late Precambrian glaciation in Australia. *Nature, Lond.* **231**, 498–502.

DZERDZEEVSKII, B. L. (1961). The general circulation of the atmosphere as a necessary link in the sun-climatic variations chain. *Ann. N.Y. Acad. Sci.* **95**, 188–199.

EASTON, C. (1928). "Les hivers dans l'Europe Occidentale". E. J. Brill, London.

EASTON, W. H. and OLSON, E. A. (1976). C^{14} profile of Hanauma reef,

Oahu, Hawaii. *Bull. Geol. Soc. Am.* **87,** 711–719.
EGYED, L. (1961). Temperature and magnetic field. *Ann. N.Y. Acad. Sci.* **95,** 72–77.
ELTON, C. S. (1924). Periodic fluctuations in the numbers of animals, their causes and effects. *J. exp. Biol.* **2,** 119–163.
ELTON, C. S. (1929). The relation of animal numbers to climate. *Conf. Emp. Met.* 1929. Agric. sect. pp. 121–129.
ELVIN, M. (1973). "The Pattern of the Chinese Past". Eyre Methuen.
EMILIANI, C. (1954). Temperatures of the Pacific bottom waters during the Tertiary. *Science,* **119,** 853–855.
EMILIANI, C. (1955a). Pleistocene temperature variations in the Mediterranean. *Quaternaria,* **2,** 87–98.
EMILIANI, C. (1955b). Pleistocene temperatures. *J. Geol.* **63,** 538–578.
EMILIANI, C. (1956). Oxygen isotopes and paleotemperature determinations. *4th Int. Quat. Cong. Rome–Pisa.* **2,** 831–844.
EMILIANI, C. (1958). Paleotemperature analysis of core 180 and Pleistocene correlations. *J. Geol.* **66,** 264–275.
EMILIANI, C. (1966). Paleotemperature analysis of the Caribbean cores P6304–8 and 9, and a generalised temperature curve for the last 425,000 years. *J. Geol.* **74,** 109–126.
EMILIANI, C., GARTNER, S. and LIDZ, B. (1972). Neogene sedimentation on the Blake plateau and the emergence of the central American isthmus. *Paleogeog. Paleoclim. Paleoecol.* **11,** 1–10.
EMILIANI, C., GARTNER, S., LIDZ, B., ELDRIDGE, K., ELVEY, D. K., HUANG, T. C., STIPP, J. J. and SWANSON, M. F. (1975). Paleoclimatological analysis of late Quaternary cores from the northeastern Gulf of Mexico. *Science,* **189,** 1083–1086.
EMILIANI, C., MAYEDA, T. and SELLI, R. (1961). Paleotemperature analysis of the Plio-Pleistocene section at La Castella, Calabria, southern Italy. *Bull. Geol. Soc. Am.* **72,** 679–688.
ERICSON, D. B. (1961). Pleistocene climatic record in some deep sea sediments. *Ann. N.Y. Acad. Sci.* **95,** 451–537.
ERICSON, D. B., EWING, M. and WOLLIN, G. (1963). Pliocene–Pleistocene boundary in deep sea sediments. *Science,* **139,** 727–737.
ERICSON, D. B., EWING, M., WOLLIN, G. and HEEZEN, B. C. (1961). Atlantic deep-sea sediment cores. *Bull. Geol. Soc. Am.* **72,** 193–286.
ERICSON, D. B. and WOLLIN, G. (1956). Micropaleontological and isotope determinations of Pleistocene climates. *Micropaleont.* **2,** 267–270.
ERICSON, D. B. and WOLLIN, G. (1964). "The Deep and the Past". Alfred A. Knopf, New York.
EVANS, M. E. (1976). Test of the dipolar nature of the geomagnetic field throughout Phanerozoic time. *Nature, Lond.* **262,** 676–677.
EVERNDEN, J. F. and EVERNDEN, R. K. S. (1970). The Cenozoic time-scale. *In* Radiometric dating and paleontologic zonation (Bandy, O. L., Ed.). *Geol. Soc. America. Special paper,* **124,** 1–247.
EVERNDEN, J. F. and JAMES, G. T. (1964). K/Ar dates and the Tertiary floras of N. America. *Am. J. Sci.* **262,** 945–974.
EVERNDEN, J. F. and RICHARDS, J. R. (1962). Potassium-argon ages in eastern Australia. *J. Geol. Soc. Aust.* **9,** 1–50.
EVERNDEN, J. F., SAVAGE, D. E., CURTIS, G. H. and JAMES, G. T. (1964). K/Ar

dates and the Cenozoic mammalian chronology of North America. *Am. J. Sci.* **262**, 145–198.

EWING, M. and DONN, W. L. (1956). A theory of ice-ages I. *Science*, **123**, 1061–1066.

EWING, M. and DONN, W. L. (1958). A theory of ice-ages II. *Science*, **127**, 1159–1162.

FAIRBRIDGE, R. W. (1960). The changing level of the sea. *Scient. Am.* **202**, 70–79.

FAIRBRIDGE, R. W. (1961a). Eustatic changes in sea-level. *In* "Physics and Chemistry of the Earth", pp. 99–185. Pergamon Press, Oxford.

FAIRBRIDGE, R. W. (1961b). Convergence of evidence on climatic change and ice ages. *Ann. N.Y. Acad. Sci.* **95**, 542–579.

FAIRBRIDGE, R. W. (1964). African ice-age aridity. *In* "Problems in Paleoclimatology" (Nairn, A. E. M., Ed.), pp. 356–360. John Wiley, New York and London.

FAIRBRIDGE, R. W. (1965). Eiszeitklima in Nordafrika. *Geol. Rundschau.* **54**, 399–414.

FAIRBRIDGE, R. W. (1967). Carbonate rocks and paleoclimatology in the biogeochemical history of the planet. *In* "Carbonate Rocks" (Chilingarian, G. V., Bissell, H. J. and Fairbridge, R. W., Eds), pp. 399–432. Elsevier, Amsterdam.

FAIRBRIDGE, R. W. (1969). Early Paleozoic south pole in northwest Africa. *Bull. Geol. Soc. Am.* **80**, 113–114.

FAIRBRIDGE, R. W. (1973). Glaciation and plate migration. *In* "Implications of Continental Drift to the Earth Sciences", pp. 503–515. Academic Press, London and New York.

FAIRBRIDGE, R. W. and KREBS, O. A. Jr. (1962). Sea-level and the southern oscillation. *R. Astron. Soc., Geophys. J.* **6**, 532–545.

FAUL, H. (1960). Geologic time-scale. *Bull. Geol. Soc. Am.* **71**, 637–644.

FIRBAS, F. (1949). "Spät und Nacheiszeitliche Waldgeschichte Mitteleuropas nordlich der Alpen", Vol. 1. Jena.

FIRBAS, F. and LOSERT, H. (1949). Untersuchungen uber die Entstehung der Heutigen Waldstufen in den Sudeten. *Planta*, **36**, 478–506.

FISHER, A. G. (1965). Brackish oceans as the cause of the Permo-Triassic marine faunal crisis. *In* "Problems in Paleoclimatology" (Nairn, A. E. M., Ed.). Interscience, London.

FITZGERALD, C. P. (1961). "China, a Short Cultural History" (2nd ed.). Cresset Press, London.

FITZGERALD, C. P. (1966). "A Concise History of East Asia." Heinemann, London.

FLEMING, N. C. (1973). Tectono-eustatic changes in sea-level and sea-floor spreading. *Nature, Lond.* **243**, 19–22.

FLEMMING, M. C. (1972). Relative chronology of submerged Pleistocene marine erosion features in the western Mediterranean. *J. Geol.* **80**, 633–662.

FLESSA, K. W. and IMBRIE, J. (1973). Evolutionary pulsations. *In* "Implications of Continental Drift to the Earth Sciences" (Tarling, D. H. and Runcorn, S. K., Eds), pp. 247–285. Academic Press, London and New York.

FLINT, R. F. (1971). "Glacial and Quaternary Geology." John Wiley, New York.

FLOHN, H. (1951). Solare Vorgänge im Wettergeschehen. *Arch. Met. Geophys. Biokl.* **A3**, 303–329.
FORD, E. B. (1965). "Ecological Genetics". Chapman and Hall, London.
FOSTER, J. H. and OPDYKE, N. D. (1970). Upper Miocene to Recent magnetic stratigraphy in deep sea sediments. *J. Geophys. Res.* **75**, 4465–4473.
FRAKES, L. A. and KEMP, E. M. (1972). Influence of continental positions on early Tertiary climates. *Nature, Lond.* **240**, 97–100.
FRAKES, L. A., KEMP, E. M. and CROWELL, J. C. (1975). Late Paleozoic glaciation VI Asia. *Bull. Geol. Soc. Am.* **86**, 454–464.
FRENZEL, B. (1966). Climatic change in the Atlantic/sub-Boreal transition. *Proc. Int. Symp. World Climate 8000–0 B.C.* (Sawyer, J. S., Ed.), pp. 99–123. Royal Meterological Society.
FRITTS, H. C. (1962). In *Proc. Conf. Climates 11th and 16th centuries.* N.C.A.R. Tech. Notes, 63.
FROGET, C., THOMMERET, J. and THOMMERET, Y. (1972). Molluscs septentrionaux en Meditérranée occidentale, datation par le C^{14}. *Paleogeog. Paleoclim. Paleoecol.* **12**, 285–293.
FUNNELL, B. M. (1964). The Tertiary Period. *Q. Jl geol. Soc. Lond.* **120** (supplement), 179–191.
GARLAND, G. D. (1971). "Introduction to Geophysics". Saunders Company, Philadelphia.
GARRETT, H. B., DESSLER, A. J. and HILL, T. W. (1974). Influence of solar wind variability on geomagnetic activity. *J. Geophys. Res.* **79**, 4603–4610.
GASJUKOV, P. S. and SMIRNOV, N. P. (1967). Pressure-field oscillations over the northern hemisphere within the 11 year cycle of solar activity. *Dokl. Akad. Nauk SSSR*, **173**, 567–569.
GEYH, M. A. and JÄKEL, D. (1974). Lateglacial and Holocene climatic history of the Sahara desert region from a statistical assay of C^{14} dates. *Paleogeog. Paleoclim. Paleoecol.* **15**, 205–208.
GIBSON, T. G. (1967). Stratigraphy and paleoenvironment of the phosphatic Miocene strata of North Carolina. *Bull. Geol. Soc. Am.* **78**, 631–650.
GIDON, P. (1970a). Glaciations majeures and révolutions galactique du système solaire. *C.r. hebd. Séanc. Acad. Sci., Paris*, **271**, 385–387.
GIDON, P. (1970b). L'alternation glaciaire-interglaciaire au cours d'une glaciation majeure. *C.r. hebd. Séanc. Acad. Sci., Paris*, **271**, 1493–1494.
GILL, E. D. (1961). The Climates of Gondwanaland in Cenozoic times. In "Descriptive Paleoclimatology" (Nairn, A. E. M., Ed.), pp. 332–355. Wiley Interscience, New York.
GILL, J. B. and McDOUGALL, I. (1973). Biostratigraphic and geological significance of Miocene–Pliocene vulcanism in Fiji. *Nature, Lond.* **241**, 176–180.
GILLULY, J. (1949). Distribution of mountain building in geological time. *Bull. Geol. Soc. Am.* **60**, 561.
GILLULY, J. (1963). The tectonic evolution of the western U.S. *Q. Jl geol. Soc. Lond.* **119**, 133.
GIMPEL, J. (1977). "The Medieval Machine". Gollancz, London.
GINSBURG, L. (1965). Les régressions marines et le problème du rénouvellement des faunes au cours des temps géologiques. *Bull. Soc. géol. Fr.* **6**, 13–22.

GLAESSNER, M. F. (1962). Pre-Cambrian fossils. *Biol. Rev.* **37,** 467–494.
GLASS, B., ERICSON, D. B., HEEZEN, B. C., OPDYKE, M. D. and GLASS, J. A. (1967). Geomagnetic reversals and Pleistocene chronology. *Nature, Lond.* **216,** 437–442.
GLEISSBERG, W. (1944). A table of secular variations of the solar cycle. *Terr. Magn. Strn. Telectr.* **49,** 243.
GODWIN, H. (1940a). Pollen analysis and forest history of England and Wales. *New Phytol.* **39,** 370.
GODWIN, H. (1940b). Studies of the Post-glacial history of the British vegetation III. *Phil. Trans. R. Soc. Ser. B.* **230,** 239–303.
GODWIN, H. (1943). Coastal peat beds of the British Isles and North Sea. *J. Ecol.* **31,** 199.
GODWIN, H. (1956). "The History of the British Flora". Cambridge University Press, London.
GODWIN, H. (1961). The Croonian lecture. *Proc. R. Soc. Ser. B.* 287–320.
GODWIN, H. (1973). "The History of the British Flora" (2nd ed.). Cambridge University Press, London.
GODWIN, H., SUGGATE, R. P. and WILLIS, E. H. (1958). Radiocarbon dating of the eustatic rise in sea-level. *Nature, Lond.* 1518–1519.
GODWIN, H., WALKER, D. and WILLIS, E. H. (1957). Radiocarbon dating and Post-glacial vegetational history. *Proc. R. Soc. Ser. B.* **147,** 352–366.
GODWIN, H. and WILLIS, E. H. (1959). Radiocarbon dating of prehistoric wooden trackways. *Nature, Lond.* **184,** 490–491.
GOLIK, A. (1968). History of Holocene transgression in the gulf of Panama. *J. Geol.* **76,** 497–507.
GORDON, W. A. (1973). Marine life and ocean surface currents in the Cretaceous. *J. Geol.* **81,** 269–284.
GOW, A. J. (1970). "International Symposium on Antarctic Glaciological Exploration" (Gow, A J., Keeler, C., Lanway, C. C. and Weeks, W. F., Eds), Vol. 86, p. 78. *Internat. Publ. Hydrology.*
GRABERT, H. (1965). Klimazeugan im Paläzoikum Brasiliens. *Geol. Rundschau.* **54,** 165–192.
GRASTY, R. L. (1967). Orogeny, a cause of world wide regression of the seas. *Nature, Lond.* **216,** 779.
GREEN, F. H. W. (1975). The February–June weather relationship. *Nature, Lond.* **253,** 522–523.
GRIBBIN, J. (1976a). "Our Changing Universe". Macmillan, London.
GRIBBIN, J. (1976b). "Forecasts, Famines and Freezes". Wildwood House, London.
GRIFFIN, J. B. (1961). Some correlations of climatic and cultural changes in eastern North American prehistory. *Ann. N.Y. Acad. Sci.* **95,** 710–717.
GROMOV, I. (1970). The Tiraspol faunal complex. *Paleogeog. Paleoclim. Paleoecol.* **8,** 187–196.
GROUSSET, R. (1941). "L'Empire Mongol". Paris. 339 pp.
GRUGER, J. (1973). Studies on the late Quaternary vegetation history of N.E. Kansas. *Bull. Geol. Soc. Am.* **84,** 239–250.
GUILCHER, A. (1969). Pleistocene and Holocene sea level changes. *Earth Sci. Rev.* **5,** 68–97.
GUMILYOV, L. N. (1964). Khazaria and the Caspian. *Vest. Lenin. Univ. Ser. Geog.* **19,** 83–95.

Gumilyov, L. N. (1966a). English translation of foregoing. *Soviet Geog.* **7**, 34–45.
Gumilyov, L. N. (1966b). Heterochronism in the moisture supply of Eurasia in the Middle Ages. *Vest. Lenin. Univ. Ser. Geog.* **21**, 81–90.
Gurnett, D. A. and Akasofu, S. I. (1974). Electric and magnetic field observations during a substorm on February 24th 1970. *J. Geophys. Res.* **79**, 3197–3200.
Hall, J. W. and Norton, N. J. (1967). Palynological evidence of floristic change across the Cretaceous–Tertiary boundary in eastern Montana. *Paleogeog. Paleoclim. Paleoecol.* **3**, 121–131.
Hallam, A. (1963). Major epeirogenic and eustatic changes since the Cretaceous, and their possible relationship to crustal structure. *Am. J. Sci.* **261**, 397–423.
Hallam, A. (1969a). Tectonics and eustasy in the Jurassic. *Earth Sci. Rev.* **5**, 45–68.
Hallam, A. (1969b). Faunal realms and facies in the Jurassic. *Paleontology*, **12**, 1–18.
Hallam, A. (1971). Mesozoic geology and the opening of the North Atlantic. *J. Geol.* **79**, 129–157.
Hamilton, W. L. (1970). The Uralides and the motion of the Russian and Siberian platforms. *Bull. Geol. Soc. Am.* **81**, 2553–2576.
Hamilton, W. L. (1973). Tidal cycles of volcanic eruptions—fortnightly to 19 yearly periods. *J. Geophys. Res.* **78**, 3363–3375.
Hamilton, W. L. and Krinsley, D. (1967). Upper Paleozoic glacial deposits of South Africa and Southern Australia. *Bull. Geol. Soc. Am.* **78**, 783–800.
Hamilton, W. L. and Seliga, T. A. (1972). Atmospheric turbidity and surface temperature on the polar ice sheets. *Nature, Lond.* **235**, 320–322.
Hansen, B. L. and Langway, G. C. Jr. (1966). Deep core drilling in ice, and core analysis at Camp Century, Greenland. *Antarctic J. (U.S.)*, **1**, 207.
Haram, O. J. and Pearson, R. G. (1967). The distribution of some freshwater biota in Fennoscandia. *Arch. Hydrobiol.* **63**, 135–142.
Harland, W. B. (1964a). Evidence of late Precambrian glaciation and its significance. *In* "Problems of Paleoclimatology" (Nairn, A. E. M., Ed.), pp. 150–155. Wiley Interscience, New York.
Harland, W. B. (1964b). Critical evidence for a great infra-cambrian glaciation. *Geol. Rundschau.* **54**, 45–61.
Harland, W. B. and Herod, K. N. (1975). Glaciations through time. *In* "Ice Ages Ancient and Modern" (Wright, A. E. and Moseley, F., Eds), pp. 189–216. Seel House Press, Liverpool.
Harris, D. L. (1963). Characteristics of the hurricane storm surge. *U.S. Weather Bur. Tech. Pap.* **48**, 139 pp.
Harrison, C. G. A. (1968). Evolutionary processes and reversals of the earth's magnetic field. *Nature, Lond.* **217**, 46–47.
Hart, M. B. and Tarling, D. H. (1974). Cenomanian paleogeography of the North Atlantic and possible mid-Cenomanian eustatic movements and their implications. *Paleogeog. Paleoclim. Paleoecol.* **15**, 95–108.
Hartz, N. and Milthers, V. (1901). Det senglaciale leri Allerød Teglvaerksgrav. *Medd. Dansk. geol. Foren.* **8**, 31.
Harwood, J. M. and Malin, S. R. C. (1976). Present trends in the earth's magnetic field. *Nature, Lond.* **259**, 469–471.

Hatfield, C. B. and Camp, M. J. (1970). Mass extinctions correlated with periodic galactic events. *Bull. Geol. Soc. Am.* **81,** 911–914.
Hawson, C. L. (1974). Five year climatic trend in the northern hemisphere. *Nature, Lond.* **249,** 540–541.
Hays, J. D. (1965). Radiolaria and late Tertiary and Quaternary history of Antarctic seas. *Am. Geophys. Union. Antarct. Res. ser.* **5,** 225–184.
Hays, J. D. (1971). Faunal extinctions and reversals of the earth's magnetic field. *Bull. Geol. Soc. Amer.* **82,** 2433–2447.
Hays, J. D. and Berggren, W. A. (1971). Quaternary boundaries and correlations. *In* "Micropaleontology of the Oceans" (Funnell, B. M. and Riedel, W. R., Eds), pp. 669–691. Cambridge University Press, London.
Hays, J. D. and Opdyke, N.D. (1967). Antarctic Radiolaria, magnetic reversals and climatic change. *Science,* **158,** 1001–1011.
Hays, J. D., Saito, T., Opdyke, N. D. and Burckle, L. H. (1969). Pliocene–Pleistocene sediments of the equatorial Pacific. *Bull. Geol. Soc. Am.* **80,** 1481–1514.
Heape, W. (1931). "Emigration, Migration and Nomadism." Heffer, Cambridge, 369 pp.
Hédin, S. (1903). "Central Asia and Tibet" (2 volumes). Hurst and Blackett, London.
Heirtzler, J. R., Dickson, G. O., Herron, E. M., Pitman, W. C. III, and Le Pichon, X. (1968). Marine magnetic anomalies, geomagnetic field reversals and motions of the ocean floor and continents. *J. Geophys. Res.* **73,** 2119.
Helsley, C. E. and Steiner, M. B. (1969). Evidence for long periods of normal polarity during the Cretaceous period. *Earth Planet. Sci. Lett.* **5,** 325–332.
Henriksen, K. (1933). Undersøgelser over Danmarks Skane kvartaere Insektfauna. *Vidensk. Meddr. dansk. naturh. Foren.* **96,** 77–355.
Herm, D. (1965). Mikropalaontologisch-stratigraphische Untersuchungen im Kreideflysch zwischen Deva und Zumaya. *Z. dt. geol. Ges.* **115,** 277–348.
Herschel, J. (1830). On the astronomical causes which may influence geological phenomena. *Trans. Geol. Soc. 2nd ser.* **3,** 293.
Heusser, C. J. (1973). Age and environment of allochthonous peat clasts from the Bogachiel River Valley, Washington. *Bull. Geol. Soc. Am.* **84,** 797–804.
Hibbert, F. A., Switsur, V. R. and West, R. G. (1971). Radiocarbon dating of Flandrian pollen zones at Red Moss, Lancashire. *Proc. R. Soc.* **177,** 161–176.
Hoffman, R. S. (1974). Terrestrial vertebrates. *In* "Arctic and Alpine Environments" (Ives, J. D. and Barry, R. G., Eds), pp. 475–568. Methuen, London.
Hollin, J. T. (1962). On the glacial history of Antarctica. *J. Glaciol.* **4,** 173–195.
Holmes, A. (1959). A revised geological time-scale. *Trans. Edin. Geol. Soc.* **17,** 183–216.
Holmes, A. (1965). "Principles of Physical Geology" (2nd ed.). Nelson, London.
Holmsen, A. (1961). "Norges Historie". Universitetsboklaget. Oslo.

HOUSE, M. R. (1967). Fluctuations in the evolution of Paleozoic invertebrates. In "The Fossil Record" (Harland, W. B., et al., Eds), pp. 41–56. Geological Society of London.

HOUTEN, F. B. VAN (1976). Late Variscan non-marine deposits: implications for pre-Drift, North Atlantic reconstructions. Am. J. Sci. **276,** 671–693.

HOYLE, F. and LYTTLETON, R. A. (1939). The effect of interstellar matter on climatic variations. Proc. Camb. phil. Soc. biol. Sci. **35,** 405–415.

HUGHES, N. F. (1976). "Paleobiology of Angiosperm Origins". Cambridge University Press, London.

HUMPHREYS, W. J. (1913). "Physics of the Air" (3rd ed. 1940). McGraw Hill, New York.

HUNTINGTON, E. (1907). "The Pulse of Asia". Houghton Mifflin, Boston.

HUNTINGTON, E. (1911). "Palestine and its Transformation". Houghton Mifflin, Boston.

HUNTINGTON, E. (1914a). The solar hypothesis of climatic changes. Bull. Geol. Soc. Am. **25,** 477–590.

HUNTINGTON, E. (1914b). "The Climatic Factor as Illustrated in Arid America". Carnegie Inst. Publ. **192,** 330 pp.

HUNTINGTON, E. (1917). The geographical work of Dr M. A. Veeder. Geog. Rev. **3,** 188–211.

HUNTINGTON, E. and VISHER, S. S. (1923). "Earth and Sun". Yale University Press, New Haven, Connecticut.

HUNTINGTON, E., JONES, J. C. and ANTEVS, E. (1925). "Quarternary Climates". Carnegie Institute, Washington.

IRVING, E. (1964). "Paleomagnetism and its Application to Geological and Geophysical Problems". John Wiley, New York.

IRVING, E. and BROWN, D. A. (1964). Abundance and diversity of the labyrinthodonts as a function of paleolatitude. Am. J. Sci. **262,** 689–708.

IRVING, E. and ROBERTSON, W. A. (1968). The distribution of the continental crust and its relation to ice ages. In "The History of the Earth's Crust" (Phinney, R. A., Ed.), pp. 168–177. Princeton University Press, Princeton.

IVANOVA, E. A. (1955). Concerning the problem of the relations of the evolutionary stages of the organic world with evolutionary stages of the earth's crust. Dokl. Akad. Nauk SSSR, **105,** 154–157.

IVERSEN, J. (1947). Plantevaekst, Dyreliv og Klima i det senglaciale Danmark. Geol. Foren. Stockholm. **69,** 67.

JANSEN, H. S. (1970). Secular variations of radiocarbon in New Zealand and Australian trees. In "Radiocarbon Variations and Absolute Chronology", Nobel Symposium 12 (Olsson, I. U., Ed.), pp. 261–274. Wiley Interscience and Almqvist and Wiksell, Uppsala.

JARDETZKY, W. S. (1961). Investigations of Milankovitch and the Quaternary curve of effective solar radiation. Ann. N.Y. Acad. Sci. **95,** 419–423.

JEANNEL, R. G. (1942). "La Genèse des Faunes Terrestres". Institut Maritime.

JELGERSMA, S. (1960). Die palynologische und C^{14} untersuchungen. Kon. Ned. Geol. Mijnb. Verhandl. **19,** 25.

JELGERSMA, S. and PANNEKOEK, A. J. (1960). Post-glacial rise of sea-level in the Netherlands. Geol. en. Mijnbouw, **16e,** 156.

JENKINS, D. G. (1971). Stratigraphic position of the New Zealand

Pliocene–Pleistocene boundary. *N.Z. Jl Geol. Geophys.* **14,** 418–420.
JESSEN, K. (1935). The composition of the forests in northern Europe in Epipaleolithic time. *K. danske Vidensk. Selsk. Biol. Meddel.* **12,** 1–64.
JESSEN, K. (1949). Studies in Late Quaternary deposits and floral history of Ireland. *Proc. R. Ir. Acad.* **52B,** 85–290.
JOHN, B. S. (1970). "The Ice-Age". Collins, London.
JOHNSON, J. G. (1971). Timing and coordination of orogenic, epeirogenic and eustatic events. *Bull. Geol. Soc. Am.* **82,** 3263–3298.
JOLY, J. (1930). "The Surface History of the Earth." Clarendon Press, Clarendon.
JORDAN, P. J. (1971). "The Expanding Earth" (Beer, A., trans.). Pergamon Press, Oxford and New York.
JOSEPHY, A. M., Jr. (1972). "The Indian Heritage of America". Jonathan Cape, London.
JULIAN, P., RUFF, I. and NORDØ, J. (1957). Possible responses of terrestrial atmospheric circulation to changes in solar activity. *Tech. Rep. 1.* Boulder Institute for Solar-Terrestrial Research.
KAMEI, T. and MAEDA, H. (1976). Lunar effect in the quiet time D_{st} index. *Nature, Lond.* **259,** 644–645.
KEMPTON, J. P. and GROSS, D. L. (1971). Rate of advance of the Woodfordian glacial margin. *Bull. Geol. Soc. Am.* **82,** 3245–3250.
KENDALL, R. L. (1969). An ecological history of the Lake Victoria basin. *Ecol. Monogr.* **39,** 121–176.
KENNETT, J. P. and WATKINS, N. D. (1976). Regional deep-sea dynamic processes recorded by late Cenozoic sediments of the southeastern Indian ocean. *Bull. Geol. Soc. Am.* **87,** 321–339.
KENNETT, J. P., WATKINS, N. D. and VELLA, P. (1971). Paleomagnetic chronology of Pliocene–early Pleistocene climates and the Plio–Pleistocene boundary in New Zealand. *Bull. Geol. Soc. Am.* **82,** 2741–2754.
KENT, D., OPDYKE, N. D. and EWING, M. (1971). Climatic change in the North Pacific using ice-rafted detritus as a climatic indicator. *Bull. Geol. Soc. Am.* **82,** 2741–2754.
KETTLEWELL, H. B. D. (1942). A survey of the insect *Panaxia dominula*. *Trans. S. Lond. ent. nat. Hist. Soc.* (1942–3). 1–49.
KETTLEWELL, H. B. D. (1955a). Recognition of appropriate backgrounds by the pale and black phase of Lepidoptera. *Nature, Lond.* **175,** 934.
KETTLEWELL, H. B. D. (1955b). Selection experiments on industrial melanism in the Lepidoptera. *Heredity*, **9,** 323–342.
KETTLEWELL, H. B. D. (1957a). The contribution of industrial melanism in the Lepidoptera to our knowledge of evolution. *Adv. Sci.* **52,** 245–252.
KETTLEWELL, H. B. D. (1957b). Industrial melanism in moths and its contribution to our knowledge of evolution. *Proc. R. Instn Gt. Br.* **36,** 1–14.
KETTLEWELL, H. B. D. (1958a). A survey of the frequencies of *Biston betularia* (L.) and its melanic forms in Great Britain. *Heredity*, **12,** 51–72.
KETTLEWELL, H. B. D. (1958b). Industrial melanism in the Lepidoptera and its contribution to our knowledge of evolution. *Proc. 10th Int. Congr. Ent.* (1956). **2,** 831–841.
KETTLEWELL, H. B. D. (1961a). The phenomenon of industrial melanism in the Lepidoptera. *Ann. Rev. Ent.* **6,** 245–262.

KETTLEWELL, H. B. D. (1961b). Geographic melanism in the Lepidoptera of Shetland. *Heredity*, **16,** 393–402.
KETTLEWELL, H. B. D. (1961c). Selection experiments on melanism in *Amathes glareosa. Heredity*, **16,** 415–434.
KETTLEWELL, H. B. D. (1965). Insect survival and selection for pattern. *Science*, **148,** 1290–1296.
KETTLEWELL, H. B. D. (1973). "The Evolution of Melanism". Clarendon Press, Clarendon.
KHUDOLEY, K. M. (1974). Circum-pacific Mesozoic ammonoid distributions: relation to hypotheses of continental drift. *In* "Plate Tectonics: Assessments and Reassessments" (Kahle, C. F., Ed.), pp. 295–330. Amer. Ass. Petrol. Geol. Tulsa, Oklahoma.
KING, J. W. (1974). Weather and the earth's magnetic field. *Nature, Lond.* **247,** 131–134.
KOCH, L. (1945). The east Greenland ice. *Meddr. Grønland*, **130,** 373 pp.
KÖPPEN, W. and WEGENER, A. (1924). "Die Klimate der Geologischen Vorzeit." Borntraeger, Berlin.
KRENKE, A. N. (1974). Climatic conditions for the existence of glaciers. *In* "Meteorology and Climatology" (Danilina, I. P. and Kapitsa, A. P., Eds), vol. 1, pp. 179–224. Hall and Co., Massachusetts.
KRIVSKY, L. (1953). The long range variability of annual precipitation in Prague–Klementinum 1805–1951, and its relation to solar activity. *Publ. Astrophys. Obs. Czech. Acad. Sci.* **23,** 37–72.
KROPOTKIN, P. (1899). "Memoirs of a Revolutionist" (2 volumes). Smith, Elder, London.
KRUTZSCH, W. (1957). Sporen- und pollengruppen aus der Oberkreide und dem Tertiär Mitteleuropas und ihre stratigraphische Verteilung. *Zeit. Angewandte. Geol.* **3,** 509–548.
KUKLA, G. J. and KUKLA, H. J. (1974). Increased surface albedo in the northern hemisphere. *Science*, **183,** 709.
KULLMER, C. J. (1933). The latitude shift of the storm track in the 11 year solar period. *Smithson. Inst. misc. Colls*, **89,** 1–34.
KULP, J. L. (1961). Geologic time-scale. *Science*, **133,** 1105.
KURTEN, B. (1971). "The Age of Mammals". Weidenfeld and Nicolson, London.
KUTZBACH, J. E., BRYSON, R. A. and SHEN, W. C. (1968). An evolution of the thermal Rossby number in the Pleistocene. *Meteorol. Monog.* **8,** 134–138. (Amer. Met. Soc.)
LABEYRIE, J., DELIBRIAS, G. and DUPLESSY, J. C. (1970). The possible origin of natural carbon radioactivity fluctuations in the past. In Olsson (1970). 539–547.
LADURIE, E. L. (1971). "Times of Feast and Famine". Allen and Unwin, London.
LAMB, H. H. (1961). Climatic change within historic time as seen in circulation maps and diagrams. *Ann. N.Y. Acad. Sci.* **95,** 124–161.
LAMB, H. H. (1965). The early Medieval warm epoch and its sequel. *Paleogeog. Paleoclim. Paleoecol.* **1,** 13–37.
LAMB, H. H. (1966). Climate in the 1960's. Changes in the world's wind circulation reflected in prevailing temperatures, rainfall patterns and the levels of African lakes. *Geogr. J. Lond.* **132,** 183–212.

LAMB, H. H. (1967). Volcanic dust, melting of ice-caps, and sea-levels. *Paleogeog. Paleoclim. Paleoecol.* **3,** 222–226.

LAMB, H. H. (1968). "The Changing Climate". Methuen, London.

LAMB, H. H. (1969). Volcanic dust in the atmosphere; with a chronology and assessment of its meteorological significance. *Phil. Trans. R. Soc. Ser. A.* **266,** 425–533.

LAMB, H. H. (1971). Volcanic activity and climate. *Paleogeog. Paleoclim. Paleoecol.* **10,** 203–230.

LAMB, H. H. (1972). "Climate: Present, Past and Future" (2 volumes). Methuen, London.

LAMB, H. H. (1974). The current trend of world climate—a report on the early 1970's and a perspective. *Climatic Research Unit Res. Publ.* **3,** 1–27. University of East Anglia.

LAMB, H. H. (1975). "Climatology and Climatic Research". Booklet, University of East Anglia.

LAMB, H. H. (1976). Climate in the 1970's. *Nature, Lond.* **259,** 606.

LAMB, H. H. and JOHNSON, A. I. (1966). Secular variations of the atmosphere circulation since 1750. *Geophys. Mem., Lond.* **110.** Met. Office.

LANDSBERG, H. E. (1962). Biennial pulses in the atmosphere. *Beitr. Physik. Atmosphare,* **35,** 184–194.

LANDSBERG, H. E., MITCHELL, J. M. Jr. and CRUTCHER, H. I. (1959). Power spectrum analysis of climatological data for Woodstock College, Maryland. *Mon. Weather Rev.* **87,** 283–298.

LARSON, R. L. and PITMAN, W. C. (1972). World wide correlations of Mesozoic magnetic anomalies. *Bull. geol. Soc. Am.* **83,** 3645–3662.

LATTIMORE, O. (1938). The geographical factor in Mongol history. *Geographical Journal,* **91,** 2–3.

LATTIMORE, O. (1941). "Inner Asian Frontiers of China" (2nd edition, 1950). Beacon Press, Boston.

LEOPOLD, E. B. (1969). Late Cenozoic palynology. *In* "Aspects of Palynology" (Tschudy, R. H. and Scott, R. A., Eds). Wiley Interscience, New York.

LE PICHON, X. (1968). Sea floor spreading and continental drift. *J. Geophys. Res.* **73,** 3661–3698.

LEQUEUX, J. (1972). "On the Origin of the Solar System" (Reeves, H., Ed.). Paris.

LERMAN, J. C., MOOK, W. G. and VOGEL, J. C. (1970). C^{14} in tree rings from different localities. *In* "Radiocarbon Variations and Absolute Chronology", Nobel Symposium 12 (Olsson, I. U., Ed.), pp. 275–301. Wiley Interscience and Almqvist and Wiksell, Uppsala.

LIBBY, W. F. (1967). *In* "Proc. Symp. Radiocarbon Dating and Methods of Low Level Counting", IAEA, Vienna.

LINDEN, W. J. M. VAN DER (1975). Mesozoic and Cainozoic opening of the Labrador Sea, Atlantic and the Bay of Biscay. *Nature, Lond.* **253,** 320–324.

LINDSAY, J. F. and SRNKA, L. J. (1975). Galactic dust lanes and lunar soil. *Nature, Lond.* **257,** 776–777.

LINGENFELTER, R. E. and RAMATY, R. (1970). Astrophysical and geophysical variations in C^{14} production. *In* "Radiocarbon Variations and Absolute Chronology", Nobel Symposium 12 (Olsson, I. U., Ed.), pp. 513–537. Wiley Interscience and Almqvist and Wiksell, Uppsala.

LINK, F. (1958). Kometen, Sonnentätigkeit und Klimaschwankungen. *Die Sterne*, **34**, 129–140.
LINK, F. (1964). Manifestations de l'activité solaire dans le passé historique. *Planet. Space Sci.* **12**, 333–348.
LIPPS, J. H. (1970). Plankton evolution. *Evolution*, **24**, 1–22.
LIVINGSTONE, D. A. (1975). Late Quaternary climatic change in Africa. *A. Rev. Ecol. Syst.* **6**, 249–280.
LLOYD, J. J. (1963). Tectonic history of the south central American orogen. *In* "Backbone of the Americas" (Childs, O. E. and Beebe, B. W., Eds). *Am. Ass. Pet. Geol. Mem.* **2**, 88–100.
LOVENBURG, M. F., DELL, C. I. and JOHNSON, M. J. S. (1972). Effect of a shorter day upon biotic diversity. *Bull. geol. Soc. Am.* **83**, 3529–3530.
LOWENSTAM, H. A. (1961). Mineralogy, $^{18}O/^{16}O$ ratios, and strontium and magnesium contents of recent and fossil brachiopods and their bearing on the history of the oceans. *J. Geol.* **69**, 241–260.
LOWENSTAM, H. A. (1964). Paleotemperatures of the Permian and Cretaceous periods. *In* "Problems in Paleoclimatology" (Nairn, A. E. M., Ed.). Wiley Interscience, New York.
LOWRY, W. P. (1967). "Weather and Life: an Introduction to Biometeorology." Academic Press, New York and London.
LUNGERSHAUZEN, G. F. (1957). The periodic change of climate and the earth's gigantic glaciation. *Sov. Geol. Sbornik.* **59**, 88–115.
LUYENDUK, B. P., FORSYTH, D. and PHILLIPS, J. D. (1972). Experimental approach to the paleocirculation of the oceanic surface waters. *Bull. geol. Soc. Am.* **83**, 2649–2664.
MAACK, R. (1964). Characteristic features of the paleogeography and stratigraphy of the Devonian of Brazil and South Africa. *In* "Problems in Paleoclimatology" (Nairn, A. E. M., Ed.). Wiley Interscience, New York.
MABESOONE, J. M. (1966). Relief of northeastern Brazil and its correlated sediments. *Z. Geomorph.* **10**, 419–453.
MACGINITIE, H. D. (1937). The flora of the Weaverville beds of Trinity County, California. *Carnegie Inst. Washington Publ.* **465**, 83–151.
MACHADO, F. (1967). Geological evidence for a pulsating gravitation. *Nature, Lond.* **214**, 1317–1318.
MACINTYRE, R. M. (1971). Apparent periodicity of carbonatite emplacement in Canada. *Nature, Lond.* **230**, 23–24.
MAEZAWA, K. (1976). Magnetospheric convection induced by the positive and negative Z components of the interplanetary magnetic field. *J. Geophys. Res.* **81**, 2289–2303.
MAKSIMOV, I. V. and SLEPTSOV, B. A. (1963). Study of eleven year variations in atmospheric pressure over the Antarctic. *Soviet Antarctic Expedition Reps.* No. 43. English version.
MALEY, J. (1973). Mécanisme des changements climatiques aux basses latitudes. *Paleogeog. Paleoclim. Paleoecol.* **14**, 193–227.
MALIN, S. R. C. (1973). Worldwide distribution of geomagnetic tides. *Phil. Trans. R. Soc. Ser. A.* **274**, 551–594.
MANLEY, G. (1961). Late, and Postglacial climatic fluctuations and their relationship to those shown by the instrumental record of the last 300 years. *Ann. N.Y. Acad. Sci.* **95**, 162–172.

Manley, G. (1971). Interpreting the meteorology of the Late, and Postglacial. *Paleogeog. Paleoclim. Paleoecol.* **10,** 163–175.

Mann, J. C. (1972). Faunal extinctions and reversals of the earth's magnetic field; Discussion. *Bull. geol. Soc. Am.* **83,** 2211–2214.

Manten, A. A. (1967). Palynology and environmental geology. *Paleogeog. Paleoclim. Paleoecol.* **3,** 7–15.

Margolis, S. V. and Kennett, J. P. (1970). Antarctic glaciation during the Tertiary recorded in sub-Antarctic deep sea cores. *Science,* **170,** 1085–1087.

Markham, S. F. (1942). "Climate and the Energy of Nations" (2nd ed., 1947). Oxford University Press, London.

Marshall, J. F. and Thom, B. G. (1976). The sea level in the last interglacial. *Nature, Lond.* **263,** 120–121.

Martin, P. S. and Wright, H. E. Jr. (1967). "Pleistocene Extinctions". Yale University Press, New Haven, Connecticut.

Marvin, V. B. (1973). "Continental Drift. The Evolution of a Concept." Smithsonian Press, Washington.

Mason, B. J. (1971). Global atmospheric research programme. *Nature, Lond.* **223,** 382–388.

Mayr, E. (1942). "Systematics and the Origin of Species". New York.

Mazullo, S. J. (1971). Length of the year during the Silurian and Devonian periods. *Bull. geol. Soc. Am.* **82,** 1085–1086.

McCartney, W. D., Poole, W. H., Wanless, R. K., Williams, H. and Loveridge, W. D. (1966). Rb/Sr age and geological setting of the Holyrood granite. *Can. J. Earth Sci.* **3,** 947.

McClure, H. A. (1976). Radiocarbon chronology of lake Quaternary lakes in the Arabian desert. *Nature, Lond.* **263,** 755.

McCrea, W. H. (1975). Ice ages and the galaxy. *Nature, Lond.* **255,** 607–609.

McCrea, W. H. (1976). Glaciations and dense interstellar clouds. *Nature, Lond.* **263,** 260.

McDougall, I. and Page, R. W. (1974). Toward a physical time-scale for the Neogene. *In* "Late Neogene Epoch Boundaries", pp. 75–84. American Museum of Natural History.

McElhinny, M. W. (1971). Geomagnetic reversals during the Phanerozoic. *Science,* **172,** 157–159.

McKenzie, D. P. and Sclater, J. G. (1971). The evolution of the Indian ocean since the Late Cretaceous. *Geophys. J.R. Ast. Soc.* **24,** 437–531.

Mercer, J. H. (1968). The discontinuous glacio-eustatic fall in Tertiary sea-level. *Paleogeog. Paleoclim. Paleoecol.* **5,** 77–86.

Mercer, J. H. (1970). Variations of some Patagonian glaciers since the late-glacial II. *Am. J. Sci.* **269,** 1–25.

Merriam, D. F. and Sneath, P. H. A. (1967). Comparison of cyclic rock sequences using cross correlation. *In* "Essays in Paleontology and Stratigraphy" (Teichert, C. and Yochelson, E. L., Eds). University of Kansas Press.

Mesolella, K. J., Matthews, R. K., Broecker, W. S. and Thurber, D. L. (1969). The astronomical theory of climatic change: Barbados data. *J. Geol.* **77,** 250–274.

Milankovič, M. (1930). Mathematische Klimalehre und astronomische Theorie der Klimaschwankungen. *In* "Handbuch der Klimatologie"

(Köppen, W. and Geiger, R., Eds). Borntraeger, Berlin.
MILANKOVIČ, M. (1938). Astronomische Mittel zur Erforschung der Erdesgeschichtlichen Klimate (also 1920 etc.). *Handb. Geophysik.* **9**, 593–698.
MILES, M. K. and FOLLARD, C. K. (1975). Changes in the latitude of the climatic zones of the northern hemisphere. *Nature, Lond.* **252**, 616.
MILLER, M. M. (1964). Inventory of terminal position changes in Alaskan coastal glaciers since the 1750's. *Proc. Am. phil. Soc.* **108**, 257–273.
MILLIMAN, J. D. and EMERY, K. O. (1968). Sea levels during the past 35,000 years. *Science*, **162**, 1121–1123.
MITCHELL, G. F. (1956). Post-Boreal pollen diagrams from Irish raised bogs. *Proc. R. Irish Acad.* **57B**, 185–251.
MITCHELL, J. M. (1963). On the world wide pattern of secular temperature change. *In* "Changes of Climate", Vol. 20, pp. 161–181. Arid Zone Research Series Unesco, Paris. **20**.
MITCHELL, J. M. (1965). The solar inconstant. *Proc. Seminar on possible responses of weather phenomena to variable extraterrestrial influences. NCAR. Tech. notes.* Boulder, Colorado.
MOCK, S. J. and HIBLER, W. D. III (1976). The 20 year oscillation in eastern North American temperature records. *Nature, Lond.* **261**, 484–486.
MOORES, E. M. (1970). Ultramafics and orogeny, with models for the U.S. Cordillera and the Tethys. *Nature, Lond.* **228**, 837–842.
MORAN, J. M. and BLASING, T. J. (1972). Statistical approaches to "alpine" glacier response. *Paleogeog. Paleoclim. Paleoecol.* **11**, 237–246.
MULLER, J. (1970). Palynological evidence on early differentiation of angiosperms. *Biol. Rev.* **45**, 417–450.
MUNK, W. and MACDONALD, G. J. F. (1960). "The Rotation of the Earth". Cambridge University Press, London.
MURPHY, R. (1951). The decline of North Africa since the Roman occupation: climatic or human? *Ann. Ass. Am. Geog.* **41**, 116–132.
NAYLOR, R. (1970). Continent collision and the Acadian orogeny. *Geol. Soc. Am. Abs.* **7**, 634–635.
NEAVERSON, E. (1955). "Stratigraphical Paleontology". Clarendon Press, Clarendon.
NEEDHAM, J. (1954). "Science and Civilisation in China" (vol. 1). Cambridge University Press, London.
NELSON, J. H. (1952). Planetary position effect on the short-wave signal quality. *Electron. Engng*, **71**, 421–424.
NELSON, J. H. (1962). Do the planets cause sunstorms? *Saturday Rev.* 6 Oct. 1962, 63–66.
NEWELL, N. D. (1952). Periodicity in invertebrate evolution. *J. Paleont.* **26**, 371–385.
NEWELL, N. D. (1962). Paleontological gaps and geochronology. *J. Paleont.* **36**, 592–610.
NEWELL, N. D. (1963). Crises in the history of life. *Scient. Am.* **208**, 76–92.
NEWELL, N. D. (1967). Revolutions in the history of life. *Geol. Soc. Am. Spec. Pap.* **89**, 63–91.
NEWELL, R. E. (1973). Climate and the Galapagos Islands. *Nature, Lond.* **245**, 91–92.
NEWELL, R. E. (1974). Changes in the poleward energy flux by the

atmosphere and ocean as a possible cause for ice-ages. *Quatern. Res.* **4,** 117–127.
NICHOLS, H. (1969). Chronology of peat growth in Canada. *Paleogeog. paleoclim. paleoecol.* **6,** 61–65.
NICHOLS, H. (1974). Arctic North American paleoecology. *In* "Arctic and Alpine Environments" (Ives, J. D. and Barry, R. G., Eds). Methuen, London.
NICOL, D. (1961). Biotic association and extinction. *Syst. Zool.* **10,** 35–41.
NILSSON, E. (1968). Södra Sveriges senkvartära historia. *K. svenske Vetensk Akad. Handl.*, ser. 4, **12** (1), 117 pp.
NISHIDA, A., KOKUBUN, S. and IWASAKI, N. (1966). Annual variation in the magnetosphere configuration. *Rep. Ionos. Space Res. Jap.* **20,** 73–78.
NORDHAGEN, R. (1928). Rypear og baerar. *Bergens Mus. Arb.* (Naturvid. Rekke), **2,** 1–52.
O'BRIEN, B. J. (1967). Energetic charged particles in the magnetosphere. *In* "Solar-Terrestrial Physics" (King, J. W. and Newman, W. S., Eds). Academic Press, London and New York.
OLIVEIRA, A. I. DE (1956). *In* "Handbook of South American Geology" (Jenks, W. F., Ed.), *Geol. Soc. Am. Mem.* Vol. 65, 378 pp.
OLSSON, I. U. (Ed.) (1970). "Radiocarbon Variations and Absolute Chronology". Nobel Symposium 12. Wiley Interscience and Almqvist and Wiksell, Uppsala.
OPDYKE, N. D. (1972). Paleomagnetism of deep sea cores. *Rev. Geophys. Space Phys.* **10,** 213–249.
OPDYKE, N. D., GLASS, B., HAYS, J. D. and FOSTER, J. H. (1966). Paleomagnetic study of Antarctic cores. *Science,* **154,** 349–357.
OSMOND, J. K., MAY, J. P. and TANNER, W. F. (1970). Age of the Cape Kennedy barrier and lagoon complex. *J. Geophys. Res.* **75,** 469–479.
OUTI, M. (1961). Climatic variations in the north Pacific subtropical zone and solar activity during the past ten centuries. *Bull. Kyoto Gakugei Univ.* B, **19,** 41–61; **20,** 25–48.
OVERBECK, F., MUNNICH, K. O., ALETSEE, L. and AVERDIECK, F. R. (1957). Das Alter des Grenzhorizonts norddeutscher Hochmoore nach Radiocarbon Datierung. *Flora,* **145,** 37–71.
PANNEKOEK, A. J. (Ed.) (1956). "The Geological History of the Netherlands" (2 volumes). State Press.
PARKIN, D. W. and SHACKLETON, M. J. (1973). Trade wind and temperature correlations down a deep-sea core off the Saharan coast. *Nature, Lond.* **245,** 455–456.
PAVLOV, A. P. (1924). About some still little studied factors of extinction. *In* "Causes of Animal Extinction in Past Geological Epochs." State Publishing House, Moscow.
PEARSON, R. (1962). The Coleoptera from a detritus mud erratic of Full-glacial age at Colney Heath, St. Albans. *Proc. Linn. Soc. Lond.* **173,** 38–55.
PEARSON, R. (1963). Coleopteran associations in the British Isles during the late Quaternary period. *Biol. Rev.* **38,** 334–363.
PEARSON, R. (1964). "Animals and Plants of the Cenozoic Era". Butterworths, London.
PEARSON, R. (1965). Problems of Post-glacial refugia. *Proc. R. Soc.* B, **161,**

324–330.
PEATTIE, R. (1940). "Geography in Human Destiny" (re-issued 1970). Kennikat Press, New York.
PEKERIS, C. L., ACCAD, Y. and SHKOLLER, B. (1973). Kinematic dynamos and the earth's magnetic field. *Phil. Trans. R. Soc. Ser. A.* **275,** 425–461.
PENCK, A. and BRUCKNER, E. (1909). "Die Alpen im Eiszeitalter". Tauschnitz, Leipzig.
PENNINGTON, W. and LISHMAN, J. P. (1971). Iodine in lake sediments in northern England and Scotland. *Biol. Rev.* **46,** 279–314.
PENNY, J. S. (1969). Late Cretaceous and early Tertiary palynology. *In* "Aspects of Palynology" (Tschudy, R. H. and Scott, R. A., Eds). Wiley Interscience, New York.
PETROV, O. M. (1963). The stratigraphy of the Quaternary deposits of the southern part of the Chukotsk peninsula. *Moscow Acad. Sci. Comm. for study of the Quaternary Period. Bull.* 28. English version.
PETROV, O. M. (1967). Paleogeography of Chukotka during late Neogene and Quaternary time. *In.* "The Bering Land Bridge" (Hopkins, D. M., Ed.). Stanford University Press, Stanford.
PHILLIPS, E. D. (1965). "The Royal Hordes; Nomad Peoples of the Steppes". Thames and Hudson, London.
PHILLIPS, J. D. and FORSYTH, D. (1972). Plate tectonics, paleomagnetism and the opening of the Atlantic. *Bull. geol. Soc. Am.* **83,** 1579–1600.
PIANKA, E. R. (1966). Latitudinal gradients in species diversity: a review of concepts. *Am. Nat.* **100,** 33–46.
PISIAS, N. G., HEATH, G. R. and MOORE, T. C. Jr. (1975). Lag-times for oceanic responses to climatic change. *Nature, Lond.* **256,** 716–717.
PITRAT, C. W. (1970). Phytoplankton and the late Paleozoic wave of extinction. *Paleogeog. Paleoclim. Paleoecol.* **8,** 49–66.
PITRAT, C. W. (1973). Vertebrates and the Permo-Triassic extinction. *Paleogeog. Paleoclim. Paleoecol.* **14,** 249–264.
PLASS, G. N. (1956a). The influence of the 9·6 micron ozone band on the atmospheric cooling rate. *Q. Jl R. met. Soc.* **82,** 30–44.
PLASS, G. N. (1956b). The carbon dioxide theory of climatic change. *Tellus*, **8,** 140–154.
PLASS, G. N. (1961). The influence of absorptive molecules on the climate. *Ann. N.Y. Acad. Sci.* **95,** 61–71.
PLUMSTEAD, E. P. (1969). Gondwana floras, geochronology and glaciation in South Africa. *22 Int. Geol. Cong. New Delhi*, **9,** 303–319.
POKROVSKAYA, I. M. (1956). Atlas of Miocene spore pollen complexes of various areas. *Vse. Geol. Inst. Mat.* new series. **13,** 1–460.
PORTER, S. C. and DENTON, G. H. (1967). Chronology of neoglaciation in the North American cordillera. *Am. J. Sci.* **265,** 177–210.
POTBURY, S. S. (1935). The La Porte flora of Plumas County, California. *Carnegie Inst. Washington Publ.* **465,** 29–81.
PRESS, F. and BRIGGS, P. (1975). Chandler wobble, earthquakes, rotation and geomagnetic changes. *Nature, Lond.* **256,** 270–272.
RAFTER, T. A. and O'BRIEN, B. J. (1970) Exchange rates between the atmosphere and the ocean as shown by recent C^{14} measurements in the South Pacific. *In* "Radiocarbon Variations and Absolute Chronology", Nobel Symposium 12 (Olsson, I. U., Ed.), pp. 355–377. Wiley Inter-

science and Almqvist and Wiksell, Uppsala.
RALPH, E. K. and MICHAEL, H. N. (1967). Problems of the C^{14} calendar. *Archeometry*, **10**, 3–11.
RANKAMA, K. (Ed.) (1967). "The Quaternary" (2 volumes). Wiley Interscience, New York.
RASOOL, I. and SCHNEIDER, S. H. (1971). Atmospheric carbon dioxide and aerosols. *Science*, **173**, 138–140.
RASTOGI, R. G. (1974). Westward equatorial electrojet during daytime hours. *J. Geophys. Res.* **79**, 1503–1512.
RATCLIFFE, J. A. (1970). "Sun, Earth and Radio". Weidenfeld and Nicholson, London.
READING, H. G. and WALKER, R. G. (1966). Sedimentation of Eocambrian Tillites. *Paleogeog. Paleoclim. Paleoecol.* **2**, 177–212.
REGER, R. D. (1968). Recent history of Gulkana and College Glaciers, Alaska. *J. Geol.* **76**, 2–16.
REID, E. M. and CHANDLER, M. E. J. (1933). "The London Clay Flora". British Museum (Natural History), London.
REID, G. C., ISAKSEN, I. S. A., HOLZER, T. E. and CRUTZEN, P. J. (1976). Influence of ancient solar-proton events on the evolution of life. *Nature, Lond.* **259**, 177–179.
RHODES, F. H. T. (1967). Permo-Triassic extinction. *In* "The Fossil Record" (Harland, W. B. *et al.*, Eds), pp. 57–76. Geological Society of London.
RICHTER-BERNBURG, G. (1964). Solar cycle and other climatic periods in varvitic evaporites. *In* "Problems in Paleoclimatology" (Nairn, A. E. M., Ed.), pp. 510–519. John Wiley, New York.
RIEDEL, W. R. (1957). Radiolaria—a preliminary stratigraphy. *Swedish Deep Sea Exped. Rep.* **6**, 61–96.
RIEDEL, W. R. and FUNNELL, B. M. (1964). Tertiary sediment cores and micro-fossils from the Pacific ocean floor. *Q. Jl geol. Soc. London.* **120**, 305–368.
RIEDEL, W. R., PARKER, F. L. and BRAMLETTE, M. N. (1963). Pliocene–Pleistocene boundary in deep sea sediments. *Science*, **140**, 1238–1240.
ROBERTS, D. F. (1973). "Climate and Human Variability". Benjamin/Cummings Publishing Company, Menlo Park, California.
ROBERTS, W. O. and OLSON, R. H. (1973). New evidence for effects of variable solar corpuscular emission on the climate. *Rev. Geophys. Space Res.* **11**, 731–741.
ROBINSON, P. L. (1971). A problem of faunal replacement on Permo-Triassic continents. *Paleontology*, **14**, 131–153.
ROBINSON, P. L. (1973). Paleoclimatology and continental drift. *In* "Implications of Continental Drift to the Earth Sciences" (Tarling, D. H. and Runcorn, S. K., Eds), Vol. 1, pp. 451–476. Academic Press, London and New York.
RONAI, A. (1970). Lower and Middle Pleistocene flora in the Carpathian basin. *Paleogeog. Paleoclim. Paleoecol.* **8**, 265–285.
ROOSEN, R. G., HARRINGTON, R. S., GILES, J. and BROWNING, I. (1976). Earth tides, volcanoes and climatic change. *Nature, Lond.* **261**, 680–682.
ROSENBERG, R. L. and COLEMAN, P. J. Jr. (1974). 27 day cycle in the rainfall at Los Angeles. *Nature, Lond.* **250**, 481–484.
ROSENBERG, R. L. (1975). On the 27 day cycle in the rainfall at Los Angeles.

A reply. *Nature, Lond.* **258**, 457–458.

ROSHOLT, J. N., EMILIANI, C., GEISS, J., KOCZY, F. F. and WANGERSKY, P. J. (1961). Absolute dating of deep-sea cores. *J. Geol.* **69**, 162–185.

ROWAN, W. (1950). Canada's premier problem of animal conservation: a question of cycles. *New Biol.* **9**, 38–57.

RUBASHEV, B. M. (1964). "Problems of Solar Activity". Astron. Obs. Moscow (Trans. NASA programme: NASATTF-244, Washington).

RUNCORN, S. K. (1964). Changes in the earth's moment of inertia. *Nature, Lond.* **204**, 823–825.

RUNCORN, S. K. (1965). Paleomagnetic comparisons between Europe and North America. *In* "A Symposium on Continental Drift". *Phil. Trans. R. Soc., Ser. A*, **258**, 1–11.

RUSSELL, R. J. (1964). Techniques of eustasy studies. *Z. Geomorph.* N.F. **8**, 25–42.

RUTTEN, L. M. R. (1949). Frequency and periodicity of orogenic movements. *Bull. geol. Soc. Am.* **60**, 1755.

RUTTEN, M. G. (1966). Geologic data on atmospheric history. *Paleogeog. Paleoclim. Paleoecol.* **2**, 47–57.

SAHNI, A. and KUMAR, V. (1974). Paleogene paleobiogeography of the Indian subcontinent. *Paleogeog. Paleoclim. Paleoecol.* **15**, 209–226.

SAITO, T., BURCKLE, L. and HAYS, J. D. (1974). Micropaleontologic and paleomagnetic data on the Miocene/Pliocene boundary. *In* "Late Neogene Epoch Boundaries" (Saito, T. and Burckle, L., Eds), pp. 226–244. American Museum of Natural History.

SALINGER, M. J. (1976). New Zealand temperatures since 1300 A.D. *Nature, Lond.* **260**, 310–311.

SALINGER, M. J. and GUNN, J. M. (1975). Recent climatic warming around New Zealand. *Nature, Lond.* **256**, 396–398.

SANBORN, E. I. (1935). The Comstock flora of west central Oregon. *Carnegie Inst. Washington Publ.* **465**, 1–28.

SANDERS, H. L. (1968). Marine benthic diversity: a comparative study. *Am. Nat.* **102**, 243–292.

SAUER, C. O. (1936). American agricultural origins. *In* "Essays in Anthropology Presented to A. L. Kroeber", pp. 279–297. University of California Press, Berkeley.

SAVIN, S. M., DOUGLAS, R. G. and STEHLI, F. G. (1975). Tertiary marine paleo-temperatures. *Bull. geol. Soc. Am.* **86**, 1499–1510.

SAWYER, J. S. (1972). Man-made carbon dioxide and the greenhouse effect. *Nature, Lond.* **239**, 23–26.

SCHATZ, A. (1957). Some biochemical and physiological considerations regarding the extinction of the dinosaurs. *Proc. Acad. Sci. Pa.* **31**, 26–36.

SCHELL, I. I. (1961). Recent evidence about the nature of climate changes and its implications. *Ann. N.Y. Acad. Sci.* **95**, 251–270.

SCHIEGL, W. E. (1975). Climatic significance of deuterium abundance in growth rings of *Picea*. *Nature, Lond.* **251**, 582–583.

SCHINDEWOLF, O. H. (1955). Uber die möglichen ursachen der grossen erdgeschichtlichen Faunenschnitte. *Neues Jahrb. Geol. Paleontol.* 457–465.

SCHMID, F. (1959). Biostratigraphie du Campanien-Maastrichtien du NE de la Belgique sur la base des Belemnites. *Ann. Soc. geol. Belg.* **82**, 235–256.

SCHNABLE, J. E. and GOODELL, H. G. (1968). Pleistocene–Recent stratigraphy, evolution and development of the Apalachicola coast, Florida. *Geol. Soc. Am. Spec. Papers.* **112,** 72 pp.

SCHOPF, T. J. M. (1974). Permo-Triassic extinctions: relation to sea-floor spreading. *J. Geol.* **82,** 129–143.

SCHOVE, D. J. (1954). Summer temperatures and tree rings in north Scandinavia A.D. 1461–1950. *Geogrl Ann. Stockholm,* **36,** 40–80.

SCHOVE, D. J. (1955). The sunspot cycle 649 B.C.–A.D. 2000. *J. Brit. Astron. Ass.* **66,** 59–61.

SCHOVE, D. J. (1961). Tree rings and climatic chronology. *Ann. N.Y. Acad. Sci.* **95,** 605–622.

SCHUSTER, A. (1889). The diurnal variation of terrestrial magnetism. *Phil. Trans. R. Soc. Ser. A.* **180,** 467.

SCHUTZ, S., ADAMS, G. J. and MOZER, F. S. (1974). Electric and magnetic fields measured during a sudden impulse. *J. Geophys. Res.* **79,** 2002–2004.

SCHWARTZ, M. L. (1967). The Bruun theory of sea-level rise as a cause of shore erosion. *J. Geol.* **75,** 76–92.

SCHWARZBACH, M. (1961). The climatic history of Europe and North America. *In* "Descriptive paleoclimatology" (Nairn, A. E. M., Ed.), pp. 255–291. Wiley Interscience, New York.

SCHWARZBACH, M. (1963). "Climates of the Past". Van Nostrand, New York.

SCHWARZBACH, M. (1976). Late Paleozoic glaciation: Part VI, Asia. *Bull. Geol. Soc. Am.* **87,** 640.

SCLATER, J. G. and FISHER, R. L. (1974). Evolution of the east central Indian Ocean. *Bull. Geol. Soc. Am.* **85,** 683–702.

SEIBOLD, E. and WIEGERT, R. (1960). Untersuchungen des zeitlichen Ablaufs der Sedimentation im Malo Jezero auf Periodizitäten. *Z. Geophys.* **26,** 87–103.

SELLERS, A. and MEADOWS, A. J. (1975). Long term variations in the albedo and surface temperature of the earth. *Nature, Lond.* **254,** 44.

SELLI, R. (1970). Report on the absolute age. *G. Geol. Ser. 2,* **35,** 51–59.

SHACKLETON, N. J. (1967). Oxygen isotope analyses and Pleistocene temperatures re-assessed. *Nature, Lond.* **215,** 15–17.

SHACKLETON, N. J. and OPDYKE, N. D. (1973). Oxygen isotope and paleomagnetic stratigraphy of equatorial Pacific core V 28-238. *Quatern. Res.* **3,** 39–55.

SHAPLEY, H. (1921). Note on a possible factor in changes of geological climate. *J. Geol.* **29,** 502–504.

SHEEHAN, P. M. (1972). Quoted by Berry and Boucot 1973.

SHELFORD, V. E. (1943). The Abundance of the collared lemming in the Churchill area. *Ecology,* **24,** 472–484.

SHEPPARD, P. M. (1951a). A quantitative study of two populations of the moth *Panaxia dominula. Heredity,* **5,** 349–378.

SHEPPARD, P. M. (1951b). Fluctuations in the selective value of certain phenotypes in the polymorphic land snail *Cepaea nemoralis. Heredity,* **5,** 125–134.

SHEPPARD, P. M. (1952a). A note on non-random mating in the moth *Panaxia dominula* (L.). *Heredity,* **6,** 239–241.

SHEPPARD, P. M. (1952b). Natural selection in two colonies of the polymorphic land snail *Cepaea nemoralis. Heredity,* **6,** 233–238.

SHEPPARD, P. M. (1953). Polymorphism and population studies. *Symp. Soc. exp. Biol.* **7**, 274–289.
SHEPPARD, P. M. (1956). Ecology and its bearing on population genetics. *Proc. R. Soc. Ser. B.* **145**, 308–315.
SHEPPARD, P. M. (1958). "Natural Selection and Heredity". Hutchinson, London.
SHOTTON, F. W. and WEST, R. G. (1969). Stratigraphic table of the British Quaternary. *Proc. Geol. Soc. Lond.* **1656**, 155–157.
SIMBERLOFF, D. S. (1974). Permo-Triassic extinctions: effects of area on biotic equilibrium. *J. Geol.* **82**, 267–274.
SIMPSON, G. C. (1929). Past climates. *Mem. Manchester Lit. Phil. Soc.* **74**, 1–34.
SIMPSON, G. G. (1952). Periodicity in vertebrate evolution. *Bull. Geol. Soc. Am.* **26**, 359–370.
SIMPSON, G. G., PITTENDRIGH, C. S. and TIFFANY, L. H. (1957). "Life, an Introduction to Biology". Harcourt, Brace Jovanovich, New York.
SINGH, G. and AGRAWAL, D. P. (1976). Radiocarbon evidence for deglaciation in northwestern Himalaya. *Nature, Lond.* **260**, 232.
SLOSS, L. L. (1972). Concurrent subsidence of widely separated cratonic basins. *Abs. Geol. Soc. Am.* **4**, 668–669.
SMILEY, C. J. (1974). Analysis of the crustal relative stability from some late Paleozoic and Mesozoic floral records. *In* "Plate Tectonics; Assessments and Re-assessments" (Kahle, C. F., Ed.), pp. 331–360. Amer. Ass. Petrol. geol. Tulsa, Oklahoma.
SMITH, A. G. and HALLAM, A. (1970). The fit of the southern continents. *Nature, Lond.* **225**, 139–144.
SMITH, P. J. (1976). Assumed dipolar geomagnetic field. *Nature, Lond.* **262**, 643.
SOUTHWARD, A. J., BUTLER, E. I. and PENNYCUICK, L. (1975). Recent cyclic changes in climate and in abundance of marine life. *Nature, Lond.* **253**, 714–717.
SPROLL, W. P. and DIETZ, R. S. (1969). Morphological continental drift fit of Australia and Antarctica. *Nature, Lond.* **222**, 345.
SRIVASTAVA, S. K. (1967). Palynology of late Cretaceous mammal beds, Montana. *Paleogeog. Paleoclim. Paleoecol.* **3**, 133–150.
STACEY, F. D. (1969). "Physics of the Earth". John Wiley, New York.
STARR, V. P. and OORT, A. H. (1973). Five year climatic trend for the northern hemisphere. *Nature, Lond.* **242**, 310–313.
STEINEN, R. P., HARRISON, R. S. and MATTHEWS, R. K. (1973). Eustatic low stand of sea-level between 125,000 and 105,000 B.P. *Bull. Geol. Soc. Am.* **84**, 63–70.
STEINER, J. (1967). The sequence of geological events and the dynamics of the Milky Way Galaxy. *J. geol. Soc. Australia*, **14**, 99–132.
STEINER, J. and GRILLMAIR, E. (1973). Possible galactic causes for periodic and episodic glaciations. *Bull. geol. Soc. Am.* **84**, 1003–1018.
STEWART, R. J. (1975). Late Cainozoic explosive eruptions in the Aleutian and Kuril Island arcs. *Nature, Lond.* **258**, 505–506.
STILLE, H. (1924). "Grundfragen der Vergleichende Tektonik". Gebruder Borntraeger, Berlin.
STILLE, H. (1940). "Einfuhrung in den Bau Amerikas". Gebruder Borntraeger, Berlin.

STIPP, J. J., CHAPPELL, J. M. A. and McDOUGALL, I. (1967). K/Ar age estimate of the Pliocene–Pleistocene boundary in New Zealand. *Am. J. Sci.* **265**, 462–474.

STRAUCH, F. (1968). Determination of Cenozoic sea-temperatures using *Hiatella arctica*. *Paleogeog. Paleoclim. Paleoecol.* **5**, 213–233.

STREET, E. A. and GROVE, A. T. (1976). Environmental and climatic implications of late-Quaternary lake-level fluctuations in Africa. *Nature, Lond.* **261**, 385–390.

STRINGFELLOW, M. F. (1974). Lightning incidence in Britain and the solar cycle. *Nature, Lond.* **249**, 337.

STUART, A. J. (1974). Pleistocene history of the British vertebrate fauna. *Biol. Rev.* **49**, 225–266.

STUBBLEFIELD, C. J. (1960). Sessile marine organisms and their significance in Pre-Mesozoic strata. *Q. Jl geol. Soc. Lond.* **116**, 219–238.

STUCKENBERG, B. R. (1969). Effective temperature as an ecological factor in southern Africa. *Zool. Africana*, **4**, 145–197.

STUIVER, M. (1965). C^{14} content of 18th and 19th century wood; variations correlated with sunspot activity. *Science*, **149**, 533.

STUIVER, M. (1970). Long term C^{14} variations. *In* "Radiocarbon Variations and Absolute Chronology", Nobel Symposium 12 (Olsson, I. U., Ed.), pp. 197–213. Wiley Interscience and Almqvist and Wiksell, Uppsala.

STUIVER, M. (1971). Evidence for the variation of atmospheric C^{14} content in the late Quaternary. *In* "Late Cenozoic Glacial Ages" (Turekian, K. L., Ed.), pp. 57–70. Yale University Press, New Haven, Connecticut.

SUESS, H. E. (1965). Secular variations of the cosmic-ray-produced C^{14} in the atmosphere and their interpretations. *J. Geophys. Res.* **70**, 5937–5950.

SUESS, H. E. (1967). Bristle-cone pine calibration of the radiocarbon time-scale from 4100 B.C. to 1500 B.C. *In* "Radioactive Dating and Methods of Low Level Counting", pp. 143–151. I.A.E.A., Vienna.

SUESS, H. (1970a). Bristlecone pine calibration of the ^{14}C timescale 5200 B.C. to the present. *In* "Radiocarbon Variations and Absolute Chronology", Nobel Symposium 12 (Olsson, I. U., Ed.), pp. 303–312. Wiley Interscience and Almqvist and Wiksell, Uppsala.

SUESS, H. (1970b). The 3 causes of the secular C^{14} fluctuations, their amplitudes and time constants. *In* "Radiocarbon Variations and Absolute Chronology", Nobel Symposium 12 (Olsson, I. U., Ed.), pp. 595–612. Wiley Interscience and Almqvist and Wiksell, Uppsala.

SUESS, H. E. (1971). Climatic changes and the atmospheric C^{14} level. *Paleogeog. Paleoclim. Paleoecol.* **10**, 199–202.

SUTCLIFFE, R. C. (1966). "Weather and Climate". Weidenfeld and Nicolson, London.

SVALGAARD, L. (1973). Polar cap magnetic variations and their relationship with the interplanetary magnetic sector structure. *J. Geophys. Res.* **78**, 2064–2078.

SZAFER, W. (1946). The Pliocene flora of Krościenko, in Poland. *Roz. Wydz. mat. przy. Akad. Um.* **72**, 2 vols.

SZAFER, W. (1971). Miocenska flora ze Starych Gliwic na Slasku. *Geol. Prace.* **33**, 1–205.

TALBOT, M. R. (1973). Major sedimentary cycles in the corallian beds of southern England. *Paleogeog. Paleoclim. Paleoecol.* **14**, 293–317.

TALBOT, R. J. Jr., BUTLER, D. M. and NEWMAN, M. J. (1976). Climatic effects during passage of the solar system through interstellar clouds. *Nature, Lond.* **262,** 561–563.

TALLANTIRE, P. A. (1972). Spread of spruce (*Picea abies*) in Fennoscandia, and possible climatic implications. *Nature, Lond.* **236,** 64–66.

TALWANI, M., WINDISCH, C. C. and LANGSETH, M. G. Jr. (1971). Reykanes Ridge crest: a detailed geophysical study. *J. Geophys. Res.* **76,** 473–517.

TAMRAZJAN, G. P. (1967). The global historical and geological regularities of the earth's development as a reflection of its cosmic origin. *Ostr. Vys. Skola. Banska. Storn.* **13,** 5–24.

TAMRAZYAN, G. P. (1968). Principal regularities in the distribution of major earthquakes relative to solar and lunar tides and other cosmic forces. *Icarus*, **9,** 574.

TANAI, T. and HUZIOKA, K. (1967). Climatic implications of Tertiary floras in Japan. *11th Pacific Sci. Cong. Tokyo 1966*, Symp. 25, pp. 77–87.

TANNER, W. F. (1968). Cause and development of an ice age. *In* "Causes of Climatic Change" (Mitchell, J. M. Jr., Ed.). *Am. Met. Soc. Meteorol. Mon.* **8,** 126–127.

TAPPAN, H. (1968). Primary production, isotopes, extinctions and the atmosphere. *Paleogeog. Paleoclim. Paleoecol.* **4,** 187–210.

TAPPAN, H. (1970). Phytoplankton abundance and late Paleozoic extinctions: a reply. *Paleogeog. Paleoclim. Paleoecol.* **8,** 49–66.

TARLING, D. H. (1971). "Principles and Applications of Paleomagnetism". Chapman and Hall, London.

TARLING, D. H. (1971). Gondwanaland, paleomagnetism and continental drift. *Nature, Lond.* **299,** 17–21.

TAUBER, H. (1970). The Scandinavian varve chronology and C^{14} dating. *In* "Radiocarbon Variations and Absolute Chronology", Nobel Symposium 12 (Olsson, I. U., Ed.), pp. 172–196. Wiley Interscience and Almqvist and Wiksell, Uppsala.

TEIS, R. V., CHUPAKHIN, M. A. and NAIDIN, D. P. (1957). Determination of paleotemperatures from the isotopic composition of oxygen in calcite of certain Cretaceous fossil shells from Crimea. *Geokhimiya*, **9,** 323–329.

TERMIER, H. and TERMIER, G. (1973). The early climatic history of the earth. *In* "Implications of Continental Drift to the Earth Sciences" (Tarling, D. H. and Runcorn, S. K., Eds), Vol. 1, pp. 475–484. Academic Press, London and New York.

TETRODE, P. (1952). Sunspots and the occurrence of unprecedented excesses of mean temperature over a wide area. *Weather*, **7,** 14–15.

THOMAS, C. and BRIDEN, J. C. (1976). Anomalous geomagnetic field during the late Ordovician. *Nature, Lond.* **259,** 380–382.

THOMAS, R. H. (1976). Thickening of the Ross Ice Shelf and equilibrium state of the West Antarctic ice sheet. *Nature, Lond.* **259,** 180–182.

TOBIEN, H. (1970). Biostratigraphy of the mammalian faunas at the Pliocene–Pleistocene boundary in central and western Europe. *Paleogeog. Paleoclim. Paleoecol.* **8,** 77–94.

TOYNBEE, A. (1934). "The Study of History", Vol. 3. Oxford University Press, London.

TOYNBEE, A. (1975). "Mankind and Mother Earth". Oxford University Press, London.

TREVISAN, L. (1958). "La Terra", Vol. 1. Turin.

TROITSKAYA, V. A. (1967). Micropulsations and the state of the magnetosphere. *In* "Solar–Terrestrial Physics" (King, J. W. and Newman, W. S., Eds). Academic Press, London and New York.

TSUKADA, M. (1967a). Vegetation in sub-tropical Formosa during the Pleistocene glaciations and the Holocene. *Paleogeog. Paleoclim. Paleoecol.* **3,** 49–64.

TSUKADA, M. (1967b). Vegetation and climate around 10,000 B.P. in central Japan. *Am. J. Sci.* **265,** 562–585.

TUREKIAN, K. L. (Ed.) (1971). "Late Cenozoic Glacial Ages". Yale University Press, New Haven, Connecticut.

TURNER, C. and WEST, R. G. (1968). The subdivision and zonation of interglacial periods. *Eiszeitalter Gegenew.* **19,** 93–101.

TURNER, D. L. (1970). K-Ar dating of Pacific Miocene foraminiferal stages. *Geol. Soc. Am. Special paper,* **124,** 91–129.

TURNER, P. (1975). Paleozoic secular variation recorded in Pendleside limestone. *Nature, Lond.* **257,** 207–208.

TYNDALL, J. (1861). On the absorption and radiation of heat by gases and vapours and on the physical connection of radiation absorption and conduction. *Phil. Mag.* **22,** 169–194; 273–285.

UFFEN, R. J. (1963). Influence of the earth's core on the origin and evolution of life. *Nature, Lond.* **198,** 143.

UMBGROVE, J. H. F. (1947). "The Pulse of the Earth". Martinus Nijhoff, The Hague.

UPSON, J. E., LEOPOLD, E. B. and RUBIN, M. (1964). Postglacial change of sea level in New Haven Harbour, Connecticut. *Am. J. Sci.* **262,** 121–132.

UREY, H. C., LOWENSTAM, H. A., EPSTEIN, S. and MCKINNEY, C. R. (1951). Measurements of the paleotemperatures of the Upper Cretaceous of England, Denmark, and the south eastern United States. *Bull. Geol. Soc. Am.* **62,** 399–416.

VALENTINE, J. W. (1973). "Evolutionary Paleoecology of the Marine Biosphere". Prentice Hall, Eaglewood Cliffs, New Jersey.

VALENTINE, J. W. and MOORES, E. M. (1970). Plate tectonic regulation of biotic diversity and sea level: a model. *Nature, Lond.* **228,** 657–659.

VALENTINE, J. W. and MOORES, E. M. (1972). Global tectonics and the fossil record. *J. Geol.* **80,** 167–184.

VAN DER HAMMEN, T. (1961). Upper Cretaceous and Tertiary climatic periodicities and their causes. *Ann. N.Y. Acad. Sci.* **95,** 440–448.

VAN DER VLERK, I. (1959). Problems and principles of Tertiary and Quaternary stratigraphy. *Q. Jl geol. Soc. Lond.* **115,** 49.

VAN DER VLERK, I. and FLORSCHUTZ, R. (1950). "Nederland in Het Ijstijdvak". de Haan, Utrecht.

VAN GEEL, B. and HAMMEN, T. VAN DER, (1973). Upper Quaternary vegetation and climatic sequence of the Fuqeuene area (eastern Cordillera, Colombia). *Paleogeog. Paleoclim. Paleoecol.* **14,** 9–92.

VANGENGEIM, E. A. and SHER, A. V. (1970). Siberian equivalents of the Tiraspol faunal complex. *Paleogeog. Paleoclim. Paleoecol.* **8,** 197–208.

VEBAEK, C. L. (1962). *In* Proceedings of Conference on Climates of the 11th and 16th centuries. *Natl. Centre Atmos. Res. Boulder Colorado. Technical notes,* 1.

VEEH, H. H. and CHAPPELL, J. (1970). Astronomical theory of climatic

change—support from New Guinea. *Science*, **167**, 862–865.
VELLA, P. (1963). Plio–Pleistocene cyclothems, Wairarapa, New Zealand. *Trans. R. Soc. N. Z. geol.* **2**, 15–50.
VESTINE, E. H. (1961). Solar influences on geomagnetic and related phenomena. *Ann. N.Y. Acad. Sci.* **95**, 3–16.
VIBE, C. (1967). Arctic animals in relation to climatic fluctuations. *Meddr Grønland*, **170**, 227 pp.
VINE, F. J. and HESS, H. H. (1970). Sea-floor spreading. *In* "The Seas" (Maxwell, A. E., Ed.), Vol. 4, pp. 587–622. John Wiley, New York.
VOGEL, J. C. (1970). C^{14} trends before 6000 B.P. *In* "Radiocarbon Variations and Absolute Chronology", Nobel Symposium 12 (Olsson, I. U., Ed.), pp. 313–325. Wiley Interscience and Almqvist and Wiksell, Uppsala.
VOLTZINGER, N. E. *et al.* (1966). The internal structure of natural climatic series exposed by a periodogram analysis technique. *Arkt. Antarkt. Inst. Issled.* **277**, 147–157.
VORONOV, P. S. (1960). Attempt to restore the Antarctic ice sheet at the epoch of the earth's maximum glaciations. *Sov. Antarct. Exped. Inf. Bull.* **23**, 15–19.
WAHL, E. W. and BRYSON, R. A. (1975). Recent changes in Atlantic surface temperatures. *Nature, Lond.* **254**, 45–46.
WALKER, G. T. (1924). World weather II. *Mem. 24 India Meterol. Dept.* p. 275.
WANLESS, H. R. (1960). Evidence of multiple late Paleozoic glaciation in Australia. *21st Inst. Geol. Cong. Copenhagen*, pt. 12, 104–110.
WARD, F. and SHAPIRO, R. (1961). Solar, geomagnetic and meteorological periodicities. *Ann. N.Y. Acad. Sci.* **95**, 200–224.
WARNKE, D. A. (1970). Glacial erosion, ice-rafting and glacial marine sediments. Antarctica and the southern ocean. *Am. J. Sci.* **269**, 276–294.
WATKINS, N. D. (1972). Review of the development of the geomagnetic polarity timescale. *Bull. geol. Soc. Am.* **83**, 551–574.
WEERTMAN, J. (1976). Milankovitch solar radiation variations and ice age ice sheet sizes. *Nature, Lond.* **261**, 17–20.
WELLS, J. W. (1963). Coral growth and geochronometry. *Nature, Lond.* **197**, 948–950.
WEST, R. G. (1968). "Pleistocene Geology and Biology". Longmans, London.
WEST, R. G. (1970). Pleistocene history of the British flora. *In* "Studies in the Vegetational History of the British Isles" (Walker, D. and West, R. G., Eds), pp. 1–11. Cambridge University Press, London.
WEST, R. G. (1970). Pollen zones in the Pleistocene of Great Britain and their correlation. *New Phytol.* **69**, 1179–1183.
WEST, R. G. (1972a). Relative land-sea-level changes in south eastern England during the Pleistocene. *Phil. Trans. R. Soc. Ser. A.* **272**, 87–98.
WEST, R. G. (1972b). The stratigraphical position of the Norwich Crag in relation to the Cromer Forest Bed series. *Bull. Geol. Soc. Norfolk*, **21**, 17–23.
WESTERN, D. and PRAET, C. VAN, (1973). Cyclical changes in the habitat and climate of an east African ecosystem. *Nature, Lond.* **241**, 104–106.
WHILLANS, I. M. (1976). Radio echo-layers and the recent stability of the West Antarctic ice sheet. *Nature, Lond.* **264**, 152–155.

WIEDMANN, J. (1959). Le Cretacé supérieur de l'Espagne et du Portugal et ses Céphalopodes. *Compt. Rend. 84th Congr. Soc. sav. Dijon. Sect. Sci.*, 709–764.
WIEDMANN, J. (1969). The heteromorphs and ammonoid extinction. *Biol. Rev.* **44,** 563–602.
WIESENFELD, S. L. (1969). Sickle cell trait in human biological and cultural evolution. *In* "Environment and Cultural Behaviour" (Vadya, A. P., Ed.), pp. 308–331. American Museum of Natural History.
WILCOX, J. M., SCHERRER, P. H., SVALGAARD, L., ROBERTS, W. O. and OLSON, R. H. (1973). Solar magnetic sector structure: relation to circulation of the earth's atmosphere. *Science*, **180,** 185.
WILLETT, H. C. (1953). *In* "Climatic Change" (Shapley, H., Ed.). Harvard University Press, Cambridge, Massachusetts.
WILLETT, H. C. (1961). The pattern of solar climatic relationships. *Ann. N.Y. Acad. Sci.* **95,** 89–101.
WILLETT, H. C. (1964). Evidence of solar climatic relationships. *In* "Weather and our Food Supply". Iowa State University CAED 20, 123–151.
WILLIAMS, D. (1961). Sunspot cycle correlations. *Ann. N.Y. Acad. Sci.* **95,** 78–88.
WILLIS, E. H. (1961). Marine transgression sequences in the English fenlands. *Ann. N.Y. Acad. Sci.* **95,** 368–376.
WILLIS, E. H. and TAUBER, H. (1970). Contributions to discussion *in* "Radiocarbon Variations and an Absolute Chronology" (Olsson, I. V., Ed.), pp. 610–611. Wiley Interscience and Almqvist and Wiksell, Uppsala.
WILLIS, E. H., TAUBER, H. and MUNNICH, K. O. (1960). Variations in the atmospheric C^{14} concentration over 1300 years. *Radiocarbon*, **2,** 1–6.
WILSER, J. L. (1931). "Lichtreaktionen in der Fossilen Tierwelt." Gebruder Borntrager, Berlin.
WING, L. W. (1935). Wild cycles in relation to the sun. *Trans. Am. Game Conf.* **21,** 345–363.
WING, L. W. (1961). Latitudinal passage: a principle of solar terrestrial cycle behaviour. *Ann. N.Y. Acad. Sci.* **95,** 381–417.
WINKLESS, N. and BROWNING, I. (1975). "Climate and the Affairs of Men". Peter Davies, London.
WINSTANLEY, D. (1973). Rainfall patterns and general atmospheric circulation. *Nature, Lond.* **245,** 190–194.
WOLFE, J. A. and HOPKINS, D. M. (1967). Climatic changes recorded by Tertiary land floras in northwestern North America. *11th Pacific Sci. Cong. Tokyo 1966. Symp.* 25, 67–76.
WOLLIN, G., ERICSON, D. B. and RYAN, W. B. F. (1971). Variations in magnetic intensity and climatic changes. *Nature, Lond.* **232,** 549.
WOLLIN, G., KUKLA, G. J., ERICSON, D. B., RYAN, W. B. and WOLLIN, J. (1973). Magnetic intensity, climatic changes and evolution. *Nature, Lond.* **242,** 34–36.
WRIGHT, A. E. and MOSELEY, F. (Eds) (1975). "Ice Ages; Ancient and Modern". Seel House Press, Liverpool.
WRIGHT, H. E., Jr., BENT, A. M., HANSEN, B. S. and MAHER, L. J., Jr. (1973). Present and past vegetation of the Chuska Mountains, N.W. New Mexico. *Bull. geol. Soc. Am.* **84,** 1155–1180.
YAMAMOTO, T. (1967). On the climatic change along the current of

historical times in Japan and its surroundings. *Jap. Phil. Mag.* **76,** 115–141.
YORK, D. and FARQUHAR, R. M. (1972). "The Earth's Age and Geochronology". Pergamon Press, Oxford and New York.
ZAGWIJN, W. H. (1957). Vegetation, climate and time correlations in the early Pleistocene of Europe. *Geol. Mijnbouw.* **7,** 233–244.
ZAGWIJN, J. W. (1960). Aspects of the Pliocene and Pleistocene vegetation in the Netherlands. *Meded. Geol. Sticht.* C3, **1,** 1–78.
ZAGWIJN, W. H. (1976). Variations in climate as shown by pollen analysis, especially, in the Lower Pleistocene of Europe. *In* "Ice Ages; Ancient and Modern" (Wright, A. E. and Moseley, F., Eds), pp. 137–152. Seel House Press, Liverpool.
ZAGWIJN, W. H., MONTFRANS, H. M. VAN and ZANDSTRA, J. G. (1971). Subdivision of the Cromerian in the Netherlands. *Geol. Mijnbouw.* **50,** 41–58.
ZAKLINSKAIA, E. D. (1967). Palynological studies on late Cretaceous–Paleogene flora history. *Rev. Paleobot. Palynol.* **2,** 141–146.
ZEUNER, F. E. (1945). "The Pleistocene Period". Ray Soc. Publ. London. New edition (1959). Hutchinson, London.
ZEUNER, F. E. (1952). "Dating the Past" (3rd ed.). Methuen, London.

Subject Index

Italicised page numbers refer to figures.

A

Acanthosphaera, 175
Acer, 162, *184*
Acrocoelites, 144–145
Aeolianites, 151–*152*
Africa, 31, 35, 99, 117, *121*, 193
Agathis australis, 95
  palmerstoni, *95*
Ailanthus, 162
Alnus, 161, 163, *184*, 201–202
Alpine–Dinaride–Tauride belt, 174
America, 18, 24, *30*, 39, 45, 49, 77, 99, 108, 110, 117, *121*, 123, 124, 139, 142, 146, *153*, 161, 165, 167, 172, 178, 192–193, 195–196, 205, 215, 224–227
Ammonites, *125*, 129, 137, 154–158
Amphibia, 129
Ancylus lake, 203
Anoplotherium, 7
Antarctica, 39, 121, 124, 170, 192
Anticyclones, 31, *36*, 45, 192,
  belt, 31–32, 195
Apaches, 225
Apatemyidae, 159
Apocynaceae, 162
Apogalacticum, *104*
Apsides, 103–105
Arabs, 58, 215
Aralia, 161
Aramaeans, 215
Archeocyathida, 133
Arctic ocean, 58, 61, 181, 192
  region, *38*, 41, 154
Arctica arctica, 187
Armeria, 199

Artemisia, 199
Artiodactyla, 178
Asia, 23, 31, 215
Athrotaxis selaginoides, 95
Atlantic ocean, 39–41, 58, 138–140, 174, 181, 189
Atmosphere, 67, 69–71
Atmospheric dynamo, 65, 69–71
Aurorae, 64
Avars, 215

B

Baffin island, 39
Balanus, 50
Barbados, 119
Barometric depressions, 31
Basin, Karroo, 124
  Parana, 122
Bays, *82*
Belemnites, *125*
  hastatus, 146
Belemnitella americana, 147
Belemnopsis canaliculatus, 145
Benthos, 157
Betula, 184, 199–200, 202
  nana, 198–199
Betulaceae, 162
Biometeorology, 12
Biston betularia, 15–16
Black death, 59
Blastoids, 125
Bovoidea, 160, 178
Brachiopoda, 116, *125*, 129
Britain, 31, 59, 184–186, 197–202, 227–228

268   INDEX

Brontotheres, 160
Bryozoa, 116, *125*, 129

C

[14]C, 93–96, 202–205, 208–210
California, 27
Cambodia, 221
Camelidae, 178
Camp Century ice core, 53–57, 191
Canada, 40, 192
Cannartiscus marylandicus, 175
Carbonate, 190
Carpinus, 162, *184*
Carya, 162
Castanea, 162
Castanopsis, 193
Catastrophism, 1–2, 157
Cenosphaera nagata, 171
Cenozoic Era, 3, 118, 135, 141
Cepaea nemoralis, 15–16
Cercidiphyllum, 161
Cervoidea, 160
Chalicotheres, 160
Chama macerophylla, 147
Chenopodiaceae, 162
Cherts, 137
China, 30, 220–224
  dynastic history of, 220–223
Chlamys, 169, 187
Chromyechinus antarctica, 171
Chthamalus, 49
Cimmerians, 215
Circulation, 153, 190, 200
Circumpolar vortex, 40–43, 192
Cladium mariscus, 201
Climatic determinism, 212–213
  optimum, *191*
  periodicity, *see* Cycles
CO_2, 126
Coal, 151
Cod, 49–50
Commodity prices, 51
Continental drift, 105–108, 117–119, 138–140, 148–149, 158
Corals, *125*, 129
Corylus, *184*, 201–202
Cosmic year, 103
Crag, Norwich, 183
  Red, 183

Weybourn, 183, 185
Crinoidea, 116, *125*, 129
Cromer Forest Bed, 185
Cryptostomata, 133
Cunninghamia konishii, 193
Currents, Californian, 154
  Caribbean, 172
  Circumpolar, 167
  Mozambique, 154
  Peruvian, 154
Cycles, 43–57
  5·115 days, 44
  3·635 quarter year, 44
  4·465 quarter year, 44
  1·7 year, 18
  2·1 year, 18, 31
  26 month, 46
  2·3 year, 46
  2·5 year, 46, 140
  2·7 year, 46
  4 year, 15
  4·222 year, 44
  $c.4·7$ year, 18, 31
  5·7 year, 45, 120
  6 year, 50, 140
  7–8 year, 120, 140
  $c.9·5$ year, 18, 31, 44
  10 year, 15, 49, 120, 140
  11–12 year, 18, 29, 44, 46, 47, 49, 50, 72, 120, 141
  18 year, 47
  19 year, 31
  22–23 year, 44, 49, 120
  33 year, 18
  63–66 year, 53
  78 year, 53
  80–90 year, 44, 49, 120
  170–200 year, 52, 53, 120, 141
  400 year, 120
  900 year, 52
  1,325 year, 57
  2,000 year, 55
  4,000 year, 55
  40,000 year, 22
  90,000 year, 22
Cyclones, *36*, 47–48
Cylindroteuthis puzosiana, 146
Cyrthocapsella tetrapera, 175
Cystoids, *125*

INDEX

D

Dacrydium cupressinum, 95
Daniglacial retreat phase, 197
Deltatheridea, 159
Depressions, 31, 41
Desmospyris spongiosa, 171, 175
Diploplegma banzare, 171
D layer, 71–73
Dromomeryx, 160
Droughts, 49, 226
Dryas octopetala, 198–199
Dwyka series, 123, 135
Dynamo theory, 65, 69

E

Earthquakes, 2, 111–112
East Greenland current, 31, 40
Echinoids, *125*
Ecliptic, 19–22
E layer, 71–73
Elephantidae, 176
Empetrum, 199
Emys orbicularis, 201
Engelhardtia, 162
Eucyrtidium calvertense, 175
Evaporites, 137, 152
Extinctions, 3, 124–134, 155–158

F

Fagaceae, 162
Fagus, 162–163
Fayette ice, 195
Fish, *127–128*
F layer, 71–73
Foraminifera, *125*, 172

G

Galactic factors, 101–105
Gastropods, *125*
Geomagnetic field, 62–69, 73–88, 93, 96
  reversals, 3, 81, 84–91, *133*, 142–144
Ginkgo, 161
Giraffoidea, 160, 178
Glaciation, *33*
  Anglian, 183

Baventian, 183–186
Beestonian, 183, 185
Blancan, 182
Carboniferous, 29
Cenozoic, 98, *104*–105, 180 *et seq.*
Devensian, 183, 185, 189–195
Donau, 163, 182
Egan–Marinoan, 103
Elster, 183, *186*
Eocambrian, *99*–100, *104*–105
Gowganda, *99*–100
Gunz, 163, 182
Illinoian, 183
Infracambrian, *99*–100, *104*–105
Kanzan, 182
Menapian, 182, *186*
Mindel, 163, 183
Nebraskan, 182
Ordovician, 99, 122
Paleozoic, 98
Permo-Carboniferous, *99, 104*–105
Porikan, 183
Precambrian, 103
Quaternary, 29, 179–210
Riss, 163, 183
Saalian, *186*
Siluro-Ordovician, *99, 104*–105
Sturtian, 100
Thurnian, 183, 186
Varangian, *100*
Waimaungan, 183
Waimean, 183
Weichselian, 187
Wisconsinian, 55, 187
Wolstonian, 183, 185
Wurm, 163, 183, 187
Glacial pavements, *121*
Glaciers, 51, 205
Globoquadrina altispira, 173
  dehiscens, 174
Globotoralia fistulosa
  menardii, 74, 180
  triloba, 180
  truncatulinoides, 174, 180
Glycimeris, 169
Gnaphalium norvegicum, 14
  supinum, 14
Gondwanaland, *121*, 123, 149, 151
Gotiglacial retreat phase, 197

Gramineae, 162
Graptolithina, 123, *125*
Grenz-horizont, *see* Recurrence surfaces

H

Hale cycle, 45, 48
Harvests, 37
Hastites umbilicatus, 144
Hawaii, 204
Helotholus vema, 175
Heterochronism, 27
Heteromorphs, 154–158
Heterospory, 115
Hiatella arctica, 165, 206
Hippophae, 199
Holland, 57
Homo erectus, 177
Hopewellian culture, 224
Hsiung Nu, *214–215*, 218
Huns, *see also* Hsiung Nu, 215

I

Ice age, *see* Glaciations and Little Ice Age
Icebergs, 58, 122
Ice cores, 53–57, 189, 191
Iceland, 40, 46, 58
Ice rafting, 170, 181
  retreat, 57, 195, 197, 203, 205
Ilex, 162
Interglacials, 33
  Aftonian, 182
  Antian, 183, 185–*186*
  Blancan, 182
  Cromerian, 183, 185
  Holstein, 183
  Hoxnian, 183
  Ipswichian, 183
  Ludhamian, 183, *186*
  Pastonian, 183, 185
  Sangamonian, 183
  Tiglian, 182–183
  Waalian, 182
  Yarmouthian, 183
Intertropical convergence, 150–151, 189
Isotherms, 13–14, 21
Isotope dating, 4–6, 86, 160, 182, 193–195, 202–203

J

Japan, 172
Jet stream, 36
John Dory, 49
Juglandaceae, 162
Juglans, 162, 193
Jupiter, 27

K

K-Ar, 5–6, 86, 160
Karroo Basin, 124

L

Labyrinthodonts, 137
Lahillia, *169*
Lake Chad, 61
  Victoria, 18
Latitudinal passage, 44
  variation, 145
Lauraceae, 162
Laurasia, 149
Leguminosae, 162
Libyans, 215
Ligustrum, 193
Liquidambar, 162
  formosa, 193
Little Ice Age, 40, 53, 205, 221, 228–229
Lychnocanium grande, 175

M

Magnetic, disturbances, 26, 66–69
  field and climate, 73–81
  interplanetary field, 80
  poles, 62–63
Magnetosphere, *64*
Magyars, 215
Malaria parasite, 16
Mallotus paniculatus, 193
Manchurians, 213
Mediterranean, 43, 61, 138, 162–*163*
Megateuthis giganteus, 145
Megrim, 49
Meridional circulation, 27, 45
Mescaleros, 225
Mesopause, 37
Mesozoic Era, 3, 133, 135–159

Metasequoia, 161
Mexico, 225–226
Microcachrydites, 163
Microchaeridae, 159
Middle Ages, 59–60, 215, 228
Middle East, 61
Milankovič theory, 19–23, 33, 188
Mixtecs, 226
Modiolus, 187
Mongols, 215
Monocolpites medius, 141–142, 161
Monsoon, 41–43, 151, 167
Moraceae, 162
Moraines, 197
Mullet, 49
Mya pseudarenaria, 206
   truncata, 206
Mytilus, 206

N

Nannobelus, 144
Nautiloidea, 116, *125*
Navahos, 225
Negroes, 11
Nekton, 157
New Zealand, 37, 121, 183, 198
Nomads, 17, 213–219
Norwich Crag, 183
Nothofagus, 163
Notostrea, 169
Nuphar, 193
Nyssa, 162

O

^{18}O, 53–57, 114, 144
Ocean floor, 87, 151
Ommatocampe hughesi, 175
Orogeny, Accadian, 108–110
   Appalachian, 108–110
   Cascadian, *109*
   Cenozoic, 108
   Laramide, *109–110*
   Mesozoic, 108
   Nevadan, *109*
   Palisadean, *109*
   Taconic, 109–110
   Taxonian, 108–*110*
Oroscena carolae, 175

Ostracoda, *125*, 172
Ostrea, 169
Overkill, 178
Oxygen depletion, 126
Oxyria, 199
Ozone, *37*, 71

P

Paleoclimates, 119–124, 144–154, 165–168, 206–208, 212
Paleolithic, 199–200
Paleomagnetic epochs, 90–91, 173–174
   Brunhes, *90*, 171, 181–183
   Gauss, *90*, 171
   Gilbert, *90*
   Matuyama, *90*, 171, 181–183
Paleomagnetic events
   Cochiti, *90*
   Gilsa, *90*, 171, 183
   Jaramillo, *90*, 181, 183
   Kaena, 171
   Laschamp, *90*
   Mammoth, 86, *90*
   Nunivak, *90*
   Olduvai, 86, *90*, 171
   Reunion, 171
Paleotemperatures, 119, 144–149, 168–173, 208
Paleotherium, 7
Paleozoic Era, 3, 115–134, 158
Palmae, 141–142, 162
Pangaea, 117, 138–140
Pantotheres, 136
Paratethys, 174
Park-Tundra, 199
Passaloteuthis, 144
Peat, 57
Pelecypods, *125*
Perigalacticum, *104*
Period, Aalenian, *145*
   Albian, *91*, *136*, 148, *155*, 159
   Allerød, *191*, 193, 197, 203
   Aptian, *91*, 148, 159
   Artinskian, 119
   Bajocian, 145–146
   Barremian, 91
   Baventian, 183
   Bølling, 57, *191*, 197, 203

Period (*contd.*)
   Calabrian, 176
   Callovian, 145, 149
   Cambrian, 2, 4–6, *92*, *109*, 115, 122, 128, 134
   Campanian, *91*, 148, *155*
   Carboniferous, 6, 29–30, *92*, 116, *118*, 120, 122, *127–128*
   Cenomanian, *91*, *136*, 147, *155*
   Coniacian, *91*, 148, *155*
   Cretaceous, 2, 6, *92*, *109*, 136–138, 143, 148, 151–158, 160, 166
   Danian, 155, 158, 160
   Devonian, 2, 6, *92*, 109, 115–116, 120, *127–128*, 134
   Dryas, *191*, 193, 197–200, 203
   Dzhulfian, 129
   Eburonian, *186*
   Emsian, 115
   Eocene, *91*, 136, 141, 159, 161–162, 164
   Fammenian, 116
   Flandrian, 22, 184, 200–210
   Frasnian, 116
   Gedinnean, 115
   Hauterivian, *91*
   Holocene, 55–56, *191*, 197
   Jurassic, 2, 6, *91–92*, *109*, 135–136, 138, 143, 145–146, 148, 154
   Kimmeridgian, 146–147
   Late Weichselian, 22, 197–200
   Liassic, 145
   Maestrichtian, *91*, 141, 155, 160
   Miocene, *6*, *91*, 136, 141, 159–160, 163–165, 168, 173
   Mississippian, 2, 6, 128
   Neogene, 154, 163, 173–176
   Oligocene, *91*, 136, 141, 159–160, 162–163, 168
   Ordovician, 2, 6, *92*, *109*, 116, 122–123
   Oxfordian, 147
   Paleocene, 6, *91*, *136*, 140–141, 159, 164
   Paleogene, 154, 162, 172
   Pennsylvanian, 2, 128
   Permian, 2, 6, *92*, 119–122, 127–128, 134–135
   Piacenzian, 176
   Pleistocene, 6, 178–210
   Pliensbachian, 145–*146*
   Pliocene, 6, *91*, 160, 164–165, 168, 174
   Pre-boreal, 203
   Pretiglian, 182, 185
   Purbeckian, *91*
   Quaternary, 6, 122, 177–210
   Ruscinian, 176
   Ryazanian, *91*
   Santonian, *91*, 148–149
   Senonian, *136*
   Serravalian, 176
   Siegenian, 115
   Silurian, 2, 6, *109*, 115, 116, 120, 134
   Sub-Atlantic, 95
   Sub-boreal, 95
   Tertiary, 2, 6, *92*, *109*, 159–176
   Tiglian, 182
   Toarcian, 145–*146*
   Tortonian, 176
   Tremadocian, 115–116
   Triassic, 2, 6, *109*, *127–129*, 134–136, 149–152, 158
   Turonian, *91*, *136*, 147, 155
   Varangian, *91*
   Zanclian, 176
Perissodactyls, 159
Persicaria, 193
Pezon, *157*
Picea, 50, *184*
Pinus, *184*, 198, 200, 202
   chinensis, 193
   sylvestris, 50
Plankton, 126, 157
Platanus, 161
Plate tectonics, 3
Plesiadapidae, 159
Pluvial period, 33
Podocarpaceae, 164
Podosporites, 163
Pollen, 141, 161, 184, 197, 200–205
Polygonaceae, 162
Populus, 161
Primates, 178
Proboscidea, 178
Productivity, 125–126
Prunopyle titan, 175
Pterocanium trilobum, 175
Pterocarya, 162

Pullieniatina obliquiloculata, 174
Pulse of Asia, 23
Pygmies, 11

Q

Quercetum mixtum, 185
Quercus, 162, *184*, 193, 202

R

Rainfall, 18, 40, 60, 151
Ranunculus glacialis, 14
Rb–Sr, 5
Recurrence surfaces, 205, 212
Red-beds, 151–*152*
Red Crag, 183
Remanent magnetism, 83–84
Reptiles, 116–117, 159
Rhamnaceae, 162
River Nile, 31, 61, 189
Rules, Allen's, 10–12
  Bergmann's, 10–12
  Gloger's, 10–12
Rumex, 199

S

Sahelian region, 35
Sahul shelf, 194
Sakas, *214*
Salinity, 194
Salix, 193
Salt production, 57–58
Sapindaceae, 162
Sapotaceae, 162
Sarmatians, *214*
Saturnulus planetes, 175
Scythians, 215
Sea-level, 57–59, 108–110, 142, 166, 187–189, 204–206
Secular change, 37, 95
Sedum rosea, 13
Selaginella, 199
Sequoias, 18
Shallow seas, 131
Siberia, 46, 49
Sivatherium, 160
Snow cover, *33*, 38

Solar-cyclonic hypothesis, 27
Solar wind, 62, 64, 67
Somerset levels, 58
Sphaerodinellopsis seminulina, 173
Sphaeroidinella dehiscens, 174
Spongoplema antarcticum, 175
Spongopyle osculosus, 171
Storminess, 26, 227–228
Stratopause, *37*
Stratosphere, *37*
Stromatoporoids, 116
Stylatractus neptunus, 171
Sunspots, 18–19, *25*–28, 33, 45–47, 63, 67, *82*, 94–96
  maxima, 18–19, 26, 45
  minima, 45
Symmetrodonts, 136
Symplocus, 193

T

Tabulata, 133
Tarim Basin, 23
Tectonic events, *132*
Tertiary floras, 160–164
Tethys Sea, 121, 146, 154
Thalassemia alleles, 16
Thalictrum, 199
Theocyrtis redondoensis, 175
Thermosphere, *37*
Thunderstorms, *32*–33, 45
Tilia, 202
Tillites, 122–123, 137
Time scale, 6, 176
Tiraspol fauna, 179
Toltecs, 226
Trade winds, 137, 149–151, 189
Transformism, 6
Trapa natans, 193, 201
Tree rings, 18, 50, *97*
Trema occidentalis, 193
Triceraspyris, 175
Triconodonta, 136
Trilobita, *125*
Tritylodonta, 136
Trochodendron, 161
Tropopause, 36
Troughs, 76–77
Tsuga, 193
Turkestan, 23

U

Ulmus, 162, *184*, 193

V

Varves, 96, 203
Viburnum, 161
Vikings, 53, 58
Vineyards, 59–*60*
Vitis,
Volcanoes, 28, 112–114, 127
Vorticity, 76–78, 81, 151
Vulcanism, 2, 27, 108–114

W

Weybourn Crag, 183, 185
Wheat, 51
Wine vintages, 46

Y

Year length, 120
Yoldia Sea, 203

Z

Zelkova, 162, 193
Zonal circulation, 41–43
Zones, interglacial, 184
    postglacial, 200–202